Democracy in Europe

Democracy in Europe

The EU and National Polities

Vivien A. Schmidt

OXFORD
UNIVERSITY PRESS

OXFORD
UNIVERSITY PRESS

Great Clarendon Street, Oxford OX2 6DP

Oxford University Press is a department of the University of Oxford.
It furthers the University's objective of excellence in research, scholarship,
and education by publishing worldwide in

Oxford New York

Auckland Cape Town Dar es Salaam Hong Kong Karachi
Kuala Lumpur Madrid Melbourne Mexico City Nairobi
New Delhi Shanghai Taipei Toronto

With offices

in Argentina Austria Brazil Chile Czech Republic France Greece
Guatemala Hungary Italy Japan Poland Portugal Singapore
South Korea Switzerland Thailand Turkey Ukraine Vietnam

Oxford is a registered trade mark of Oxford University Press
in the UK and in certain other countries

Published in the United States
by Oxford University Press Inc., New York

© Vivien A. Schmidt

The moral rights of the author have been asserted
Database right Oxford University Press (maker)

First published 2006

British Library Cataloguing in Publication Data
Data available

Library of Congress Cataloging in Publication Data
Data available

Typeset by SPI Publisher Services, Pondicherry, India
Printed in Great Britain
on acid-free paper by
Biddles Ltd., King's Lynn, Norfolk

ISBN 978-0-19-926697-5
ISBN 978-0-19-926698-2 (Pbk.)

To Jolyon

Contents

Preface

Democracy in Europe is about the impact of European integration on national democracies. It argues that the oft-cited democratic deficit is indeed a problem, but not so much at the level of the European Union per se as at the national level. This is because national leaders and publics have yet to come to terms with the institutional impact of the EU on the traditional workings of their national polities.

The book begins with a discussion of what the EU *is*—a new form of *regional state* in which sovereignty is shared, boundaries are variable, identity composite, and democracy fragmented. But the main focus of the book is on how the EU has altered national governance practices, thereby challenging national ideas about democracy. It finds in particular that the EU's *'policy without politics'* has led to *'politics without policy'* at the national level. The book also shows that institutional 'fit' matters. The *compound* EU, in which governing activity is highly dispersed among multiple authorities, is more disruptive to *simple* polities like Britain and France, where governing activity has traditionally been more concentrated in a single authority, than to similarly *compound* polities like Germany and Italy. But the book concludes that the real problem for member-states is not so much that their democratic practices have changed as that national ideas and discourse about democracy have not. The failure has been one of the *communicative* discourse to the general public—a problem which again has been more pronounced for simple polities, despite political leaders' potentially greater capacity to communicate through a single voice, than for compound polities, where the *coordinative* discourse among policymakers predominates.

This book, then, goes beyond the usual discussion of European integration in terms of policy and politics to focus on *polity* issues. It offers theoretical insights into the democratic implications of the EU's international organizational form, the interactions between the EU and national institutions, and the role of ideas and discourse in democratic adjustment. But it also provides detailed empirical studies of matched pairs of cases to elucidate the differential impact of the EU on its member-states.

The book has had a long gestation. It began in the mid-1990s as part of a larger project to examine the political economic and institutional impact of the EU on its member-states. The economic project came to fruition earlier in *The Futures of European Capitalism*, which appeared in 2002. It examines the impact of Europeanization on political economic policies, practices, and discourse in France, Britain, and Germany. *Democracy in Europe* can be seen as complementary to the first, as what happens to national democratic practices and discourse as a result of the new political institutional arrangements that are the context within which the new political economic realities have developed.

The book has benefited greatly from those who have listened and commented on my many papers and presentations as the project has unfolded. Various parts of the book have been presented at conferences and seminars in the US and Europe. I have benefited the most from discussions held at the European University Institute in Florence, Sciences Po in Paris, the University of Florence, the Max Planck Institute in Cologne, and the Center for European Studies at Harvard University. Special thanks go to Beate Kohler-Koch and the participants in the ECPR workshop in Oslo in 1996 and the follow-up meeting in Mannheim in 1997, where I first presented the ideas at the heart of the book. I am also grateful for stimulating discussions with Fritz Scharpf, Adrienne Héritier, Philippe Schmitter, Gerda Falkner, Joseph Weiler, George Ross, Kalypso Nicolaïdis, Gary Marks, Liesbet Hooghe, Bo Rothstein, Maurizio Ferrerra, Stefano Bartolini, Wolfgang Wessels, Jane Mansbridge, Renaud Dehousse, Craig Parsons, Nicolas Jabko, Mark Thatcher, David Coen, Ian Bache, Alberta Sbragia, Ulrike Liebert, Pierre Rosanvallon, and Sergio Fabbrini.

The project received support from a variety of institutions. I would like to thank in particular the Rockefeller Foundation Conference Center at Bellagio for a month spent in something near to paradise in 2003—other than the heat wave that engulfed Europe that summer; the Fulbright Foundation, which provided me with a European Union Research Scholar Award in Fall 2001; and Nuffield College, Oxford University, my host for the Fulbright. I would also like to thank the Centre Européen at Sciences Po in Paris, which has constituted my European base for the past seven years in late spring and early summer, offering not only a stimulating environment but also, last year, a bird's-eye view of the French referendum on the Constitutional Treaty.

On the other side of the Atlantic, I would like to thank my home institution, Boston University, for its supportive environment while I am there and its generous leave policy which has allowed me to be in Europe to carry out the necessary research. I am also grateful to the Center for European Studies at Harvard, and Peter Hall in particular, for creating a vibrant environment for intellectual exchanges on Europe. I would also like to thank Renée Haferkamp for having brought so many members of the European Commission and other EU institutions to Boston, to Harvard as well as to Boston University. A special note of thanks also goes to Irena Gross and Kryszctof Michalski of the Institute for Human Sciences at BU for public events that have brought European and American public figures to Boston for stimulating exchanges. Interaction with the wide range of European public figures, through talks as well as private conversations, have given me invaluable insights into the internal workings of the EU and the issues of concern in national capitals. I'd like to thank in particular Joaquin Almunia, Elmar Brok, John Bruton, Jorgo Chatzimarkakis, Pascal Lamy, Mario Monti, Karel Van Miert, Eva Nowotny, Chris Patten, Michel Petite, Quentin Peel, Philippe de Schootheete, Stephen Wall, and David Williamson.

Special thanks also goes to those who closely read portions of the final manuscript, in whole or in part: Tanja Börzel, Furio Cerutti, David Coen, Paulette Kurzer, Fritz Scharpf, and Mark Thatcher. My research assistants also made valuable contributions with regard to bibliographic research and the collection of qualitative data, including Jesse Kalata, George Tsinias, Laure Wagener, Karen Sigiemund, and Eloisa Devietti. Finally, the book is dedicated to Jolyon Howorth, who gets special thanks not only for closely reading the final manuscript but for being there through it all.

List of Figures

List of Tables

Introduction: Democracy in Europe

Democracy has become an issue for Europe. Concerns with the 'democratic deficit' in the European Union (EU) have been building. They began with calls for greater power for the European Parliament (EP) and greater transparency from the European Commission (EC) and the Council of Ministers. These were followed by questions of accounting and accountability related to the Commission under President Santer, and culminated with the demand for institutional reform in light of enlargement to the east. In response came the intense debates about what form a more democratic European governance system should take in the Constitutional Convention, leading to its blueprint for a Constitution for Europe, then the bargaining in the Intergovernmental Conference that produced the Constitutional Treaty. The Treaty itself was a compromise where all EU-level institutions were to be strengthened even as the delicate balance was to be maintained between the EU and member-state power and the authority. The suspension of the ratification process following the failures of the referenda in France and the Netherlands suggests that democracy will remain an unresolved issue for Europe in the near term, regardless of how bits and pieces of the Treaty are salvaged.

The institutional reforms envisioned in the Treaty could indeed have gone some way toward reducing the perceived problems of EU democracy. But they would not in any case have solved the real problem of democracy in the EU: the democratic deficit at the national level. EU member-states have yet to come to terms with the impact of the EU on the traditional workings of their national democracies. Whereas all attention has been focused on the future of European integration, or the process of building a more 'democratic' European public sphere, it is what has been called 'Europeanization,' or how member-states adapt their democracies to this evolving European public sphere, that holds the real key to the future.

The Challenges to National Democracies

Europeanization has brought radical change to all national governance practices. The workings of national institutional structures, policymaking processes, and representative politics have all been greatly affected by the addition of an EU layer of structures, processes, and politics. The locus of governmental power and authority has shifted to the EU. National executives now deliberate as twenty-five—soon to be twenty-seven, then thirty-three (and how many more?)—in the EU on issues previously decided solely within the national context. National parliaments translate EU decisions into national legislation. National judiciaries interpret EU laws and subnational regions implement EU regulations. Moreover, the focus of interest access and influence has moved from national capitals to Brussels. National interests have become enmeshed in an EU policy-formulation process which involves a vast array of actors in a highly complex set of interactions with multiple points of entry. National administrations have been pressed into more regulatory and legalistic modes of enforcement in place of administrative discretion and self-regulation. Finally, national partisan politics has been marginalized. Ministers speak in the Council more in the name of the national interest than for governmental majorities. Members of the EP speak more in terms of the public interest than for electoral majorities. Citizens have more influence in Brussels when lobbying as organized interests than when voting or protesting in national capitals.

Such changes in governance practices, however, are not the source of a national democratic deficit per se. After all, European integration, meaning the building of the EU level of governance, has served to promote member-states' democratic purposes in a whole host of ways. It has ensured that member-states have had a better chance to achieve collectively what would have been more difficult to attain individually: regional peace, economic prosperity, and world power. Although national governments have transferred large amounts of power and authority to the EU, their shared authority and participation in the joint actions of the EU have brought policy innovation and economic progress to an ever growing number of areas, ranging from monetary and industrial policy to labor and social policy. Moreover, although organized interests may have lost some measure of *national influence* as policy formulation has moved up to the EU level and some measure of flexibility as implementation has become more regulatory, they have been gaining an appreciable measure of *EU influence* while benefiting from greater equality and predictability in the application of the rules. Finally, despite the fact that national partisan politics is submerged by the EU's politics of interest, citizens' votes and voices are increasingly finding expression in the EU nevertheless.

What, then, is the problem with Europeanization? The changes in national practices are not in and of themselves a problem. Rather, it is that national conceptions of democratic power and authority, access and influence, and vote and voice remain largely unchanged. This disjunction between new practices and old ideas is at the root of questions raised about the legitimacy of the new patterns of governance and confusion over who is responsible or accountable for EU-related policies. The political fallout from such questions can be found in the razor-thin wins, and in the defeats, of Treaty referenda. This feeds the rise of the extreme right on the back of anti-immigrant sentiment. It fuels the concerns on the left about the impact of economic neoliberalism on social welfare. And it adds more generally to the political disaffection that comes from the loss of trust in government and of confidence in national political leaders.

But national leaders continue to project traditional visions of national democracy, speaking as if they fully retained their former authority and citizens, their influence. That national leaders have chosen not to engage their publics in deliberations about the effects of Europeanization on national democracy attests to the fact that the short-term political costs are high and the benefits low. Ironically, this failure allows national publics to hold their leaders accountable for policies for which they are not fully responsible, over which they may not have much control, and to which they may not even be politically committed. It also contributes to citizens' disenchantment and provides populists with grist for their mill. Were national leaders instead to engage their citizens in deliberations in light of the new realities, they well might generate new legitimizing ideas and avoid the populist extremes, thereby enabling a clearer and 'truer' assessment of the EU's impact on national democracy. Such ideas might even point to remedies via new national practices more adapted to the new realities.

The range of issues that contribute to the democratic deficit for national democracies cannot be attributed to the EU alone. Forces other than Europeanization have also been at play, including external pressures related to globalization and internal dynamics related to modernization, devolution, corruption, and even 'postindustrial' values. However, because the EU has been the focal point for change in member-states, it has become the focus for concern and for the search for remedies. But at the EU level no conceivable remedies can successfully address these problems. Only national leaders and publics through national discourse and deliberation can reevaluate their own national democracies in light of Europeanization. Without it, even the most brilliant of solutions for EU-level democracy may fail.

However, there is a further complicating factor. The EU has had a differential impact on its member-states' governance practices, largely as a matter of institutional 'fit' (or lack thereof). The EU is a highly *compound* polity in which governing activity is highly dispersed among multiple authorities. As such, it has been somewhat less directly disruptive to the compound polities of countries like Germany or Italy, where governing activity is similarly dispersed through multiple authorities, than to the more *simple* polities of countries like Britain or France, where governing activity is traditionally channeled through a single authority. For simple polities, the EU has served to diffuse the traditional concentration of power in the executive, opened up the traditionally limited interest access in policy formulation, diminished the traditional interest accommodation in policy implementation, and submerged their traditionally polarized, partisan politics. By contrast, for compound polities, the EU has mainly added to the traditional diffusion of power, further opened up interest access, allowed corporatist implementation to stand, and reinforced their consensus-oriented (albeit partisan) politics. As a result, the challenges to national ideas about democracy are concomitantly greater for the leaders of simple national polities than for those of compound polities. Therefore, the need for legitimating discourse is the greater in simple polities.

At least with regard to discourse, however, institutional architecture actually is advantageous for simple polities. This is because their leaders have greater capacity to speak to the challenges of Europeanization, were they to so choose, because of the very same concentration of authority that makes the changes in governance practices more disruptive. In simple polities, where a restricted governmental elite tends to coordinate policy construction, national leaders are better able to communicate their ideas to the public, by projecting a clear message in a single voice. By contrast, in compound polities where a much wider range of actors is involved in the *coordinative* discourse, it is harder for national leaders to develop a clear *communicative* discourse, given the number of potentially authoritative voices with differing messages. In the compound EU, these problems are multiplied by the larger range of national and EU-level actors involved in the coordinative discourse with little communicative voice of their own, since they depend on national leaders for communication to national publics. The fact that national leaders have tended not to speak to the democratic challenges, therefore, is arguably more serious for simple polities than compound polities, but serious nonetheless for all member-states and especially for the EU as a whole.

The democratic deficit thus results not so much because national governance practices have changed as because national leaders have bungled their communicative role. So far they have failed to generate ideas and discourse that engage national publics in deliberations about the EU-related changes to national democracies. Nor have they generated the ideas and discourse that would enable each member-state to fashion its own new, distinct 'democratic compromise' to legitimize the new realities of its more Europeanized polity.

How, then, should national leaders proceed in such deliberations? First and foremost, they have to decide what the EU *is*, in order to assess correctly what their countries are *becoming*. Without some clear idea about this, they are likely to compare the EU to the nation-state. The pro-Europeans will always find the EU wanting in power and democracy. For Euroskeptics, such a comparison raises the red flags of 'federalism' and 'superstate', with threats to sovereignty and identity.

In this book, I propose a more helpful way of thinking about the EU, as a *regional state*. By this I mean that the EU is best understood as a regional union of nation-states in which national differentiation persists alongside regional integration. In this regional state, sovereignty is shared with its constituent member-states and contingent on internal acceptance and external recognition; boundaries are variable with regard to policy reach and not as yet fixed with regard to geography; identity is composite in terms of 'being' and 'doing', given EU, national, and subnational levels; and governance is highly compound as a result of the dispersion of power, access, and voice through quasi-federal structures, quasi-pluralist processes, and consensus-oriented politics. Finally, democracy is fragmented between a national level that ensures government *by* and *of* the people through political participation and citizen representation and an EU level that involves primarily governance '*for* the people' through effective government and '*with* the people' through consultation with organized interests.

In such a fragmented democracy, the EU's legitimacy has been in question. But this is because the EU is compared to the ideal of the nation-state. Instead, were it to be reconceived of as a regional state, the democratic deficit would turn out not to be as great as it is sometimes made to appear. But the problems for national democracy turn out to be much greater. This is because while the EU makes *policy without politics*, given the marginalization of national partisan politics, its member-states suffer from having *politics without policy*. As increasing numbers of policies are removed from the national political arena, national citizens are left with little direct input into the EU-related policies that affect them, and only national politicians to hold to account for them. This has contributed to the problems of voter dissaffection and political extremism plaguing EU member-state democracies today.

The only solution is for member-states to come up with new national ideas and discourse that come to terms with these EU-related changes to the traditional workings of their national democracies. To do so, however, we must first understand how institutions affect European democracy at EU and national levels.

Institutional structures set the overall patterns for democracy. Federal structures ensure a greater diffusion of power among multiple authorities; unitary structures generate a greater concentration of power in a single authority. Such state structures combine with societal structures to shape policymaking processes which are pluralist, corporatist, or statist depending on their mix of diffusion or concentration. Representative politics in turn affects how institutional structures function and how policymaking proceeds, with majoritarian representation fostering a more competitive environment, proportional representation a more cooperative one. This institutional mix is also affected by culture, which frames all institutions, as does history, making for different ideas infusing actors' understandings of their actions and interests within institutions. Discourse, finally, is essential to actors' ability to maintain or change their politics, processes, and structures.

The Organization of the Book

This book, then, is about the nature of the EU governance system and its effects on national democracies. I begin in Chapter 1 with a discussion of the

EU as a regional state in terms of sovereignty, boundaries, identity, economy, governance, and democracy and highlight how this affects national democracies in terms of institutions, ideas, and discourse. In Chapters 2–4, I examine more closely the differential impact of the EU on national institutions by considering in turn the institutional structures, the policymaking processes, and the representative politics of the EU and its member-states. Chapter 5 provides an overview of the main arguments I developed tied to the main theoretical and methodological issues raised by the interplay of institutions, ideas, and discourse. In the conclusion, I discuss the future prospects for democracy in Europe.

I illustrate my argument with examples of four countries: Britain and France, as cases of simple polities, Germany and Italy, as compound polities. These countries not only are the four largest in Europe, accounting together for over half the population of the EU (in 2004, 68% of the EU15, 55% of the EU25), but also can fruitfully be compared and contrasted as matched pairs of cases with regard to governance practices. On a continuum between simple and compound polities, Britain and France are closer to the simple end of the continuum, as countries in which power, access, and voice have traditionally been channeled through a single authority. Germany and Italy are situated at the compound end of the continuum, where power, access, and voice have traditionally, and legitimately, been dispersed through multiple authorities. Thus, the two groups represent 'most different' cases for the purposes of comparison. But within each of the two groups, we also find ourselves with most different cases, given the significant differences in history, culture, institutional capacity, and politics as well as in responses to Europe between Britain and France on the one hand, Germany and Italy on the other. This enables me to provide not only a double 'contrast of contexts' which demonstrates my theory about the differential impact of Europeanization on simple and compound polities but also a 'parallel demonstration of theory' which shows how my theory about the general impact of Europeanization holds good across contrasting contexts.[1]

Other country contrasts are also highly revealing, such as large countries as opposed to smaller countries, economically advanced countries versus less developed ones, newer member-states versus older ones. Where possible, I also consider these dimensions by bringing in other examples. However, the impact of Europeanization on its member-states' institutions is best demonstrated by these four countries' experiences while making it possible to control for the most significant possible variations. These countries are more or less comparable in population size; levels of economic development—since these have the highest GDP among European member-states; and length of EU membership—since three of the four are original members while Britain came in with the first wave of enlargement. The cases lend themselves to

---

[1] Skocpol and Somers (1980).

other contrasts as well, such as between historically older nation-states like France and Britain and newer ones like Germany and Italy, or even between countries having greater or lesser administrative capacity, with Italy a stand-in for the newer Central and Eastern European member-states.

Methodologically, I use a mix of 'new institutionalist' approaches to develop my arguments, with 'soft' rational choice institutionalist assumptions about actors' interests and motives, historical institutionalist attention to how institutions shape such interests, sociological institutionalist awareness of how cultural rules and norms frame both interests and institutions, and my own 'discursive institutionalist' approach which adds the dimension of ideas and discourse to illuminate the dynamics of change in interests, institutions, and culture. My methodological approach is deliberately heterogeneous. I have long believed that to understand the complexity of reality requires as many perspectives as possible and thus as many methods as appropriate. I show this more explicitly in the last theoretical chapter, where I separate out institutions, ideas, and discourse. In the other chapters, these methods are intertwined in substantive considerations of the EU.

My evidence is based on extensive primary and secondary source materials, some quantitative analysis, much qualitative analysis, and some interviews. Although in the past I have used a large number of elite interviews to supplement other investigative methods, I have done this only to a minor extent in this work. When one's argument is that no one is talking about the topic being investigated, then elite interviews will yield rather thin results, that is, confirmation that no one is indeed talking about what they are not talking about. Still, I have spoken with a random sample of national and EU leaders who corroborate the fact that there is little discussion of the impact of the EU on national democracies—either because they are not talking about it themselves or because they agree that it is something others do not talk about. I have further confirmed this through content analyses of newspapers in all four countries.

One last comment: this book is about '*polity*' issues rather than about '*policy*' issues or '*politics*' per se. It concentrates on the major questions about institutions and democracy that are generally bundled up with the notion of polity rather than on the decisions and rules that make up EU and national policies or the elections, negotiations, and conflicts that make up EU and national politics. This is not to say that EU and national policies or politics should, could, or are being ignored. Rather, these are being considered only insofar as they raise polity issues. The literature is vast on the Europeanization of national policies and politics, rather thin on the Europeanization of national polities . . . which is why I set out to write this book.

1

The European Union as Regional State

When Joschka Fischer, foreign minister of Germany, made a speech on May 12, 2000 calling for a 'European federation' with a constituent treaty, a second chamber for a reinvigorated Parliament, and possibly an elected president, he did something unprecedented: he opened up a Europe-wide public debate about the future of European democracy. In the past, such a speech would more likely have remained part of confidential, intergovernmental discussions among member-states rather than becoming an opening gambit addressed to the European public as well as to member-states. Fischer's remarks spurred a generalized exchange among national leaders, then a Constitutional Convention, followed by an Intergovernmental Conference (IGC) to agree on a new Constitutional Treaty subject to parliamentary votes and national referenda.

The Constitutional Convention of the EU was an important first step in addressing the so-called democratic deficit[1] of the EU not only institutionally, with proposals for structural reform, but also procedurally, through intense deliberation and wide consultation.[2] The disappointments of the IGC, the travails of the ratification process, and the failure of the referenda in France and the Netherlands cannot detract from this. But even had the whole process been an unmitigated success, the problems of the democratic deficit would have remained because its problems and solutions are grounded in the wrong model: that of the nation-state. And they are focused at the wrong level. Whatever the problems and constitutional remedies at the EU level, they can do little to address, let alone resolve, the democratic deficit at the national level.

As everyone reminds us, the EU is certainly not a nation-state. It is *sui generis*, an 'unidentified political object' according to Jacques Delors,[3] 'less than a federation, more than a regime' for William Wallace,[4] more of a future

---

[1] There is a vast literature on the democratic deficit in the EU. See, for example, Williams (1990), Pogge (1997), Bellamy and Castiglione (2000), Greven and Pauly (2000), and Moravcsik (2002).
[2] Magnette (2003).
[3] Cited in Schmitter (1996: 1).
[4] For the first phrase, Wallace (1983), for the second, Wallace (1996).

'neomedieval empire' than a 'neo-Westphalian state' for Jan Zielonka,[5] a 'condominio' for Philippe Schmitter,[6] or maybe even 'the first truly postmodern political form' for John Ruggie.[7] And yet, in discussions of the democratic deficit, the EU is consistently (and wrongly) compared to the nation-state, and necessarily found wanting. I argue that we would do better to conceive of it as a regional state in the making, by which I mean a regional union of nation-states[8] in which the creative tension between the Union and its member-states ensures both ever-increasing regional integration and ever-continuing national differentiation.

I use the term 'regional state' deliberately here for two reasons: first, as can ideational strategy to show how the concept of the state an encompass the EU, and second, as a discursive strategy to break the hold of the nation-state concept with regard to understandings of democracy in the EU and its member-states. Thus, even if the first strategy promoting the idea of the regional state was not to win over many converts, the second strategy still serves a useful purpose, by showing how different the EU is and will remain at least for the medium term from its closest counterparts, the economically advanced, democratic nation-states such as the United States, Japan, Switzerland, or even its own member-states (leaving aside in this instance how they have themselves changed as a result of European integration).

These nation-states have had a certain finality characterized in principle by indivisible sovereignty, fixed boundaries, coherent identity, established government, and cohesive democracy. By contrast, the EU has no such finality but, rather, is better conceptualized as in a constant process of becoming.[9] What it is becoming, moreover, is not a nation-state but, rather, a regional state, given shared sovereignty, variable boundaries, composite identity, *highly compound* governance, and fragmented democracy split between government *by* and *of* the people at the national level, and governance, *for* and *with* the people at the EU level. Legitimacy, in this context, is naturally in question when the EU is compared to the nation-state. It need not be if we rethink legitimacy in terms of a regional state. However, other legitimacy problems intrude, in particular, with regard to the EU's nation-state members. The problems for national democracy result from EU-related changes in national governance practices, challenges to national ideas about democracy, and the lack of discourses that sufficiently legitimate the changes. National politics in particular is affected as 'policy without politics' at the EU level makes for 'politics without policy' at the national level. All of this, however, is more of a problem for simple polities than compound

---

[5] Zielonka (2001). On the term 'neomedieval empire', see Waever (1997: 61).
[6] Schmitter (2000).
[7] Ruggie (1993: 139–40).
[8] My thanks to Renaud Dehousse for suggesting the term: regional union of nation-states.
[9] Laffan et al. (2000: 73).

polities, despite the fact that leaders in simple polities have a greater capacity to speak to the changes, given a potentially stronger communicative discourse.

In what follows, I consider in turn the EU's move to regional sovereignty, the variability of the EU's regional boundaries, the composite character of EU identity, the compound framework, and the fragmented nature of the EU's democracy. I end with a discussion of the real sources of the democratic deficit in the EU, linked to the lack of ideas and discourse about national democracy, and how this affects simple and compound national polities.

From 'Indivisible' Nation-State Sovereignty to 'Shared' Regional Sovereignty

Although it began as a regional trade association of nation-states, the EU has gone much farther than any other such association toward a formal governance system with jurisdiction over a wide range of issues and areas. Among regional trade associations, only the EU has developed a single currency, a single market, a single voice in international trade negotiation, a single anti-trust authority, common policies on environmental protection, worker safety and health, a common foreign and security policy, and even the beginnings of a common defense policy.

The EU is consequently no longer just a regional trade association made up of nation-states. But it is still very different from a nation-state. And yet, when considered in terms of its international form, it is generally compared—unfavorably—to the nation-state in terms of power and sovereignty.

Nation-states tend to be defined first of all by their sovereignty. Sovereignty, as elucidated by Stephen Krasner, is attributed to states that have international recognition from other states ('international law' sovereignty); autonomy with regard to the exclusion of external authority from their own territory ('Westphalian' sovereignty); control over activities within and across their borders ('interdependence' sovereignty); and exclusive power to organize authority within the polity ('domestic' sovereignty).[10] A nation-state such as the United States has all of these attributes at least in theory (even though in practice, autonomy and control have been eroding in response to the pressures of globalization[11]). The EU has none of these on its own, but it shares them to varying degrees and in various ways with its member-states.

The nation-states that make up the EU can no longer themselves be said to have all the attributes of sovereignty, having 'pooled their sovereignty' in the process of European integration by agreeing by treaty to share certain responsibilities that in the past were the purview of individual nations

[10] The definitions are those of Krasner (1999).
[11] There is a vast literature on this. See the discussion in Schmidt (2002a), ch. 1.

alone.[12] In pooling their sovereignty, European countries accepted limits to all four types of nation-state sovereignty in exchange for the gains that have come from the exercise of collective power and authority and the achievement of joint goals. For example, in international trade negotiations, EU member-states gave up their individual recognition by other states when they agreed to have their interests represented by the EU commissioner for international trade. In the monetary arena, most ceded their autonomy of decision-making to the independent authority of the European Central Bank (ECB), while in the single market they gave up individual control over what goes on in the national territory by agreeing to joint action initiated by the Commission.[13] What is more, across policy areas, EU member-states have given up their exclusive authority to organize the polity in the process of accepting the precedence of EU institutions in setting policy and judging compliance in an ever-widening array of domains.[14] And although such giving up of sovereignty is sometimes contested in practice, for example, when the French threatened to veto the GATT round in the early 1990s because of dissatisfaction with the agricultural aspects of the agreement or when the French and Germans do not stick to the deficit spending criteria of the Stability of Growth Pact, the general principle has been consecrated.

In short, the originally indivisible sovereignty of EU member-states has increasingly become 'divided' or shared through the transfer of nation-state competencies to different EU institutions. Sovereignty need be seen as divided, however, only if we assume the concept to be a rigid construct, indivisible, and an attribute of the nation-state alone, as defined by most realists in International Relations (IR) theory.[15] If we were to consider sovereignty instead as 'socially constructed' and evolving over time, following more constructivist IR theorists,[16] then the EU could be seen as constituting a new kind of regional sovereignty. Here, as authority has drifted upward in the process of European integration, as the countries making up the EU have moved from 'sovereign nations' to 'member-states',[17] the EU itself has been transformed from a federation of sovereign nations to a new kind of sovereign region which will continue as such so long as it is accepted on the inside by its own sovereign member-states and is recognized on the outside by other sovereign nation-states. The United States prior to the Civil War is probably the closest approximation to

---

[12] Keohane and Hoffmann (1991).

[13] For an extended discussion of the impact of the EU on national autonomy and control, see Schmidt (2002b: ch. 1).

[14] This also touches on questions of 'popular sovereignty' involving democratic access to decision-making (see Newman 1996: 12–15). But that is an issue dealt with later.

[15] If, by contrast, we were to take our definition from the federalism rather than the IR literature, divided sovereignty would be a perfectly acceptable term, and it is in fact the one traditionally applied to the United States.

[16] See Biersteker (1999).

[17] See Sbragia (1994: 70).

this state of affairs in a nation-state, since internal acceptance of sovereignty was as much an issue as was its external recognition.[18]

Sovereignty inside the EU is the product of the continuous negotiations among member-states and with EU institutions over when, how, and in which domains to allow decisions to be taken at the EU level in the exercise of regional sovereignty rather than individually at the national level in the name of nation-state sovereignty. It is important to note, however, that any shift of sovereignty to the EU level has a different significance for each of the member-states, depending on when and how the decision affected it. In the monetary policy arena, for example, although the EU's sovereignty in monetary policy was formally established as of 1979 with regard to the European Monetary System (EMS) and in 1999 for European Monetary Union (EMU), member-states' perceived loss of national sovereignty with regard to monetary autonomy came at different times. For France, the critical juncture came in 1983 with the Socialist government's 'great U-turn' in macroeconomic policy—the shift toward monetarism in order to stay in the EMS—while the public debate on sovereignty came only with the referendum on the Maastricht Treaty in 1992. For the UK, by contrast, sovereignty was less of an issue when it joined the EMS in 1979, since it did not participate in the Exchange Rate Mechanism (ERM), and the critical juncture has yet to occur, given its negotiated opt-out to EMU in the Maastricht Treaty.[19] Neither Germany nor Italy had the same kinds of defining moments with regard to monetary sovereignty. In Germany, where EMU followed the country's own patterns and prejudices, sovereignty was simply not an issue except perhaps at the very last moment, with the abandonment of the Deutschmark—arguably one of the few symbols of sovereignty in postwar Germany. In Italy, where governments have long had difficulty exercising monetary autonomy or control, EMU constituted, if anything, a reinforcement of sovereignty through the government's success in acceding to the euro. EU sovereignty from the inside, in short, results from the combination of two interconnected processes: EU-level negotiations that consecrate an EU regional sovereignty and member-states' differentiated adjustment to the development of such EU-level sovereignty.

Sovereignty from the outside, moreover, is largely the result of the continual adjustment to these internal processes by other sovereign nation-states which generally accept the EU as sovereign in areas where EU member-states have already so agreed. In this sense, sovereignty is not just 'socially constructed,' it is 'relational' in that it is realized 'through participation in the various regimes that regulate and order the international system.'[20]

---

[18] My thanks to Martin Shapiro for this insight.   [19] See Schmidt (2002a; ch. 1 and 6).
[20] Chayes and Chayes (1995: 27)—see the discussion in Slaughter (2001: 285), and in Keohane (2002: 748).

Thus, for example, the United States tacitly accepted the EU as a sovereign region in international trade negotiations beginning with the Uruguay Round and continuing with the Doha Round, with the EU international trade commissioner responsible for speaking for the EU in much the way the US Special Trade Representative speaks for the United States. In addition, the United States recognizes the competence of the EU in competition policy decisions, even when these scuttle mergers between American companies because of their anticompetitive effects on the European market, as in the case of GE's acquisition of Honeywell. And the United States of course recognizes the sovereignty of the EU in European monetary policy and the single currency.

However, the United States also considers the EU far from sovereign in security and defense policy, and lacking in any 'one telephone number to call'. And yet, EU military missions in Bosnia and elsewhere depend on both Serbian (re. US) and UN recognition of the EU as a 'sovereign' military actor. In security matters, the different approaches to sovereignty of the two powers—unitary in the United States's external authority, multiple rather than joint authority for the EU—is at the source of serious potential problems between the two.[21] In the case of Iraq, the EU, by not having resolved the question of sovereignty in the security and defense arena, left the United States to decide with whom to deal—whether 'new Europe' or 'old Europe', in the words of Donald Rumsfeld.

The security and defense arena is where the notion of a regional state, with the emphasis on state, is likely to be hardest for traditional international relations scholars, immersed in state theories based on Max Weber's classic definition of the nation-state as having a monopoly on the means of exercising coercive power. There is no doubt that the EU lacks this—but this is exactly why I emphasize the regional in *regional* state. As a regional state, coercive power is also shared by the member-states—which may or may not choose to act collectively through the EU—while the EU level on its own, separate from its member-states, does not have the means to exercise such 'hard' power (although with the member-states, it increasingly exercises hard power, with fifteen European Security and Defense Policy (ESDP) missions by the end of 2005). Instead the EU has 'soft power', a term that should be understood not just to mean that it provides humanitarian aid, or 'does the dishes', while the United States, as a 'hard power', does the fighting.[22] It also suggests the projection of power through the rule of law, both internally—since the EU, unlike any nation-state, works by relying on member-states to police themselves—and externally. This is where the EU seeks to promote international

---

[21] Keohane (2002). See also Aalberts (2004) on the constructivist view of the 'relational' nature of sovereignty, and Wendt (1995).

[22] On the extensive debates on the EU's soft power vs. the United State's 'hard' power, see Kagan (2003), Nye (2000).

governance through 'norms' and multilateral institutions as opposed to through sovereignty-based unilateralism or allowing certain countries—read the United States—to opt in and out of international treaties.[23]

Thus, we could argue that while losses of power in a Weberian sense may have undermined member-states' national autonomy and control, such losses have been offset by gains in power in a Parsonian sense, as countries have attained national goals and enhanced national influence through shared EU-level authority and control. We should not forget that individual governments have gained in powers by being able to achieve collectively that which they can no longer achieve individually. Together, through the shared supra-national authority of the EU, they can better meet the challenges of global and regional economic interdependence, find solutions to transnational problems in areas such as immigration, terrorism, the environment, and drug trafficking, and more generally develop common solutions to unanticipated problems.[24] What is more, internally, EU legislative requirements for transposition and implementation, national participation in EU networks, and the circulation of EU ideas have all served to strengthen the capacities of domestic actors and to modernize national administrations.

It is fitting that Europe, as the birthplace of the modern nation-state and of the concept of sovereignty, should build on its own inventions by becoming the birthplace of the sovereign regional state. But as a regional state, the EU's sovereignty is much more contingent than the nation-state given that it depends not only on external recognition policy area by policy area but also on internal acceptance by its member-states, and not just by its citizens. The EU already has state-like sovereignty in a range of policy areas that makes it much more than a 'neomedieval empire' but it still lacks—and may always lack—the central control and coercive power necessary to make it a neo-Westphalian state. While the use of the term state may therefore be difficult for classically trained IR theorists, there is no other word that does justice to the growing power and developing sovereignty—however contingent—of the EU. What makes the contingency of EU sovereignty a continuing reality is equally a result of the variability of the EU's boundaries.

A Regional State With Variable Boundaries

Nation-states tend to be defined also by their territoriality and their notionally fixed boundaries. The EU's regional state, by contrast, has been expanding with no clear end in view on what those territorial boundaries may ultimately be. Questions abound regarding whether Turkey will become a member and, if

---

[23] Laïdi (2005).
[24] See Moravcsik (1998), Kassim (2005: 288).

it does, what about the Ukraine or even Russia, such that the EU would extend from Land's End, Cornwall to Vladivostok, from the Baltic to the Black Sea, and from the North Cape to Central Asia. Such questions about the geographical 'ends' of Europe, however, require answers also about its 'ends' in terms of polity, economy, and society.

The EU's boundaries are not only not fixed in terms of territory, they also vary in terms of policy arenas, including areas that are ordinarily seen as essential to nation-state sovereignty such as border controls, monetary policy and the currency, foreign policy, and defense. The Schengen group of countries that eliminated internal border controls has expanded greatly since its inception in 1995, and will grow even more rapidly with the addition of the Eastern European candidate countries, but the UK and Ireland remain outside whereas Norway and Iceland are in, despite the fact that they are not member-states. The eurozone currently encompasses twelve out of fifteen member-states, and will only increase slowly, depending on the outcome of referenda in Denmark, and Britain and the economic readiness of the ten candidate countries scheduled to become members—a matter of a decade or more by most estimates. ESDP encompasses all current member-states other than Denmark, which gained an opt-out in the Amsterdam Treaty, and even non-EU members such as Switzerland and Turkey (through ESDP missions). But decisions on troop deployment (and most everything else) remain sovereign decisions of member-states, EU and non-EU, and therefore highly variable as well.[25] Only the single market seems to encompass all member-states. But even here, countries have been granted individual exemptions or delays in application, as the seven-year delay on the implementation with regard to alcohol policy in Sweden and on the freedom of movement of labor with regard to the candidate countries.

The variability of policy boundaries may increase even further if 'structured' cooperation becomes truly viable and is taken advantage of. 'Enhanced' cooperation—introduced in the Amsterdam Treaty, loosened (but not enough) with the Nice Treaty, and further loosened with the Constitutional Treaty— allows a certain number of member-states (eight under the Nice Treaty, one-third of member-states under the Constitutional Treaty) to go forward on their own with initiatives as long as the Commission deems that these do not undermine the functioning of the single market or the *acquis communautaires*. Notionally, it could mean the harmonization of welfare state policies for member-states with similar kinds of pension systems—for example, conservative welfare states with occupationally based benefit systems; or the harmonization of fiscal policies for countries with similar kinds of tax systems—say, high tax Scandinavian countries with generous welfare states. In the foreign and security area, which has been the main focus of discussions of 'structured'

[25] Howorth (2004).

cooperation, it would allow member-states with common interests to move forward, but is designed to be as inclusive as possible.[26]

This sort of differentiated integration or 'variable geometry', whether based on this or other means, has not yet gotten terribly far.[27] The obstacles to it result from two interconnected objections: First, a 'two-speed' Europe is seen as problematic because where there is an advance group there are always also those who take up the rear—this view explains criticism of the proposals for a smaller core group to go forward on EMU when this was under discussion in the mid-1990s. Second, uniformity is assumed good for its own sake because it promotes integration whereas anything else could represent moves backward into fragmentation and 'dis'-integration.[28] Both such objections have been present in particular in the Commission, with the view that for the EU to advance, it would be best served by doing so together at the same pace in the same way. Opt-outs, therefore, are seen as regrettable exceptions, for example, for the British and the Danes in the Maastricht Treaty—the first breach of uniformity—and not to be repeated if at all possible. For the candidate countries, accession means accepting all the *acquis communautaires* despite the problems these may cause, for example, in accepting Schengen—which is not only extremely costly but also creates serious problems with regard to relations with neighboring economies and labor flows, as in Poland's relations with the Ukraine. On EMU, moreover, countries like Rumania are pressed to liberalize their capital controls despite the deleterious impact on the economy because EU civil servants are focused on the EU's legal requirements, not on the health of the country.[29]

If the future of the EU is of a nation-state, then the focus on uniformity might make sense. If it is to be a regional state, then the insistence on uniformity is much more open to question. By the same token, however, too much variability could itself compromise the regional integration process. The challenge for the EU is how to strike a balance between integration and differentiation, policy area by policy area.

But whatever the EU's future variability in terms of policy geometry, and however far the extension of the EU's territory, the EU has already undermined the coherence and coincidence of the territorially based boundaries of its nation-state members not only in terms of policies but also in terms of culture, economics, governance, and military. Europeanization, as Stefano Bartolini puts it, has been a 'process of nation state *boundary transcendence*, resulting in a process of *dedifferentiation of European polities*' after a history of five centuries of progressive differentiation into nation-states.[30] And for older nation-states, such as the UK and France, such a process of boundary transcendence is arguably more difficult to countenance than for younger ones such as Germany and Italy.

[26] Howorth (2004).   [27] De Búrca and Scott (2000).
[28] See Scharpf (2003*b*), who links this to problems of democratic legitimacy in the EU.
[29] Abdelal n/a.   [30] Bartolini (2002: 2005).

The consequences of such nation-state boundary transcendence, however, cannot be fully understood without seeing how it intersects with national identities that have been at least in part forged on the basis of nation-state boundaries and notions of sovereignty.

A Regional State With a Composite Identity

Nation-states are also often defined by their sense of 'nationhood', or that which binds them through ties of collective identity, shared culture and values, common language(s), historical memories, myths of origin, a sense of membership, and a sense of common destiny. On these grounds, the EU is far from becoming, let alone being, a nation-state. The EU lacks the nation-state's 'thick identity' because it has, as Joseph Weiler put it, 'neither the subjective element (the sense of shared collective identity and loyalty) nor the objective conditions which could produce ... the kind of homogeneity of the organic national-cultural conditions on which peoplehood depends.'[31] Whereas most nation-states have a majority of citizens who have a primary or at least secondary identity tied to their nation-state, Europeans by all opinion polls identify much less with Europe than with their nation-state or subnational region, although Europeans do have multiple identities, of which being European is certainly one—just not the most salient. Only 4 percent of citizens put European as their primary sense of identity in 1999—a large number of whom I daresay cluster in Brussels—as opposed to 45 percent who identified themselves in terms of nationality alone, and 48 percent with some mix of European and national identity.[32]

However, national identity is not just a question of 'being' but of 'doing'—in the words of Jolyon Howorth—through national political, economic, and social structures and activities that build a sense of belonging across time.[33] Such doing is closely tied to notions of citizenship, the building blocks of which include rights, social as well as political; participation, political as much as social; and belonging, as part of a political community even more than of a cultural community.[34] Importantly, a political community need not be based primarily on ethno-cultural identity but rather, as Habermas argues, on 'the practices of citizens who exercise their rights to participation and communication'.[35] On these grounds, instead of finding the EU wanting as a 'community of identity', we might do better to speak of its prospects as a 'community of fate', in the sense of Raymond Breton, in which a political community arises out of people's 'experience of interdependence', which 'grows out of politics, instead of preceding it', and which combines perceptions of distributive

---

[31] See Weiler (1995).   [32] Eurobarometer (52: 10).   [33] Howorth (2000).
[34] Bellamy (2004: 6–11).   [35] Habermas (1996: 495); see also Cerutti (2003: 28–9).

justice with a commitment to collective ends.[36] The doing in any such community of fate, however, is not only the product of citizens acting in the world but also of governments acting on it.

More specifically, the state in modern history has actively taken a role in constructing a sense of nationhood. If the nation is, as Benedict Anderson suggests, an 'imagined political community' in which people imagine that they form a community with ties of fraternity limited by territorial boundaries and endowed with sovereignty, then the nation was largely the creation of states which have used mass communication, mass education, historiography, and conscription to consolidate the nation.[37] Historical memories and traditions have often been 'invented' rather than 'discovered',[38] with much 'forgotten' in the process, as Ernest Renan has reminded us,[39] and with nations invented even 'where they do not exist', as Ernest Gellner has noted.[40] The oft-quoted phrase that sums up the process is from Massimo d'Azeglio who, on the successful unification of Italy in 1871, said: 'We have made Italy, now we must make Italians.' In France, where the state was in the business of nation-building for a much longer time, the modern sense of nationhood was nonetheless forged around the same time as Italy, during the Third Republic, which turned 'peasants into Frenchmen', in Eugen Weber's words.[41]

The EU has also begun to use such tools, but to much less effect for a number of reasons, not the least of which is the fact that the nation-states that make up its members continue to be engaged in the self-same task. The EU can be no more than an add-on for three reasons. First, because it depends in large measure on its member-states to build a sense of Europe, given the lack of a common language, Europe-wide mass communication system, political leadership with Europe-wide election campaigns, and so forth. Second, because it is imagined mainly through the different lenses of national identity and purposes. Finally, because it lacks the levers of constraint used by states, such as conscription, forced language and educational policies, and so on.

The Europe represented in the public imagination, at least as portrayed by national leaders, is different from one country to the next. For the French, Europe is to be like France, with an effective governance authority, a defense identity, clearly defined borders, and a cultural mission that promotes a high European culture and democratic values. By contrast, for the British, Europe is more of an addition to the nation-state than a clone of it, with undefined boundaries expandable as far as possible, with limited governance authority to promote commerce and trade but not to impose a cultural mission or too

---

[36] Breton (1995: 42). See also the discussion of Choudry (2001: 395–6).
[37] Anderson (1983: 6–7).
[38] Hobsbawn and Ranger (1983).
[39] Renan (1947 (1): 892)—cited in Anderson (1983).
[40] Gellner (1964: 169)—cited in Anderson (1983).
[41] Weber (1976). For a short account of the long history, see Jenkins (2000).

many statutory rules, and not to interfere with its other relationship—the Trans-Atlantic one.[42] For the Italians, Europe is the opposite of Italy, and therefore to be embraced for its effective governance, rule of law, transparency with regard to decision-making, and more. Finally, for the Germans, Europe is less defined by what it does than what it is, as a larger entity which subsumes German being under its doing, thereby protecting the country from its own past and bringing it into the future as part of a larger imagined community.

As a result of this plurality of nationally imagined Europes, it is very hard for the EU to have a common identity or a sense of 'regionhood' equivalent to member-states' senses of nationhood. Complicating this even further is that in some nation-states, subnational regionhood constitutes a local territorial identity which outweighs the national. Here, European identity may even come before the national, and just after the subnational regional, as in the Basque Country, Corsica, Scotland, and arguably Northern Ireland.[43] But building a sense of European identity is still possible if one accepts its necessarily composite nature—with national (and subnational regional) constructions of Europeanness alongside EU constructions of Europeanness.

'Inventing' Europe at the EU level has been a slow process, however. Although one could argue that the sense of common destiny has been growing for a long time, given the European project since the 1950s, conscious attempts to build other aspects of a European identity started late. They began with just a nod to the need to create a European identity in the final communiqué of the 1969 Hague Conference and the 1983 'Solemn Declaration of European Identity', which was consolation for the failure yet again to create a common foreign policy. They have picked up speed since the mid-1980s, though, with the creation of symbols with which people can identify, such as the European passport, European license plates, the European flag, the European anthem 'Ode to Joy', and most recently the euro, arguably the single most important identity-creating symbol for Europe yet. The EU has also built European identity by reinforcing ties among citizens, such as through school exchange programs like Erasmus and Socrates and Jean Monnet awards; by encouraging research on 'European' problems through a vast number of cross-national research projects—which has the double function of increasing knowledge of Europe while reinforcing ties; with school textbook projects to rewrite European history, by emphasizing the progress toward integration while downplaying the wars, making heroes of Schuman and Monnet; by increasing awareness of Europe through public awareness campaigns, awards such as the 'European Woman of the Year', the European library and museum; through signs on roads on highways in Greece, Spain, and Portugal built

---

[42] This comes out strongly when reading Siedentop (2000), Shor (2000). See also Brewin (2000).

[43] See Keating and Jones (1995), Keating (2000).

with the help of EU structural funds; and much, much more.[44] Such constructions of identity, focused on creating a sense of being European, are underpinned by the fact that Europeans are doing more and more as part of the EU decision-making process, and thereby becoming more European.

Thus, a composite European identity is being built through the process of doing, but has yet to get very far with regard to being. Any such identity, moreover, is unlikely ever to become anything like that of a nation-state. This is not only because of the EU's variable boundaries in terms of policies as well as territory and its divided, two level sovereignty. It is also for historical reasons related to the priority of nationally-based identities as well as the 'post-modern' nature of EU politics. Moreover, although the plurality of nationally imagined Europes means that it is harder for the EU to have the equivalent of a nation-state's sense of nationhood built on a community of identity, the kind of composite identity built in the EU may very well be the essence of a regional state's sense of regionhood built on a community of fate. What is more, if we note that doing involves not just creating EU symbols but also working toward greater integration in economic endeavors and political action—through cross-border national interactions as well as through the EU—we can expect that a sense of regionhood will only be reinforced as the EU regional state continues to develop economically and politically.

A Regional State With Highly Compound Governance and Fragmented Democracy

If democratic legitimacy in a nation-state is predicated on a country's indivisible sovereignty within a fixed set of boundaries with a coherent national identity enabling the expression of a collective will, then the EU is clearly very far from achieving nation-state legitimacy. But this does not mean that the EU lacks democratic legitimacy. Much the contrary, since it can be shown to pass most of the legitimacy tests required of nation-states in terms of political participation, citizen representation, effective government, and interest consultation—only in somewhat different ways with different emphases. This is because the EU has a more *highly compound* governance system than any nation-state, with governing authority much more dispersed among multiple authorities, and with institutions more fully 'multilevel'[45] and more 'multi-centered'[46] than those of any nation-state. This makes for a more fragmented democracy in which legitimacy depends on both EU and national levels.

[44] Shor (2000).
[45] See Marks et al. (1996).
[46] See Nicolaïdis and Howse (2001).

EU Governance by, of, and for the People

More ink has been spilt in recent years over the issue of the democratic deficit in the EU than just about any other, so I will not even attempt to lay out the full range of the debates or the literature. Briefly put, increasing numbers of democratic theorists have pointed to a democratic deficit in the EU mainly because of the lack of 'input democracy' through political participation and the impossibility of such given the lack of a collective will and identity or a common political space.[47] Only a few defend the EU as providing 'output democracy' through effective regulatory governance or as no worse than other democracies, given its checks and balances and delegated authorities.[48]

Most see the main answer to the problem of the democratic deficit as the development of EU-level institutions that are more participatory and representative, thus the focus on a new Constitutional Treaty intended to strengthen the democratic status of the EU.[49] But this is not so easy.

The central problem for the development of more democratic EU institutions has to do with the fragmented nature of democracy in the EU. Democratic legitimacy in the nation-state has traditionally been seen as depending on, in the phrase coined by Abraham Lincoln, 'government *by* the people, *of* the people, and *for* the people.' This means that citizens are guaranteed political participation, citizen representation, and effective government.[50]

In the EU, 'governance *by* and *of* the people' has generally been much weaker than 'governance *for* the people', since political participation and citizen representation are situated primarily at the national level. EU-level representative politics are in fact very far from that of any nation-state, given the lack of EU-wide elections for a president and/or a prime minister and for a legislature with vigorous political parties in a competitive electoral system. Instead, the EU has the indirect representation afforded by nationally elected executives through the Council and the much weaker direct representation of the EP, given the 'second-order' nature of EP elections, in which citizens' voting has long focused more on national than European issues.[51] EU elections to the EP do not make the grade as governance *by* and *of* the people also because they do not reflect or express a collective will, as elections in principle do in a nation-state democracy. But how could they, since the EU has no collective identity, which is a *sine qua non* to constitute a *demos*[52] or to express

---

[47] Scharpf (2000), Weiler (1995), Grimm (1995), Habermas (1996), Greven (2000).

[48] Majone (1998), Moravcsik (2002).

[49] See, for example Collignon 2004.

[50] Often, this is summarized in the distinction between input democracy—consisting of government *by* the people, focused on political participation, and generally traced back to Rousseau—and output democracy—consisting of government *for* the people, focused on government effectiveness, and traced back to Montesquieu. See Scharpf (1999: ch. 1).

[51] See Reif and Schmitt (1980), van der Eijk and Franklin (1996).

[52] See Weiler (1999).

a collective will. Any 'government *by* and *of* the people' based on the electoral politics of the kind found in the nation-state—in particular where this involves elections of representatives by majority rule[53]—is not possible in the EU at the moment.

What is more, unlike in any nation-state, where party politics and partisan competition is ever-present, in the EU, partisan differences and political contestation have been submerged by the general quest for consensus and compromise. In the EU, the Council tends to be dominated by the politics of national interest or even European interest, as national ministers are expected to speak for their country or the EU as a whole rather than for the political party or coalition of which they are a member. Moreover, the EP is primarily focused on the politics of the public interest, as members of the European Parliament (MEPs) are more likely to coalesce around 'citizen' issues rather than party politics, given the difficulties of party organizing.[54] Finally, the Commission is mostly concerned with the politics of organized interests, as Commission officials seek input from 'civil society'—meaning the vast range of interest groups that seek access and influence in Brussels—as well as from government actors.[55] This results in *policy without politics*, meaning that policymaking at the EU level goes on without the kind of political competition, partisanship, and party politics typical of the national political arena.

But this does not mean that 'democracy beyond the nation-state' is impossible,[56] or that the EU is necessarily democratically illegitimate. As Kalypso Nicolaïdis puts it, although there may be no *demos*, or a single people, there are *demoi*, or peoples, who make up the EU '*demoicracy*'.[57] The 'will *of* the peoples' can still be expressed, and is—indirectly and strongly through the national executives sitting in the Council of Ministers; directly but much more weakly through the elected members of the EP. Moreover, that the EU lacks a full-fledged parliamentary democracy of the kind found in the member-states ought not in any case be used as the normative standard by which to measure the EU, since the member-states themselves have not agreed on the legitimacy of any further parliamentarization of the EU.[58]

What is more, if legitimacy means legislating in such a way as to safeguard minority rights while responding to the majority will, then the EU, if anything, governs *for* the people in a way that better protects against abuses of power than most nation-state democracies. Any decision subject to the unanimity rules means that national executives can veto it.[59] And the consensus

---

[53] Kielmansegg (1996), Offe (1998), Scharpf (1998).
[54] Schmidt (1999*b*). On the difficulties of building party politics at the EU level, see Ladrech (1999), Mair (1995). See also the discussion in Chapter 4.
[55] See Imig and Tarrow (2001), Goetz and Hix (2001).
[56] See the discussion on the possibilities by Zuern (2000).
[57] Nicolaïdis (2003). On the nature of the *demoi*, see Pogge (1998).
[58] See Majone (1998), Schmitter (1998).
[59] For Furio Cerutti (2005), however, this rule is the source of a second 'democratic deficit', since any one government can frustrate the will of the Europeans as a whole.

rule—by which any issue with high political saliency is not forced on the concerned member-state—serves to safeguard any minority rights that would not already be protected by the supermajorities (of over 70%) required in qualified majority voting.[60] On top of this, the EP has powers of oversight over appointments to the EU Commission and over legislation—in particular with the every-expanding codecision procedure, which enables it to block as well as amend Council decisions.[61] In addition, there are a number of conflict minimizing mechanisms which also act as safeguards, such as the 'proportionality' doctrine in which the European Court of Justice (ECJ) can invalidate any decision which involves a trade off between values where the imposition of one value is not the 'absolute minimum infringement necessary to serve the other value'.[62] On these grounds, any fears of 'bureaucratic despotism'[63] coming from a federal 'superstate' may be exaggerated, as Andrew Moravcsik reminds us, especially if one adds that the EU has much less in the way of taxing, spending, implementing, and coercive powers than any nation-state.[64]

The dangers of any federal superstate are also diminished by the EU's quasi-federal institutional arrangements, which contain even greater checks and balances than in national federal systems. In the EU, the vertical division of powers between EU federal and sub-federal levels is more tipped in favor of the sub-'federal', that is, of the EU member-states, than of any federal nation-state. The EU guarantees its constituent members much greater independent powers than those of any federal nation-state in policy formulation, to shape as well as to veto legislation, and in policy implementation, to transpose EU directives and to administer them (along with the regions).[65] This is reinforced by the principle of subsidiarity as well as by the horizontal 'confusion of powers' among branches of EU governance, in which the Council, Commission, EP, and ECJ have overlapping competences and oversight.[66] The very multiplicity of authorities engaged in EU decision-making, together with the vast range of interests engaged in the EU interest consultation process, establishes a kind of mutual horizontal control.[67] In this kind of federal legitimacy *for* the people— in which the system of checks and balances ensures against the excesses of a superstate—the EU leads all nation-states, given the need for a very high consensus among institutional actors for anything to be agreed.

By the same token, however, this very system of checks and balances can potentially undermine governing effectiveness '*for* the people' as a result of the immobility that comes in the case of lack of agreement on rules. This is a potential problem not only with regard to rules not agreed but also to those formerly agreed but now no longer accepted. The problem is that rules once made are very difficult to reverse in the absence of an EU politics or strong

---

[60] Scharpf (2003*b*). [61] Shackleton (2005). [62] Stone Sweet (2000: 98).
[63] Siedentop (2000). [64] Moravcsik (2002: 606–10). [65] Schmidt (2003).
[66] Schmidt (1999*a*). [67] Héritier (1999).

political participation '*by* the people' akin to that of the United States—in which an activating popular consensus can overcome all the checks and balances through the election of a president with an overriding majority in the House and the Senate, able to threaten to pack the Supreme Court, as did Roosevelt.[68] This leaves the EU at risk of implementing rules that are no longer seen as legitimate, and even of provoking member-states to defy the rules, thereby risking a crisis of legitimacy. The restrictive criteria of the Stability and Growth Pact of EMU and the subsequent actions by France and Germany forcing the suspension of the rules are cases in point.

It is in the supranational governance mode, in which certain authorities have delegated powers to act for the EU, that the EU runs the greatest risk of being accused of being a 'federal superstate'. However, here, if there are dangers from a superstate, then this is something all nation-states also face. The kinds of delegated authority given over to the Commission, the ECB, the Competition authority, the International Trade representative, or the ECJ are the same given over to independent bodies everywhere. These are the ones in which independent authorities are believed to take the most legitimate set of actions because they are in potentially contested and politicized areas where citizens remain 'rationally ignorant or nonparticipatory', as in monetary policy; where impartiality is needed to safeguard minority rights; or where majorities require 'unbiased representation', as in antitrust policy.[69] In the EU, democratic legitimacy by such supranational governance *for* the people is based on the fact that all actions follow from the legitimate decisions of the member-states as the outcome of Treaty negotiations, with 'expertocracy', as Giandomenico Majone argues, providing for a kind of 'ouput' legitimacy based on delegated responsibility, or governing effectiveness *for* the people.[70]

The legitimacy problems for the EU in this domain come not some much from any potential violation of political rights but rather from the potential clash between two other kinds of rights which also underpin democratic legitimacy in advanced industrialized democracies. These consist on the one hand of economic rights grounded in private property, market economies, and the 'four freedoms' of movement of goods, capital, services, and people and on the other hand of social rights based in the postwar welfare state that sought to ensure universal access to food, shelter, employment, education, and health care. While economic policies have increasingly grown together, with the EU Commission having had an obligation to promote convergence through the 'market-making' envisioned in the Treaty of Rome and reinforced by subsequent treaties, social policies have remained largely divergent, with minimal provisions in the treaties for 'market-correction' to deal with the spillover effects from the economic policies.[71] Moreover, while 'negative integration'

---

[68] My thanks to Fritz Scharpf for this example.   [69] Moravcsik (2002: 613–14).
[70] Majone (1998).   [71] See Scharpf and Schmidt (2000), Ferrera et al. (2000).

has been comparatively easy—given the market-making powers of the Commission and the ECJ that follow from the treaties—'positive integration' to correct for market spillovers is difficult in a situation where member-states' preferences with regard to social policy are so different, given their divergent social systems.[72]

EU Governance With the People

Avoiding abuses of power and guaranteeing minority rights while ensuring democratic participation, representation, and effective government are not the only means of reinforcing legitimacy in nation-state democracies. Another kind of democratic legitimacy has come to be added to the original formulation of 'government *by*, *of*, and *for* the people', which I call 'government *with* the people' because its opens decision-making up to citizens *qua* organized interests as opposed to *qua* voters. This kind of democracy through interest intermediation has gained its greatest support from democratic theorists in the United States such as David Truman and Robert Dahl, with roots traced back to Madison's Federalist no. 10, who have portrayed pluralist policymaking as complementing 'democracy *by*, *of*, and *for* the people'. It represents a way in which minority interests can gain a voice even without a majority vote, through a kind of consultative democracy. But more recently, in the theory of 'associative democracy', it has been also seen as another form of democracy in its own right, as well as a corrective to representative democracy.[73] For the EU, governance *with* the people through pluralist-type consultation—mainly through joint decision-making involving a wide range of governmental and nongovernmental actors in a process commonly known as the 'Community Method'—has deliberately been encouraged as a way of counterbalancing the paucity of governance *by* or *of* the people through political participation and citizen representation. But it is only in recent years that such 'functional representation' through interest groups has come to be seen as an additional form of democratic legitimization in the EU.[74]

In governance systems with pluralist policymaking processes such as the United States but also in the EU's 'semipluralist' system,[75] the problem for democratic legitimacy raised by government '*with* the people' is that it can interfere with government '*by* and *for* the people' by catering to the demands of interests rather than the wishes and welfare of voters. Moreover, the sheer complexity of any such consultation system can lead to a kind of opaqueness

---

[72] Scharpf (2003*a*, 2003*b*).
[73] See Cohen and Rogers (1992), Hirst (1994).
[74] See Andersen and Burn, (1996), Wessels, (1999), Smismans (2003), Lord and Beetham (2001), Greenwood (n/a).
[75] See Schmidt (1999*b*, 2001).

with regard to who is responsible for decisions and who benefits. This is all the more problematic in the EU given that there are no EU-wide elections *by* the people to set the parameters for the consultations *with* the people. The (partial) solution to this problem in the United States has been citizen activism and grass roots mobilization to balance out the power of special interests. In the EU, the (partial) solution has been Commission activism to mobilize civil society in order to make policymaking 'more inclusive and accountable' (as per the *White Paper on European Governance 2001*)[76] and to create 'grassroots' interest groups (e.g. of women and consumers) at the EU level to counterbalance the more powerful, already present business groups as well as to increase transparency.[77]

It is important to note that the Commission's particular use of the word *civil society* actually blurs distinctions between special interests and activist citizens. This was apparent in the *White Paper on European Governance, 2001* where civil society is used to refer mainly to functional groups with particular ends, going from business and labor groups all the way through to NGOs, grassroots and community-based organizations, charities, religious communities—but no political parties.[78] It has also been prevalent in Commissioners' discourse, as when Pascal Lamy welcomed the participation of NGOs in the European Services Forum (ESF) stating that 'it is a *forum* open to all stakeholders, including civil society', meaning the European employers' federation (UNICE), consisting only of organized business interests.[79] This usage of the term has represented an effective discursive strategy to promote the EU's democratic legitimacy by creating the impression that more open interest consultation '*with* the people' in the policy sphere counteracts the lack of political participation '*by* the people' in the political sphere—which is where civil society is ordinarily located. Significantly, prior to the *White Paper on Governance*, the Commission mainly legitimated itself through arguments based on governance *for* the people because, as Prodi himself argued: 'at the end of the day, what interests them (the citizens) is not who solves the problems but the fact that they are being solved.'[80]

But openness to civil society is of course not just a discursive strategy. It is a political strategy to increase legitimacy of decision-making. Bringing civil society back in by increasing the number of interests represented in the policymaking process has been one way in which the Commission has sought to remedy the 'democratic deficit'—not only as a way to increase legitimacy among the groups most affected but also to improve public awareness of the entire process, and thus dissipate suspicions that deals are being struck behind closed doors.[81]

---

[76] European Commission (2001), see also the discussion in Magnette (2003*b*).
[77] Young (1998), Mazey (1995), Héritier (1999).
[78] See the discussion by Magnette (2001).   [79] Cited in Guiraudon (2003).
[80] Cited in Magnette (2003*b*).   [81] Curtin (1998).

While such governance *with* the people no doubt adds to democratic legitimacy, it is no panacea. It still faces a number of legitimacy problems, including questions of access and influence: Business is better organized and more present at the EU level than other economic groups, let alone noneconomic groups that have difficulties with transnational organization and mobilization, as we shall see below.

Moreover, the Commission's increasingly demanding criteria for representation focused on numbers of members and countries set hurdles that nationally based public interest groups often have difficulty meeting.[82] Such requirements are likely to increase the professionalization of the organizations representing civil society[83] and to decrease the purported goal of increasing inclusiveness, which is to give a voice to those not often heard.[84] Moreover, it does not really address the problem of how to ensure that NGOs democratically represent their membership and promote an effective EU political socialization function.[85] The goal of increasing input legitimacy through greater interest group participation does not necessarily help legitimacy if there is little link between the groups representing citizens at the EU level and those they are meant to represent at the national level.[86]

Such groups' independence can also be undermined by the substantial funding a large majority receive from the EU itself—to the tune of approximately one billion euros per year, with €50 million going to educational NGOs alone, €70 million to social NGOs.[87] Tellingly, all five NGOs asked to speak directly to the Convention on the Future of Europe were handsomely funded by the Commission, and all argued for 'the government of the Union to be in the hands of the Commission'.[88] Moreover, the European Women's Lobby, which played a leading role in the Amsterdam Treaty by actively campaigning across the member-states in favor of the gender equality plank, receives about 85 percent of its funding from the EU.[89] But this is arguably a trade-off with regard to ensuring that all groups have the resources to represent their interests in Brussels.

Other problems in the interest articulation process involve the 'comitology' system—in which expert committees engage in rule making once formal legislation has been passed. While a certain 'deliberative democracy' may be achieved,[90] other problems remain. These are related to questions of transparency, given the vast number of expert committees meeting behind closed doors with little public awareness; accountability, given that they are generally

---

[82] Curtin (2003: 60).   [83] See Saurugger (2003).   [84] Smismans (2003: 490–2).
[85] Warleigh (2001).   [86] Greenwood (n/a).
[87] According to Romano Prodi (2000)—*The Economist*, Oct. 23, 2004, p. 54.
[88] *The Economist*, Oct. 23, 2004, p. 54.
[89] Greenwood (n/a), Helferich and Kolb (2001).
[90] Joerges and Vos (1999).

not subject to parliamentary review or other forms of public scrutiny; and access—since it is still the Commission that chooses which groups to include and which to exclude. On this last point, without a guarantee of participation enshrined in a constitutional treaty, rights to participation remain the arbitrary decision of the Commission.[91] In other words, governance *with some* of the people and possibly not *for all* of the people is meant to make up for the lack of government *by* and *of* the people.

On this score, the EU and its interest groups could in fact gain greater legitimacy by taking a page from the US experience. Pluralist consultation *with* the people, enthroned in the 1950s as the answer to the drawbacks of electoral politics *by* and *of* the people, was found in the 1960s to lack legitimacy because it was only *with some* of the people—excluding the poor, minorities, nonvoters, immigrants, and so on. By the 1970s and 1980s, these groups had learned the lessons of pluralism, organizing themselves as interests to pressure and protest even as they sought to increase government *by* and *of* the people by way of voter registration drives, running candidates of their own, and grassroots mobilization. But this, as we shall see below, requires greater awareness and organizational capacity of member-state citizens, something which has been rather slow in developing.

The EU also suffers from the fact that its governance *with* the people targets only groups of people. Individual citizens *qua* citizens have arguably had the least access to EU decision-making, since petitioning through the EP was the only official vehicle for direct citizen representation up until the Maastricht Treaty, when the EU Ombudsman became the new avenue for citizen complaints.[92] A lack of transparency and accountability have been additional problems, although new information campaigns such as 'Citizens First' and greater public access to EU documentation through the internet and the development of e-government have somewhat alleviated the first problem,[93] the EP's greater vigilance and active investigations of the Commission and the Council, the second.

All in all, then, the EU confronts a range of potential problems of legitimacy. But it is not therefore necessarily much more or less democratically legitimate than nation-states unless it is held to the nation-state's particular mix of democratic legitimizing mechanisms. Indeed, one could argue—along with Christopher Lord and Paul Magnette—that democratic legitimacy in the EU, rather than being diminished by being based on multiple and often seemingly contradictory principles, is actually enhanced by this, especially if the contradictions are the basis for an informed and full deliberative process.[94] One study, in reviewing the findings of a number of quantitative analyses, rates

---

[91] See the discussion in Dehousse (2003), pp. 151–4.
[92] Magnette (2003).
[93] See Leitner (2003).
[94] Lord and Magnette (2002).

the EU as largely on a par with the United States and Switzerland among others in terms of all the measures of democracy.[95] Although the EU lacks the collective identity and collective will as well as the representative politics that would make it fit the legitimacy requirements of a nation-state, it nonetheless can attain a kind of legitimacy as a regional state in which its legitimizing mechanisms are split between EU and national levels. As a regional state, it makes up for its limits with regard to government *by* and *of* the people—which it leaves largely to the member-states—with more governance *for* and *with* the people through a wide variety of policymaking processes that ensure against federal excesses.

Thus, the problems of an EU level democratic deficit may not in fact be as great as many seem to think, although they cannot be shrugged off. But why, then, do people persist in talking of the democratic deficit?

The Democratic Deficit Resulting From the EU's Impact on National Democracy

In the popular mind, the EU is seen as having insufficient political participation or 'government *by* the people', which it sees as possible only through the EP. It is also 'guilty' of too much 'government *for* the people' through excessively technocratic decision-making by the Commission. And it has insufficient transparency and accountability with regard to the Council of Ministers or the Commission engaged in interest consultation *'with* the people'.[96] To counter these perceptions is not easy (especially since they are true). But even were it possible to convince the public of the legitimacy of the EU, there would still be problems. These result from the impact of the EU on national democratic practices as well as from the fact that the EU's highly compound governance system is not only multilevel and multicentered but also 'multiform',[97] given member-state governance systems which are themselves either *compound* or *simple* in institutional setup.

The EU's Impact on National Democratic Practices

The main problem for the EU is that even if it may govern effectively *for* the people and consult *with* the people (or at least some of the people), it still does not have sufficient participation *by* and representation *of* the people. However much the EU Commission improves accountability and transparency, whatever the growth in Commission-led interest consultation *with* the people, and regardless of the increases in governing effectiveness *for* the people provided

---

[95] Zweifel (2002).
[96] On the range of criticisms, see discussion in Moravcsik (2002).   [97] Schmidt (1999*a*).

by an 'expertocracy', this does not solve the fundamental problems of democratic legitimacy because it does not respond to desires for clear participation *by* and representation *of* the people, or, put more succinctly, for 'input-oriented' democracy.[98] The EU, as Michael Th. Greven argues, lack 'a common political space in which competition among political elites and elections for government could take place, a "body politic" of citizens to which it would be responsible, and, finally, a political space and public sphere of its own.'[99]

Put more simply, the problem is that people miss the simplicity of a system in which one can 'throw the bastards out', even if in the EU one does not really need to (since it has little opportunity to impose, given the consensus model) and one cannot (since the main decision-makers are the nationally elected executives of the member-states acting in the Council of Ministers and the appointed EU Commission officials). But because the EU, in essence, involves *policy without politics*, it means that the lack of politics at the EU level puts tremendous pressure on national politics.

Perversely, government *by* the people might mean holding national politicians accountable for EU policies over which they may have little control. This is particularly problematic in areas of supranational governance. In monetary policy, for example, while the ECB's role in monetary policy, together with the restrictive terms of the Stability and Growth Pact, limit national governments' ability to take effective demand-side action in times of economic downturn, national constituencies still hold national authorities solely responsible for the state of the economy. At the same time that the Commission held Chancellor Schröder to task for risking breaching the 3 percent deficit criteria, the German public held him to blame for high unemployment and the declining state of the economy. Given this, it should come as no surprise that Germany, and France for similar reasons, chose to buck the Stability Pact when their economies were in a state of downturn, and then sought to amend the rules of the Stability and Growth Pact. Where such defiance does not work, as in the case of the UK on mad cow disease in 1996—when Prime Minister Major disrupted the regular operations of the Council through his 'policy of non-cooperation' (in which he vetoed over 70 EU decisions)—or France on agricultural concessions in the Uruguay Round in 1993—when Prime Minister Balladur threatened to veto the EU's agreement in the Uruguay Round of trade negotiations for the sake of French farmers—national leaders have at least sought to convince the public that they have been making a good faith effort to fight the policy at the EU level while moderating its impact at the national level—mainly by buying off the most affected interests. The French government did this by offering subsidies to their farmers after the Uruguay Round, the British, by gaining EU recompense for their farmers in the mad cow crisis.[100]

---

[98] Scharpf (1999).   [99] Greven (2000: 54).   [100] Bush and Simi (2001).

Other disjunctions affect consultative democracy '*with* the people' in the EU. Although Brussels holds the key to decision-making in increasing numbers of policy areas, national interest groups in a large number of these areas mostly still organize, pressure, and protest primarily at the national level, with relatively little transnational coordination, with the notable exception of business.[101] The problem for nonbusiness interests is that the possible payoffs from EU level lobbying are not always as clear as for business interests while organizing across borders is much more difficult. Public interest groups in particular are hampered by such factors as the differing levels of interest aggregation among member-states, the difficulties of developing cross-national ties, the expense of getting to Brussels versus the proximity of national capitals, and the difficulties in arriving at a consensus on issues that often divide more than they unite on the basis of interest, culture, or politics. National governments remain the natural target because they still have an important intergovernmental role to play, they are closer at hand, easier to influence, and are politically sensitive to interest pressures, whether through lobbying or protests. Significantly, direct European protests with 'marches on Brussels', have been a relatively rare phenomenon, especially by comparison with the United States. Europrotests, in which the EU was both the source and the direct target, are infrequent (17%) compared to 'domesticated' protests in which the EU was the source but the national state or one of its components was the direct target (83%).[102]

In immigration policy, for example, nationally based interests organize, lobby, and protest for the most part domestically, despite the fact that since the Amsterdam Treaty decision-making has been increasingly focused on the EU level with the policy area's move from the third pillar to the first.[103] Even farmers, for whom one would expect that the long experience of the Common Agricultural Policy (CAP) would have redirected attention to Brussels, continue to focus their attention on national authorities, with surprisingly little transnational organization or even mobilization, despite the fact that most of their reasons for protest have their source in EU decisions.[104] They mostly demonstrate in their own countries, as when French farmers demonstrated in France against the changes in the CAP and the implementation of the GATT or British beef farmers protested in Britain against the measures related to 'mad cow disease',[105] although there has been the occasional mass demonstration in Brussels. Labor, similarly, has had little clout at the EU level, even though it has had official representation through the European Trade Union Conference (ETUC) starting in 1973 and has most recently been part of quasi-corporatist consultation processes for the formulation of EU directives on labor and social

---

[101] Imig and Tarrow (2001*a*).   [102] Imig and Tarrow (2001: 34–7).
[103] Guiraudon (2001).   [104] Klandermans et al. (2001).   [105] Bush and Simi (2001).

policy.[106] The ETUC is hampered by the lack of a pan-European labor movement, and remains much like 'a head without a body', lacking real representative power or authority at the national levels, whatever its successes in negotiations at the EU level.[107] There are signs, however, of growing trans-European coordination among labor unions on strikes and protest action, as when several thousand dockers converged on the EP in Strasbourg in January 2006 to protest a proposed port liberalization directive at the same time that major strikes were held in ports in France, Belgium, Spain, Portugal, and Greece, with shorter work stoppages in Germany, Sweden, Denmark, and The Netherlands.[108]

Social movements *qua* social movements, finally, are barely represented in EU policymaking. This is in large measure because at the same time that the EU is generally much more open to transnational social movements' representations than national governments, it is also a more uncertain target for the kind of grassroots mobilization and street protests that works at the national level—both because it is harder for social movements to mobilize against it and because it is harder for the EU to respond quickly or directly.[109] Other than the big anti-globalization demonstrations at the times of major EU summits, social movements have engaged in relatively little direct protest but have rather tended to follow traditional interest group practices—as in the case of the environment.[110] This said, some MEPs have been members of social movements, as in the case of the French-origin group ATTAC.[111] And some social movement leaders have access to the highest levels of the Commission. This can lead to strange situations, such as when, as Pascal Lamy recounts, leaders of NGOs were in the plane with Commission officials on a trip to the Cancun WTO meeting even as their own members were protesting outside the plane, refusing to allow it to leave. When asked where they stood on this, the NGO leaders' responses were, 'we are ambivalent'.[112]

Most problematic, however, are the effects of Europeanization on government 'by the people' when national governments, elected on a political platform at the national level, must speak and act at the EU level as representatives of national territorial interests or even national organized interests about policies which, once passed, they then must speak for and act on at the national level in their capacity as political representatives. The result is that they are therefore held accountable not only for which they may not be entirely responsible but also for that to which they may not be politically

---

[106] Falkner (1998). [107] See Martin and Ross (2001).
[108] *Le Monde* January 17, 2006.
[109] Della Porta and Kriesi (1999: 20), Marks and McAdam (1999: 98–102).
[110] Webster (1998), Rucht (2001: 137).
[111] 75 MEPs in the early 2000s, only 18 of whom were French—Sommier (2003: 162–6). See further discussion in Chapter 3, in the section on France.
[112] Informal conversation with EU official.

committed. The French government's implementation of EU-led deregulation in electricity is a case in point.[113] Partisan politics seems to be lost in this maze.

Electoral politics also suffers. National elections tend to be focused on substantive policy issues that increasingly can only be fully addressed at the EU level, such as immigration, food safety, environment, or economic growth, while European Parliamentary elections tend to focus on more general polity issues that can only be resolved by nationally based actors, such as how to reform EU institutions—where, that is, they are concerned with EU issues at all, given the second order nature of EU elections. The result, as Peter Mair argues, is that voters have voice over questions that do not count at the level at which they voice them. This runs the risk of political disaffection, as decisions are seen to be made by the government and bureaucracy, and of demobilization through decreasing citizen engagement in traditional politics, with a concomitant turn to identity politics, issue politics, and even extremist politics.[114] But it also can lead to unexpected and unwelcome results when citizens do get a chance to make their views known directly on the EU, such as in the 'no' votes on the referenda on the Constitutional Treaty in France and the Netherlands.

All in all, then, while the EU has *policy without politics*, the member-states end up with *politics without policy* in EU-related areas. And this makes for major problems for national democracy. Until citizens begin to see Brussels as equally important a place to voice their concerns, to apply pressure, and to protest as part of a pluralist policymaking process akin to that which developed in the United States in the 1970s and 1980s, national politics will continue to suffer from the bottleneck caused by national governments being the main conduit for the representation of national concerns and the main focus of national discontent. But while a fuller democracy *with* the people at the EU level would help alleviate some of the problems at the national level, it cannot solve them entirely. This is because the EU alters the traditional workings of national institutions and challenges traditional ideas about national democracy. What is more, the EU has a differential impact on its member-states depending on their particular mix of institutions and ideas about democracy.

The Differential Impact of the EU on Simple and Compound National Polities

The EU's impact on its member-states is only made more complicated by the fact that member-states' government systems themselves vary greatly along a continuum from simple polities such as France and Britain, where governing activity has traditionally been channeled through a single authority, to more compound polities such as Germany and Italy, where governing activity has traditionally been much more diffused through multiple authorities.[115] Such

---

[113] See Eising and Jabko (2001).   [114] Mair (2001).   [115] See Schmidt (2003, 2005).

differences in national institutional design make for differences not only in the way member-states interact with the EU—in 'uploading' their preferences (for European integration) or 'downloading' EU rules (in policy implementation)—both of which are arguably easier for simple polities where power is more concentrated in the executive.[116] It also makes for differences in how they adapt their institutions to the EU—which is arguably easier for compound polities as a result of greater institutional fit.

To begin with, although the EU 'federalizes' all member-states' institutional structures by diffusing power through multiple authorities, it has had a greater impact on simple polities with unitary states than on compound polities with federal or regionalized structures. The EU's quasi-federal diffusion of power through its multiple authorities fits well with the already diffused power of institutional authorities in compound polities at the same time that it reinforces organizing principles that assume that democracy '*by* the people' is best served by the dispersion of government power and authority, such that citizens' rights are protected from government excess through institutional checks and balances. In federal Germany, this sits well with a centuries-old history of regional power and a postwar federal constitution written to ensure against any possible return to the excesses of a centralized power. By contrast, the EU's federalizing effects undermine the traditional concentration of power of the unitary structures of simple polities while it challenges organizing principles which assume that democracy is better served by the concentration of governmental power and authority, such that the government has the sole responsibility as well as the capacity to respond to citizens' wants and needs effectively '*for* the people'. For unitary France, the EU challenges the country's Jacobin philosophical foundations that concentrate power and authority in the 'one and indivisible' Republican state. For unitary Britain, it undermines the authority of the executive as the embodiment of parliamentary sovereignty. For regionalized Italy, which has a weak, formally unitary state but strong regional authorities, the EU reinforces the capacity of the central state at the same time as the increasingly regionalized practices that promote the dispersion of power and authority.

Similarly, although the EU 'pluralizes' all member-states' policymaking processes by including interests in policy formulation and excluding them in implementation through regulatory or legalistic enforcement, it has had a greater impact on simple polities with statist processes, where interests have generally been excluded from policy formulation but included in policy implementation, either through administrative discretion (in France) or self-regulation (in Britain). EU-related openness to interests in policy formulation clashes with the assumptions of simple polities that the executive governs most effectively *for all* the people by being closed to interest consultation *with* the

---

[116] See Chapter 2 for empirical illustration and Chapter 5 for further theoretical discussion.

people. For France, open interest consultation offends ideas prevalent since the Revolution that see it as illegitimate; in Britain, it also clashes with ideas of executive autonomy—although parliamentary lobbying has been acceptable so long as the government keeps its distance. In the implementation process, moreover, the EU's regulatory denial of flexibility in applying the rules through interest consultation *with* the people clashes with simple polities' assumption that such flexibility is required in order to respect the specific wishes and welfare of minority interests. For France, the EU's disallowing of any exceptions to the rules compromises the executive's governing effectiveness *for* the people by denying it the ability to accommodate minority interests negatively affected by majority decisions. And it increases the risks of confrontation when interests cut out of policy formulation no longer find accommodation in policy implementation. For Britain, by making statutory what were voluntary rules and replacing 'private self-government' with regulatory agencies or legalistic rules, the EU has expanded as it has rigidified the public sphere to the detriment of the private sphere which governments see as their duty to protect.

By contrast, the EU's pluralizing of policymaking reinforces the corporatist policymaking processes of compound polities like Germany and Italy, where certain privileged interests have traditionally been involved in policy formulation and implementation. In policy formulation, the EU bolsters the view in compound polities that effective governing *for* the people demands openness to a multiplicity of intermediate interests via consultation *with* the people through multiple centers of power. For both Germany and Italy, the EU only reinforces these organizing principles, by reducing the risk of producing policies only *for some* of the people. But whereas for Germany, this mainly increases legitimacy by opening up corporatist processes, for Italy, it also serves to delegitimize clientelistic practices. In policy implementation, moreover, the EU again tends to reinforce legitimacy by promoting governing effectiveness *for* the people through regulatory and legalistic processes that also predominate in Germany, by allowing corporatist processes to continue in both Germany and Italy, or by substituting regulatory enforcement for a discredited clientelism in Italy. This said, because the 'micro' patterns of policymaking in any given sector at the EU or national level may not conform to the 'macro' processes just discussed, the EU can have a varied impact, depending upon its own particular sectoral pattern as well as the national one[117]

Finally, although the EU 'depoliticizes' all member-states' representative politics by way of interest-based, consensus-oriented politics, this has tended to put more of a damper on the more highly polarized, politically charged politics of the majoritarian representation systems of simple polities than on the more consensus-oriented (albeit partisan) politics typical of the proportional systems of more compound polities. The EU's 'politics' clashes with the

---

[117] See the discussion in Chapter 3.

expectation in simple polities that only political leadership by a single authority, elected *by* the people and representative *of* the people, closed to consultation *with* the people, can truly express the *will* of the people. In Britain and
France, where majoritarian electoral systems generally provide for stronger
governments with little need to negotiate or to find consensus, the ambiguity
of EU-related compromises is likely to cause more problems for politicians and
greater disaffection in electorates used to more politically demarcated policies
and positions. Moreover, unpopular EU-related policies can easily trigger
questions of democratic legitimacy, since national electorates expect their
governments to be fully responsible for, in control of, and politically committed to whatever policies they propose.

By contrast, the EU sustains the assumption in compound polities that
political compromise among the plethora of authorities representative *of* the
people, elected *by* the people, and open to consultation *with* the people is
the best way to express the *will* of all the people. In Germany and Italy, the
complex negotiations and search for consensus and compromise that go on in
the EU are not so different from their own politics. Compromise in negotiated
settings has always been a *sine qua non* of proportional representation systems,
however partisan the politics, especially since the government generally does
not have the power to impose. EU-related policies, therefore, are less likely to
trigger questions of democratic legitimacy, since national publics know that
their politicians are never fully responsible for or fully in control of any
decisions, even when they are fully politically committed to them. Legitimacy
comes up only where the people lose trust in the system as a whole—the
problem for Italy in the postwar period but less so today, where the EU has
contributed to greater governing effectiveness. The risk is greater for Germany,
where the perception of a dissipation of authority as a result of its greater
diffusion through the EU can be problematic.

Such questions of legitimacy only add to the problems that come from the
fact that national sovereignty is now shared, national territorial and policy
boundaries are in the process of 'de-differentiation', national identity is no
longer exclusively national, national government structures and rules have
changed through absorption into the EU's multilevel and multimodal governance system, and national politics is under pressure.

The National Sources of the Democratic Deficit: The Lack of New Ideas and Discourse

The central problem for the EU, however, is not so much the changes in
national democratic practices *per se* as that they have gone unrecognized or
unaccepted. And this is *the* problem, because mainstream political leaders,
instead of acknowledging the changes and seeking to redefine national

democracy in light of them, have instead tended to hold on to traditional ideas about their country's democracy—seeming to suggest that nothing has changed, even though everything has.[118] Although EU-related policy issues are often at the forefront of national discourse, as national politicians blame the EU for unpopular policies or take credit for the popular ones (often without mentioning the EU's role), EU-related changes in governance practices are in fact mostly passed over in silence. Even though this pattern is understandable—politicians, after all, are not likely to use their scarce political resources to speak about changes that are complicated and difficult to 'sell', especially since there are no electoral incentives to do so—it adds to the problems of the democratic deficit. These problems have been dramatized most recently by the fiasco of the ratification of the Constitutional Treaty.

The Lack of New Ideas in the Discourse

Mainstream national leaders have mostly been loath to broach the topic of national democracy, seeing it as a Pandora's box. In the postwar period, the 'permissive consensus' that allowed political elites to build the EU largely outside the public eye was buoyed by national discourses that in most countries presented further European integration as having little negative effects on national sovereignty, identity or citizenship, and with little mention of any deep-seated changes to traditional democracy. Most leaders said little about the potential challenges of EU-related changes in governance practices to the institutionally grounded organizing principles of national democracy. Only in national referenda and certain 'defining moments'—at times of accession to membership, de Gaulle during the 'empty chair' crisis, the referenda on the Maastricht Treaty in France and Denmark, the Nice Treaty for Ireland, and the referenda on the Constitutional Treaty in France and the Netherlands—have changes in national practices that challenge national ideas about democracy been explicitly addressed. Otherwise, member-states have experienced the institutional creep of EU governance, with national adaptation a continuing process without significant deliberation or debate as to its impact on the polity. But where polity issues did come up, most mainstream political leaders—with the exception of the British—have tended to highlight the polity-enhancing aspects of European integration while downplaying any disruptive impact on democratic organizing principles.

In France, for example, national leaders tend to ignore the impact of the EU on the national polity, focusing instead on France's influence in the EU. Thus, they have presented European integration as an extension of national sovereignty through the country's leadership in Europe, and as an enhancement of identity by serving to renew the country's *grandeur* while projecting its

[118] Schmidt (2002*b*, 2003*b*).

universalistic values, without admitting that Europeanization has undermined the unitary nature and powers of the 'Republican state.' Leaders still speak as if the state were unitary, despite the federalizing trends related not only to the EU but also to internal reforms, and as if France still led Europe, despite the fact that France has followed much more than led since the early 1990s, and sometimes quite reluctantly—as in the deregulation of public infrastructural services. The problems with this kind of discourse, touting France's leadership in the EU while ignoring its impact on the national polity, came home to roost with the no vote in the referendum on the Constitutional Treaty in 2005.

In Germany, too, national leaders have mostly focused on the positive effects of Europeanization, up until recently presenting it as the basis for a new German identity, out of a troubled past *being* into an economically prosperous *doing*. Even here, however, debate on certain sensitive, polity-defining topics, such as giving up the Deutschmark, has been avoided. But when debate has been engaged, as when the Länder demanded new powers in exchange for the ones they had lost before they would ratify the Maastricht Treaty, the discourse focused mainly on how to recreate an appropriate institutional rebalancing rather than challenging Europeanization. The problems for Germany, in fact, are likely to arise less from polity issues per se than from policies that challenge practices seen as fundamental to the polity, such as threats to the foundational bases of the social market economy, of which the decision by the Competition Authority against the low cost lending practices of the regional state-owned savings and loan banks was a foretaste.

In Italy, national leaders have developed an even more positive discourse, presenting European integration as a reinforcement of sovereignty through the rescue of the nation-state, a guarantor of political rights, and an embellishment of national identity.[119] For Italy, where the state until the 1990s had been characterized by paralysis along with clientelism, moreover, Europeanization could only rectify the problems of a democracy unable to govern effectively *for* the people. This includes forcing the state to implement the rules, welcome in principle but not always in practice, since they are disruptive of citizens' informal political 'right' to the derogation of the rules—and something which largely goes unmentioned by Italian politicians.

In Britain, by contrast, there has been very little discourse on the polity-enhancing aspects of European integration. While national leaders opposed to European integration have focused on the polity issues, presenting Europeanization as a threat to parliamentary sovereignty, to the 'historically established rights of Englishmen', and to an identity constructed with Europe as 'the other', those in favor have tended to emphasize the economic benefits without confronting the polity issues. The result is that the public has been made maximally aware of the drawbacks to Europeanization with regard to sovereignty and

---

[119] See, for example, Ferrera and Gualmini (1999).

identity without being presented with any countervailing, positive vision of Britain in Europe. This helps explain why the referendum on the Constitutional Treaty would have been very hard to win, even were Blair to have couched it as the question of whether Britain was to be in or out of Europe. As it turns out, the no votes in France and the Netherlands let Blair off the hook.

The referenda on Europe were very much a wake-up call to national leaders that the democratic deficit that they were trying to remedy at the EU level through the Constitutional Treaty was a more serious concern at the national level. The referenda were in fact all about politics—national electorates' concern with the lack of government *by* the people at the EU level and their desire, once they finally had the chance, to make their views heard on the EU generally as well as in particular on policies over which they have had very little direct say, including economic integration, enlargement, and democracy in Europe. The irony is that the no vote in the referenda stopped the EU level institutional reforms that might have introduced more politics into the process and, thereby, made it possible for their policy concerns to be addressed.

Moreover, the political fallout from the European integration process which culminated in the Constitutional Treaty has been significant, as it has increasingly split mainstream political parties down the middle—into pro-and anti-Europeans —leaving an opening to the extremes on both sides of the political spectrum to exploit for their own purposes. Such increasing polarization has gone hand in hand with the public disaffection that has increasingly characterized national democracies in the last decade of the twentieth century and at the beginning of the twenty-first century, with citizens' loss of trust in national governments as well as in EU institutions,[120] their rampant cynicism about national leaders, and their growing apathy as voters, apparent in higher and higher rates of abstentionism—with the exception of the no votes in the referenda.[121]

The democratic deficit, in short, is a significant problem at the national level, whatever one thinks of it at the European. And it will remain a problem so long as national leaders and citizens in each and every one of the member-states do not start reevaluating what they mean by national democracy today, even before they decide how to democratize the EU for tomorrow. The EU is no longer an elite project supported by a permissive consensus. But it is not yet a peoples' project grounded in a 'democratic consensus'.

But how to build such a consensus? For this, we need to consider public discourse in Europe at both the EU and national levels.

The Importance of Communicative Discourse

One of the main challenges for Europe is the fact that while large numbers of policy actors are debating and deliberating policy issues on an everyday basis,

---

[120] Reynié and Cautrès (2001: 243–4), Bréchon (2002: 103).
[121] Klingemann (1999), Dalton (1999), Pharr and Putnam (2000), Newton and Norris (2000).

few political actors are addressing the polity issues that follow from EU-related practices. Put in the more theoretical terms of my framework for the analysis of discourse,[122] while in the *coordinative* discourse of policy construction, policy actors have been engaged in an extensive process of deliberation about their ideas' soundness and appropriateness, in the *communicative* discourse of political legitimization, political actors have rarely informed the public about the EU-related changes in national democratic practices, let alone debated their soundness or appropriateness. Moreover, as we have just seen, when national leaders have broached such topics, rather than seeking to reconceptualize national ideas about democracy in light of the new practices, they have tended mainly either to deny or to decry their impact.

The problem for member-state democracies with regard to discourse is not only a question of ideas, that is, of how sound their cognitive arguments in terms of technical norms and scientific principles or how appropriate their normative arguments in terms of democratic values and political principles. It is also a matter of discursive interaction, that is, of how ideas that are discursively constructed and communicated at the EU level affect the ways in which they are constructed and communicated at the national level. Because the EU has the most elaborate of coordinative discourses among policy actors and the thinnest of communicative discourses between political leaders and the public, it disrupts all member-states' discursive patterns of interaction.

The EU, as the most compound of governance systems, naturally has a highly developed coordinative discourse. Through its coordinative discourse, consultation *with* the people adds deliberation to the (pluralist) procedural foundations of democratic legitimization. Here, policies are generated by the ideas of the 'epistemic communities' of, say, the central bankers, economists, and financial reporters who convinced policymakers of the merits of EMU.[123] They are elaborated through the discursive 'policy networks' that have brought together EU, national, and regional actors in the development and implementation of structural and cohesion policies.[124] They are promoted by the 'advocacy coalitions' which have had the power to push their ideas in particular in those areas covered by the joint decision mode of policymaking.[125] They are decided in the 'supranational deliberative democracy'[126] or the 'directly deliberative polyarchy'[127] of the EU-anointed national experts, government representatives, and interests meeting in 'comitology' committees; they are critiqued through the 'strong publics' constituted by the Parliament;[128] and so on. Moreover, civil society—as defined by the EU Commission—has become increasingly a part of this coordinative discourse through the creation of 'forums' on issues of interest to business and society.[129]

[122] See: Schmidt (2002*a*), Chapter 5, and the discussion in this book, Chapter 5, pp. 249–58.
[123] Verdun (2000).   [124] Kohler Koch (2002).   [125] Sabatier (1990).
[126] Joerges and Neyer (1999).   [127] Gerstenberg and Sabel (2000).
[128] Fraser (1992: 134), Erikson and Fossum (2002).
[129] See the discussion in Chapter 3.

But while the EU has the most elaborate of coordinative policy discourses, it has the thinnest possible of communicative discourses. This is to be expected, of course, given not only institutions that ensure a high diffusion of power among multiple authorities but also the lack of a European public sphere underpinned by a substantial EU-level representative politics and the paucity of EU-political actors able to speak directly to a European public in a common language, reported by a European media, and considered by a European public opinion.[130] Instead, the communicative discourse comes largely by way of national political actors speaking to national publics in national languages reported by national media and considered by national opinion.

The absence of a European communicative arena is not only a problem for creating a sense of European identity, since there are relatively few European political actors *saying* to a general European public what the EU is *doing*, which means that it may have little effect on *being* European. It is also a problem for crafting a Europe-wide sense of legitimacy in terms of governance '*by* the people'—let alone *of* the people. The legitimacy problems are admittedly attenuated if one argues that there is indeed a developing European public sphere, only one made up of European member-state 'publics' rather than some idealized single public in which national publics are increasingly aware of European issues and the views of other member-state publics on those issues.[131] However, this does not get around the fact that without a Europe-wide representative politics to focus debate, European political leaders have little opportunity to speak directly to the polity issues and European publics have little ability to deliberate about them or to state their conclusions directly—through the ballot box.

Moreover, this situation allows national leaders to continue to say and do one thing at the EU level and to say (although no longer necessary do) another at the national. Thus, in the Council, as Dominique de Villepin, French foreign minister at the time, noted: 'when they talk to one another around the table, the men and women who represent their countries at the same time that they are Europeans and wish to do the right thing are just about in agreement on the basics. But when they separate each to their own press conference at the end of the meeting, they communicate on the basis of what separates them from the decision that was just taken or the course that was chosen. This means that communication about Europe is based more on what divides us than on what brings us together'.[132] There are constant reports of ministers in the Council agreeing with their colleagues on one or

---

[130] Many note these problems. See for example: Grimm (1995), Meyer (1995), Weiler (1995, 1999).

[131] See Risse (2003), Koopmans (2004).

[132] Dominique de Villepin, remarks during the closing session of the Proceedings of the European Students Conference (Assises de la Convention des Etudiants Europeens) at the Institut d'Etudies Politiques, Paris January 18, 2003.

another reform, then claiming to their own national press that they had vehemently opposed it in the meeting. Moreover, they do little to correct national media that promulgate ludicrous rumors about what the EU is up to, for example, in Britain, that the EU is outlawing square gin bottles and curved bananas; in France that the EU is reducing the diameter of cigarettes, requiring firefighters to wear navy blue pants, and protecting maggots by banning their use in fishing.[133] All of this causes problems not just for European policymaking but also for EU legitimacy.

This said, the beginnings of a truly European public sphere have been emerging. Evidence can be found in news media coverage of the EU as well as of other member-states, which has been on the rise over the years, showing a slowly growing interest in more than just the national public sphere.[134] But the best evidence can be found in the process engaged during the Constitutional Convention[135]—even if 55 percent of the populations of the EU 25 had never even heard of it.[136] This was the first truly European communicative discourse about questions of polity in a fully European public space—and this in and of itself has served to contribute to the legitimacy of the EU in terms of governance *by* the people.[137] This is where individuals came together as political actors—representatives of national parliaments and the EP, national governments and the EU Commission, special interests and public interests—to deliberate about the EU's future architecture. Most importantly, what made this a kind of deliberative democracy rather than simply an interest-based bargaining session among nationally focused, EU-anointed, rational actors, is that the political actors 'argued' as well as 'bargained' with one another,[138] and as often as not changed their positions because they were persuaded of the soundness as well as the appropriateness of institutional reforms that they had heretofore rejected out of hand.

For the president of the Convention and former president of France, Valéry Giscard d'Estaing, the Convention constituted a truly deliberative process in which a genuine exchange of ideas was generated, similar to the Philadelphia Convention that established American democracy.[139] Although some might quibble with Giscard about how open and democratic the process,[140] none

---

[133] *Le Point* (1995), as reported in the *New York Times*, February 20, 1997.

[134] See the results of the massive Europub research project, Koopmans (2004).

[135] See Magnette (2003*a*).

[136] Flash Eurobarometer 142 'Convention on the Future of Europe' (23.06.2003–1.07.2003).

[137] See Magnette (2003*a*).

[138] See discussion in Chapter 5.

[139] Giscard d'Estaing, Talk at Harvard JFK school of government, October 8, 2003.

[140] Many complained about how Giscard controlled the process in the Consilium, deciding which proposals reflected the sense of the meeting while rejecting others out of hand. Giscard himself claims to have partially ensured the openness of the process by seating people in alphabetical order rather than by affinity or grouping, and addressing one another by their names, not titles. Talk at Harvard JFK school of government, October 8, 2003.

could deny how much deliberation there was. The measure of their deliberative output can be judged by the 16,365 speeches, and 35,000 documents on
the Internet alone, not to mention the countless months of meetings in the
Convention and outside the proceedings, with NGOs and other groups, as well
as in member-states, through government-sponsored informational meetings
and debates even prior to the start of the Convention.[141] The political evidence of the Convention's success can be seen in the fact that, halfway
through the process, national governments began to take the Convention
seriously, and to replace junior representatives with foreign ministers. But
this also undermined the fully deliberative nature of the process, with arguing
giving way to bargaining by the simple fact that the discussions were taking
place in the shadow of the potential veto of member-states.[142] This was
nothing like the IGC under the Italian Presidency that was to agree on the
Constitutional Treaty, however, which turned into a typical bargaining
session, and a failed one at that.

In other areas, albeit in a more limited way, the EU has also been developing
more communicative public discourses that flow out of coordinative policy
discourses. Across a wide variety of areas, Commission officials have been
increasingly seeking to communicate European policy views to a larger public
through editorials and the like on such issues as security and defense, international trade, and the EU's institutional architecture. The current Commission now even has a Commissioner responsible for Communications. How
successful Commission strategies can be on their own, however, is open to
question: The communications strategies proposed by the *White Paper on
Governance,* for example, were mainly top-down, focusing on institutional
provision of citizen information, and professional communications, whereas
bottom-up communication limited itself to 'media gadgets'.[143] A stronger
communicative discourse is likely only if and when the new institutional
arrangements laid out in the Constitutional Treaty—with a new foreign minister and president of the Council in addition to a stronger Commission
president—are fully in place.

The Importance of Communicative Discourse in Simple and Compound Polities

But whatever the recent improvements in the EU's communicative discourse,
its inherent weakness demands much stronger national communicative discourses to legitimize EU-related changes. And here, the problems come not
only from the lack of new ideas but also from problems with national communicative discourses that differ in simple and compound polities. In compound

---

[141] On French government-sponsored information meetings, see: Weisbein (2002, 1998).
[142] Magnette (2003*a*).
[143] Magnette (2001).

polities such as Germany and Italy, the diffusion of power in multiple authorities ensures that the coordinative discourse is most elaborate, the communicative discourse very thin. Here, the large number of policy actors involved in decision-making demands extensive deliberation among those actors as well as with their own policy constituencies to coordinate agreement. Political leaders then tend to communicate these agreements to the general public only in vague terms, since any detailed discussion could risk unraveling the compromises reached in private. By contrast, in simple polities such as Britain and France, the concentration of power in the executive ensures that the coordinative discourse is very thin, the communicative discourse most elaborate. Here, political actors have greater need to legitimate any new ideas directly to the general public in the absence of widespread policy coordination and in the face of certain opposition from other parties and minority interests.[144]

In simple polities, as a result, where a restricted, governmental elite tends to coordinate the construction of the ideas and then to 'communicate' them to the public for discussion and deliberation, political leaders are schooled in projecting a clear message to the public. The strength of the communicative discourse means that political leaders in simple polities have the capacity to speak eloquently to Europeanization—itself a good and necessary thing in light of its challenge to simple polities' foundational organizing principles of democracy. The problem, however, as we have already seen, is that political leaders have not addressed these issues. Had they done so, we might have avoided the communicative discourses that, as in France, reiterated the fictions of a unitary state and an all-powerful executive immune to the pressures of interests, or, as in Britain, railed against the EU's incursions on sovereignty (as in the Thatcher years) or fell totally silent on the EU's impact on the polity (as today). Instead, we might have seen communicative discourses that legitimized the greater division of powers as a check on executive excesses; the greater openness to interest representation in policy formulation as promoting citizen access; regulatory implementation as ensuring greater equality and predictability in policy implementation; and consensus-oriented politics as more likely to produce policies that gain the acceptance of large majorities of voters.

But who would say this? There are no incentives for French leaders to admit that they have lost their powers in an increasing number of areas, or to say that they are no longer responsible or in control, but still have to implement policies to which they are not necessarily politically committed. Instead, we see leaders increasingly focusing on purely national issues for which they can be responsible, which they can control, and to which they are politically committed. These are the focus of national discourse, whether public services in Blair's second term or the 35-hour work week in Jospin's prime ministership. This is perhaps politically useful in the short term, but in the long term this

---

[144] See Schmidt (2002*a*: Chapter 5); and see the discussion in this volume, Chapter 5.

dearth of substantive discourse and deliberation about the impact of Europeanization on the polity—even as policy change is the focus of an extensive but mixed press—only contributes to public disaffection and depoliticization, while it leaves the issue open to exploitation by the political extremes. The referendum in France is a case in point. Because the political elites were split, and therefore unable to speak in one voice to the general public about the reasons to vote 'yes', it left open field to the political extremes on the right and the left.

Compound polities confront a different set of problems since, as in the EU, the communicative discourse is very thin. Political leaders are schooled in communicating only in vague terms on the agreements reached among the wide range of actors involved in the coordinative discourse of policy construction. Here, it is a good thing that Europeanization has been less of a challenge to compound polities' foundational organizing principles of democracy. As it is, where Europeanization challenges other nationally specific democratic values—whether political, economic, or social—the general poverty of the communicative discourse may raise major red flags for the public. And here, public discussion and deliberation through the kind of deliberative democracy that Habermas[145] has consistently called for is very difficult, given the range of voices speaking at the same time and seeking to be heard, without any one having any more of an authoritative voice than any others. Reaching a consensus in this context may therefore be quite long and difficult compared to any simple polity, mainly because the ideas communicated to the public can get lost in a cacophony of voices if there is no consensus, which will in any case take time to build. This was clearly the problem in the Dutch referendum.

Conclusion

As a developing regional state, in short, the EU confronts major problems of democratic legitimacy at the national level, and more in simple polities than in compound ones. These involve not only questions of institutions but also the ideas that infuse them and the discourse that legitimizes them. To elucidate, in the next three chapters, we begin with the institutional structures that determine the architecture of the EU and its member-states, follow with how those institutional structures are operationalized by policymaking processes, to end with how they are given meaning by representative politics. Each chapter first focuses briefly on EU-level dynamics, then examines its comparative impact on the member-states, and concludes with a more nuanced consideration of each of the four country cases: France, Britain, Germany, and Italy.

---

[145] Habermas (1996).

2

The European Union and National Institutions

In the constitutional debates about the future institutional design of the EU, national leaders' initial propositions tellingly projected deeply traditional visions of national democracy onto the EU. The German proposal that launched the constitutional debates was particularly federalist, with a 'European Federation' to consist of a second chamber with powers like those of Germany's Bundesrat, and a 'European Constituent Treaty' much like the German Basic Law which would set out EU-level competencies while leaving everything else to the member-states.[1] The French counterproposal was more intergovernmental, with a 'union of nation-states' in place of a federation that would do nothing to threaten the unitary nature of the French state, with a constitution that would be no more than a simplification of the treaties, with no second chamber, and no competencies that would increase the powers of the regions to the detriment of the center.[2] The British offering was equally intergovernmental, but it rejected not only the idea of a federation but also that of a constitution—in line with the country's own lack of a written constitution—suggesting instead a charter of nonbinding competencies and a second chamber similar to the House of Lords in its political powers of review.[3] The Italians, after waiting for a time, produced a vague set of statements that seemingly endorsed all of the above, reflecting the ambiguities of their own system. Most subsequent propositions on institutional reform followed a similar pattern in the four countries. But what none of these leaders considered as they sought to redesign the EU's architecture in keeping with national visions of democracy is not only that the EU has already become something akin to a federal system but that it has also already substantially altered the national institutions on which each and every one of their visions are based.

---

[1] Joschka Fischer, speech at Humboldt University in Berlin, May 12, 2000.
[2] Jacques Chirac, speech to the Bundestag, June 27, 2000.
[3] Tony Blair, speech to the Polish Stock Exchange, Warsaw, October 6, 2000.

The EU comes closest to a 'quasi-federal' system characterized vertically by a division of powers between supranational and national levels and horizontally by a 'dynamic confusion of powers' between executive, legislature, and judiciary. As such, it provides for the kind of democratic legitimacy through effective governing *for* the people generally found in federal systems, where the checks and balances among various governing authorities ensures against abuses of power. By superimposing this system on top of those of its member-states, the EU has federalized its member-states' institutional structures through the diffusion of their power in its multiple authorities. This has served to diminish national executives' autonomy and to reduce national parliaments' powers while increasing the independence of the regions and the courts. Complicating this general set of effects, however, has been the EU's differential impact on its member-states' institutional structures depending on where they sit along a continuum from unitary to regionalized to federal states. Overall, Europeanization has caused unitary states to lose more autonomy and control than federal states, whereas it has had mixed effects on regionalized states. By the same token, however, unitary states have for the most part been better able to project their preferences in the process of European integration than either federal or regionalized states.

The chapter begins with a brief discussion of EU institutional structures in comparison with national institutional structures. It then examines the EU's comparative effects on unitary, regionalized, and federal member-states by considering in turn its impact on national executives, parliaments, subnational authorities, and courts. It follows with a more detailed exploration of the EU's effects on each of our four country cases, France, Britain, Germany, and Italy. Here, we find further differentiations. Although Europeanization has been more disruptive to the unitary structures of France than to those of Britain, Britain has had a harder time accepting EU-related changes and yet has had a better compliance record. And despite the fact that Europeanization has been least disruptive to Germany's federal structures and most reinforcing to the regionalized structures of Italy, Germany's compliance record is little better than that of France while Italy's is the worst. Finally, in the legitimating discourse of Europeanization, whereas the French emphasize the country's leadership in Europe while denying the EU's structural impact, the British decry that impact when Europe leads while the Germans embrace it as identity-enhancing and the Italians, as capacity-building as well.

The EU's Quasi-Federal Institutional Structures

To the casual observer, the EU's basic institutional structures seem to resemble those of a typical federal system constituted on the basis of the division of power between the central and lower level units and the separation of powers between the executive, legislature, and judiciary. On closer look, however, it becomes clear that the EU fits no traditional model of governance.[4] While the legislative decisions adopted at the center are the supreme law of the land for all constituent members, as in any federal state, only in the EU are the constituent members almost completely in control of the legislation, both in terms of its approval (as members of the European Council and the Council of Ministers) and its implementation. Moreover, only the ECJ has the power typical of the supreme judicial courts in a federal system. The EP is weak in legislative power, given the primacy of the EC in the initiation and elaboration of legislation and of the Council of Ministers in its approval. The Council of Ministers is weak in executive power, given the role of the EU Commission in legislative initiative and enforcement. As the late Daniel Elazar has noted, the EU constitutes an even more complex governance matrix than any purely national, federal system, and is certainly even less of a 'power pyramid' than any national system.[5]

Defining the EU's institutional structures has been a problem from the very beginning, largely because of the different perceptions of what the EU is and views of what it should be and/or become. The federalists of the early years, men like Paul-Henri Spaak, Altiero Spinelli, or Jean Monnet, learned very quickly that their federal visions threatened national leaders' attachment to the integrity of the nation-states which they were intent on rebuilding following the devastation of the Second World War.[6] The founders therefore chose not to specify what they were building but to name instead the process of building itself—first as the 'functionalist' process of 'spillover' from one functional area to the next in the European Coal and Steel Community (ECSC) and, later, the 'Community Method' for the European Economic Community (EEC). As a result, the EU developed without any clear set of ideas or discourse about what it was or would be, just how it would proceed. This more readily allowed national leaders from different countries to project their own national visions onto the EU, and to promote European integration without having to consider the EU's impact on national institutional structures—a boon in the early years, much more problematic today.

The first difficulty for democratic theorists, then, is to define the EU's governance structure, which conforms neither to that of a traditional unitary state nor to that of a federal state, although it is closest to the latter.[7] Federalism is ordinarily defined as a system with a formally established, vertical division of power such that the central governing body incorporates subnational units in its

---

[4] See Hoffmann (1989: 41), Sbragia (1993: 24), and Schmitter (1996).
[5] See Elazar (2001).
[6] See Unwin (1995: ch. 1).
[7] There is an immense literature on the federal characteristics of the European Community/European Union and its similarities with as well as differences from other federal systems. See, for example: Scharpf (1988, 1994), Sbragia (1993), Gunlicks (1989), and Wincott (1996).

decision procedures on a constitutionally entrenched basis.[8] In most federal systems, moreover, subnational units generally have independent legislative powers of their own as well as separate domains of competence—as in the United States, Canada, and Spain—and some degree of financial independence (taxing and spending). In some federal systems, however, instead of this jurisdictional separation of responsibilities, there is a functional division in which subnational governments are charged with the implementation of nationally formulated policies—as in Germany. In at least one federal system, moreover, the territorial division of political power is complemented by a further territorial division in cultural and educational authority—as in Belgium, which has arguably the most complex federalism in existence.

The unitary state, by contrast, typically has no constitutionally guaranteed, vertical division of power. Instead, it has a vertical integration of powers centered in the executive. The executive has formal control over subnational units which have at best limited legislative powers and fiscal discretion, even though they may have substantial autonomy based on national legislation or informal practice. In recent years, as central governments everywhere have increasingly devolved political power, administrative functions, and financial resources to the periphery, the central control of the unitary state has softened, although some countries, like Spain and Italy, have gone much farther along the continuum toward federalism, becoming 'regionalized' states, than others, such as France or the UK (see Figure 2.1).[9] But all such formerly unitary states remain formally unitary to the extent that the central government retains significant control over the periphery at least in principle, if only because without the protection of constitutional guarantees, that which it has given to subnational authorities, it can always take back. In practice, however, taking power back would be very difficult indeed, especially for regionalized states like Spain and Italy not only because of the political ramifications but also because of how much institutional and legislative power has already been transferred. For countries that remain closer to the unitary end of the continuum such as Britain and France, power remains largely in the center— although even here, what powers have been devolved or decentralized would be very difficult to take back.

Given these definitions, the EU clearly has nothing in common with the unitary state (see Table 2.1). It is weak in central control, with the 'periphery'

---

[8] King (1982: 77).

[9] Lijphart's quantitative approach puts this more precisely using indicators such as the functional separation of power between parliament and government—where the UK (with a score of 20) followed by France (19) sit at one end, Spain is not much farther along (17) while Germany (12) and Italy (8) sit at the other—and degree of federalism and decentralization— where the UK (with a score of 1) is followed by France (1.3) and Italy (1.3) while Spain (3) sits closer to Germany (5) at the other end (Lijphart 1999: 97, 209)—as elaborated by Della Porta 2003: 14–15).

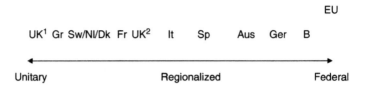

Figure 2.1. Simple and Compound Polities along a continuum between unitary, regionalized, and federal structures (UK[1] under Thatcher; UK[2] beginning with the devolutionary reforms of Blair)

of member-states also a collective central authority in the EU through the Council of Ministers and the European Council. For intergovernmentalist theorists, this member-state authority is such that it precludes seeing the EU as anything more than a 'confederacy' in which states, represented by state executives, are the primary movers in the EU, acting as rational, unitary actors with an inherent desire to defend and enhance their own central power.[10] However, this view of EU member-states as consisting of unitary actors, even if useful at high levels of theoretical abstraction, encounters three major problems when dealing with the EU. First, it generally overlooks the fact that even member-states that are unitary in structure are not necessarily unified in action, given conflicting agendas and interests within the state executive as well as counterpowers exercised by other governmental authorities and societal groups (although here 'liberal' intergovernmentalism covers itself).[11] Second, it ignores the fact that even if executives of many unitary member-states can act with relatively little constraint, those of federal member-states cannot, given the stronger, constitutionally based counterpowers of other branches and levels of government. Finally, and most importantly, it does little to account for the multifarious ways in which institutional and other actors at EU, national, and subnational levels interrelate, and which make the institutional structures of the EU more akin to those of a federal system than any confederation of states—except when it comes to the negotiation of the major EU treaties. This is why the EU has been variously described as a 'federal union',[12] 'cooperative federalism',[13] 'cooperative federalism without a state',[14] or, in the most prevalent of terms used in recent years, 'multilevel governance'.[15]

---

[10] Hoffmann (1966), Moravcsik (1991), and Milward (1992).

[11] See Moravcsik (1991, 1998).

[12] Pinder (1994).

[13] Wessels (1990).

[14] Mény, Muller, and Quermonne (1996).

[15] See, for example, Benz and Eberlein (1999), Jachtenfuchs and Kohler-Koch (1995), Jeffery (1996), Kohler-Koch (1996), Marks (1993), Marks and Hooghe (2001), Marks, Hooghe, and Blank (1996), Scharpf (1994, 1998, 1999), and Wallace (1994).

Table 2.1. Institutional structures of simple and compound polities

	Structures	Power	Authority	Vertical relations b/w center and periphery	Horizontal relations among functional branches
Simple polities (Fr, UK)	Unitary	Concentrated	Single	Vertical integration of powers focused on center	Integration of powers among functional branches with executive in control
Compound polities (Sp, It)	Regionalized	Partially diffuse	Somewhat multiple	Partial vertical division of powers b/w center and periphery with legislative guarantees for periphery	Integration of powers among functional branches with executive in control
Compound polities (Ger, US)	Federal	Diffuse	Multiple	Vertical division of powers b/w center and periphery with constitutional guarantees for periphery	Separation of powers among functional branches with little executive control
Highly compound polity (EU)	Quasi-federal	Highly diffuse	Highly multiple	Vertical division of powers focused on periphery	Confusion of powers among separate functional branches with no control

But although there is no question that the EU resembles more closely the model of a federal system, it is its own particular brand of federalism. It is not all that close to the federalism of the United States.[16] Germany is perhaps a more apt comparison when it comes to institutional structures,[17] or even Switzerland when adding fiscal matters.[18] In Germany as in Europe, decision-making effectiveness depends on negotiations among politically autonomous governments. But in Germany, the federal government has political and fiscal resources to impose its will in ways that the EU does not, and can depend on a shared national politics and public opinion; viable political parties to balance out state power; and a high degree of economic and cultural homogeneity, none of which exist in Europe at large.

Moreover, European federalism is a 'balancing act' between the representation of territorial and nonterritorial interests, with territorial interests much more fully embedded in every institution than in the United States or Germany: National governments appoint the judges of the ECJ and the commissioners of the EU Commission; national ministers compose the Council of Ministers; members of the EP are elected by national electorates. And these national governments are involved in the enforcement as much as the initiation of 'federal' policies through regulations enforced by national executives and directives that are transposed into national law by national parliaments.[19]

The EU, in short, has a vertical confusion of powers between federal and 'subfederal' governing authorities. A similar such confusion characterizes the EU's horizontal interrelationship of powers between governing branches of authority.

Although not part of the traditional definition of federalism, which limits itself to the vertical division of power, the horizontal division of power, commonly known as the 'separation of powers', is also a characteristic of most federal systems, whether the United States, Canada, Germany, or Belgium. What this means is that the federal executive has relatively little autonomy of action given a legislature and judiciary each with its own independent authority. But there are differences of degree, with greater independence for some legislatures where the political majority differs in a second house (the United States and Germany) and for some judiciaries (Germany vs. Belgium). This is in contrast to unitary states such as France, Britain, The Netherlands, Denmark, and Sweden, which have a horizontal integration of power. In such states, the centralization of power in the executive ensures it a great deal of autonomy, since the legislature and judiciary are largely subordinated to it. Even here, however, there are differences of degree, since some legislatures

---

[16] Its development from confederal to federal over time bears greatest resemblance to the US, however. See Fabbrini (2004b); Sbragia (1993).
[17] See: Sbragia (1993), Gunlicks (1989), and Scharpf (1994).
[18] McKay (2000).   [19] Sbragia (1993: 28).

have traditionally had greater powers of oversight (Denmark and Britain more than France) or the judiciary greater independent authority (Britain more than France). But this horizontal separation of powers is also in contrast to the EU.

In the EU, instead of the relatively clearly defined, constitutionally fixed, and formally unchanging separation of powers between executive, legislative, and judicial branches of government, as found in the US or German federal systems, the EU exhibits a *dynamic confusion of powers*.[20] This confusion involves not only the lack of traditional separation among the various EU institutions but also the mixing up of their very roles. The legislative function is more the domain of the formal executive, the Council of Ministers made up of (mostly) elected national executives, than of the directly elected legislature, the EP, which has at best the secondary legislative powers of most second houses of national parliaments with regard to amendment, review, and coagreement. The executive function is more the purview of the unelected bureaucracy, the Commission, which has powers of both initiation and enforcement, than of the formal executive to which it reports, the Council. And the judicial function, although the only one performed by the expected institution, the ECJ, encroaches on the executive and the legislative functions through the judiciary's activism.

But who then is in charge? Principal–agent theory does not help us much here, since there are too many principals as well as too many agents, with those technically definable as agents often acting as principals and vice versa. For example, while the Commission is in principle the agent and the member-states collectively the principal, in practice the member-states are themselves also agents to the Commission, which acts as the principal with regard to holding the member-states collectively to task for their decisions in the Council or individually to task for their implementation of EU directives.[21] And where does the EP fit here? As the weakest of principals? Even the ECJ and the national courts, which can certainly be seen as the 'agents' of the member-states, are less and less effectively controlled by these 'principals', whether the member-states in the Council when it comes to the ECJ or the member-state governments when it comes to national constitutional courts, since these judiciary agents at both EU and national level have gained greater and greater autonomy vis-à-vis their principals.[22]

When all is said and done, while principal–agent theory is useful for descriptive purposes, to illustrate the difficulties of sorting out who delegates to whom on what, with what kinds of tools and sanctions,[23] it cannot answer

---

[20] Schmidt (1999a). This is as distinguished from the 'fusion of powers', the term used by Wessels (1997) to explain continuing integration.

[21] For more detailed discussion of the problems, see Marks and Hooghe (2001).

[22] Stone Sweet (2000).

[23] See Pollack (1997).

the question of who is in control. But this is not in any case the most important question—despite the never-ending debates on just this point between the 'intergovernmentalists' who claim the member-states to be more in control and the neofunctionalists of various stripes who see the supranational institutions as increasingly in charge.[24] Much more interesting is to ask for the reasons why principals might willingly give up control, as do Gary Marks and Liesbet Hooghe;[25] and much more useful is to take the complexity of multiple principals and agents as a given, and to work out the decision-making traps that follow therefrom, as does Fritz Scharpf.[26] For our purposes, however, the most important question is to ask not who is in charge but how all of this affects the member-states.

The EU's Impact on Institutions in Unitary, Regionalized, and Federal States

The EU's federalizing of its member-states' institutional structures has altered the nature and balance of powers of national branches and levels of government. National executives have all given up a measure of autonomy in favor of a shared supranational authority in Brussels and of control as national courts and regions have gained in independence. National legislatures have lost traditional powers of policy initiation and approval as increasing numbers of policies are agreed in Brussels by national executives, although the legislatures have replaced these with greater powers of oversight and review. For the regions, gains in autonomy vis-à-vis national executives as a result of EU-related resources and access have been offset by their responsibilities with regard to the implementation of EU-mandated policies. For the courts, similarly, gains in autonomy vis-à-vis national executives have been offset by their subordination to the ECJ.

Such Europeanization, however, has been more disruptive to simple polities with unitary structures like France and Britain, where the traditionally powerful executive has given up significant autonomy and control as a result of the diffusion of decision-making upward to the EU, downward to more autonomous regional authorities, and sideways to more independent judicial authorities. Compound polities with federal structures like Germany, Belgium, and Austria, instead, have largely maintained an equilibrium between executive, legislature, and judiciary as well as between center and periphery—although

---

[24] The neofunctionalists encompass a wide range of scholars including 'neofunctionalists' such as Haas (1958), Lindberg (1963), and Schmitter (1970), neofunctional 'supranationalists' such as Sandholtz (1996), Stone Sweet and Brunnell (1996), Stone Sweet and Sandholtz (1997), and the supporters of multilevel governance, cited earlier.

[25] For an excellent discussion of these reasons, see Marks and Hooghe (2001: 71–7).

[26] Scharpf (1997, 2000b).

not without some renegotiation of powers. The impact has been mixed with regard to regionalized states such as Italy and Spain, where the EU has served to reinforce executive power and regional autonomy at one and the same time—although not without a struggle between center and periphery.

One caveat, though. Even though unitary states may have lost comparatively more autonomy and control than either federal or regionalized states in the process of Europeanization, unitary executives still have more autonomy and control over other national authorities than do federal and regionalized states. This in turn ensures that unitary executives are better able to project their preferences onto the EU in the process of European integration.

National leaders' communicative discourse in response to the impact of Europeanization has varied greatly: the French seek to gloss over the loss of executive autonomy at the national level by touting their leadership at the EU level, claiming that it provides national economic and political benefits while adding to the grandeur of France. British leaders instead claim to retain as much executive autonomy and control as possible while getting as much as they can in economic benefits from the EU. For the Germans, by contrast, executive autonomy has not been at issue in this 'semisovereign' state, and their discourse has instead focused on showing that they were good Europeans. For the Italians, executive autonomy has, if anything, been enhanced through Europeanization, such that they use the EU's leadership in their discourse to legitimize the executive's empowerment at the national level as well as to reinforce identity.

National Executives and the Loss of Governmental Autonomy

National executives, to begin with, have all given up significant autonomy in exchange for the shared authority and control of the EU. National executives have been one of six, then twelve, fifteen, now twenty-five, and soon more in the Council in deciding on policies that had in the past been theirs to decide alone or in tandem with other national authorities. Similarly, they have delegated to a range of EU institutions authority over policy areas that used to be sovereignty-defining tasks of the nation-state, whether in monetary policy or international trade. Moreover, not only has the ECJ taken jurisdiction over the final interpretation and the enforcement—along with the Commission—of agreed rules and laws, it has also acted as a 'purposeful opportunist'[27] by setting precedents that have expanded its own powers as well as those of the Commission in cases such as the mutual recognition of products, equal pay for women, and migrant workers' benefits.[28] In addition, not only does the Commission set the agenda by drafting the directives that executives pass in the Council of Ministers and then push through national

[27] Wincott (1995).   [28] Conant (2002).

parliaments and put into practice, it also rules on, and overrules, actions that executives used to decide unilaterally in areas such as industrial policy (especially state subsidies) and regional policy.[29] Finally, the Commission's regulatory powers ensure that it has tremendous impact despite its relatively small budget, mainly because the costs of regulation are borne by national public institutions—which must transform the rules devised in Brussels into national public policies—as well as by national economic actors and consumers.[30] In other words, the Commission has the advantage of, in Laura Cram's words, 'calling the tune without paying the piper'.[31]

National executives have not only lost autonomy in consequence of the shift of decision-making upward to the EU but they have also lost control as a result of the shift of decision-making power downward to subnational authorities, through processes of devolution and decentralization, and outward to independent regulatory agencies. The move to regulatory agencies in particular—the response to globalization pressures beginning in the 1980s and EU mandates beginning in the 1990s—has produced a weakening of the state qua central actor, although it at the same time could be seen as a strengthening of public action and effective governance *for* the people. Moreover, such agencies increasingly constitute a Europe-wide force, independent of national governments, as a result of the EU's creation of formalized networks of national regulatory authorities in sectors such as energy, telecommunications, railways, financial services, and competition policy. These provide regulators not only with new ideas through the creation of 'epistemic communities' but also a set of allies for support against national governments and the businesses they regulate.[32]

Despite all of these shifts in executive autonomy and control, intergovernmentalist theorists, focusing on national executives' role in the Council, have argued that the EU's national impact is one that has served to 'strengthen the state' by enhancing the powers of the executive to the detriment of national legislatures and societal interests.[33] If what they mean by this is that the EU has 'rescued the nation-state' by enabling national executives to push through economic reforms that might have been impossible otherwise, this is no doubt true. Moreover, if they wish to claim that national executives have gained in power with regard to the most 'heroic' of policies, such as Treaty negotiations, this is not wrong. The problem is that the claim is too general, and does not specify the conditions where this is—and is not—the case.[34]

---

[29] See Cini (1996), Ludlow (1991), Nugent (1994), Marks, Hooghe, and Blank (1996), Schneider (1995), Garrett and Tsebelis (1996), Peters (1992), and Kerremans (1996: 225).

[30] See the discussion in Mény, Muller, and Quermonne (1996).

[31] Cram (1993).

[32] Coen and Héritier (2005), Eberlein (2004), Wilks (2005), and Coen and Thatcher (2005).

[33] Milward (1992), and Moravcsik (1994).

[34] Although Moravcsik (1994) does not argue that the EU strengthens the state under all conditions, he specifies no conditions where this is not the case.

If one considers the most 'heroic' of European initiatives, whether the Single Market Act or the Maastricht Treaty, the argument that the executive gains in power by way of a 'two-level strategy' to overcome domestic opposition—first, through its mantle of legitimacy and, second, through the creation of policies by way of an insulated process that offers national legislatures and societal interests few opportunities for comment or change[35]—seems to have a lot to recommend it. This is where the executive appears most to impose, negotiating behind closed doors for long nights, with no minutes of the meetings and no obligations for transparency, and making deals that national legislatures and societal interests appear bound to accept. Even here, however, the executive has had less and less autonomy, especially since the Maastricht Treaty, with the growth of interest participation and public scrutiny through ratification debates and referenda. Moreover, in everyday policymaking, qualified majority voting in the Council places significant limits on individual member-state control; parliamentary codecision procedures limit member-states' collective control; comitology brings in a wider range of experts and interests that further limits individual national governments' control through the Council—although it at the same time also constrains Commission decision;[36] while the weight of Commission technical expertise makes member-state objections on purely political grounds difficult.[37] The confusion of powers in the EU, in short, ensures that national executives acting together in the Council of Ministers cannot control policymaking, even if they do control the agenda and the big issues.

Intergovernmentalist theorists also overlook the fact that executives of different countries differ in the comparative 'strengthening' of the state. If anything, Europeanization weakens the strong executives of unitary states, while it has comparatively little impact on federal executives. Only for regionalized executives, as in Italy, could one agree that the EU strengthens the state.[38]

Here, mind you, we have to differentiate between the process of Europeanization and European integration. Adapting national structures to the developing European polity as part of a top-down process of Europeanization is different from projecting preferences from national capitals to the EU through the bottom-up process of European integration.[39] Most significantly, while the unitary state can be seen to have been weakened through its top-down adaptation to the EU, it retains greater bottom-up ability to project its preferences onto the EU than federal or regionalized states. This stands to reason, since the

---

[35] Putnam (1988), and Moravscik (1993: 515).
[36] Pollack (1997: 115–16).
[37] See Marks and Hooghe (2001: 4–10), and Egan and Wolf (1999: 254).
[38] Jeffery (1999) and Fabbrini (2003).
[39] See the more extensive discussion of the theoretical literature on Europeanization in Chapter 5.

executives in unitary states are in principle (if not always in practice) better able to control the various ministries involved in European policymaking by creating unified coordinating structures that express national preferences through a single voice at the EU level. Unitary states like France, Britain, and Denmark all benefit from unified structures that serve to promote their strategic ambitions to influence the EU across policy areas.[40] But this is not generalizable to all unitary states. In Greece, a lack of administrative capacity has ensured that national coordination of EU policy has been piecemeal, conducted by way of irregular ad hoc meetings or personal contacts.[41] In the Netherlands, by contrast, the presence of coalition governments ensures a more decentralized, ministerial approach to coordination. In regionalized states, moreover, where the executive is formally unitary but the regions strong, central coordination also depends on administrative capacity, and/or coalition governments. Here, while Spain has largely been able to speak in one voice, Italy has had a more decentralized approach. In federal states, however, the formal structure alone makes central coordination difficult, given the autonomous powers of the different branches of national authority on top of regional participation in EU-level decisions.[42] This helps explain why Germany has hoped that 'hundreds of arrows may be more effective than one shot with Big Bertha'.[43]

This division between unitary, regionalized, and federal state ability to project preferences is replayed in the the Committee of Permanent Representatives (COREPER), where influence depends on internal coordination as well as the quality of the ambassador. Here, in the words of former Belgian COREPER ambassador, Philippe de Schoutheete, the British were generally 'practically perfect', the French for the most part good, and the Germans typically bad, given rivalries between federal ministries and the Länder;[44] Italy did not even bear mentioning. Whereas the British COREPER actively lobbies EU institutions, attempts to set the EU policy agenda for high and low politics, coordinates intersectorally, and maintains contact with private interests, the French COREPER does all of these except for intersectoral coordination, the German COREPER is like the French except that it attempts to set the EU agenda only for high politics, and the Italian COREPER does none of these.[45]

Differences in member-states' institutional structures also affect their capacity to project their own grand strategies onto the EU, although other factors, such as country size, political power, economic weight, leaders' ideas and

---

[40] Kassim (2003a: 157–8), and Pederson (2000).

[41] Dimitrakopoulos (1997: 181)—cited in Page (2003: 171).

[42] See Kassim (2000).

[43] Derlien (2000).

[44] Remarks of Baron Philippe de Schoutheete, permanent representative from Belgium, interview with author, Cambridge, MA, October 15, 1997.

[45] Kassim (2003b: 98–101), and Kassim et al. (2001).

personality, or control of the EU presidency also play a role. For countries in which size, power, and weight are not so different, as is the case of our four countries, unitary states seem more likely to try to develop and project preferences in terms of grand strategies onto the EU than regionalized or federal states. This can be explained not simply as a natural follow-on from national experiences of executive power but also as a consequence of the greater need to offset the loss of autonomy and control related to Europeanization with greater say in European integration.

Thus, in unitary France, national leaders have often sought to impose their preferences—whether by proposing grand initiatives as part of the Franco-German partnership, by maneuvering to maintain CAP subsidies for French farmers, or by insisting that Europe-based institutions such as the ECB or NATO's southern command be led by Frenchmen. In unitary Britain, by contrast, while national leaders have occasionally sought to engage in grand initiatives, as in Blair's great leap forward on European security and defense in St. Malò in 1998, they have more often resisted the EU because they were not leading it, as in the case of Thatcher on monetary union and social policy, even though this consecrates the UK as the EU's 'awkward partner.'[46] In federal Germany, by contrast, exercising leadership has been difficult except in the context of the Franco-German partnership. In regionalized Italy, where exercising leadership domestically has itself been a near impossible task until the 1990s, given state paralysis, national leaders have rarely sought to propose any grand initiatives, and have been content to follow rather than lead.

Institutional structure also helps explain member-states' differential capacity to apply EU decisions, both with regard to transposition of EU directives and their implementation. Unitary states have a potentially greater capacity to apply EU decisions because of the concentration of power in the executive and the executive's little need to negotiate with subnational regional authorities, as in federal or regionalized states. Other factors, however, also come into play. This is because institutional capacity to apply EU decisions does not necessarily ensure the political will to apply them—if national executives are opposed to the measures—or the administrative capacity—if national executives are not efficient or effective in transposing or implementing the measures. Generally speaking, whereas institutional design provides a plausible explanation for the poor compliance record of Germany and the stellar record of the UK, the absence of political will better explains the French case, the absence of administrative capacity, the Italian case. Infringement proceedings against member-states provide a very rough bit of statistical evidence for this (see Figure 2.2).[47] In infringement cases between 1978 and 1999, the UK began

---

[46] George (1990).
[47] Whether these are a fair indicator of compliance failure is another matter—for this, see Börzel (2001). For us, what matters is that it suggests patterns of response to EU directives.

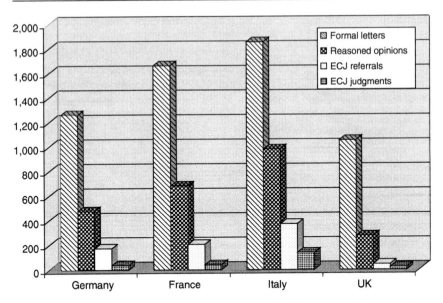

Figure 2.2. Infringements of the internal market classified by stage of ECJ proceedings (1978–99).

Source: European University Institute (compiled by Tanja Böerzel) http://www.iue.it/RSCAS/ Research/Tools/ComplianceDB/Index.shtml

with the fewest openings of proceedings against it (1,056 formal letters), reduced them most quickly, and ended up with the least ECJ judgments (23) whereas Germany, which began only slightly above the UK, with 1,262 formal letters, dropped more slowly to end with more negative ECJ judgments (37)—suggesting that institutional design matters.[48] But Italy, which was the worst offender—with 1,856 formal letters dropping very slowly, to end up with 139 ECJ judgments against it—suggests that in addition to institutional design comes the lack of administrative capacity to respond even when faced with the possibility of court action. France, initially not so far behind Italy, at 1,664 formal letters, dropped much more quickly and successfully, to end up with forty-one judgments—suggesting that it had the institutional capacity to respond quickly when forced but lacked the political will to comply.

Compliance patterns for 1998–2004 tell a similar story. Italy was again the worst offender generally with regard to ECJ judgments, followed by France, Germany, and, way behind the others, the UK—although the areas of infringement differed, with Italy topping the chart on ECJ judgments on free movement and social policy, France on the environment and taxation (see Figure 2.3).[49]

[48] European University Institute (compiled by Tanja Börzel) http://www.iue.it/RSCAS/ Research/Tools/ComplianceDB/Index.shtml
[49] ECJ (cases as up to February 2004) http://europa.eu.int/eur-lex/en/index.html

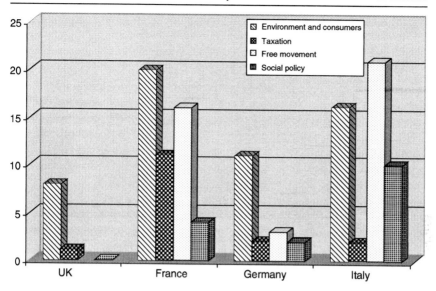

Figure 2.3. European Court of Justice Judgments, 1998–2004
Source: Compiled from ECJ http://europa.eu.int/eur-lex/en/index.html (cases up to February 2004)

Qualitative studies tend to provide further corroboration of the statistical patterns. This is a necessary addition since the statistical data on compliance alone is not a very reliable source of information, given that EC oversight suffers from a scarcity of resources and inconsistency in enforcement.[50] One such study of compliance patterns in the social policy arena by Gerda Falkner, Oliver Trieb, Miriam Harlapp, and Simons Lieber should suffice to show how complex the picture is, but also how it confirms our general argument about the underlying structural factors.

First of all, the Falkner et al. study shows that misfit in terms of policy legacies, the main focus of the compliance literature, is not a major explanatory factor. The UK, with one of the highest degrees of misfit for a wide range of social policy directives, was nevertheless the fastest of our four countries in transposing social policy directives correctly (and fourth among the EU15) whereas France, with one of the lowest degrees of policy misfit in this area, was one of the slowest in transposition, with Germany and Italy not much better.[51] Second, the study finds that politics is a better explanatory variable than policy misfit, with shifts in government majority, say, from the center-right to the center-left, a better predictor of a shift from resistance to compliance, as was the case for Italy and Germany with the Parental Leave Directive or for the UK with regard to bringing on board EU social policy when the Blair government

---

[50] See the critique in Falkner et al. (2005: ch. 11).
[51] Falkner et al. (2005: ch. 14: 294).

came to power.[52] But while politics affects all countries, it is not always the most significant explanatory variable.

In the Falkner et al. study, our four countries fall into two of three 'worlds' of compliance: The UK and Germany fall into the world of domestic politics because delays are only related to partisan politics. France and Italy fall into the world of neglect, France because of its consistent unwillingness to comply, regardless of the politics, Italy, because of its incapacity to comply, even when politics is not at issue (the other world, of law, is limited to Nordic countries).[53] But how then do we further differentiate among countries in the two worlds? Institutional design helps explain the differences between Britain and Germany. The former has good scores because it can readily comply where politics is not an issue, given a unitary state (enhanced by one party government and limited social partner involvement). Germany, however, has bad scores on compliance as a result of its federal structure (further complicated by coalition governments and social partner involvement), which tends to increase the political problems. Political will rather than institutional design helps differentiate unitary France from unitary Britain. 'National arrogance' characterizes French attitudes to compliance on all social policy directives, since French governments of left and right have consistently resisted transposition of EU directives because they saw French laws as at least as good as if not better than EU laws. But once pushed, they implemented quickly, attesting to the benefits of unitary institutional design. This stands in contrast to Italy, where the lack of administrative capacity, which made for often slow and flawed transposition as well as enforcement even where politics and political will were favorable to compliance, came on top of the complications arising from its regionalized institutional design (not to mention coalition governments and social partner involvement). This made for a compliance record worse than that of Germany as well as France.

In the application of EU policy, then, once we control for politics, political will, and administrative capacity, unitary institutional design ensures faster compliance by national executives than regionalized or federal design. Similarly, in the projection of national preferences onto the EU, unitary structures make for national executives' greater potential voice. But the very unitary structures that make for national executives' greater powers of preference projection and policy application by comparison with those of regionalized or federal states also ensure them a greater overall loss of power than federal or regionalized states when it comes more generally to adapting to the EU. This is because the higher levels of national autonomy and control diminish comparatively more in the face of increased shared EU authority and control (see Table 2.2).

---

[52] Falkner et al. (2005: ch. 14: 297).
[53] The following discussion is based on Falkner et al. (2005: ch. 15).

Table 2.2. The differential effects of the EU on national executives' powers, projection of preferences, and compliance patterns related to institutional structure

National executives	Europeanization Top-down impact on autonomy/control	European integration Bottom-up ability to project preferences		Europeanization Top-down impact on patterns of compliance	
		Administrative capacity	Voice	Transposition	Enforcement
Unitary France	Weakened	Strong	Strong	Slow (bc lacks political will)	Fast
Unitary Britain	Weakened	Strong	Strong	Fast (if politics not at issue)	Fast
Federal Germany	Neutral	Weak	Weak	Fast (if politics not at issue)	Slow
Regional'd Italy	Strengthened	Very Weak	Very Weak	Slow (bc lacks administrative capacity)	Very Slow (also bc lacks administrative capacity)

What does this tell us about the 'EU strengthening the state' hypothesis? That the hypothesis sheds little light on preference projection or policy application, since long-standing national institutional design characteristics sufficiently account for national executives' strength or weakness in both cases. But it also suggests that no such general claim can explain adaptation to the EU, since while unitary executives have weakened, regionalized executives may have been strengthened and federal executives have neither appreciably weakened nor strengthened. To demonstrate this, however, we need to look more closely at the other branches and levels of government and their relationship with the executive.

National Parliaments and the Loss of Legislative Power

Although the EU may not have strengthened the state, understood as the executive, it has certainly weakened national parliaments. National parliaments have been the biggest losers in Europeanization, as the EU has taken over powers of initiative and approval that had been the domain of national legislatures.[54] This is related not so much to the presence of the EP as to the way in which the EU has gained legislative powers traditionally exercised by national parliaments in such areas as economic policy, trade policy, tariff policy, and agricultural policy. The contribution of national parliaments in areas of EU competence has become primarily one of transposing into national law EU directives elaborated in the EU Commission and approved by national

---

[54] See Maurer and Wessels (2001) and Maurer (2001).

executives in the Council of Ministers. In economic legislation alone, the EU is now responsible for over 75 percent of the laws passing through member-state parliaments,[55] 80 percent of environmental laws, and 90 percent of consumer protection legislation.[56]

In addition, national parliaments suffer from a lack of authoritative power over transnational policymaking, which is generally the domain of the national executives; they labor under the burden of a lack of information on EU developments; and they lack control over policy decisions made in the Council by their own member governments. National parliaments have been ill-informed, if they have been informed at all, not only of government positions before the decision but also of what stance they took in the negotiations, given the secrecy rule that forbids even minutes being taken during the meetings. This means that they have not been able to anticipate and respond to EU initiatives before they come to the Council. But even if national parliaments were kept informed—and reforms in various countries have improved this in recent years—it would not necessarily affect the outcome, given the ability to agree to 'package deals', or logrolling, and qualified majority voting.[57] Moreover, once directives are agreed, national parliaments have little choice other than to transpose them. And even here, executives can circumvent parliamentary oversight by using delegated legislation, or implementing rules by decree.[58]

The extent to which the EU alone can be blamed for 'deparliamentarization', or national parliaments' loss in power, is questionable, however. This is because parliaments generally have lost power over the years to national executives for a range of reasons, including the increasing complexities of modern governing activities and the growing importance of technical expertise, the wide use of specialized agents within ministries and the move to independent regulatory agencies which are less directly accountable to parliaments than executive agencies, the increasing organizational power of political parties and their imposition of party discipline to shore up government power, the demands of national security, the rise of international organizations and global interdependence, and more.[59]

This said, national parliaments still have a role to play—new ones as 'regulators of society'[60] and reinforced ones with regard to oversight—as part of a process of 'reparliamentarization'.[61] Although the EU may have taken over

---

[55] Greenwood (2003).
[56] This according to German MEP Jorgo Chatizmarkakis, talk at Boston University, October 6, 2005.
[57] Norton (1996*b*).
[58] Dimitrakopoulos (2001).
[59] See Raunio and Hix (2001), Anderson and Burns (1996), and Norton (1997).
[60] Duina and Oliver (2004).
[61] Raunio and Hix (2001).

policy initiation from national parliaments in an ever-growing number of areas, EU-related legislation has often acted as a spur to national parliaments and governments to legislate in areas not subject to EU rulings, either by setting precedents—the case of antitrust legislation in Italy and the Netherlands—or by providing opportunity for policy transfer—the case of National Action Plans (NAPs) in the Open Method of Coordination (OMC).[62]

Most importantly, however, in place of their decreasing powers of initiative in areas of EU-related legislation, parliaments have increased their oversight functions. Legitimacy now comes less from proposing legislation than from raising issues, holding hearings, proposing amendments, and voicing concerns and complaints. Moreover, even if members of parliament may not be informed as much as one might wish, they have been increasing their access to information. Since the Maastricht Treaty, most parliaments have developed mechanisms and rules that force governments to explain EU-related policies and actions in the parliamentary arena.[63] In addition, the growing importance of European Affairs Committees in all the member-states has provided members of parliament with more information on European policy initiatives at earlier stages of the process.[64] And information represents power—or at least more power than before, in particular for members of the opposition and Euroskeptics.[65] However, this is still a lot less power than in the past, in particular given the increase in executive power related not just to general trends but also to the process of European integration.

But although all national parliaments have lost legislative power as a result of the EU, different countries' parliaments have experienced differing degrees of loss of powers. In federal states, national parliaments' actual loss of power has been less than one might have expected, mainly because parliaments were able to negotiate a reequilibration of powers with the central executive. In Germany, the opposition-controlled, regionally based second chamber of the legislature was instrumental in forcing the issue at the time of the Maastricht Treaty,[66] with Belgium following suit, while in Austria, the Länder insisted on having a procedure for intrastate participation in EU decision-making even prior to EU accession in 1995.[67] In Germany, the degree of control of the executive by parliament has remained quite strong, in particular on the part of the upper chamber of the regions (Bundesrat) whereas it has been more moderate for the lower chamber (Bundestag); in Austria, only the lower house (Nationalrat) is strong.[68] Belgium's parliament, by contrast, traditionally weak because highly divided along political, religious, and linguistical lines, has remained weak.

---

[62] See Duina and Oliver (2004), and the discussion in Chapter 3.
[63] Raunio and Hix (2001: 163).   [64] See Maurer and Wessels (2001).
[65] Raunio and Hix (2001: 155–63).   [66] Saalfeld (1996).
[67] Morass (1997).   [68] Kassim (2005).

In unitary states, by contrast, the actual loss of parliamentary power has been greater because legislatures have weaker constitutional bases than in federal states to force a rebalancing with the executive. And they have less political independence, given the traditional weakness of the second chamber and control of the first by the executive as representative of the majority party. As a result, in France the parliament's traditionally highly limited powers have remained limited, despite reforms, with both houses of parliament exercising only very weak control over the executive with regard to oversight.[69] In Britain the parliament has by comparison managed to retain its traditionally greater powers of oversight and voice, allowing the House of Commons to exercise moderate control over the executive.[70] The case of Denmark, however, where the traditionally strong parliament has had significant oversight over the executive in EU policymaking, shows that unitary structure is not in and of itself an impediment to strong control.[71] Almost all other unitary states in the EU15, however, have either moderate (Sweden and Finland) or weak control, as is also the case for regionalized states such as Spain and Italy.[72]

The differences among unitary, regionalized, and federal states with regard to the powers of national parliaments also tend to color national executives' preferences with regard to the powers of the EP in the process of European integration.[73] Unitary states like France and Britain have tended to promote an intergovernmental view of European integration in which they have sought to maintain the power of the member-states in the Council and resisted increasing the powers of the EP or the EC (e.g. de Gaulle's 'empty chair' crisis). Federal or regionalized states like Germany and Italy, by contrast, have tended to promote a more federal vision which gives more power to the EP as well as to the EC (as have smaller states more generally). Other preferences may complicate this picture, however. Thus, national executives' preferences for an economic community in which legitimacy has its basis in effective solutions to problems via market mechanisms or nonmajoritarian institutions like regulatory agencies may override intergovernmental preferences, as was the case for Britain with regard to the Single Market.[74] This also applies to executives' desire to ensure greater democratic legitimacy, as was the case for Giscard d'Estaing with regard to the direct election of the EP.

---

[69] Rizzuto (1996), Maurer and Wessels (2001), and Kassim (2005).

[70] Norton (1996b), Maurer and Wessels (2001), and Kassim (2005).

[71] See Laursen (2001), Sørensen and Waever (1992) and Nehring (1992). See also the discussion in Newman (1996: 192–3).

[72] Kassim (2005), and Maurer and Wessels (2001).

[73] Rittberger (2003).

[74] Rittgerger (2003). See also Jachtenfuchs et al. (1998).

Subnational Authorities and the Gains in Territorial Autonomy

The involvement of subnational authorities in EU decision-making represents arguably the greatest challenge to the traditional institutional balance of all of the member-states, by loosening the hierarchical authority of central governments vis-à-vis the periphery. European integration has engendered a system of multilevel governance in which subnational authorities no longer have to channel all their demands through central authorities and are no longer only responsible to these authorities. Instead, they operate in a broader system in which, although national governments remain the central authority, subnational authorities may deal with EU institutions, other national authorities, as well as with other subnational authorities in decision-making at the same time that they are also often responsible for EU policy implementation.[75] Seeing the EU as a system of 'multilevel governance' represents a useful corrective to intergovernmentalist theories focused exclusively on member-states' powers or supranationalist theories which privilege EU institutions.[76] But it is no substitute for them, as studies of multilevel governance themselves demonstrate that the powers of regional authorities not only remain relatively modest but they also differ across member-states as well as within them.

Regional authorities participate as members of the Committee of the Regions, of relevant EU level committees, and in 'cohesion' policy and the structural funds. These involve Commission, national, regional, and local officials as well as the social partners at all levels and stages of the policy process. Moreover, regional authorities are increasingly responsible for the implementation of EU-related policy, including not only the structural funds but also other policies over which they mostly have had no input, such as environmental regulation, the application of technical and safety standards, workplace requirements, public procurement, and regional aids to industry. As a result, at the same time that Europeanization has increased regional authorities' autonomy from the national executive, by providing them with new access to EU-level policy formulation processes and resources, it has undermined this autonomy with respect to supranational authority, by making regional authorities responsible for the implementation of EU-related policies.[77]

But although all regional authorities have experienced increasing autonomy from national authorities and greater subordination to EU authorities in the process of Europeanization, the amount of autonomy and/or subordination differs across and even within member-states. In federal states, regional authorities have generally been able to count on their substantial, constitutionally based powers, complemented in most European countries with their

---

[75] See Marks (1992), Hooghe (1996), John (2000), and Kassim (2005).
[76] See Marks and Hooghe (2001), Kohler-Koch (2000), and Jachtenfuchs (2000).
[77] On the whole range of issues involving Europe and the regions, see, for example: Jones and Keating (1994) and du Granrut (1994).

domination of a second parliamentary chamber, to maintain their balance of power with the executive. We have already seen that in Germany, Belgium, and Austria, the regions' parliamentary powers, through control of the second chamber, enabled them to force a rebalancing. In federal Germany, the Länder, after an initial loss in power as a result of the executive deciding at the EU level on policies that had long been their domain, were compensated for the loss with a seat at the table in the EU on issues that affect them and maintained major responsibility in policy implementation.

In regionalized states, regional authorities have no such constitutionally based powers, nor do they predominate in a second parliamentary chamber, and therefore have a more difficult time negotiating any rebalancing. Because they have for the most part only relatively recently benefited from the decentralizing or 'federalizing' legislation that effectively transformed unitary states into regionalized ones, any loss in powers to the executive due to their EU level role was certain to be highly contested politically by regional authorities.[78] Moreover, any new gains in power of the still formally unitary executive would likely be defended. This has been the case for the Italian regions, where decentralizing reforms began in the early 1970s, as much as for the Spanish 'Autonomous Communities', which gained quasi-federal autonomy in the early 1980s.[79] In Spain, historically conflictual relations combined with 'asymmetical federalism' ensured that it took a long time for cooperation to replace the conflictual interactions between the national executive responsible for ensuring implementation and the recently empowered regions seeking to protect their new autonomy from the encroachments of the EU as much as the national executive.[80] Thus, unlike in federal states, in regionalized states regional authorities were not given a seat at the table in the Council (nor did they necessarily want one) and generally had to struggle with the center on policy area after policy area to retain or regain the preexisting equilibrium in center-periphery relations.

In unitary states, the regions have little autonomous power and certainly neither the constitutionally based nor legislatively derived powers to force any renegotiation of powers with the executive. This is why the EU has constituted a much greater potential source of autonomy. Because the regional authorities of unitary states have been largely dependent on the executive, any increase in supranational access and funding clearly made for an increase in their independence. However, by the same token, any increase in such regions' independence would be likely to be circumscribed by the executive. This has been as true for unitary France, in which regional authorities gained some measure of autonomy from the executive only in the decentralizing reforms of the

---

[78] Börzel (2002).
[79] On the Spanish reforms, see: Agranoff (1996), and Keating (1998).
[80] Börzel (2002).

1980s,[81] as for the newly emancipated 'regions' of Britain, beneficiaries of the devolution that started only in the late 1990s for Scotland, Wales, and Northern Ireland with elected legislatures, but which has yet to begin for the recently created English regions.[82]

These differential patterns of responses to the EU's impact on regional authorities are played out in a number of areas. In regional planning, for example, the most federal states, Germany and Belgium, made their regional authorities responsible for regional development plans while in regionalized Spain, the central government framed the process, despite much regional involvement in planning, as was also the case in Italy. By contrast, in the more unitary states such as France, Greece, Ireland, and the UK, the central governments dominated, with regional actors playing a weak or insignificant role.[83]

With the EU policy formulation process, moreover, unitary states have often been more wary of their regional authorities' EU access, fearful of a loss of control. Most, however, did not go quite as far as the French state, which put a subprefect in Brussels in 1988 in order to ensure against the regions making European policy 'behind the back of the state'.[84] This, needless to say, did not stop the French regions from establishing representation in Brussels through lobbies (by the mid-1990s, 17 of the 22 regions) as well as through various nongovernmental regional interests and regional and local associations that lobby, of which regions are members.[85] Italy, by contrast, despite being more decentralized than the French state, did stop its regional governments from setting up offices in Brussels, although this was for political reasons, mainly the concern about Communist-controlled regions trying to make their own foreign policy (it was only in 1995 that the proscription was removed, with by 1996 only two regions having established themselves in Brussels). Even the German federal government, however, initially disapproved of the Länder's establishing a presence in Brussels (which they did earlier than any other subnational authorities) for fear of their conducting auxiliary foreign policy.[86] The greatest fears with regard to EU access, of course, have been by states with strong regional autonomy movements, concerned that the closer relationship with Europe would only encourage the concerned regions to challenge the state's power over them, and even their territorial integrity. Scotland, Catalonia, the Basque region, and Corsica are cases in point.[87]

Subnational authorities' greater independence from central executives depends not only on the executive's granting of permission on EU access but

---

[81] Schmidt (1990).   [82] See Loughlin (2001).   [83] Marks (1996).
[84] Schmidt (1990: 300). France did finally officially acknowledge their right to be in Brussels with the law of 6 February 1992.
[85] Mazey (1995a).   [86] Anderson (1996: 173).
[87] See, for example, Keating (1988).

also on subnational authorities' own interest and capacity. Here, regions' experiences have much to do with what they bring to the process, with the richer regions with greater administrative capacity likely to do better than the poor ones with lesser capacity. But the personality of the heads of the regions also makes a difference, with the more powerful personages better able to make themselves heard at the EU level.[88] The German Länder, for example, are well-represented on a wide range of committees, but that representation comes primarily from the richest of the three Länder operating (purportedly) in the interests of the rest. And it does not involve all member-states. The British had no subnational representation until devolution because they had no elected regional authorities as such (although they did institute regional administrative units to deal with the structural funds). Moreover, although the French regions have been well-represented, they have tended to be very light structures, often set up in conjunction with other regions, with no more than three employees, such as Brittany sharing an office with the Loire.[89]

Whatever the representation of the regions at the EU level, however, their influence in policy formulation remains minimal outside the regional policy arena. This is not only because the regions as a group have little formal role but also because the regions often seem more focused on keeping tabs on their own national governments in Brussels, and in influencing their positions on matters of domestic importance, than on having a larger impact on the EU more generally—including the German and Spanish regions.[90] What is more, after an initial period where the Commission had encouraged greater regional independence, it seems to have been going back to a focus on national executives. This also makes sense since, ultimately, the executive is responsible for regions' performance in implementation while the regions, as relative newcomers to EU-level policymaking, have fewer points of access than organized interests such as business, and less well-developed circuits of influence. But all of this suggests that multilevel governance is not quite as multilevel as the theory suggests.

Judicial Authorities and the Gains in Court Independence

The European Court of Justice represents a further source of encroachment on the powers and prerogatives not only of national executives and legislatures but also of the judiciaries. However, at the same time that the ECJ has served to subordinate national judicial authorities to itself, it has increased their independence from national executives as well as from one another, with lower courts emancipated from their hierarchical superiors through their recourse to

---

[88] Keating (1998: 134).   [89] Pasquier (2004: 131).
[90] David Williamson, Secretary General of the EU Commission, interview with author, September 30, 1997.

the ECJ. This is all the more notable once we remember that although the ECJ has been acting as if it were the supreme court of a federal system in which it is the guardian of an entrenched written constitution by which it had been empowered, it is in fact the court of a loose economic federation which, although its decisions are binding on national governments, has no formal power over national legal systems and no enforcement powers.[91] It is national courts, in fact, that do the ECJ's work, by acting as 'agents of the Community order' to ensure conformity with EC law.[92] The national courts do this not only by following the ECJ's rulings but also by seeking preliminary rulings by the ECJ, thus establishing a unitary system of judicial review.[93]

The source of the ECJ's powers follows from two main doctrines, those of 'supremacy' and of 'direct effect'. The doctrine of supremacy establishes the primacy of European law over national rule or practice. The doctrine of direct effect establishes that EU rules confer rights on individuals that can be invoked against their own governments in national courts.[94] Both doctrines together have had significant impact on national autonomy generally, by giving individuals recourse against their own governments, whether they seek to alter national economic practices that they find not in conformity with EU laws or to provide protections for citizens that the national government refuses, by forcing them to implement EC legislation.

The ECJ now serves as a superior level of judicial review, capable of vetting all national laws and policies for their conformity with EU law. But at the same time that this has effectively reduced national courts' autonomy vis-à-vis the ECJ, it has given national courts new powers and autonomy vis-à-vis the executive. Because they have been able to choose to seek 'authoritative guidance' from the ECJ (as per Article 234, ex. 177), the courts have the opportunity of changing national law (since ECJ interpretations are generally accepted as precedent-setting). For the lower courts, this also means circumventing their own national judicial hierarchy.[95] Such referrals began in 1961, reaching 100 per year in the 1970s, over 175 in the 1980s, and over 250 annually by the late 1990s.[96]

There are various theories as to why the courts have referred cases in increasing numbers, thus fueling European integration through the courts. The 'judicial empowerment thesis' suggests that European legal integration is the result of judges having sought referrals as a way to increase their own power over other actors, whether the national executives, parliaments, or other

---

[91] Stein, (1981), and Garret and Weingast (1993: 195–6).
[92] Stone Sweet (1998: 163–4; 2004: 69).
[93] Weiler (1991: 2430).
[94] See Craig and de Búrca (1998), and Stone Sweet (2004).
[95] Burley and Mattli (1993), and Weiler (1994).
[96] Stone Sweet and Brunnell (1998).

judges.[97] Another approach builds on this, but adds the role of private actors in instigating litigation as a way to promote their own interests.[98] Yet another focuses on the differences between lower courts, interested in asserting their independent power from the higher courts, and the higher courts, concerned to thwart the penetration of EC law into the national legal order.[99] But whatever the reasons, the result is the increasing independence of national judiciaries from other national authorities and their increasing incorporation into an EU system of adjudication.

This said, there are factors that limit the impact of EU judicialization. First, national courts are most often likely to apply ECJ law by direct reference to the treaties, directives, or regulations, without appeal to the ECJ for a preliminary ruling or even reference to ECJ case law. Thus, for example, in the years 1983–97, German courts made 3,388 decisions on European law and only 657 preliminary references; Italy 2,039 decisions and 407 references; France 2,525 decisions and 414 references; and the UK 1,150 decisions and only 198 references.[100] This leaves open the likelihood of significant divergence in national judgments on European law.

But it also shows the differences among countries in terms of how much EU law national courts take on board, with Germany generally making the most EU law-related decisions, Britain the least. This is also apparent with regard to national courts' references to the ECJ for preliminary rulings—as can be seen in the figures up until 1999 in terms of the number of references from the lower courts and the proportionately fewer from courts of last instance. Here again, Germany was highest, with 812 lower courts' references and 350 Courts of Last Instance; then came Italy with 532 and 93 respectively and France, at 534 and 77; followed far behind by Britain at 255 and 36.[101] With regard to preliminary references specifically, in the period between 1988 and 1997, Germany averaged 48.6 annual references, Italy 33.1, France 25.9, and the UK 16.9.[102]

The reasons for the differences in recourse to preliminary rulings have many possible sources. Stone Sweet and Burrell argue that such differences are related to the combined size and openness of a member-state's economy.[103] But this cannot be generalized to cases of social or labor law.[104] Moreover, it does little in any event to explain differences among our four countries, all of which are both big and open. Better to mention instead the long-standing

---

[97] Stein (1981) and Weiler (1981, 1991, 1994).
[98] Burley and Mattli (1993), and Stone Sweet and Brunell (1998).
[99] Alter (1998: 242).
[100] Conant (2002: 80–2).
[101] Conant (2002: 85).
[102] Hix (2005: 129), calculated from the Stone Sweet and Brunell 1999 dataset.
[103] Stone Sweet and Brunell (1998).
[104] Conant (2001: 88).

importance of a legalistic culture for a long-independent judiciary in Germany; the growing independence of the formerly subordinated judiciary in Italy and France; and the UK's Euroskeptic culture. But none of these is entirely satisfactory either.

Quantity of references, after all, says nothing about the quality of references, that is, which preliminary rulings made a bigger difference in terms of national law. For this, we could argue that although the UK referred fewer cases, those that have been referred have had a greater impact than in, say, France in areas like gender policy.[105] And to explain such an impact, we have to turn to questions of political opportunity structures and, again, to legal culture. In the case of equal pay, for example, in the UK well-organized women's interest groups and committed public agencies actively pursued the legal route with judges open to referring such cases through the ECJ in the absence of UK law. In France, by contrast, equal pay got little boost from the ECJ in the absence of well-organized interest groups, committed public agencies, or referring judges; but it also needed it less given more progressive laws and less of a pay gap.[106]

Generalizations by reference to the structural differences between unitary and federal states also do not take us very far. Although we could show that Germany is more open to the ECJ because of its federal structure by comparison with regionalized Italy, which in turn is more open to the ECJ than France or the UK, this generalization does not hold once we look across countries. Federal Belgium, for example, has fewer references for preliminary rulings from the lower courts (333) or from the Courts of Last Instance (77) than Italy or France, although more than the UK.[107] Moreover, although we can suggest that in principle the ECJ's empowerment of national courts to the detriment of the executive is of greater consequence for unitary than federal states, this is more difficult to demonstrate in practice. First of all, the EU-related empowerment of national courts pales in comparison to the national dynamics of empowerment in countries like unitary France and regionalized but formally unitary Italy. And second, in France and Britain national judges have contained the impact of EU law on the unitary state by restricting their own rulings to the individual cases under consideration and avoiding generalizing them to similar classes of cases.[108] In other words, although the ability to refer cases to the ECJ may have empowered national courts more in unitary states vis-à-vis the executive, those courts have used that power to protect the executive's administrative autonomy.

We can also make no such structure-related generalizations about national constitutional courts' responses to their subordination to the European court. The national constitutional courts of each of our four countries have had different kinds of difficulty with regard to the doctrine of supremacy, and all have left

---

[105] See Tesoka (1999).   [106] Tesoka (1999).   [107] Conant (2002: 85).
[108] Conant (2002: 90), and Chalmers (2001).

open legal avenues to future refusal of EU authority.[109] France saw a clash between high courts with regard to accepting ECJ supremacy, with the highest ordinary judicial court accepting it early on, the highest administrative court rejecting it until quite late. The British high court (the Law Lords) resisted accepting the ECJ's authority until equally late because of its challenge to parliamentary sovereignty. Italy's constitutional court resisted early because of the direct challenge to its authority as the sole arbiter of compatibility between EU and national law if ordinary courts were to decide on EU matters, but then capitulated.[110] And Germany left the question open because of concerns about the democratic legitimacy of subordinating national authority to the EU.[111]

The four countries' responses to the EU's growing judicial authority, in short, must be understood in terms of their very different histories and concerns. In France, for example, the courts' increasing independence from executive control has been the result of internal dynamics related to the rise of the Constitutional Court and the growing investigative powers of the magistrates and not just of their empowerment as an enforcement arm of the EU. Such independence has been particularly unsettling to the executive, concerned about holdups to reform initiatives due to Constitutional Court decisions or ministerial resignations due to magistrates' corruption investigations. In Italy, where the courts have traditionally been even more subordinated to the executive than in France, a similar dynamic has taken place. In Britain, where the courts have always been relatively independent and the precedent-setting approach of British common law matches EU practice, the executive found it easier to accept the growing independence of the judiciary, although not the proliferation of EU laws. But the courts bristled at giving up their long-established prerogatives and have referred many fewer questions to the ECJ.[112] In Germany, where the courts are even more independent than they are in Britain and the importance of law as a regulatory instrument parallels EU practice, the problem has been neither with the even greater independence of the courts nor with the proliferation of EU laws. Rather, it has been with constitutional issues related to the precedence of EU law over German.

The EU's Impact on Institutional Structures in France, Britain, Germany, and Italy

The discussion of the differential effects of Europeanization on the member-states shows that the EU has had a comparatively more disruptive impact on the institutional balance and constitutive bases of unitary states than on those

---

[109] See Alter (1998).   [110] See Raderchi (1998).   [111] Stone (2001).
[112] See Chalmers (2001).

of federal or regionalized states. But what do these comparative systemwide effects of Europeanization entail for the internal workings of national institutions? And to what extent do they challenge national ideas and discourse about the structural bases of democracy? A closer look at the particular country cases shows a highly nuanced picture.

France

French responses to the structural impact of the EU have to be understood in terms of the country's long history as a unitary state. The move toward a unitary state began in the late seventeenth and early eighteenth century, as the absolute monarchy sought to complete political unity with administrative unity. But it was the French Revolution that consecrated the unitary state—centralizing political power while creating an efficient, centralized administrative system which was consolidated under Napoleon. With this came the Jacobin notion of the role of the 'Republican state' as the direct representative of the people, to do its bidding without obligation to any other authorities (which are to be subordinate to it, whether judiciary, legislature, or subnational units).

Beginning at this time, moreover, local liberty (meaning everything from the local election of the mayor on up) came to be seen as a threat to national unity. But federalism was seen as the greatest threat largely because support for it, after the defeat of the Girondins in the Constituent Assembly, was associated with the extreme right—first the royalists at the time of the Revolution, then the ultras during the Restoration who called for the recreation of the old provinces, followed by the legitimists beginning under Louis-Philippe's reign who saw the center as controlled by the left.[113] During the Third Republic, the opposition to federalism continued unabated, with the focus now on consolidating republican national unity against regional diversity, which also meant trying to suppress all regional languages. During the twentieth century, federalism in the form of regionalism, moreover, as in the case of Corsica's struggle for independence, represented a new threat to the unitary state. It is telling that decentralization has itself had a relatively short history, since it was not until the 1880s, one century after the French Revolution, that the local election of the mayor was allowed (although not in Paris), and not until the 1980s, two centuries after the French Revolution, that the prefect's *tutelle* (or a priori review powers) over the mayor was abolished and executive power transferred from the prefect to the presidents of the councils of the departments and the regions.[114]

It should come as no surprise, therefore, that over time French leaders have been wary of any increases in the power of EU institutions because of its

[113] Schmidt (1990: ch. 1).   [114] Schmidt (1990).

potential effects on the unitary state, and have had difficulty accepting any federalism for the EU. They have nonetheless been one of the major players—with Germany—in the construction of Europe. They recognized that only in building Europe could France enhance its own power and objectives, even if this entailed pooling a certain measure of national sovereignty and, thereby, executive autonomy. In their communicative discourse to the public, national leaders have consistently sought to obscure this by presenting France as maintaining autonomy and extending sovereignty through its leadership of Europe. Their constant refrain has been that France's leadership has enabled it to protect its national interests while projecting its values onto the rest of Europe and, indeed, the world.[115]

With regard to federalism specifically, moreover, although some leaders expressed support for a federal Europe embracing Germany (and containing it) during the Fourth Republic, since the inception of the Fifth Republic government leaders have been adamant in rejecting the notion of a 'federal' Europe, even though what they have meant by this has changed somewhat over time.[116] Charles de Gaulle resisted any notion of a federal Europe in favor of *une Europe des patries* (a Europe of nations). By this, he meant a political union which, as he wrote in a letter from Algiers in February 1944, would constitute a 'strategic and economic *fédération* which would not, as he insisted in a letter a month later, be a *bloc* of nations'.[117] Rather, as de Gaulle suggested in 1958, it was to be a union of nations with their own 'national personalities' which would gain 'the habit and desire to cooperate in all domains' and eventually become 'perhaps the united Europe about which the sages dream'.[118] This Europe, then, was to be much more than the vast free-trade zone that Britain had proposed and de Gaulle resisted in 1958.[119] But it was to be much less than what the Commission—whom de Gaulle saw as 'stateless functionaries without faces'[120]—seemed to be pushing for in 1965, which is what had precipitated the 'empty chair' crisis.

President Georges Pompidou was no more of a federalist than de Gaulle, but was willing to go farther with political union through a strengthening of both the Council and the Commission. In his view, the debate about federalism versus 'confederalism' was unhelpful, and best avoided in favor of the expression 'EU' which had 'the merit of being Delphic' because it 'indicated that all of this would in the end work together one day'.[121] President Giscard d'Estaing, who had long been even more of a federalist than Pompidou, let alone de

---

[115] See the discussion in Chapter 4.

[116] For the full discussion of French political debates, see the discussion in Chapter 4. Here, I focus on leaders' communicative discourse on the construction of European institutions.

[117] Jouve (1967: 111, 112). See also Howorth (1996: 10–11).

[118] De Gaulle (1970: 200–2) (author's translation).

[119] Howorth (1996: 11).

[120] *New York Times*, Feb. 20, 1997.

[121] Roussel (1994: 523)—cited in Howorth (1996: 14).

Gaulle, proved willing to the increase supranational powers of the EU even more, through the direct election of the Parliament and the creation of the European Council.[122] François Mitterrand went even farther, having been willing to suggest the beginnings of a more federal Europe in which Europe and France were increasingly conjoined as units since *tout se rejoint, notre patrie, notre Europe, l'Europe notre patrie* (everything comes together, our nation, our Europe, Europe our nation).[123] But Mitterrand thought that none of this would affect France's institutional structures, which he continued to see as unitary, despite also having initiated major decentralizing reforms because, as he consistently reiterated, he was the garantor of *l'unité nationale et la solidarité sociale*.[124]

Jacques Chirac went only slightly farther in his concept of the EU as a 'federation of nation-states', which he borrowed from former Commission President Jacques Delors. In his response to Fischer's call for a more federal Europe, moreover, Chirac insisted that any Constitution was to be a simplified statement of the existing treaties and not a new constituent treaty creating a political federation, while he did not even go so far as to suggest a second chamber for the EP, although he did argue for a 'pioneer group' to push ahead on integration. Most importantly, he made clear that France would not support any new vertical division of powers to the benefit of the regions since although a federal system was fine for Germany, it was not for France which 'has succeeded in maintaining a unitary tradition which helps to preserve the cohesion of its national community'.[125] Lionel Jospin's response was similarly intergovernmental, although he did not endorse Chirac's notion of a pioneer group. He was also careful to note that he was 'never partisan of a Europe of the regions' but rather of a 'union of nations' because 'Europe is not meant to replace the nations. It can, however, be their extension'.[126]

But even though all French leaders resisted the vision of a federal Europe, France has not, for all this, been spared the federalizing effects of the EU. The French executive has given up a significant amount of autonomy to the EU in a wide range of policy areas in exchange, however, for a shared EU control. For example, at the same time that giving over monetary policy authority to the ECB represents a loss in autonomy, it constitutes a gain in shared control over something that France had lost to globalization in the 1970s and to the German Bundesbank in the 1980s and 1990s.[127] Similarly, trade negotiations have been made the responsibility of the international trade commissioner who makes deals on agriculture that France then finds itself constrained (fortunately) to accept, as in the Uruguay Round. The loss of autonomy was

---

[122] See Parsons (2003). [123] Mitterrand (1986: 15, 104).
[124] Cited in Labbé (1990: 157–8).
[125] Speech to the Bundestag, June 27, 2000.
[126] Speech to the Socialist Party's Summer University, La Rochelle, September 3, 2000.
[127] See Schmidt (2002: ch. 1).

dramatized in the French presidential election campaign of 2002, when Chirac promised to reduce the value-added tax (VAT) on restaurants (at 19.5%) in order to bring it down closer to the level of fast-food establishments (at 5.5%), only to find that he could not do so because this came under the European VAT regime.[128] But it has also been clear in state aid cases such as French plans to bolster the textile industry or to aid urban areas in crisis, when the EU Commission harshly sanctioned French civil servants' blatant disregard of EU state aid rules in the mid-1990s under a somewhat Euroskeptic, right-wing government.[129]

Moreover, France's leadership role in Europe has been slipping. Although in the past, as part of the Franco-German partnership, France has been a 'motor' for Europe, bringing such grand initiatives as the EMS, the Single Market, and the Single Currency,[130] it is no longer. Beginning in the 1990s in particular, French leaders had to give up on their initiatives on EU-level industry policy and to give in on deregulation in the *services publics* (public utilities) arena with regard to telecommunications and electricity. In this latter area, the best they could wring out of the EU was language in the directives with regard to obligations for universal access. Most importantly, however, France has lost its claim to leadership in an enlarged EU, largely as a result of the geopolitical shift toward Germany.

This said, the French executive still manages quite well in projecting its particular policy preferences onto the EU. It is aided in this by the coordination of EU policy under the prime minister through the General Secretariat for Interministerial Cooperation on European Affairs (SGCI), a unit of 150 elite civil servants which serves as a secretariat to interministerial committees including ministers and civil servants.[131] But although France gets high marks on its centralized domestic EU-related policymaking process, despite interministerial rivalries, it gets lower ones with regard to linking the development of particular preferences with any grand strategy.[132] It also risks problems with grand strategy in times of cohabitation, when president and prime minister are from opposing parties and both therefore participate in the European Council and Treaty negotiations. This was particularly true for the highly conflictual cohabition of Mitterrand and Chirac (1986–8) and the sometimes conflictual one of Chirac and Jospin (1997–2002), although not for the highly consensual one of Mitterrand and Edouard Balladur (1993–5).[133] But everyday policymaking in the process of joint decision is another matter entirely. Ironically, the very attributes that have ensured French leaders a

---

[128] Change had still not yet occurred by June 2006.
[129] Le Galès (2001).
[130] Ross (1995), and Grant (1994).
[131] Menon (2000), and Kassim (2003a).
[132] Menon (2000).
[133] Elgie (2002), and Portelli (1999).

preeminent role in the initiation and negotiation of major EU treaties—the great autonomy and the grand style—have undermined its ability to predominate in Europe's more everyday policymaking, where close relations with societal interests are key—as we shall see in the next chapter. Projecting preferences and getting what you want, after all, are two very different things.

The French executive, in short, has given up a significant amount of national autonomy in the process of Europeanization in exchange for a supranational leadership in the process of European integration that has been on the wane over the past decade. The legislature, by contrast, never had much autonomy to give up.

The traditionally weak legislature, which never had much independent power as long as the government had a solid majority, has lost significant legislative powers to the EU and, thereby, become even weaker legislatively next to the executive at the same time that its powers of oversight have increased.[134] Significantly, the loss of legislative power became a matter of concern or debate comparatively late. In the mid-1970s, of all the parliaments of the nine member-states, the French alone was seemingly little bothered by the possible encroachment of the EC on its legislative powers and its lack of information.[135] Only in the late 1970s was a formal procedure established to ensure that the Parliament was informed of European Community activities, although this did not have much effect. But only in the early 1990s was the government obligated as a result of a constitutional amendment to inform Parliament of all European Community legislative proposals prior to a decision of the Council of Ministers, enabling deputies and senators not just to express opinions but to vote on nonbinding resolutions.[136] Delays on receiving information nevertheless continued—in some cases taking several months, or arriving after decisions had already been made in Brussels—until 1999, when a revision of the Constitution together with a circular from the prime minister ensured that parliament would receive all relevant texts within a month. But although these changes have increased the French parliament's powers of oversight appreciably while also enabling legislators to express their views through putting resolutions on the table,[137] the parliament continues to be something of a rubber stamp for directives issued from Brussels negotiated by the French executive in the Council of Ministers.

The regions, by contrast with the parliament, have gained in autonomy from the center as a result of their ties to Europe, primarily through the resources provided by the structural funds and the direct contact through lobbying in Brussels. But internal reform dynamics have played a much more significant role in the regions' increasing autonomy, namely the decentralization reforms in the early 1980s that devolved competencies and

---

[134] Rizzuto (1996), and Ladrech (1994).   [135] Frears (1975).
[136] Rizzuto (1996), Ladrech (1994), and Oberdorff (1994).   [137] Szukala (2003: 222–6).

resources with regard to economic development, infrastructure, and professional training to the regions[138] and the constitutional amendment in 2003 that constitutionalized these reforms. Europeanization has added to this autonomy, by providing the regions with new administrative responsibilities and greater financial autonomy as well as by diminishing their exclusive reliance on the French state for information and expertise.[139] Increased autonomy is most apparent with regard to the structural funds in terms of land-use planning and economic development, for which it gets approximately a third of its money from the French state, a third from the EU, and the rest from its own resources.

At the same time that the regions have gained in competencies and resources, however, the French executive continues to retain ultimate control. In regional economic development policy in particular, the state has simply created a less centralized and less *dirigiste* control compared to the past, creating state-centered networks ensuring the regionalization of the state rather than a growing regionalism.[140] Moreover, the French executive does not involve the regions in the formulation of EU policy, leaving this to the DATAR, the territorial planning commission, and other central ministries, while the regional prefect is ultimately responsible for the submission of applications for EU structural fund support, and the funds received are funneled through the appropriate ministries.[141] In other words, the 'regionalized state' remains more powerful than the regionally elected officials, and understandably so, since the prefect has much greater sources of power—in terms of expertise and resources, both financial and administrative.[142] What is more, the regions also find themselves subordinated to the EU and not just the French state. This is not only because they have to implement policies decided in Brussels, often with highly technical specifications, but also because they are subject to EU sanctions.[143] For all this, however, some regions have been able to interact with regional prefect, national ministry, and Brussels highly effectively, getting mostly what they wanted in terms of the structural funds— the case of Brittany—whereas others have been highly ineffective—the case of Languedoc-Rousillon.[144]

By contrast with the national parliament and much like the regions, the traditionally subordinated judiciary has been gaining in independence from the executive. This results only in part, however, from the judiciary's empowerment by the ECJ to uphold decisions even against the executive. Internal dynamics play an equally if not more important role in the growing autonomy of the judiciary, in particular since the 1980s. These dynamics

---

[138] See Schmidt (1990).   [139] Lavignote (1999: 290).
[140] Balme and Jouve (1996), Mazey, 1995a, and Biancarelli (1991).
[141] Mazey, 1995a, 147–50.
[142] Balme and Jouve (1996), and Dupoirier (2004).
[143] Mazey, 1995a, 137.   [144] Pasquier (2003).

include the magistrates' increasing activism in the pursuit of malfeasance in high political and business circles alike—a matter of distress for the executive—and the Constitutional Council's growing influence in settling disputes between executive and legislature, or majority and opposition.[145] The higher courts' influence has also been expanding as they have been learning to work together more. The Conseil d'État (Council of State), once hostile to seeing the Constitutional Court's case law as binding on it, now seeks to harmonize its own judgments with those of the Constitutional Court.[146] But the lack of agreement between the courts in the past has been a significant issue with regard to the doctrine of supremacy, accepted by the Cour de Cassation (the highest of the ordinary judicial courts) as of 1975 but not accepted by the Conseil d'Etat (the supreme administrative court) until the *Nicolo* decision of 1990.[147] And here, the French Council of State accepted EU legal supremacy only on the grounds that all treaties ratified by the French parliament were sovereign over French law—thus putting the emphasis on French parliamentary ratification rather than on EU supremacy per se.

The EU, in short, has altered the unitary architecture of the French state by undermining executive autonomy and reducing legislative power while increasing the independence of subnational authorities and the judiciary. This has, thereby, challenged traditional unitary ideals about the structural bases for democracy, to wit, that power and authority are legitimately concentrated both vertically and horizontally in the 'one and indivisible' Republican state, which is also the embodiment of national sovereignty. But the discourse of national leaders has tended to ignore these effects while emphasizing, instead, France's leadership in Europe.

Britain

British responses to the EU have to be understood in terms of the country's long history as a unitary state, much as in the case of France. But although Britain has as long such a history as France, if not longer, it has not centralized political power and administration in the same way. This is because Britain, rather than having had a centralizing monarchy followed by a centralizing revolution that concentrated power in a Republican state, has had a centralizing monarchy that ever since the Magna Carta has found its executive power tempered by the historically evolving legislative power of parliament. This has meant that sovereignty, rather than being focused solely on the executive as the embodiment of the state, as in France, was long vested in the duality of the 'Crown in Parliament,' constituting a sovereignty shared between the executive—which in the twentieth century came to mean the prime minister rather

---

[145] See Stone (1992).   [146] Stone Sweet (2000: 129).
[147] See discussion in Craig and de Búrca (1998: 264–8).

than the king or queen—and the legislature. Local liberty, moreover, was not abrogated as much in Britain in the pursuit of national unity. Local governments were allowed a certain amount of local self-government, as were certain regions (in the case of Scotland, including distinct educational and legal systems), despite the fact that these regions, including Scotland, Wales, and Ireland (until the early twentieth century) were an integral part of the UK's unitary state. Federalism, in consequence, was just as anathema to the British as the French, and a much greater danger to the unity of the British state, given the long years of struggle for independence in Ireland and, to a lesser extent, Scotland.

It stands to reason that British leaders would therefore be as wary as the French of any increases in the power of EU institutions as well as of federalism because of its potential effects on the unitary state's autonomy and control. But whereas in France the difficulties of adjusting to the loss of autonomy have been focused primarily on the executive, in Britain they have included parliament as well. Because the British notion of sovereignty, the Crown in Parliament, means the executive which equals the government which represents the political majority in the parliament, when governments invoke parliamentary sovereignty against the EU, the British executive is protesting incursions on its own autonomy at one and the same time as on parliamentary powers and prerogatives.[148] For the British, therefore, a federal Europe—as a 'superstate'—constitutes a danger even greater than for the French.

Complicating matters is the fact that, unlike France, which took a lead in Europe as one of the early members of the community, Britain has been a latecomer, having joined the EEC in 1973, and has been a 'reluctant partner' at that. And national leaders have always been much more divided on the very fact of EU membership than the French. Those opposed have focused on losses of national sovereignty and identity, seeing European integration not as an extension of national sovereignty, as do the French, but rather as a threat to it.[149] Those in favor have instead concentrated on the gains in economic interest, and have largely remained silent on the polity issues. Prime ministers, whether Conservative or Labour, have consistently legitimated further integration primarily in economic terms, whether Harold Macmillan who saw it as a 'commercial move' or Harold Wilson who presented it as 'defending the national interest'; whether Margaret Thatcher who sought to 'stand up for our interests' or Tony Blair who spoke primarily of how it furthered the country's economic interests, even if he sometimes also claimed to want to play a central political role.[150]

---

[148] Pilkington (1995: 98).   [149] Lynch (1999).
[150] See the discussion in Chapter 4.

Regarding the institutional structures, moreover, all were agreed that the EU could not be federalist.[151] Only Edward Heath might be counted as an exception. Macmillan argued specifically that the kind of Europe he wanted to lead Britain into was not at all the 'federalist solution' of those who 'would like Europe to turn itself into a sort of United States' but rather, 'a confederation, a commonwealth... what I think General de Gaulle has called *Europe des patries*—which would retain the great traditions and the pride of individual nations while working together in clearly defined spheres for their common interest.'[152] Macmillan even tried to sell de Gaulle on admitting Britain into the EEC on the strength of the French–British compatibility! In her memoirs, Thatcher picked up on the same idea, presenting the Conservative Party's ideal of Europe as a 'free enterprise *Europe des patries*',[153] and otherwise tirelessly warning of the dangers of an EU superstate, calling EU civil servants 'federasts'.[154] When Blair fully and directly addressed the institutional issues in his response to Fischer's initial proposal for a more federal Europe, he was even more equivocal than the French. Blair rejected the notion of federation, which he equated with a 'superstate', but insisted that the EU was already a 'superpower' through the economic and political strength that resulted from the pooling of sovereignty of 'free independent sovereign nations'. Blair, moreover, opposed a 'single, legally binding document called a Constitution', while he proposed that a second chamber be used only 'to implement the agreed statement of principles', as a political review instead of a judicial review by a European constitutional court—much like the role of the House of Lords.[155]

Whatever the specifics of their institutional vision of Europe, then, British leaders have opposed the development of any kind of European 'superstate', and voiced concerns about European economic policies reducing flexibility, increasing red tape, and thereby destroying British competitiveness. And yet, Britain has felt the Europeanizing effects of EU-related policies very little by comparison with France.[156]

The British opt-out from EMU has ensured that no European regulations or directives have had a direct impact on monetary policy in Britain[157]—even though the government has granted the central bank a certain independence in view of eventually joining the single currency, and the Commission has lately scolded Britain for its budget deficit. Moreover, in the industrial policy arena, Britain privatized and deregulated ahead of the other countries, with regulatory arrangements and rules that EU policymakers often adopted for the

---

[151] For the full discussion of the British political debates about the EU, see the discussion in Chapter 4.
[152] Smith, G. (1992: 5).   [153] Thatcher (1993: 536).
[154] *New York Times*, February 20, 1997.
[155] Speech to the Polish Stock Exchange, Warsaw, October 6, 2000.
[156] See Schmidt (2002).
[157] Artis (1998).

EU as a whole.[158] As a result, Britain has been only minimally affected by the EU deregulatory policies which the French so strongly resisted in areas such as telecommunications, electricity, and air transport.[159] This is not to say that Britain has gotten off scot-free with regard to policy reform. In environmental policy, for example, it has had to undergo major transformation.[160] But generally speaking, it is striking that the British have protested so many policies that in the end have done so little to change actual British policy practices. Institutional practices are another matter, however. One way of interpreting the British decibel level on EU-related policy change, however minor, is to understand its incursion on executive autonomy.

What is more, for all their complaints, the British have also done remarkably well in the EU with regard to projecting their preferences in a wide range of policy areas as well as in complying with EU policies. On grand initiatives, they have promoted greater integration in security and defense together with France, starting with the St. Maló initiative, and they have pushed evermore enlargement to the east, despite periodic resistance from other member-states, whether France in the early 1990s with regard to the Central and East European countries or Germany most recently in the case of opening accession talks with Turkey. But the British have also done very well in more everyday policymaking.[161] This is largely due to the centralized organization and proactive role of the UK Permanent Representation, which seeks to push its agenda across all sectors and stages of the policy cycle even as it cultivates relations throughout the EU, including the Commission and the Parliament at the same time that it has close coordination with London.[162] Centralized coordination also has its disadvantages, however, since positions crafted in Whitehall can act as a straitjacket for negotiations in Brussels, undermining bargaining ability.[163] This aside, Britain's success also owes much to its more productive, closer relations of the government with business interests lobbying in Brussels, by comparison with France—elaborated in the next chapter.

Britain also has a much better record of compliance with EU policies than France, Britain, or Germany (as we have already seen). This is explainable in large part by Whitehall cultural norms that emphasize effective transposition of EU legislation and timely implementation, as well as the more general British legal culture that assumes that laws once passed should be applied, regardless of the source (especially since the EU source is not always clear).[164]

---

[158] The fact that the EU rules tend to be statutory rather than voluntary, however, has been a problem for the British, as discussed in Chapter 3.

[159] Thatcher (1999), Eising and Jabko (2001), and Kassim (1998). See the discussion in Schmidt (2002).

[160] Jordan (2002). And see the discussion in Chapter 3.

[161] Wallace (1996), and Kassim (2003b).

[162] Kassim (2000), and Kassim (2003a: 157).

[163] Kassim (2000).

[164] Bulmer and Burch (1998: 621).

But for all its successes, Britain has accomplished much less than it might have in terms of leadership in Europe. Where the French executive has sought a greater EU 'heroism' to cover for its loss of autonomy at the national level, the British executive has resisted 'heroically' any European incursions on national autonomy. The British not only have a bargaining style that makes greater resort to brinkmanship but also an agenda that is more focused on protecting their own prerogatives than in advancing any particular EU-wide set of reforms other than the deregulatory ones that fit their own institutional model. As a result, they often not only push the envelope much farther than other, less ambivalent member-states but also feel no compunctions, in the face of defeat after a long and arduous bargaining process, to pick up their marbles and leave—the Social Chapter of the Maastricht Treaty is a case in point. While Britain's self-styled role as reluctant partner has undermined its ability to have significant influence over grand strategy, such a role has made it very effective not only in gaining opt-outs but also in pushing a more neoliberal agenda in industry deregulation.

The executive, then, for all its complaints, has not appreciably lost in powers. The same cannot be said for the British parliament.

In unitary Britain, where Parliament has always had greater powers of over-sight and has always exercised more voice than in France, the erosion of powers has been a consistently greater cause for concern. The unitary nature of the British state which concentrates power in the executive, together with a majoritarian electoral system that produces single party government in control of the House of Commons (the Westminster model), ensures that so long as the government has a solid majority there is little that members of parliament can do.[165] The reform of the House of Lords under the Labour government has, if anything, increased this power.[166] But unlike France, where parliamentary committees had little information and paid little attention to European matters until relatively recently, the British parliament for most of UK membership in the EU has sought to scrutinize EU documents and to influence deliberations in the Council of Ministers.[167] Although this has not in fact had much direct effect on executive action, by exercising its voice on European integration, the British parliament has had more influence over public opinion and, therefore, indirectly over the executive than in France.

The regions, by comparison with the parliament, have only gained in powers. But this is also because they had nothing to lose. Recentralizing reforms under Thatcher ensured that Britain did not even have any elected bodies to represent themselves in the Committee of the Regions. Until the late 1990s, in fact, only Britain remained without significant regional authorities. Very recent devolutionary reforms begun under the Labour government in the late 1990s have changed this, as national assemblies have been set up in Scotland, Wales, and Northern Ireland while London has become

[165] See discussion in Chapter 4.   [166] See Flinders (2005).
[167] Norton (19996a).

self-governing. Only the English regions have no elected representation, as the referendum on the issue failed. These reforms have made for a state that is much less unitary in its vertical relationships with lower levels of government. However, notwithstanding arguments from some that the UK has become a quasi-federal system in consequence of such reforms, it remains highly unitary. The bulk of the British population (85%) is in centrally governed England. Only Northern Ireland, Scotland, and Wales have elected bodies with legislative independence—and this only in a limited number of areas, mainly in education, local economic development, and social policy—while budgetary autonomy comes with no control over revenue (which comes from a government block grant). This still goes farther than France, however, where the regions all have elected bodies with jurisdiction and budgetary autonomy over a similar range of policy areas but no legislative independence, with the exception of Corsica and New Caledonia.

Although these devolutionary reforms are primarily the result of internal dynamics, European integration has nevertheless served as an additional impetus for reinstating local autonomy and instituting regional authorities. Already under the Conservatives, the principle of subsidiarity had become increasingly difficult to reconcile not only with Britain's own policies toward local governments but also with its use of the subsidiarity principle to defend against the further shift of powers to EU institutions.[168] The Conservative government's creation of regional administrations, moreover, was largely in response to the EU's push for regional development plans.[169] But the central government has also tended to dominate structural fund partnerships between its functional and territorial administrations and local authorities.[170]

Britain has arguably been most affected by the EU's increasing judicial presence. This is evident in the sheer volume of EU law, which has been seen, in the words of Lord Denning, no longer like 'an incoming tide flowing up the estuaries of England. It is now like a tidal wave bringing down our sea walls and flowing inland over our fields and houses'.[171] For a country that has traditionally sought to limit the amount of law in order to leave as much freedom to the private sphere as possible, the EU's growing judicial authority has been resisted not only for its encroachments on executive autonomy and for its disruption of judicial hierarchies but also for its increasing judicialization of the private sphere.[172] This helps explain why UK courts have tended to be more ready to enforce EC law when it served to reinforce private legal relationships—as in cases of sex discrimination, which reinforce legal contracts—and more resistant when it destabilized them—as in environmental

---

[168] See: Scott, Peterson, and Millar (1994).   [169] Wilks (1996: 164).
[170] Bache, George, and Rhodes (1996).   [171] Alter (1998: 135).
[172] Chalmers (2001).

law cases, which interfere with private contracts.[173] It also more generally helps explain the lower number of preliminary references to the ECJ. But it does not explain the growing recourse to judicial decisions in Britain at large.

The increasing litigiousness of Britain began with the Thatcher government, and had a lot to do with its more adversarial style and its ideologically driven policies.[174] Societal interests and public agencies used their access to the ECJ under the doctrine of direct effect to overcome national executive resistance to implementing EU laws, in particular in environmental and social policy. Their success has been evident in landmark decisions on the quality of drinking water and equality between working women and men.[175] What is more, ever since the UK passed the Human Rights Act which incorporates the European Convention on Human Rights, national courts and/or the European Court of Human Rights (ECHR) have ruled against ministers on such questions as the rights to asylum, to liberty (in the case of prisoners), to a fair trail (in the case of the continued detention of prisoners when they have fully served their term) and to respect for private life (in the case of homosexual group sex).[176]

But as a country with a strong history of parliamentary sovereignty and without a tradition of judicial review—since the House of Lords has always been the final arbiter—the doctrine of supremacy was the most difficult for Britain to accept. Whereas Britain accepted the doctrine of direct effect on accession to the EU, it was not until 1990 that the House of Lords accepted EU supremacy on the grounds that this did not compromise parliamentary sovereignty since a British parliament had agreed to it in the 1972 act of accession and a future British parliament could always repeal that act.[177]

Thus, although the EU has affected Britain's unitary architecture by reducing executive autonomy and legislative power while increasing subnational and judiciary independence, this has affected the executive less than in France. This is because the executive has opted out of numerous policy areas, parliament retains more voice, the judiciary has always been more independent, and the subnational authorities less. And yet, the British have nevertheless felt more strongly the challenges to traditional unitary ideals of democracy, that is, to the authority of the executive as the embodiment of parliamentary sovereignty. And they have complained much more loudly.

Germany

Unlike France or Britain, with long histories as unitary states, Germany has a relatively recent history as a federal state, preceded by a much longer history of

---

[173] Chalmers (2001), and Conant (2000: 87).
[174] Johnson (1998: 151–2).
[175] Mazey (1988), Mazey and Richardson (1993: 15–16), and Caporaso and Jupille (2001).
[176] Woodhouse (2001).
[177] See Craig and de Búrca (1998).

smaller state principalities, duchies, city-states, and other forms of small state-like entities. Federalism came with the establishment of the German nation-state in the late-nineteenth century, as a way to gain the acquiescence of the long independent subnational state authorities.[178] Although Bismarck had the power to impose a unitary state, he decided instead to create a federal system with a relatively weak central state based in public law in order to ensure the cooperation of the strong Länder and to gain from their administrative competence.[179] With the reestablishment of a federal system in the postwar period following the centralized state of the Nazi period, the powers of the regions were reaffirmed along with a stronger federal system, with checks and balances to ensure against any return to the excesses of the recent past.

It stands to reason that a federal state such as Germany would have had fewer lasting problems with regard to the impact of the EU on its institutional structures than unitary states such as France and Britain, and that it would therefore favor the development of the EU into a federal system. The EU's quasi-federal structure sits well on top of a centuries-old history of regional power and a postwar federal constitution established to guard against any return to the centralized excesses of the power of the Nazi period. Germany's better fit in institutional structures is complemented by broad-based congruence resulting from reciprocal influence and adjustment in a wide range of policy areas.[180] Moreover, national sovereignty has never been the issue in the postwar period for Germany that it has been for France and Britain. Because the state has never been more than at best 'semisovereign', given the structure of its institutions,[181] Germany lacks the French conception of national sovereignty as an embodiment of state power or the British equation of national sovereignty with the country's self-sufficiency. Moreover, Europe could never represent a threat to national sovereignty, as in Britain, since the executive has never had the autonomy of the British executive. Nor could it represent an extension of national sovereignty, as in France, since postwar German ambitions could certainly never countenance such a thing.

Instead, European integration was consistently presented by Chancellor after Chancellor, from Konrad Adenauer through Helmut Kohl to Gerhard Schröder and on to Angela Merkel, in terms of its identity-enhancing qualities, with a German-as-European identity the main construct through which to explain Germany's relationship to Europe.[182] Tied with the identity-enhancing aspects of Europe has been the promotion of 'ever closer union', of a federalism that Kohl in his early years had been promoting in terms of a 'United States of Europe'.[183] Chancellor Schröder himself sought to promote increasing integration via a federalist model, although he never went quite as

---

[178] Lehmbruch (1997).   [179] See Ziblatt (2003).
[180] See Bulmer (1997), and Katzenstein (1997*b*).
[181] See Katzenstein (1989).   [182] See the discussion in Chapter 4.
[183] Anderson (2005).

far as to argue for a United States of Europe. Fischer's vision for the future of Europe, moreover, which launched the constitutional debates, was particularly federal following the German model. The European Federation was to have a second chamber with the powers of the Bundesrat (although Fischer left open the possibility that its composition could instead parallel that of the US Senate) while the 'European Constituent Treaty', much like the German Basic Law, would set out the 'core sovereignties and matters which absolutely have to be regulated at the European level', while leaving everything else to the 'responsibility of the member-states'.[184]

For Germany, sovereignty has not even been a constitutional issue, since the German Basic Law (Article 24) explicitly allows the transfer of sovereign rights to international organizations.[185] If sovereignty is seen to be situated anywhere, it is probably in the Basic Law itself, as reflected in the reverence in which it is held and the vigilance with which it is protected, which extends to the institutional balance of powers which it consecrates. In consequence, if there is any concern about sovereignty, it mainly involves the organization of domestic authority in German federal institutions. This helps explain why the protection of the powers of the country's various domestic institutional structures has been a major issue for Germany in all negotiations at the EU level, much more so than for either France or Britain.

Sovereignty as an issue has actually otherwise only come up with regard to economic issues. The abandoning of the Deustchmark, the only other postwar symbol of sovereignty, although contested at the very end of the process,[186] was not so much at issue during the run-up to EMU because the EU had generalized German macroeconomic patterns and prejudices in the process of monetary integration. In most other economic policy areas, moreover, Germany has not been nearly as concerned about the impact of EU-related change as the French either because its policies already fit better with EU requirements or because German national actors changed their preferences mid stream in favor of greater deregulation, as was the case in telecommunications (also true for the French), electricity, and air transport policies.[187] This said, sovereignty as an issue has come up in EU decisions on state aid, much as in France. The EU's decision against Saxony's aid to Volkswagen, for example, nearly precipitated a crisis of national sovereignty. Even more importantly, the decision against the *Landesbanken*, the regional, publicly owned banks, on grounds that their state-guaranteed, low-cost loans to small and medium enterprises constituted unfair competition for private banks, has been seen as threatening the very foundations of the social market economy. These cases speak to the increasing challenges to German economic practices resulting

[184] Speech in Berlin, May 12, 2000.
[185] See: Saalfeld (1999: 12–13).
[186] Thiel and Schröder (1998: 115).
[187] See Thatcher (1999), Eising and Jabko (2001), and Kassim (1998).

from EU-related policies of economic liberalization. But institutional practices, our major focus here, are another matter.

The executive, in the first place, has not experienced as much loss of executive autonomy as France or Britain because of its semisovereign status not only externally, given constitutionally based acceptance of supranationalism, but also internally. The core executive has little hierarchical authority and can do little to impose policies in the manner of unitary executives but must instead negotiate within the executive and across other governmental authorities in a complex process of joint decision-making (*PolitikVeflectung*) that depends for success on a culture of consensus and cooperation, backed by constitutional law.[188] The EU has therefore only further diminished an autonomy that was already limited by the executive's integration into a multilateral, intergovernmental bargaining system and polycentric regional networks.[189]

This lack of internal hierarchical authority not only makes it hard for the German executive to impose internally but also makes it difficult for the German executive to establish its preferences with regard to EU policies, let alone project them onto the EU. The wide range of governmental actors involved in policymaking, where interministerial as well as intergovernmental rivalries are rife, with no central coordinating agency let alone a central, hierarchical commanding authority, has ensured against any common or comprehensive German strategy in Brussels.[190] The fact that since 1992 Länder representatives also sit and speak for Germany in the Council of Ministers has made coherence in German European policy even more difficult to achieve at the same time that it has generally slowed executive response time and diminished its initiative and bargaining independence. Moreover, periodic attempts to exercise clearer leadership by centralizing European policy initiatives and grand strategy in the Chancellor's office, as during Schroeder's second mandate, have not done much to alter this state of affairs.

It should come as no surprise, therefore, that the German executive has not exercised much leadership when it comes to grand strategy in the EU, where France excels, or managed to forcefully resist policy initiatives of which it disapproves, where Britain is past master. But what Germany loses in policy initiative due to the decentralization and fragmentation of its policymaking in the EU, it more than makes up for in influence on policy outcomes due to its size and importance in the EU. The successes of the Franco-German partnership until relatively recently are testimony to this. But it is also important to note that what Germany lacks in prior centralized domestic policy coordination it may make up for after the fact in its more reactive style, something well-suited to the EU's incremental kind of decision-making.[191] Moreover, its

[188] See Scharpf (1988), Maurer (2003), and the discussion in Chapter 3.
[189] Lehmbruch (1996).
[190] See: Wessels and Rometsch (1996), Bulmer et al. (2001), and Maurer (2003).
[191] Derlien (2000).

greater general consensus on the EU also enhances its influence, especially by contrast with the UK when it has lacked a firm consensus on EU policies, as during the Major Government.[192] What is more, whatever Germany's difficulties in exercising leadership with regard to grand strategy, it excels in everyday policymaking because of the very presence of ministry officials as well as of societal interests.[193]

In short, the EU has had a relatively minor lasting impact on the German executive's institutional practices. This is equally true for other institutional actors in the German system, whether the parliament, the regions, or the courts.

The German parliament—like all other national parliaments in the EU—has lost in powers, but it has nevertheless retained more control over the executive than in either France or even Britain. Much like these other two countries, the parliament has lost legislative initiation, deliberation, and approval powers to Brussels and is also at a disadvantage with regard to information on EU developments and on its own government's actions in the Council of Ministers.[194] But the constitutive nature of the German federal executive alone ensures greater consultation with parliament in negotiations before the executive signs anything. What is more, such consultation also generally encompasses the opposition. This is a result both of the mostly cooperative, consensus-building approach to legislating, in which the opposition seeks to influence legislation through technical rather than political considerations, and of the split in power between the Bundestag and the Bundesrat, which is often controlled by the opposition.[195] This contrasts greatly with Britain, for example, where the opposition is generally kept in the dark as to developments in negotiations (and often have to hear from their German opposition colleagues as to what has been going on behind closed doors during negotiations).[196]

For the German parliament, moreover, some of the most serious problems with the loss of power and control were reduced with the reforms following the Massatricht Treaty. Prior to this, the Bundestag had very limited powers of scrutiny. Moreover, subsequent to the Single Market Act of 1986, the Bundesrat in particular had experienced a significant loss in power, as the policy areas in which it previously had held legislative power were often decided in the Council of Ministers with only the federal government representing German interests, leaving the Länder with no say in the formulation of policy that they would then have to implement.[197] The new Article 23 of the Basic Law, passed in December 1992, remedied some of these problems by increasing the

---

[192] Derlien (2000), and Kassim (2000).
[193] See the discussion in Chapter 3.
[194] See: Saalfeld (1996), Wessels and Rometsch (1996), and Maurer (2003).
[195] Maurer (2003).   [196] Maor (1998).
[197] Bulmer, (1986: 219–22), Saalfeld (1996: 15–17), and Maurer 127–31.

parliament's informational access and allowing the Bundestag an opportunity to express a view prior to decision by the Council of Ministers. Most importantly, it redressed the shift in power by ensuring that the Federal government could not transfer powers to the EU without a two-thirds majority in both the Bundesrat and the Bundestag, and that in areas of federal states' jurisdiction, the vote of the Bundesrat was binding on the Federal government.[198] As a result, the Bundesrat went from a situation of 'benevolent weakness' to a role of 'supportive scrutinizer'.[199] The empowerment of the Bundesrat, moreover, also guaranteed the Länder continued power and influence.

The Länder have always had much more significant power and autonomy than subnational authorities in unitary states because of their recognition as states in the Basic Law. The Länder have constitution, government, and parliament; sole jurisdiction in matters of education, culture, and local government; direct representation in the upper chamber of parliament (the Bundesrat); responsibility to implement federal law; and can conclude treaties with foreign governments in areas of their exclusive jurisdiction, education and culture. Their functional division of responsibilities, by contrast with the jurisdictional division of responsibilities in other federal systems, initially made the Länder more vulnerable to the EU-related loss of formulation powers, given the national government's original sole right to negotiate in Brussels. And it also subordinated the Länder to EU and federal executive oversight with regard to policies they had to implement but had no role in formulating—in the environmental arena, for example, where disputes over having to enforce the (lower) standards has been a major reason for Germany's comparatively bad compliance scores in this area; or in competition policy and state aid to industry. In these latter areas, in fact, EU intrusion has sometimes undermined not only the autonomy of Germany's Länder—the decision on subsidies to Volkswagen a case in point—but also their cooperative set of relations, as when the German executive found it necessary to adjust internal aids to correct imbalances caused by EU structural funds.[200]

The Länder's role in implementation also gave them a trump card, however, since they were able to blackmail the national government into allowing them greater influence over EU formulation in exchange for their cooperation in implementation.[201] The Länder alone, in fact, have largely been responsible for generalizing regional access and influence in the EU through their demands for incorporating the principle of subsidiarity in the Maastricht Treaty of 1991; for opening up the Council of Ministers in matters of exclusive subnational responsibility to ministers from the 'third level' (subnational); and for establishing the Committee of the Regions.[202] Another indication of

---

[198] Jeffery (1994), Saalfeld (1996: 26–29), Goetz (1995), and Maurer (2003).
[199] Hölscheidt (2001).   [200] Anderson (1996, 2005).
[201] Thaysen (1994).   [202] See Jeffery (1994).

the power of the German Länder is in their intervention in the IGC that preceded the Amsterdam Treaty, where they (or, rather, Bavaria) derailed the attempt to reach a common agreement on immigration policy.

Finally, with one of the strongest and most independent judicial systems among EU member-states, German courts have not been greatly affected by the ECJ's potential empowerment vis-à-vis the executive, since they already had significant powers. The courts' subordination to the ECJ for all but the highest court, interestingly enough, has also been relatively easy, since habits of subordination of lower to higher courts within the federal court system make this quite natural. The evidence is in the number of preliminary references alone, as noted above. But although the German courts generally have increasingly accepted EU jurisdiction, the German Constitutional Court has been somewhat recalcitrant. The issue has not been over questions of sovereignty, however, but rather over democracy, federalism, and participation, with the Court having questioned the appropriateness of the German government giving up its powers to a not-sufficiently democratic set of institutions at the supranational level in the Maastricht Treaty.[203] Although the Court allowed the German government to proceed, the issue itself remains unresolved to this day.

Thus, the EU has not significantly altered the traditional architecture of the German state. It therefore tends to complement federal ideals about democracy, in which the checks and balances resulting from the vertical and horizontal division of powers are to ensure against the encroachments of centralized power. German leaders' communicative discourse, therefore, has readily cast European integration as an add-on to German federalism while using it to enhance national identity. The main challenge for Germany with regard to Europeanization comes not from the EU's impact on the structural bases of national democracy, as it does for France and Britain, but rather from the EU-related changes in policies that challenge the bases of national economic organization, most notably the social market economy.

Italy

Italy, like Germany and unlike France or Britain, has had a relatively short history as a state, beginning also in the late nineteenth century; and it has had an even longer history of smaller state principalities, city-states, and other forms of small state-like regions. But unlike Germany, rather than instituting federalism with a weak central state, Italy established a formally unitary state, concerned that it would not be able to hold the country together without it. While Bismarck chose to create a federal system in order to benefit from the Länder's cooperation and administrative competence, Cavour had to create a

---

[203] See Weiler (1995).

unitary system with a stronger central state because the weak regions had little administrative capacity or cooperative spirit.[204]

With authority centralized in a unitary state, Italy might have come to resemble France had the state itself developed strong central power and administrative capacity. But it had neither the benefit of France's very long history of a centralizing monarchy followed by an equally centralizing Republican state nor its shorter postwar history of an elite, highly capable civil service.[205] In Italy's regionalized state, much like in Germany's federal state, the executive has not had much autonomy or control in policymaking. But unlike in Germany, where the executive's lack of autonomy and control has a constitutional basis in a federal system, in Italy, where the state is still formally unitary, the limits on executive power stem from its long-standing lack of administrative capacity, from the parliament's independence combined with its inefficiency, the regions' legislated gains in powers, and the judiciary's self-empowerment.

Italy's postwar institutions have long suffered from state paralysis, the result of a weak executive combined with a stronger but ineffective parliament riven by multiple party divisions in which *partitocrazia*—the politicization along party lines of all aspects of political and administrative life—ruled.[206] This was made worse by a generally incompetent if not also corrupt civil service, the result of the system of *sottogoverno* in which the spoils in the form of state contracts and jobs were apportioned according to the electoral weight of the parties.[207] The civil service was consequently shot through by patronage, with loyalty rewarded over and above competence. It was so bad that in a commission report in the early 1950s, the Republican party leader Ugo La Malfa, called it an 'uncharted jungle' while in the early 1960s even one of its major beneficiaries, Christian Democratic national secretary at the time Amintore Fanfani, described it as 'a clandestine organization'.[208] Only in the early 1990s did the institutions get better, with the inception of what is often called the 'Second Republic', which marks the renewal of the Italian party system after its collapse at the time of the fall of the Berlin wall in the midst of corruption scandals.[209] But administrative incompetence and corruption remain. Transparency International ranked Italy number 40 with a score of 5 (out of 10) in a 2005 corruption perceptions survey in which the UK was ranked 11 with a score of 8.6, Germany 16 with a score of 8.2, France 18 with a score of 7.5 (and the United States 17 with a score of 7.6).[210]

Given the difficulties of governing such a fragmented state, it should not be surprising that from the early postwar years on Italian leaders enthusiastically

---

[204] See Ziblatt (2003).   [205] Dente (1995).
[206] For more on this, see the discussion in Chapter 4.
[207] DiPalma (1977), Pasquino (1989), and Dente and Regonini (1989).
[208] Allum (1973: 140).   [209] See the discussion in Chapter 4.
[210] Transparency International (2005).

embraced the notion of a more federal Europe, and presented the EU as a *deus ex machina* saving Italy from itself. The EU sat well on top of a centuries-old history of regional power frustrated in the postwar period by a centralizing state suffering from paralysis, incompetence and corruption which improved only beginning in the 1990s. Italy for obvious reasons could not exercise leadership with regard to Europe in the manner of the French or Germans; instead, the Italians were the cheerleaders of further integration. The very idea of a postwar EU came from Italy with the Ventotene Manifesto of July 1941, written by Altiero Spinelli and later adopted by the Italian Resistance, which in turn led to the Geneva conference in July 1944 calling for a federal Europe with a constitution, a supranational government directly responsible to the people of Europe, an army, and a judicial tribunal.[211] A federal Europe remained Italian leaders' ultimate goal ever thereafter, so much so that they were never too concerned about the actual structure of Europe along the way. This contrasts greatly with the postwar preferences of the French for an intergovernmental union, of the British for an intergovernmental free trade area, and even of the Germans for a supranational federation. As de Gaulle commented after revealing his plan for European union in August 1958 to Italian Prime Minister Amintore Fanfani, the Italian leader's response was highly contradictory. Although he was favorable to de Gaulle's intergovernmental vision, Fanfani shared his predecessor Alcide de Gasperi's 'supranational tendency' and yet 'did not want anything done without England', despite knowing that the British were unwilling to join. At the same time that Fanfani 'was convinced that the peoples of the old world needed to be brought together, he did not envisage that this could bring about a change in their ties . . . with the United States, in particular the Atlantic Alliance', which contradicted the 'French desire to go toward a 'European Europe'.[212] Fanfani, in short, wanted everything, overlooking the incompatibilities, unwilling to choose among alternatives, but largely accepting whatever was on offer. This approach has continued to this day.

Thus, Prime Minister Silvio Berlusconi's unwillingness to commit himself to any particular design for the Constitutional Treaty was true to form. In a speech to the Chamber of Deputies on January 14, 2002, he insisted that although he joined the others in accepting that the EU 'has been authoritatively described as a federation of nation-states . . . We cannot put the cart before the horse and draw up a design for the new Europe in the abstract.' He then went on to quote Italian President Carlo Azeglio Ciampi, who similarly equivocated when he declared in Berlin in November 2001 that 'it would be counterproductive to present the vital interplay of the supranational and intergovernmental aspects in the process of European unification in terms of

[211] Unwin (1995: 8–9).
[212] De Gaulle (1970: 202–04) (author's translation).

antithesis. The two may proceed in parallel and we should not forget the insight of the Founding Fathers and the lesson they have taught us: whenever they perceived that intergovernmental cooperation was unable to ensure lasting progress, supranationality provided a way out of the difficulty'.[213] It is useful to note that the Italian government generated no overall strategy document in advance of the Convention, nor did it present one to the Convention, as did Germany and the UK, even though it did present a slew of amendments during the Convention (most of which were not accepted).[214]

For most Italian leaders, in fact, the transfer of power to the EU level has never posed the same problems with regard to national sovereignty that it has for either France or Britain. Unlike the French, who embraced Europe as an extension of national sovereignty because they saw themselves as leading European integration, or the British, who resisted European integration as an incursion on national sovereignty whenever they saw Europe as leading, the Italians were happy to follow Europe's lead, seeing national sovereignty as enhanced by being pooled in the context of European integration. Moreover, by helping the executive to govern more effectively *for* the people, it also reinforced the authority of the executive as the embodiment of national sovereignty. But although, like Germany, Italy could not therefore conceive of a threat to national sovereignty from Europe, this was not because it had a semisovereign state but, rather, because it had a 'paralyzed' state.

These differences in the nature of the state made for differences between Germany and Italy with regard to how state actors dealt with Europe. While Germany, with its semisovereign state, had greater difficulty projecting its preferences on the EU than France or Britain, it nevertheless tried to do so and largely succeeded, ensuring that much EU legislation fit its own policy preferences, in particular in the economic domain. Italy, by contrast, did not really try, and could not in any case succeed. This is because of even more highly fragmented domestic institutions in which European policy, instead of coming out of a centralized planning unit to be articulated by a strong permanent representative, as in France or Britain, emerged haphazardly from countless ministries with overlapping competencies and was only sometimes articulated by a typically weak permanent representative.[215] As a result, Italy has had little or no influence over the formulation of policies that come out of Europe. But it has nevertheless blindly accepted them—which accounts in part for its implementation difficulties, its losing out in redistributive policies such as the CAP (to France and Germany, which gained much better subsidies for wheat and cattle than did Italy for fruits and vegetables),[216] and its occasional

---

[213] Prime Minister Silvio Berlusconi, speech to the Chamber of Deputies, January 14, 2002.
[214] Hine (2004: 309).   [215] Della Cananea (2001), and Hine (2001).
[216] Sbragia (1992: 81).

strong objections, as in the case of milk quotas. Italian state actors have tended to embrace every EU-related reform as an external remedy for internal failure.

Italy may be the only country among our four cases in which the generalization about the EU's 'strengthening of the state' really does work, as it does for other Southern European countries. For Italy, the loss of government autonomy with regard to the EU has largely been experienced as a gain in government capacity, by helping it to overcome state paralysis and parliamentary divisiveness, especially since the inception of the 'Second Republic' in the early 1990s. Whereas Britain anticipated the economic policy reforms related to European integration or opted out of them while France and Germany engineered the reforms—whether the EMS, the Single Market, EMU, or (more reluctantly) deregulation in telecommunications and electricity—Italy submitted to them.[217] And it did so using the EU in its communicative discourse to the public to justify the reform as necessary—since the EU required it—and to legitimate it as appropriate—because it was part of the Italian identity as good Europeans and a question of Italian pride as founding members of the EU.[218] In so doing, the country was able to engage in the kinds of reforms of which it had heretofore been utterly incapable—successfully changing its practices despite failing to ameliorate its administrative fragmentation.[219] This is not to say, however, that Italy has been a poster child with regard to Europeanization. Much the contrary, since it has had difficulty implementing EU policies in a wide range of areas not only as a result of a continued lack of state administrative capacity but also of regional politicization and, in some cases, societal actors' resistance to EU policies, as we shall see in the next chapter.

Italy's inability to transpose and implement EU policies has much to do with the executive's inability to dominate the domestic policy process. Although there have been a number of reforms of EU-related policy formulation, transposition, and implementation processes—in particular with the 1987 Fabbri law, the 1989 La Pergola law, and the 1997 Bassanini laws—these were not very effective. With regard to policy formulation, the reforms which were intended to improve the coordination of EU policy and the sharing of information produced an even more fragmented and highly pluralistic, sector-oriented set of working arrangements at EU and domestic levels that only further complicated information-sharing and policy coordination. In policy transposition, the reforms were more effective, since they centralized responsibility under the prime minister for the newly created, annual *legge comunitaria* or community laws which grouped together all EU-related policies in a single

---

[217] See Schmidt (2002), Chapter 2.

[218] See the discussion in Chapter 3 on the discourse of economic policy reform, Chapter 4 on the issues of national identity and pride.

[219] See Giuliani (2001). For an extensive list of the benefits of EU-related reform, see Padoa-Schioppa (2001).

draft law legally mandated to go to the Italian parliament at the beginning of each year.[220] But although this was to make for more stream-lined transposition, initially at least it made for even greater delays due to political divisions and administrative snafus. The most extreme example was the 1995 Annual Community Law which, added to the 1996 bill, was then attached to the 1997 bill, to finally be approved in April 1998.[221] Things have gotten better since then, however, as the percentage of transposed EU directives went from 81.7 percent in 1990 to 96.3 percent in 2001.[222] Even today, however, transposition problems continue. Illustrative is Italy's 2005 score on the transposition of Internal Market directives, which was the very worst of the EU25, with a 4.1 percent transposition deficit leaving it with a backlog of 66 directives, by contrast with Germany's deficit of 1.4 percent for a 22 directive backlog, the UK's 1.4 percent deficit for a twenty-three directive backlog, and France's 2.4 percent for a 38 directive backlog.[223] But transposition rates in any case tell us nothing about the quality of the transposition or about implementation. These are also bad, as is quite evident from Italy's poor compliance record in implementation of EU directives, as noted earlier.

Although the Italian parliament also bears some responsibility for the slowness of transposition, the executive is largely to blame. This is because the executive has been virtually unchallenged in EU affairs, leaving the Parliament little role in EU-related policymaking. Until the late 1990s, the Italian parliament had a very low level of Europeanization in terms of participation either in the government's formulation or transposition processes, other than in approving legislation once it came to the parliament.[224] Because European affairs were initially seen as part of foreign policy, Parliament did not even have separate standing committees on EU legislation until the reforms of the late 1980s, when they were also first empowered to express their opinions on EU Commission proposals in resolutions addressed to the government. However, since the government routinely failed to inform the Parliament of such proposals, its participation in EU policy formulation remained minimal. Only a very small number of deputies were knowledgeable or active with regard to European issues,[225] and even they rarely sought to amend EU-related legislation, given their high technicality and low politicized content.[226] The Italian parliament, in short, like the French, had mainly been a rubber-stamp for an EU-related legislative process dominated by the executive. Only beginning in

---

[220] Franchini (1994), and Gallo and Hanny (2003).

[221] Giuliani and Piattoni (2001: 118).

[222] Fabbrini and Donà (2002: 41).

[223] Internal Market, Scoreboard 14, July 2005—http://europa.eu.int/comm/internal_market/score/docs/score14/scoreboard14printed_en.pdf

[224] Fabbrini and Donà (2002), and Giuliani (1996).

[225] Furlong (1996: 41), and Bindi Calussi and Grassi (2001: 281).

[226] Fabbrini and Donà (2002: 43–5).

the late 1990s did parliament gain in terms of more power and more timely information, enabling it to go from 'benevolent observer' to a more active player in Italy's EU policymaking.[227]

The Italian regions' involvement with EU policymaking has been arguably more significant than that of the parliament. They have benefited over the years from increasing EU-related responsibilities as well as internal devolutionary reforms, gaining significant powers with regard to the direct enforcement of EU directives as well as greater input into Italy's EU policymaking.[228] However, much like the Italian parliament, they suffered from a lack of information on EU developments as well as a lack of influence over government decision-making. Moreover, unlike Germany and more like France or the UK, the Italian regions still do not participate in the working groups of the Commission or the COREPER in their areas of competence, nor are they part of the national working groups sitting in the Council.[229] The regions' main problem with regard to the EU is their dismal implementation record, in particular with regard to the notoriously slow and fraud-ridden disbursement of the structural funds. Although conventional wisdom has it that the South of Italy is generally worse than the North due to either Byzantine administration, political fragmentation, and a lack of organized expertise[230] or a lack of social capital,[231] the reality is more nuanced. Some regions in the South actually do better than their more prosperous counterparts in the North as a result of better regional political leadership.[232]

Italy's difficulties in regional policy stem not just from a lack of administrative capacity. They also follow from the ambiguities of Italy's regionalized system with regard to administrative responsibility, which are often exacerbated by the highly politicized nature of center–periphery relations. Although the EU largely strengthened Italy's central state with regard to responsibility for ensuring implementation, the state still had to coordinate with the regions and the EU Commission on the details. And this has proven difficult. For example, in the case of the 2000–6 Structural Funds period in Objective 2 eligible regions, the state—in the form of the Treasury—after successfully negotiating technical standards with the EU Commission, was unable to negotiate their acceptance by the regions which, instead, bargained among themselves on the basis of partisan redistributive principles. The crisis was resolved when the government capitulated to these principles and the Commission subsequently accepted them.[233] There are signs of a growing capacity

---

[227] Bindi Calussi and Grassi (2001).
[228] Gallo and Hanny (2003: 283–85).
[229] Bindi and Cisci (2005).
[230] Desideri (1995), and Leonardi (1993).
[231] Putnam et al. (1985), and Putnam (1993).
[232] See Piattoni and Smyrl (2003), and Giuliani and Piattoni (2001).
[233] Gualini (2003).

for coordinated action between state and regional actors, however. With regard to negotiation of the 2000–7 EU structural funds, Italian central and regional actors for the first time managed not only to formulate a national position but also to promote national preferences consistently during all relevant negotiation phases.[234] Increasing Europeanization, in short, has engendered a continuing struggle between executive and subnational authorities which may only today be beginning to sort itself out, by contrast with Germany, where there was one major battle, won by subnational authorities.

Finally, the courts, which have traditionally been subordinated to the executive, have also been asserting their independence, a result not only of Europeanization but also, even more importantly, of internal dynamics of self-empowerment. Beginning in the 1970s, 'progressive judges' began to creatively interpret codes of law so as to 'adapt' them to constitutional principles, in particular with regard to individual rights issues such as equality before the law, rights to work, freedom of expression, even without referring questions to the constitutional court.[235] Moreover, the growing judicial activism of the magistrates, who went after the Mafia in the early 1980s and then, in the early 1990s, after the political and business elite through a variety of corruption investigations, in the end contributed to bringing down the entire postwar party system. To this day, they continue to bedevil the political and business establishment with investigations and trials, despite the Berlusconi government's repeated attempts to draft laws directed at curbing their powers.

The lower courts have also been highly activist with regard to the EU, having been reasonably quick to take advantage of the opportunities offered by the ECJ with regard to preliminary references. The Italian Constitutional Court has been more reticent, however. It accepted the doctrine of direct effect only in 1973, a year later than the British, and took even longer to accept the doctrine of supremacy. Despite the ECJ's 1964 decision in *Costa versus ENEL*—which was brought by an Italian citizen—that announced the principle of supremacy, the Constitutional Court continued to maintain the separation of the Italian and the EU legal systems, and waited four years to make a preliminary reference. Moreover, it was only in 1984, concerned about its isolation from other EU courts, that the Constitutional Court ruled that where EU and Italian law applied, judges should apply EU law.

The EU, in short, has tended to bolster the Italian executive's autonomy and parliament's efficiency at the same time that it has also reinforced the independence of the courts and the regions—although not without struggles between executive and regions. All of this has served Italian democracy well. Italian leaders' communicative discourse to the public has, like Germany's, embraced European integration, but in this case as much for

---

[234] Brunazzo and Piattoni (2004).
[235] Bognetti (1982)—cited in Stone Sweet (2000: 128).

Table 2.3. Relative losses and gains in power and authority of national branches and levels of government before and after the impact of Europeanization (and internal reform)

	Member-state structures	Executive autonomy		Legislative power		Subnational autonomy		Judicial independence	
		Before	After	Before	After	Before	After	Before	After
Simple polities	Unitary France	+ + +	+	− −	− − −	− − −	−	− − −	+
	Unitary Britain	+ + +	+ +	− −	− −	− − −	− −	+	+
Compound polities	Federal Germany	− −	−	+ +	+ +	+ +	+ +	+ +	+ +
	Regionalized Italy	− − −	−	+ +	+	+	+ +	− −	+

its capacity-building qualities, seeing the EU as the rescue of the nation-state and the reinforcement of national sovereignty, as for its identity-enhancing aspects.[236] The main problem for Italy with regard to the EU, unlike France or Britain, has little to do with its structural impact. Rather, its problems come from a continued lack of state capacity with regard to EU policymaking, in particular to comply with EU rules.

Conclusion

Thus, EU institutions, with their dynamic confusion of powers, have had a significant impact on member-states' national institutions. But they have had a differential impact, changing the traditional balance of power most in unitary states, then in regionalized states, and least in federal states as they have reduced executive autonomy and control, diminished legislative power, and increased judicial and subnational independence (see Table 2.3). But as we have seen, the differences in impact also depend on countries' ideas and discourse about the impact of Europeanization on the structural bases of national democracy, with Britain more concerned than France, but both much more concerned than Germany or Italy.

---

[236] See the discussion in Chapter 4.

3

The European Union and National Policymaking

When the EU Commission in the 'White Paper on Governance' in 2000 called for more transparency and openness in EU policymaking, with greater participation in EU governance by 'civil society', it was seeking to address the self-same democratic deficit in EU-level policymaking processes that the future Constitutional Convention was to attempt to address through institutional redesign. This initiative was not only unprecedented in its ambition to create a more deliberative democracy in the policy sphere but also very necessary, given public perceptions of a closed club at the EU level making policy behind closed doors, to the detriment of national policies and policymaking prerogatives. The opaqueness of the policymaking process, made worse by the complexity of the EU's institutions, led the public at large to hold the EU in growing suspicion. But greater openness in public information and access, together with efforts to galvanize societal actors to participate in decision-making at the EU level, address only part of the problem with regard to the democratic deficit in EU policymaking. This is because EU level processes have already, by their very presence, altered the procedural bases for national democracy. Europeanization of policymaking has affected not only the traditional ways in which state actors formulate and implement policy but also the traditional routes by which societal actors gain access and exercise influence in policymaking.

The EU has a 'semipluralist' pattern of policymaking in which interests have reasonably open access and influence in policy formulation but not in implementation, where regulatory and legalistic enforcement is the rule. As such, the EU provides for the kind of democratic legitimacy through interest consultation *with* the people generally found in pluralist systems, where greater minority access in policy formulation is to make up for the limitations of majority rule. In policy implementation, moreover, it provides for the kind of democratic legitimacy through effective governing *for* the people generally found in regulatory systems, where uniform enforcement safeguards against abuses of power. In laying this pattern on top of those of its member-states, the EU has effectively 'pluralized' its member-states' policy formulation processes by opening up interest access and influence, while its has 'juridified' their implementation processes with its turn to regulatory enforcement. Complicating this general set of effects, however, has been the EU's differential impact on its member-states' 'macro' patterns of policymaking, which sit along a continuum from statist to corporatist policymaking. Europeanization of national policymaking has been more disruptive to member-states with statist processes than to those with corporatist processes, mainly as a question of institutional 'fit'.

Further complicating matters, however, is the fact that the EU may also have an impact on the 'micro' patterns of policymaking in any given policy sector, with direct, diffuse, or 'knock-on' effects. As a result, the EU's sectoral effects vary greatly, with little or no predictability from one policy sector to another, leaving one to ask whether we can still talk about macro patterns in the EU and its member-states. This chapter shows that macro national patterns of policymaking still matter. Although they are less distinctive than they were in the past, they can still be distinguished along a continuum from statist to corporatist processes, even if pluralist processes are increasingly the default, catch-all category between the two.

The chapter begins with a brief overview of the EU's policymaking processes in comparison with national processes. It then outlines, first, the EU's impact on the macro patterns of its member-states' national policymaking and, second, its impact on the micro patterns of member-states' sectoral policymaking. The chapter follows with an extensive illustration of both macro and micro patterns of policymaking through considerations of our four country cases: France, Britain, Germany, and Italy. Here, too, we find further differentiations: Although Europeanization has been equally (although differently) disruptive to the statist patterns of policymaking of France and of Britain, Britain has again had a harder time accepting EU-related changes but an easier time in influencing their formulation. Europeanization has yet again been least disruptive to Germany's corporatist and legalistic patterns of policymaking and most salutary to those of Italy, by reinforcing corporatism while denying clientelism. But while Germany has had an easier time than Britain or France in accepting EU-related changes and as easy a time as Britain in influencing their formulation, Italy has been even more accepting but least influential. Finally, in leaders' legitimating discourse about Europeanization, whereas the French apply EU-mandated processes while denying their source and the British apply EU-mandated processes while decrying their source, the Germans use the EU to legitimate EU-related processes as they apply them, and the Italians use the EU in legitimation, even when they do not apply them.

The EU's Semi-pluralist Policymaking Processes

No traditional, national pattern of state–society relations quite describes the complexities of the EU, given the openness of a policymaking process managed by Commission officials in an anticipatory and cooperative manner in which interest representation is 'sectorally structured and linked with a complex and often rather incoherent issue network of groups or organizations across Europe and beyond.'[1] The EU is, above all, characterized by practices that are generally more flexible, heterogeneous, and issue-specific than in any corresponding national context,[2] while the unpredictability of the policy agenda in the EU—the result of a 'system of uncertain agendas, shifting networks, and complex coalitions'[3]—makes it akin to a 'garbage can model' of policymaking.[4]

What is more, the EU has several distinct policymaking styles rather than a single, overall one. The EU's dominant policy formulation process, the 'Community Method' of joint decision-making is most akin to the pluralist policy formulation of the United States, although it is less open, less political, and more cooperative. Its regulatory implementation process, although also similar to that of the United States, is more delegated and, in consequence, less uniform in application. Of the EU's other policymaking modes, 'intergovernmental' decision-making by member-state executives in the Council of Ministers, Intergovernmental Conferences, European Summits, and treaties make for much less capacity for unilateral action than in any nation-state; 'supranational' decision-making by delegated EU authorities such as the ECB, the ECJ, and the Competition Authority makes for more such capacity; and the 'OMC' of 'soft policymaking', found in no nation-state, creates capacity by coordinating member-state action in areas where the EU has minimal policymaking power, as in employment and social policy.

Taken together, these make for a policymaking system which is closest to a model of 'transnational pluralism'[5] and most comparable to the pluralism of the United States in its open access to interests and its regulatory and legalistic patterns of implementation. But although EU policy formulation may be more pluralist than anything else, its pluralism exhibits significant differences from that of the United States.

Overall, the EU's societal actors enjoy a pluralism that is more close and cooperative than that of the United States—as EU state actors engage with interests in the development of policy rather than keeping them at arms' length, to arbitrate among them. Despite such closeness, however, EU state actors are at the same time more insulated from the pressures of undue influence or the dangers of agency capture of the kind found in the United States.[6] This is largely as a result of the 'paradox of weakness' that follows from the plethora of public actors at the EU level,[7] and the fact that the Commission is at the center of a vast 'issues network' within which it can choose among a much wider range of ideas and proposals than is often available to national governments.[8] But it is also

[1] Mazey and Richardson (1996: 53).   [2] Schmitter (1996).
[3] Mazey and Richardson (1996: 42).   [4] Cohen, March, and Olsen (1972).
[5] Streeck and Schmitter (1991).   [6] Mazey and Richardson (1993).
[7] Grande (1996).   [8] Majone (1996: 74–5).

because the EU avoids both the politics of money and to a large extent the politics of party found in the United States. This results from the fact that apolitical EU civil servants rather than partisan legislators and their staffs are the primary drafters of legislation, and base their decisions primarily on technical and economic grounds,[9] while the EU parliament, where parties are not highly consolidated, plays a lesser role as codecision-maker and consultative body.[10]

At the same time that the EU may therefore be less politicized in its pluralism than the United States, however, it has also been less pluralistic in the kinds of interests represented as well as in their access and potential influence. While in the United States, any interest that knocks on the door is necessarily let in, in the EU, the Commission (and to a lesser extent the EP) act as 'gatekeepers', deciding which societal actors to let in and which to keep out. Whereas in the early years this gave a decided advantage to business interests, in recent years, in efforts to increase openness and transparency in response to the perceived problems of the 'democratic deficit', the EU Commission has been more and more open to any societal interests that knock on the door as well as more active in recruiting a representative set of interests in order to enhance democratic legitimacy through consultation *with* the people. In fact, the EU has represented a tremendous 'opportunity structure' for interest groups to gain access, providing new 'venues' through which to exert influence, offering new ideas that can serve to disrupt preexisting policy systems and power relationships, creating new possibilities for collective action,[11] and building a vast coordinative discourse among policy actors across policy areas.

The coordinative discourse itself takes place not just in the 'arenas' in which particular policy initiatives are debated and developed but also in the 'forums' set up by the Commission to generate ideas.[12] These encompass forums for business interests, such as sectoral 'consensus forums' on transport networks, autos, and information technology or 'high politics' forums on telecommunication policy and on energy and transport.[13] They also involve NGOs, in the 'social dialogue' forum on social policy[14] or in ad hoc meetings on trade and globalization.[15] The Charter of Fundamental Human Rights and the Constitutional Convention also provided opportunities for civil society groups to make their views known through hearings and informal channels of influence.[16]

The policy formulation process has in fact become increasingly vast and complex over the years as a result of such consultation. Commission proposals typically will have been discussed in a working group comprising national officials, submitted to an advisory board containing national experts,

---

[9] Hull (1993) and Egan and Wolf (1999: 254).   [10] See the discussion in Chapter 5.
[11] McAdam (1996), Richardson (2000), and Pollack (1997*b*).
[12] On the differences, see Jobert (1992) and Fouilleux (2001).
[13] Coen (1997: 96).   [14] Smismans (2003: 475–7).
[15] See http://www.europa.eu.int/comm/trade/csc/dcs_proc.htm
[16] Smismans (2003: 480).

considered by the COREPER, and maybe even reviewed by a committee composed of national representatives established by the Council of Ministers, before going to the EP after the Council decision. The result is that only 10–20 percent of Commission proposals are fully its own.[17]

But however open and pluralistic the process, the problem for democracy in this context is that some interests—mainly business—are always knocking at the door and coming in whereas others have had difficulty organizing themselves even to find the door, let alone to knock or to know how to act effectively once they enter.[18] Business interests make up approximately two-thirds of all interests represented in Brussels[19]—which is why David Coen has characterized the EU's interest mediation process as 'elite pluralism'.[20] Nonbusiness interests focused on consumers, women, the environment, and human rights issues, are a small minority in comparison, at about 20 percent of interests represented in Brussels.[21]

In the EU system of interest representation, as a result, the overall number and variety of interests represented is more restricted than in the United States and more heavily weighted in favor of producer interests, with comparatively few organized interests representing consumers, the elderly, immigrants, and the public interest, and many fewer protests able to galvanize public opinion. Balancing this out somewhat, however, is the fact that the system is less subject to the abuses of undue influence, and that the system itself has been generating counterweights to what might be seen as narrow business interest. It has done this either by creating more avenues for participation or by introducing considerations of the 'general interest', women's rights, consumer protection, environmental protection, and so forth, as by-products of EU Commission policy initiatives, ECJ decisions, and the generalization of prior member-state legislation. Moreover, interest group access and influence itself depends mainly on a range of factors, including how technical the area and the information required, how politically salient the issue, and what balance between 'insiders'—whose access depends on their ability to provide 'correct' information that enables the Commission to generate effective policy proposals and thereby to gain 'output' legitimacy (or governance *for* the people)—and the 'outsiders' whose access may be essential to ensure the appearance of 'input' legitimacy (or goverance *by* the people).[22]

But whereas the EU's pluralist policy formulation process may avoid some of the worst problems of the United States, even admitting the EU's own problems with regard to access and representation, in the EU's policy implementation process it courts many more problems than the United States. Although the EU's pluralism greatly resembles that of the United States at the

---

[17] Bomberg, Cram, and Martin (2003: 49).   [18] See the discussion in Chapter 1.
[19] Greenwood (2003).   [20] Coen (1997).
[21] Greenwood and Aspinwall (1998: 5).
[22] Broscheid and Coen 2004.

implementation stage, given a regulatory approach in which the rules are to apply equally to all, with any exceptions seen as illegitimate, there are significant differences. Instead of a hierarchical model of rule-making and implementation by a single bureaucracy, the EU's model tends to be coordinative. Rule-making allows wide consultation through committees making it akin to a second round of legislative review, transposition by the member-states ensures that the final law is a collaborative effort between EU and national officials, while national officials are responsible for enforcement.[23] The rule-making process itself, however, is less transparent than in the United States, given the expert-dominated 'comitology' system. But it can nevertheless be seen as legitimate insofar as it builds a kind of 'deliberative democracy', in which expert bodies deliberate on questions for which they have a clear legislative mandate in the shadow of EU law,[24] finding answers to questions that are not readily solved through voting or bargaining procedures or through passage of specific legislation (since they are in fact an answer to the lack of knowledge that makes any detailed legislation impossible).[25]

The difficulties at the transposition stage, moreover, when a directive is converted into national law by the member-states, involve not just ensuring that all member-states actually transpose the rules in keeping with the spirit of EU legislation, but also that they apply the rules uniformly—or even apply them at all. Enforcement is the black hole of the EU, since it depends not only on the Commission to take action in cases of transposition or compliance failure but also on national citizens and courts being aware of the EU rules and willing to bring cases of noncompliance to the attention of the authorities. As we have already seen in Chapter 2, compliance records are highly varied, depending not only on national citizen's awareness and willingness to bring cases to the courts but also on national institutional design, capacity, and will to implement.[26] Moreover, as we shall see below, implementation, whether in terms of transposition or enforcement, can be highly varied according to policy sector, regardless of general national patterns of policymaking.

In short, compared to the United States, the EU policy formulation process is less open in terms of interest access, given EU civil servants' gatekeeping role; more technical than political in content, given the apolitical status of EU civil servants; and more cooperative than competitive in style, given the EU's consensual culture. Concomitantly, EU regulatory implementation is less transparent in the rule-making process, given the comitology system; more delegated, given the role of member-states in transposing and enforcing the rules; and less uniform in application, given national differences in patterns of enforcement.

---

[23] Page (2001: 143–7).   [24] Joerges (1999: 317).
[25] Eriksen and Fossum (2002).   [26] See Chapter 2.

Figure 3.1. Member-states along a continuum from statist to corporatist processes

The EU' Impact on Policymaking in Statist and Corporatist Systems

The EU's policymaking pattern, then, although closest to the pluralism of the United States, departs substantially from the US pattern—thus the moniker semipluralist. For all this, however, the EU's policymaking pattern also bears some resemblance to the statist and corporatist patterns of its member-states. Most importantly, the predominance of the Commission as gatekeeper, with its greater powers of policy initiation and its greater control over the interest articulation process, introduces a statist element into the system akin to that found in France and the UK. The EU's more cooperative engagement with interests in policy formulation, by contrast, brings it closer to the corporatist patterns of interaction typical of Germany, as does the fact that the EU explicitly promotes corporatist arrangements in a number of areas.[27] These similarities are minor, however, compared to the differences between the EU's policymaking pattern and those of its member-states.

EU member-states' policymaking processes can be situated along a continuum from statist to corporatist patterns (see Figure 3.1). For member-states closer to the statist end of the continuum, simple polities like France, Britain, and Greece, state actors have traditionally provided interests with little access or influence in policy formulation but have generally accommodated them in implementation, either by making exceptions to the rules as often as not (in France) or limiting the number of rules to allow self-governing arrangements (in Britain). By contrast, for member-states closer to the corporatist end of the continuum, more compound polities like Germany, Belgium, the Netherlands, Italy, and Sweden, state actors have traditionally brought certain societal interests, mainly business and labor, into both policy formulation and implementation, although such policymaking, when not corporatist, may be legalistic (in Germany) or clientelist (in Italy).

The question here, therefore, is: How have the EU's semipluralist policymaking processes affected member-states' policymaking in the process of Europeanization? For all member-states, EU policy formulation has reduced state actors' autonomy while providing societal interests with access and influence in a policymaking process which involves a much vaster array of actors in a much more complex set of interactions with many more points of entry than that of any member-state. Societal interests have also been

---

[27] See Falkner (1998).

empowered at the national level by EU policies that mandate greater interest consultation or by EU institutions that provide new routes for redress of their complaints. EU policy implementation, moreover, has pressed state actors into taking on more regulatory and legalistic modes of enforcement—where the rules are applied without exception by independent regulators and judges—from approaches that often relied instead on administrative discretion, self-regulation, or joint regulation.

Beyond these general effects, however, are the differential effects experienced by member-states as a result of the way their particular patterns of policymaking respond to those of the EU. One of the key factors highlighted in the Europeanization literature has been the question of institutional 'fit', whether discussed as 'misfit',[28] 'mismatch',[29] or 'goodness of fit'.[30] This factor is helpful in a preliminary way to identify areas where the EU's policymaking processes may represent a challenge to its member-states' national patterns of policymaking. The argument is a relatively simple one: the closer the fit, the less disruption to traditional patterns of policymaking. A graphic illustration of the patterns of interaction between state and societal actors in the three different kinds of policymaking systems shows quite clearly that the clash between EU semipluralist and national statist patterns of policymaking is greater, since the pattern of state–societal interaction is the reverse of that of the EU, than between EU semipluralist and national corporatist patterns of policymaking, where the pattern is closer (see Figure 3.2). The impact of these differences in fit extends from policymaking processes through procedural ideas about democracy to discursive patterns of interaction.

In statist systems, the EU has generally reduced state actors' autonomy by including societal actors in policy formulation processes from which they had typically been excluded and excluding them from policy implementation processes in which they had long been included. In corporatist systems, the EU only further diffuses state actors' autonomy by adding societal actors to those already included in policy formulation while it only sometimes excludes societal actors traditionally included in policy implementation (see Table 3.1). Such changes in practice clash more with statist systems' procedural ideas of democracy—that delegitimate interest consulation in policy formulation but legitimate interest accommodation in policy implementation—than with corporatist systems' ideals—that legitimate interest involvement in policy formulation and implementation. Fit (or misfit) in practices and ideals, finally, also plays itself out in discursive patterns of interaction. The EU, by adding more voices to the coordinative discourse of policy construction, is most likely to lead to a fuller coordinative discourse in corporatist systems, as societal actors who tend to be part of both EU and national level discursive

---

[28] Börzel (1999), Börzel and Risse (2000) and Duina (1999).
[29] Héritier, Knill, and Mingers (1996).   [30] Cowles, Caporaso, and Risse (2001).

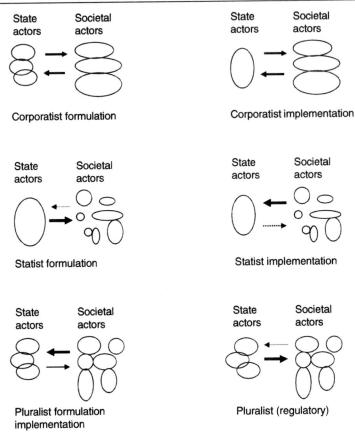

Figure 3.2. Different patterns of policy formulation and implementation in corporatist, statist, and pluralist systems

communities can better speak to their own constituencies about EU policies, thus alleviating the communicative burden of state actors. By contrast, in statist systems, although societal actors may make their views heard in the EU coordinative discourse, because they have little voice in national policy formulation, state actors are generally left alone to communicate and legitimate EU policies to the public.

Adaptation to EU policymaking processes has been particularly difficult for simple polities with statist policymaking processes, and arguably harder for France than Britain. In the policy formulation process, to begin with, state actors have lost significant autonomy in policy formulation as societal actors have increasingly become part of EU-level policymaking and, where mandated by the EU, in national policymaking. But French societal actors, used to lobbying *à la francaise* by relying on political arbitration late in the process

Table 3.1. Traditional national patterns of policymaking and the impact of the EU

Policy process	Policy formulation	Policy implementation	EU impact on policy formulation	EU impact on policy implementation
Statist	Low access	Flexible application	Opens up interest access at EU level	Reduces nat'l flexibility via legalism/regulation
France	State acts in wide sphere, society reacts	Derogation	More EU level societal input, little change at nat'l level	Eliminates derogation, less accommodation, more confrontation
UK	State acts in limited sphere, society acts on own	Self-regulation	More EU level societal input, little change at nat'l level	Eliminates self-regulation, more public 'steering'
Corporatist	Moderate access	Flexible or rigid application of rules	Adds to interest access at EU level	Flexibility where corporatism or adds to rigidity
Germany	State and society act together (corporatism)	Corporatism or legalism (Ger)	Adds to corporatist input at EU level, little change at nat'l	Maintains corporatist flexibility, reinforces legal / regulatory rigidity
Italy	State barely acts in wide sphere, society reacts, acts on own, or acts together with state (corporatism or clientelism)	Corporatism, clientelism, derogation	Adds to corporatist input EU level, denies clientelism	Maintains corporatist flexibility, eliminates derogation, more confrontation
Semi-pluralist	High access	Rigid application of rules		
EU	Open access to societal groups (with gatekeeping)	Regulatory and legalistic (except when corporatism)		

rather than getting in early with solid technical information, have had a very steep learning curve with regard to the EU lobbying process.[31] British societal actors had much less to learn, having honed their lobbying skills in their relations with parliament and their one-on-one negotiation skills with the bureaucracy; but they also gained in influence.[32] But in Britain as much as in France, nonetheless, EU policy formulation clashes with traditional ideas about procedural democracy, where governance *with* the people through lobbies is regarded as illegitimate because it undermines government *by* and *of* the people through representative politics. State actors have traditionally been expected to use their formal consultation process with a goal more toward informing than incorporating interest views;[33] and they have tended to legitimate their policies

---

[31] Schmidt (1996, 1999*b*).   [32] Greenwood (2003).
[33] Page (1995), Hayward (1995) and Schmidt (1996).

via an elaborate communicative discourse to the general public rather than through a sustained coordinative discourse with societal actors.

In policy implementation in both France and Britain, moreover, state actors have lost flexibility and societal actors their traditional accommodation as a result of the EU's regulatory and legalistic patterns of enforcement. In France, where EU requirements go against traditional state patterns of administrative discretion, those organized interests without access to EU policy formulation, finding themselves denied the accommodation of the past, engage in confrontation with national authorities.[34] In Britain, where the EU's codification of the rules goes against traditional state preferences for self-regulatory arrangements and voluntary rules, the problem has been in the increasing numbers of independent regulatory agencies and statutory rules, leaving state and societal actors to complain of the increasing rigidity of the public sphere (although this also has national sources).[35] For both countries, therefore, EU policy implementation clashes with statist ideals of flexibility in enforcement. In France, the EU makes governance *with* the people through derogation of the rules illegal. In Britain, it supplants governance *by* and *of* the people through voluntary rules and self-governing arrangements with governance *for* the people through statutory rules or regulatory agencies. All of this together help explain why in their communicative discourse French leaders tend to downplay the impact of the EU on national policy implementation where they can as they highlight their own leadership in EU-level policymaking, while British leaders play up the EU's impact on national implementation as they resist EU-level policy initiatives.

Adaptation to EU policymaking processes has been easier for more compound polities with corporatist processes, although more so for Germany than Italy. State actors in both Germany and Italy never had the autonomy of their counterparts in statist systems to lose in policy formulation, since they have long engaged in joint decision with societal actors. Societal actors in Germany have readily adapted to the EU's pluralist policy formulation process, having been schooled in the same kind of cooperative negotiating style and committee work prevalent in the EU[36]—even though some corporatist processes may have been unbalanced as business has gained greater access than labor in arenas other than labor and social policy,[37] and some businesses have gained greater access than others.[38] By comparison, Italy's organized interests have had more to unlearn rather than learn in policy formulation, given clientelistic patterns of influence peddling at the national level that are not acceptable at the EU level. The EU's semipluralism, thus, tends to complement corporatist ideals in which governance *with* the people in policy formulation is assumed to reinforce government *by* and *of* the people through representative politics. In both Germany and Italy, the legitimacy of corporatist governance

---

[34] Schmidt (1996).   [35] Schmidt (1999b, 2001).
[36] Coen (1998) and Eising (2004).   [37] Falkner (1998).   [38] Cowles (2001).

with the people through consultation with certain privileged interests is only enhanced by the EU's even greater openness to interest input while (Italian) clientelism is delegitimized. This ensures that policymaking is not limited to being only *with* some of the people and that the coordinative discourse of policy construction is expanded to a much larger number of societal interests.

In implementation, moreover, state actors have mostly been allowed their traditional flexibility where corporatist processes are already operative, since the EU generally allows corporatist implementation to stand. This serves to reinforce corporatist ideals of governance *with* the people here as much as in policy formulation, along with coordinative discourses of policy construction. But in noncorporatist areas, whereas German state actors' legalistic patterns of enforcement were little affected since they largely conform to those of the EU, Italy's often clientelistic patterns have had to change at the same time that the risks of confrontation are even greater than in France, given traditionally even greater derogation of the rules. As a result, whereas Germany still benefits from a reasonable 'goodness of fit' since it has traditionally accepted governance *for* the people through regulatory or legalistic arrangements, the adaptational problems for Italy are much greater, since its expected, if not ideal, governance *with* the people has, as in France, also become illegal. This may be why in their communicative discourse German leaders play up the EU's impact where useful to overcome any societal resistance to implementation, while Italian leaders play with the EU's impact to reinforce their own leadership, regardless of whether they implement.

An analysis in terms of macropatterns can only take us so far, however. Some policy sectors have never conformed to the general macro-policymaking pattern at either the EU or national level, while others have developed over time in ways that differentiate them more and more from the traditional pattern. In fact, the macropatterns often described in the literature—such as the 'macrocorporatism' of Austria—no longer describes the reality, although sectoral corporatism remains in a number of core areas.[39] My discussion of macronational patterns is thus not intended to deny the increasing differences in sectoral policymaking within countries but rather to point to general overall patterns of state leadership and societal involvement that are themselves evolving along with the increasing sectoral differentiation. But this is why I complement the comparative macroanalysis of overall national patterns of policymaking with a microanalysis of sectoral policymaking before turning to the country cases themselves.

The EU's Impact on Sectoral Policymaking

In the policymaking process, although the EU is semipluralist in a macrosense of policymaking, in a micro sense of sectoral policymaking it may take and/or

[39] Falkner (2001: 99–100).

mandate any number of forms, whether pluralist, statist, or corporatist. Thus, even if business lobbying in most sectors of EU policymaking, from standard setting to environmental policy, is ordinarily characterized by pluralist patterns, in some areas the EU can instead take on statist characteristics, as in competition policy and state aid while in other areas it can appear corporatist, as in employment and social policy. Similar differentiations are also found at the national level, where particular policy sectors may not follow the overall national patterns.

Complicating matters, however, is the fact that while national actors may experience one set of processes while interacting at the EU level, the EU may itself mandate or suggest another set of processes for national level policymaking. Moreover, even when the EU does little other than make a decision about national policy, say, to open a market to a particular product based on the principle of mutual recognition, or to a set of providers as part of competition policy, this can have an effect on national policymaking. What is more, the effects of the EU on national policymaking themselves vary, as national policymaking processes may be more or less adapted to EU processes and national policy actors more or less receptive. The causal connections between such potential effects have been the subject of extensive theoretical discussions among policy analysts about the kinds of adjustment pressures, adjustment mechanisms, policy outcomes, and national mediating factors that Europeanization may entail. These theoretical discussions are addressed in Chapter 5. For our purposes here, a simpler account focused on the EU's interaction effects and member-states' responses suffices to illustrate the differential impact of the EU on national patterns of sectoral policymaking.

Direct Effects

The EU has a direct effect on national policymaking processes when it mandates a particular approach to policymaking in a given sector. Where such an approach does not fit that of the member-state, the direct effect is potentially significant, leading to transformation in the sector. Although inertia is always possible, where state and/or societal actors resist compliance, this is generally limited in time, since the EU has the ability to coerce the member-state to comply through compliance procedures and the courts. Where the EU-mandated approach largely fits that of a member-state, the direct effect is likely to be minimal, as the member-state can absorb the changes without major disruption. Delays are always possible here as well, of course, because state and/or societal actors may drag their feet on complying for other reason. EU mandates cover a vast range of areas, from environmental policy processes to regional policy processes, from occupational safety and health to social policy processes, from financial market to business regulatory processes.

Examples from two policy sectors, environmental and regional policy, should be sufficient to demonstrate this.

In many areas of environmental policy, the EU's mandates for legalistic implementation in the 1980s best fit the traditional German vertical command-and-control approach whereas from the 1990s on, its mandates for more flexible and self-regulatory modes of enforcement better fit the British self-regulatory approach.[40] The 1980 Drinking Water Directive, which prescribed uniform standards and formal, legalistic patterns of interest intermediation, ensured that Germany absorbed the water pollution policy without problem. But the directive brought transformation to British and French water pollution policymaking, albeit after long periods of inertia, by forcing the UK to reverse its traditional informal and voluntary approach to implementation and by pressing France to reverse its long-standing process of administrative discretion.[41] In the case of the Waste Packaging Directive, where the EU similarly prescribed relatively high, uniform environmental protection objectives and formal, legalistic patterns of interest intermediation, the Germans again were able to absorb the policy, albeit with some delay because of objections over content, whereas British misfit forced it to transform its policymaking processes, albeit again after some initial resistance.[42] By contrast, in the 1993 Environmental Management and Auditing Systems Regulation (EAMS), which demanded a self-regulatory process of environmental auditing largely modeled on the British approach, the British easily absorbed any changes while Germany was forced to transform its more legalistic approach—although this was relatively easy because it was able to draw on its own traditional corporatist experiences.[43] In air pollution, finally, in the case of the EU Sulphur Dioxide and Suspended Particulate directive of 1981, while Britain in the end reversed its self-regulatory approach in order to comply with the EU's legalistic mandate, Italy's inertia resulted not so much from a reversal of tradition in environmental policymaking, since it barely had any, but rather from a continuing lack of state capacity and supportive societal networks.[44]

Regional policy is another area where we could expect EU-related direct effects, since the EU has mandated pluralist consultation through 'horizontal cooperation' or 'partnership' with civil society in the structural funds process.[45] But the EU's mandate to develop pluralist processes resulted in inertia at best. Statist patterns, where regional officials dominated the process

---

[40] Jordan (2002).

[41] Jordan (2002) Knill and Lenschow (1998), Knill (2001), Héritier et al. (1996) and Haverland (1999).

[42] Haverland (1999).

[43] Benz and Goetz (1996a) and Knill and Lehmkul (1999).

[44] Duina and Blithe (1999).

[45] The EU process calls for 'horizontal cooperation' between public institutions and civic associations, economic and social, which come from civil society. See Bache 1998.

and consulted little, appeared not only in French regions, where these were already prevalent. It also appeared in Germany, despite its traditional corporatist pattern and the failed attempt, in Bavaria, to institute such a pattern, as well as in the UK.[46]

Diffuse Effects

Even where the EU does not mandate change, however, it can have diffuse effects as a result of institutional learning, mimesis, and imitation,[47] or 'polydiffusion',[48] when national actors schooled in any given set of national processes gain from their close cooperative experiences of the EU or one another, and alter their behavior accordingly. The neofunctionalists' theoretical approach to integration is itself predicated on such institutional learning, which is seen to promote shared values and ideas as well as common approaches to problem-solving.[49] But participation in the EU can result in much more specific kinds of learning. Diffuse effects are most apparent where EU-related learning experiences or suggested rules lead to the diffusion of new ideas for state action. This has been the effect in tax policy, where peer review of harmful tax practices led to member-state shelving of bad practices—particularly the case for Italy;[50] in gender mainstreaming, which seeks to infuse national practices related to all aspects of work–life with EU jointly constructed ideas about gender equality,[51] or in the OMC in social and employment policy, based on self-set targets and voluntary compliance.[52]

Diffuse effects are equally apparent in interest groups' gains in organizational and communication skills as a result of EU-level lobbying experiences—which they then bring back to the national sphere. In some areas there are clear signs of growing horizontal networks across countries which have been successfully promoted by the EU through social dialogues and forums—as in the case of women's groups.[53] Moreover, all businesses gained pluralist lobbying expertise as a result of setting up shop in Brussels. However, the learning curve and thus the concomitant gains were greater for some, such as the French, little used to EU-style lobbying, than the British, consummate lobbyists as a result of their pluralist parliamentary experience, or the Germans, great at institutional relations as a result of their corporatist experience.

Such diffuse effects were not always lasting, however.[54] In banking, for example, French bankers who in the early 1990s set up shop to lobby in Brussels had left by the late 1990s, leaving lobbying to the national

---

[46] Dupoirier (2004).   [47] Falkner et al. (1999: 512).   [48] Burnham and Maor (1995).
[49] Haas (1958) and Cram (1998).   [50] Radaelli (1999).
[51] Woodward (2003) and Pollack and Hafner-Burton (2000).
[52] See de la Porte and Pochet (2002) and Mosher and Trubek (2003).
[53] Helfflich and Kolb (2001).   [54] Grossman (2003).

government which they felt more effective. British and German bankers, by contrast, went to Brussels and stayed, with the Germans, true to form, relying more on associative power, the British more on individualized lobbying.[55] And the effects were also not always beneficial. EU-level lobbying can serve to loosen national associational ties, which was the case of German firms lobbying separately from their national associations in the Trans-Atlantic Business Dialogue (TABD).[56] Moreover, although the main French business association, having experienced active participation in policy formulation at the EU level, altered its own behavior nationally, demanding more consultation, this has not guaranteed it greater access to national decision-making.[57]

As often as not, however, lobbying may have no diffuse effects at all. This is in particular the case of public interest groups whose influence comes not from European associations directly representing national member associations but rather from European NGOs—the case of immigration policy[58]—or from international nongovernmental organizations (INGOs), which have set up offices in Brussels—especially the case of the environment.[59] These groups, peopled by experts and professionals with Europe-wide or international ties, tend to be disconnected from—or to have loose connections at best with—the national and local level organizations peopled by those most affected by the policies and organized in ways that best fit national patterns and preoccupations. Environmental policy is a case in point, as INGOs tend to operate at the EU level while national NGOs remain nationally focused, so much so that even national branches of INGOs have little say over the EU-level actions of their Brussels branches, which either decide on their own or take orders from the international headquarters.[60]

What is more, diffuse effects are generally hard to establish, take time, and may be clear only in retrospect. The OMC, for example, relies on member-states' willingness to cooperate in nonbinding agreements that set targets for change, with benchmarking exercises based on common but highly vague sets of goals, in which countries learn from one another's 'best practices' and are 'named and shamed' if they fail to meet their self-set targets.[61] This makes it very difficult to establish any direct kind of causality.[62] The same events can be interpreted in any number of ways, depending on individual perceptions and positions. What does one do with the case of the top official in the French Ministry of Labor who, when asked whether European ideas connected to the OMC had an influence on French unemployment initiatives, responded

---

[55] Grossman (2003).   [56] Cowles (2001).
[57] Schmidt (1996) and Cowles (2001).   [58] Guiraudon (2001).
[59] Mazey and Richardson (1993*b*), Webster (1998), McCormick (2001), Jordan (2002*a*) and Greenwood (2003).
[60] Webster (1998).
[61] See de la Porte and Pochet (2002) and Trubek and Mosher (2001).
[62] See discussion in Erhel, Mandin, and Palier (2005).

in the negative even though the program's main objectives announced the following week turned out to be identical with those outlined by the EU?[63] Is it just because this is France, and therefore one keeps credit for policy initiatives for oneself even though the EU did have a diffuse effect? Or because France (among others) helped dictate the terms to be used by the EU, which it then applies? There can be little doubt that, at the very least, the Lisbon and Luxembourg strategies for reforms in employment and social policy via the OMC—with the demand for NAPs and the like—have led to the use of the same words and similar concepts. But such words and concepts nevertheless mostly reflect different programmatic philosophies and policies.[64]

This raises the question of how much effect the OMC really has, however diffuse. As government-centered exercises at both the EU level and the national, there has been little real deliberation with societal actors and minimal public awareness.[65] Although the OMC has great potential in areas where national divergence makes EU-level decision-making difficult if not impossible, the very vagueness of the targets and the self-reporting nature of the exercise could mean that much of it may just be smoke and mirrors. A recent study suggests that EU recommendations for corporatist consultation in the NAPs of the European Employment Strategy (EES) and for pluralist consultation in the Social Inclusion OMC have had mixed effects. They produced a new pluralist consultation in France's EES but followed traditional patterns of statist consultation in France's OMC; followed traditional patterns of statist consultation in Britain's EES but produced a new pluralist pattern of consultation in Britain's OMC; followed traditional patterns of corporatist consultation in Germany's EES and OMC; while it did not even get as far as statist consultation in either domain in Italy.[66]

Knock-on Effects

The EU has a 'knock-on' effect in policy sectors where, although the EU's policies neither demand change nor inspire it, the implementation of such policies nonetheless acts as an incentive for state and/or societal actors not to play by the old rules. Examples include EU agricultural policy reforms that affected state actors' relations with farmers and EU competition policy decisions that opened up the market, offering new opportunities for societal interests in such sectors as road haulage, public utilities, and banking. In these latter sectors, whereas existing statist processes were little affected in cases where state actors chose to maintain control, existing corporatist

---

[63] Conversation with Bruno Palier, June 2004. See also Erhel, Mandin, and Palier (2005).

[64] Barbier (2005).

[65] Smismans (2003), Jacobssen (2004), Rhodes and de la Porte (2005) and Zeitlin and Pochet (2005).

[66] Zeiltin and Pochet (2005).

processes were more vulnerable to break up where state and societal actors could not reach agreement on how to implement the policy.

Agriculture has arguably had the clearest knock-on effects, because the EU has been the main driver of policy since the beginning of the CAP. France developed a stronger quasi-corporatist pattern in the 1970s as a result of EU policy which then weakened in the 1980s as a result of greater pluralism linked to changes in the EU's approach in the CAP as well as to greater openness to other interests.[67] Similar changes were at work in British agriculture, where the traditional corporatist process was greatly loosened as a result of the reform of the CAP.[68] But in the UK, it was the mad cow crisis that had the greatest knock-on effect, forcing a reorganization of state structures which brought with it a more statist process.[69]

In the case of road haulage, too, EU deregulation produced knock-on effects for some countries. The cabotage directive which introduced the right of nonresident transport haulers to operate in foreign markets but allowed quantitative restrictions and price controls to remain had little direct effect on national regulatory policies or policymaking practices. But it did have a knock-on effect in countries where domestic coalitions were able to use the new EU rules to challenge the existing equilibria. Thus, although it had no effect in the cases of the already liberalized markets of Britain and France, in Germany, the EU rule acted as a spur to the formation of new, more pluralist coalitions for reform which then promoted liberalization while in Italy it acted as a spur to the old corporatist coalitions to create greater protectionism in the sector.[70]

Knock-on effects also occurred in the public utilities and banking sectors. In the electricity sector at the time of the EU-level negotiations of the deregulation of the sector, whereas in France statist processes were little affected as the state remained in control, in Germany the corporatist community split apart because societal actors were divided as to how to implement deregulation nationally.[71] However, even when corporatism does not break apart, associational ties based on cooperation and trust can loosen where an appeal is possible to competition authorities. This was the case of the German private banks which brought complaint against the regional public banks for unfair competition because of their state-guaranteed loans.[72] A similar pattern also occurred in France, when the private banks complained to the Commission about the preferential treatment given Crédit Lyonnais by the state bailout.[73] Britain, by contrast, experienced almost no knock-on effects because it had already deregulated and privatized these industries prior to EU-related deregulation.

[67] Roederer-Rynning (2002).   [68] Marsh and Smith (2000).   [69] Forbes (2004).
[70] Héritier et al. (1996) and Knill and Lehmkuhl (1999).
[71] Eising and Jabko (2002) and S. Schmidt (2004).
[72] Grossman (2003, 2006).
[73] Schmidt (1996) and Grossman (2003, 2006).

As a result of these variegated changes in micropatterns of sectoral policy-making, the macropatterns of policymaking have become less distinctive, with pluralism the new default option where statism and/or corporatism have been weakened in particular policy sectors. But countries nevertheless retain the essential characteristics of their traditional patterns: France and Britain are still largely statist, even though the shift to regulatory and legalistic implementation has altered the way in which the state exercises control and despite the fact that societal access in policy formulation has increased. Germany remains primarily corporatist, despite the fact that the corporatist ties have been loosening in a number of sectors, while it has become even more regulatory and legalistic in implementation. And Italy is still a mix of corporatism and clientelism, with the lack of state capacity still its main problem in implementation. This is apparent even from the eclectic set of examples we have noted above for our four country cases (see Table 3.2). But this will become clear in the four case studies elaborated below.

The EU's Impact on Policymaking in France, Britain, Germany, and Italy

The discussion of the differential effects of Europeanization on member-states shows that the EU has had a comparatively more disruptive impact on the policy formulation and implementation processes of simple polities with statist processes than of compound polities with corporatist processes, even though some policy sectors may have taken on more pluralist patterns. The full story of national adaptation to the EU for any member-state is more textured and much more complex than the macro- and micropatterns sketched out above, however. History, culture, politics, and time play a large role in explaining why, within the general categories delineated above, there is further variation in national patterns of development and adaptation to the EU.

France

In France, statist policymaking processes can be summarized as ones in which traditionally the state has acted and society reacted: state actors have formulated policies without significant input from societal actors but accommodated them in the implementation process, else risk confrontation. In Alexis de Tocqueville's oft-quoted phrase, 'the rule is rigid, the application flexible'. This means that policies decided by elected governments without consultation with the most affected interests may very well have been moderated in their application, as top civil servants have had the administrative discretion to adapt the rules in implementation.[74] But where state actors have not been

[74] Schmidt (1996a, 1999c).

Table 3.2. The sectoral effect of EU policies on national policy processes

EU effect	Policy area and potential impact	Actual outcomes in selected cases
Direct effects of EU-mandated processes	Regional policy—pluralist consultation:	Statist consultation in (statist) Fr, (corporatist) Ger, (statist) UK
	Water pollution—legalistic implementation	*Legalistic in (self-regulatory) UK; legalistic in (discretionary) Fr;* legalistic in (legalistic) Ger
	Environ'l auditing—self-regulatory implement.	Self-regulatory in (self-regulatory) UK; *self-regulatory in (legalistic) Ger*
	Air pollution—legalistic implementation	*Legalistic in (self-regulatory) UK;* not yet legalistic in It (lack of capacity)
Diffuse effects of EU-related learning experiences	Employment policy (EES)—corporatist consultation	*Pluralist consultation in (statist) Fr;* statist in (statist) UK; corporatist in (corporatist) Ger; not even statist in (corporatist) Italy
	Social Policy (OMC)—pluralist consultation	Statist consultation in (statist) Fr; *pluralist in (statist) UK;* corporatist in (corporatist) Ger; not even statist in (corporatist) Italy
	EU level pluralist lobbying experience	*Pluralist EU level lobbying by (statist) Fr bus,* except banking, and Fr bus cannot change national (statist) process; *TABD may loosen national level corporatism in Ger*
Knock-on effects from EU policies that act as incentives to competition	Electricity—pluralist formulation	*Pluralism for (corporatist) Ger;* statism for (statist) Fr
	Road haulage—pluralist formulation	*Pluralism for (corporatist) Ger;* corporatism for (corporatist) It
	Banking—pluralist formulation	*Loosening of corporatist ties in Ger; of statist ties in Fr*
	Agriculture—pluralist formulation	*More pluralism in (quasi-corporatist) Fr*

Note: Changes in direction of EU-related processes noted in italics.

accommodating, confrontation has often been the result, with social protest movements quickly organized and as quickly dispersed,[75] following either government appeasement or repression. Although this pattern has become more attenuated over time—as societal participation in decision-making has increased and state repression decreased—the balance in the state–society relationship in favor of the state has not.

France's policymaking pattern has its origins in the French Revolution, in the Jacobin understanding of the role of the state, in which elected governments are mandated to carry out the will of the people directly, without the mediation of organized interests, which are by their very nature suspect because they violate principles of democratic equality and electoral accountability.

[75] Tilly (1978).

Ever since the Revolution, Republican thought has been permeated by a fear of social pluralism leading to particularism and fragmentation, and diversity leading to inequality.[76] Although the Jacobin state of extreme centralization is long dead, the idea of it lives on through what Pierre Rosanvallon calls the political culture of 'generality'. This culture assumes an idealized relationship between the general interest embodied by the state and the particular interests of citizens, which were to be protected from the interposition of 'intermediary interests' promoting their own economic, political, or social purposes, and which was proceduralized through highly abstract laws to be applied equally to all.[77]

At the time of the Revolution, this thinking resulted in the Le Chapelier Law of 1791 outlawing all associations 'which might inspire in citizens an intermediary interest [that would] separate them from the "public sphere" (*la chose publique*) by a "spirit of corporatism"'.[78] This law was only rescinded in 1884. But even once interest groups were allowed to be formed without prior government authorization, as of the law of 1901, they continued to be viewed with suspicion not only by government but even by the population at large. Although unions had been accepted as constituting a social 'corps' by the 1920s and 1930s, the state did not really pick up on the positive contributions possible from associative life until the second part of the twentieth century. This is when the state itself began anointing certain interest associations as privileged interlocutors of the state, as associations in the 'general interest', or even devolving power to them to act in the place of the state, as in the case of the family association, UNAF. By the 1960s and especially the 1970s, the state increasingly legalized associational activity by, for example, mandating the representation of associations on urban planning commissions, environmental protection, etc. It also increasingly financed such activities—in 1995, state financing represented 58 percent of the resources of the associational world (by comparison with 64% in Germany, 47% in the UK, and 31% in the United States). By 2001, 40 percent of the population over 14 years of age belonged to one or more association, of which there were close to 700,000.[79] By the 2000s, France generally had as many associations as most other advanced industrialized countries.[80]

For all this growth in associational activity, the state retained control over policymaking. Organized interests remain less powerful than those in countries with more pluralist or corporatist processes,[81] since state-related centers of power tended to retain the upper hand, choosing with whom to consult and whom to ignore.[82] But consultation there is, and generally a lot

---

[76] Nora (1984: 653), Rosanvallon (1992: 168–71) and Laborde (1994: 55).
[77] Rosanvallon (2004).   [78] Quoted in Rosanvallon (2004: 29).
[79] Rosanvallon (2004: 417–28).   [80] Sommier (2003).
[81] Wilson (1983: 909); see discussion in Schmidt (1996a: 18–20).
[82] Hayward (1986: 39–55).

of it, as a result of a proliferation of government committees in which representatives of officially recognized groups are consulted frequently—but mainly to inform about and legitimize already formulated government policy than to coordinate policy construction. In recent years, the use of committees of *sages* (wisemen) on controversial issues, such as citizenship or the head-scarf, which consult widely before making a recommendation for government action, has softened this approach somewhat. But this is still a government-controlled process, in which government ultimately decides on action.

Lobbies in this interest consultation process continue to be seen as illegit-imate—so much so that still today, although businesses do engage in lobbying, lobbyists for big French companies are often not even mentioned on business organizational charts and do not have company business cards or e-mail.[83] Illegitimate 'lobbying', however, is differentiated from ongoing consultation on everyday policies with the 'professional organizations' legitimized by central administrators because they are seen to represent group interests acting in the 'general interest' as opposed to private interest.[84] And it is also differ-entiated from *lobbying à la française*, which involves a more subtle process of influencing one's *camarades de promotion* (classmates from elite schools) in government and encompasses no more than providing a good lunch or sending polite notes written on white paper—to ensure against even the appearance of lobbying.[85] Such lobbying remains the norm in France, given a conflictual decision-making culture where decisions are ultimately political and the most important level of decision-making is at the top, such that any decision, however technically competent, can be reversed relatively easily for purely political reasons.[86] This contrasts greatly with the EU, where the most important level is at the bottom, given that the civil servant charged with the *dossier* has the most weight and the recommendation cannot be easily reversed on other than technical grounds.[87] These differences in decision-making culture lend insight into French failures early on to lobby effectively, as epitomized by the attempted takeover of de Havilland by Aerospatiale in 1989, in which no amount of political intervention late in the process could change the negative decision.[88]

French business interests came late into the EU lobbying process, pushed by the French state, but handicapped by their dependence on it as well as their lack of experience in that kind of lobbying—so much so that the French themselves acknowledged that 'The Dutch and British are virtuosos, the Irish

---

[83] Conversation with Nicolas Dahan, assistant professor, University of Marne-la-Vallée, France.
[84] Schmidt (1996a: chs. 1 and 7) and Suleiman (1974: 337–40).
[85] Schmidt (1996a: ch. 8).
[86] See Schmidt (1996a: ch. 7).
[87] Hull (1993); Donnelly (1993).
[88] Schmidt (1996b: 234–8), Lequesne (1993) and Nonon and Clamen (1991).

excellent, the Germans (as always) efficient, and the French (as often) light-weight and late'.[89] Those days are over, however. French big business has since the early 1990s integrated itself well into the European policy formulation process, often acting as a partner of the French government in lobbying the Commission but at the same time also developing a certain autonomy that has enabled it to forge alliances with other large firms to promote its goals.[90] But although French businesses did learn quickly, attesting to the significance of the EU's diffuse effects on business lobbying, the pattern did not hold across sectors, as we have already seen in the case of French bankers. Moreover, even though French businesses have surely learned to do better over time, their traditional reliance on government and informal relationships to influence decision-making rather than on lobbies has nevertheless left them at a continuing disadvantage at the EU level by comparison with those countries with long-standing, well-developed lobbies, as in the case of the British,[91] or with cohesive peak associations, as in the case of the Germans.

At the national level, moreover, because the business–government relation-ship has remained much less equal, the diffuse effects of EU level experience has led to growing business dissatisfaction with its interactions with govern-ment. The strategy of the MEDEF, the employers' association, denied a more equal voice in the national coordinative discourse of policy construction, has been to develop a communicative voice of its own. This began when the left came to power in 1997, as the Medef pushed for more neoliberal policies and objected to a whole range of labor-related initiatives—in particular, the initia-tive to reduce the work week to thirty-five hours. The Medef at the time was often the only strong voice to be heard on the right in objection to the Socialist initiatives.[92] And it continues to be so even with the right in power, confront-ing the state, pushing for neoliberal reform and, when it has gotten it, as in the case of the Prime Minister Dominique de Villepin's measures on unemployment in January 2006, crowing about the fruits of its 'own parlia-mentary and political lobbying', much to the discomfort of the government.

While French big business has become increasingly active at the EU level, other economic interests have not. Small-and medium-sized French businesses find little representation through the main French employers' association. French trade unions, moreover, have been noticeable mainly by their absence at the EU level. The communist Confédération Générale du Travail (CGT), the second largest trade union in France, with approximately 650,000 members, was not even represented in the European Trade Union Conference (ETUC) prior to 1999.[93] The unions from corporatist countries like Germany are the ones with a real presence in Brussels.

---

[89] Fourcans (1993: 21, 32) and Schmidt (1996).   [90] Coen (1998).
[91] See Fairbrass (2003).   [92] Schmidt (2002: ch. 6).
[93] Szukala (2003: 230).

Agricultural interests, moreover, although still powerful, have had their organizational capacity and state access and influence diminish as a result of the knock-on effects of EU decisions on the CAP.[94] Between the 1970s and the late 1980s, the EU, by setting priorities and instituting a price support regime, encouraged the consolidation of a corporatist process in which a couple of large agricultural associations dominated the national scene and, through nationally integrated patterns of mobilization timed to coincide with CAP bargaining rounds, exerted significant influence on the EU and the French government.[95] Beginning in the late 1980s, however, CAP reform focused on cutting prices while the Commission opened up policymaking processes to other farming groups. This created a more pluralist process at the EU level, weakening corporatist relations at the national level even as it encouraged more contestation focused on international trade negotiations from the established farmers' unions—opposed to cuts—and from newer social movements.[96]

The new social movements include those focused on the fight against globalization and those for the *sans* (the withouts)—that is, the *sans emploi* (without employment), *sans abri* (without housing), and the *sans papiers* (illegal immigrants without papers). These, together with the older social movements, including the environmental, antinuclear, and women's movements that began in the 1970s, have galvanized a whole new set of actors in France and, increasingly, across Europe. The main social movement organizations are ATTAC, active on a whole range of antiglobalization and social justice issues, which is arguably the most successful of such movements (counting 128, or 22% of French members of the Assemblée for 1997–2002 and 60 members of the Senate, but also 75 MEPs);[97] the Confédération Paysanne, led by José Bové, with attention-getting actions, such as torching a MacDonald's and destroying fields of GMO wheat; and Solidaires, unitaires, démocratiques (SUD), a radical union, focused not only on the traditional union issues but also on social movement issues like unemployment, housing, poverty, and safety. Transnational movements are also significant mobilizers, like ACT-UP with regard to HIV, or the many other antiglobalization movements.

Thus, the reality of state–society relations has since moved very far from the initial centralizing Jacobin ideal, despite recurring complaints by intellectuals of a blocked society and of the Jacobin heritage—'le mal francais'. While the

---

[94] Keeler (1987) and Roederer-Rynning (2002).

[95] Roederer-Rynning (2002: 110–4).

[96] Roederer-Rynning (2002: 114–9), see also Coleman and Chiasson (2002) and Saurugger (2002).

[97] ATTAC (Association pour une taxation des transactions financières pour l'aide aux citoyens) began in France but now has over 30,000 members and 150 local committees in 40 countries, with 40 offices in member-states. It originally focused on the adoption of the Tobin tax but subsequently became active on a whole range of antiglobalization and social justice issues—see Sommier (2003: 162–6) and Birchfield (2004).

reality has been one of a progressive development of associations, unions, and social movements creating a significant space for society in the policy process, the rhetoric remains focused on describing only a Jacobin, centralizing state dealing directly with the citizens, undifferentiated and without intermediaries. As Rosanvallon put it, the problem is that the political culture of generality has 'stayed in the heads' with all the resulting problems with regard to conceptions of sovereignty and the general interest, along with the predisposition for the political class to assume that they alone represent the social interest. The result is that the French political class has been unable or unwilling to think through change.[98] France is no longer exceptional—it confronts the problems that all other democracies confront—except perhaps in the fact that its ideas no longer fit with reality and its discourse confuses rather than illuminates.

There is another problem, however, which involves the implementation of policy. The Jacobin logic of generality, which legitimized the production of laws without consultation with the most affected interests but which gave elite state civil servants the job of applying them, left itself open to an implementation process that allowed for a tremendous amount of derogation of the rules by those self-same servants of the state—as the interpreters of the law. The result has been a system in which consultation *with* the people was ruled out in policy formulation only to find its way into policy implementation. Interest groups were not allowed to lobby in policy formulation—although they might use informal political channels to scuttle legislation—but they were often accommodated in the implementation through exceptions to the rules. This was bad for the coherence of national administration, in which innovative solutions to particular problems could not be generalized since they were by definition illegitimate because they went against the general laws.[99] But it was good for democracy. This was a democracy which was not very open and transparent in the implementation of policy, however, and it naturally promoted contention, since where accommodation was not forthcoming, confrontation followed. The result was a pattern in which the state decided on policies without extensive consultation with societal interests, but some interests nevertheless generally got their way—business in particular, given the close business-government relationship, and agriculture until the 1990s—while others stopped much that went against their way—especially labor, students, and social movements, through strikes, protests, and 'contestation' of all sorts.

Reforms beginning in the 1980s changed much of this pattern. Citizen-focused reforms have remedied individual citizens' relations with the state administration. A variety of commissions were established to ensure free

---

[98] Rosanvallon (2004).   [99] Thoenig (1987); Schmidt (1990).

access to information, to inform the public of the information available, to control electronic eavesdropping, to set up procedural safeguards, and to limit the arbitrary power of the tax authorities with regard to criminal sanctions. And an ombudsman was appointed to mediate between the citizen and the administration. Already in 1990, there were almost twenty independent agencies that oversaw consumer protection, competition, and insurance.[100] In addition, the reform of the *services publics* or public services has led to focus on the needs of the *usagers*, the citizen 'user' of services.[101]

In the economic sphere, moreover, liberalization, privatization, and deregulation have left businesses to lead themselves at the same time that the radical decentralization of wage-bargaining, together with privatization, has reduced the strength of unions and, therefore, the threat of strikes.[102] All of this together has entailed the retreat of the state, even though the state still maintains the option of intervening where it sees the need in business as well as labor.[103] In addition, the rise of regulatory agencies—whether EU or nationally inspired—has created a more arm's-length relationship between business and government, with greater openness and transparency in the application of the rules as well as oversight over private and public sector actors. Even the national ministries have changed, taking on a more regulatory role in their relationships with still publicly owned companies, as in the case of the electricity sector.[104]

EU-mandated deregulation produced even further reform in the electricity sector by opening up the electricity market to competition—although only after the Commission overcame years of French government resistance. But deregulation has done little so far to alter national policymaking processes, attesting to the absence of EU knock-on effects in this area. The government and EDF largely decided among themselves on strategies for the EU level, leaving societal actors outside the loop.[105] This was of little concern to the large business consumers of electricity (who benefited from lower electric bills than their German competitors) but of major concern to the public sector unions, which engaged in escalating numbers of protests once liberalization had been agreed and eventual privatization seemed inevitable.[106] In response to such protest as well as to growing resistance by EDF itself to deregulation, the French government engaged in rearguard action with an elaborate communicative discourse in which it sought to demonstrate that it was doing everything to protect the *services publics* from the EU, including inserting in the directive an Article (3.2) that recognized the rights of states to impose public service obligations in the general interest.[107]

---

[100] Guédon (1991).   [101] Warin (1997).   [102] See Schmidt (1996, 2002*a*).
[103] Schmidt (1996; 2002*a*: ch. 4).   [104] Prudhomme-Deblanc (2002).
[105] Eising and Jabko (2002).   [106] Bauby and Toledo (2002: 116).
[107] See discussion in Schmidt (2002: 97–8).

In the environmental sector, France felt the EU's direct effects even more strongly, but initially responded with inertia.[108] In the case of drinking water pollution, France was very slow to comply because the new EU rules went against higher-level civil servants' administrative discretion in implementation.[109] As late as the early 1990s, the French minister of the environment claimed that his role was one of 'protecting and restoring the French model of water management'.[110] But the French model did ultimately change, albeit only after EU notifications and court rulings (as indicated in Chapter 2), leaving a highly fragmented, partially privatized system overseen by a large number of state, semipublic, and local government bodies.[111] Here, as in other low-profile areas, the French strategy was 'to lose the foreign origin of European policy by low-profile assimilation into domestic networks', despite the high political and financial costs, so much so that by the time EU legislation reached the local level, local officials were oblivious to its provenance.[112] But while state actors tried to minimize the EU's direct effects, social actors nevertheless felt empowered to press for better environmental compliance—as in Brittany, where information provided to the EU by a local interest group, frustrated by the lack of local response to its concerns, led to a landmark ECJ judgment in 2001.[113]

In regional policy, by contrast, the direct effect of EU-mandated processes did little more than create statist forms of consultation in three highly diverse regions—Alsace, Aquitaine, and Corsica. Regional officials controlled the process, organizing consultation with a 'civil society' that consisted of weak economic interests (the strong ones went directly to Paris) that were only minimally involved.[114] There was thus almost no coordinative discourse in regional policymaking, let alone any mention of the fact the EU had mandated the process.

In the EES and the Social Inclusion OMC, the diffuse effects of EU-suggested processes were mixed. In response to the EU's call for corporatist consultation in the NAPs of the EES, greater pluralism emerged instead, as social partners felt empowered through participation, even if they ultimately had little actual impact on the policies due to differences in objectives. By contrast, in response to the EU call for greater pluralism in the Social Inclusion OMC, France remained statist, with antipoverty NGOs only minimally involved in dialogue with the government on NAPs and people experiencing poverty barely brought in—in marked contrast to more pluralist national antipoverty programs.[115]

---

[108] Bodyguel (1996: 110) and Szarka (2000).
[109] Knill and Lenschow (1998), Knill (2001) and Knill and Lehmkul (1999).
[110] Buller (1998: 78).   [111] Buller (1996: 478–9).
[112] Szarka (2001: 90).   [113] Bourblanc (2005).
[114] Dupoirier (2004).   [115] Erhel, Mandin, and Palier (2005: 239–40).

In the coordinative discourse related to these and other EU-mandated or EU-suggested processes, moreover, state actors never acknowledged the EU's influence, much as in the case of unemployment policy. As a top official in the European and International Affairs Agency explained: 'In France, there is a will not to show the importance of Europe: a Brussels that regulates everything appears ominous'.[116] In high-profile areas where it is impossible not to acknowledge the EU source of a policy, especially when that policy is unpopular, French state actors are most likely to shift the blame to the EU, as we saw above in the case of the *services publics*. But wherever they can, even in high-profile areas, French officials seek to ignore the role of the EU and to frame the issue in purely French conceptual terms.

In antidiscrimination policy, for example, where the EU directive clashed with traditional French ideas about citizenship that proscribed differentiation according to race and precluded even collecting race-related statistics, the French government's discourse completely ignored the EU in its arguments, which centered around modernizing French treatment of discrimination in keeping with Republican principles of *égalité*.[117] In sexual harassment policy, moreover, success came only when the issue, originally framed by women's groups using Anglo-Saxon ideas about gender discrimination, was reframed by women legislators in more French terms of violence against women through the 'abuse of power', exploitation, and hierarchy.[118] By contrast, the notion of *parité* (equality in political office), although also EU-inspired, was more quickly accepted because this issue was readily framed in term of French universalism without dividing the Republic 'one and indivisible' or the '*peuple souverain*'[119] since, as Gisèle Halimi argued, women were *ni une race, ni une classe, ni une ethnie, ni une catégorie* because they were in all groups.[120]

Beyond these sector-specific, EU-related effects on national policymaking processes and discourse, the EU has also had a more general impact on the French implementation process. With its more regulatory and legalistic approach to implementation, the EU no longer allows the kinds of exceptions to the rules that were the stock in trade of the administrative state, where state civil servants had the administrative discretion to 'adjust' the laws to meet individual needs. This loss of flexibility is not much of an issue for businesses which have adapted to the regulatory and legalistic approach to implementation and understand that they need to go to Brussels to make their voices heard. However, for citizens with little direct access at the EU level and

---

[116] Interview January 2, 2004 in the Délégation aux affaires européennes et internationals (DAEI)—cited in Erhel, Mandin, and Palier (2005: 232).
[117] Geddes and Guiraudon (2004) and Radaelli and Schmidt (2004: 369–70).
[118] Saguy (2003).
[119] Bereni and Lépinard (2004: 17–18). My thanks to Elizabeth Simmons for this insightful comparison, as elucidated in her masters thesis for the University of North Carolina, Chapel Hill, December 2005.
[120] *Le Monde* March 7, 1997.

nonbusiness interests that remain more focused at the national level due to a lack of organizational capacity, resources, and proximity (as discussed above), the EU-related loss of flexibility is a real problem. Already denied input at the front end, in policy formulation, and now cut out at the back end, in policy implementation, because accommodation is proscribed, they are more likely to engage in confrontation. But they are no longer likely to be able to stop the policy because French governments are not longer as free to bend, or not, in response to confrontation.[121]

The farmers discovered this during the GATT negotiations of the Uruguay Round of trade negotiations, where no amount of protest could change the outcome, despite a last minute heroic gesture by the Balladur government to try to force a renegotiation of the close-to-agreed-upon treaty by threatening a veto. Public service workers have also found this out since the mid-1990s, as successive measures promoting deregulation and privatization are implemented in the face of massive strikes and repeated walkouts and despite government efforts to ensure a special regime for the *services publics* in Brussels.[122] Even truck drivers have had little impact, despite repeatedly blocking major highways and border crossings in protest against EU deregulation which has left them without protection and working long hours for little pay. Hunters in Aquitaine even formed their own party, *Chasse, Peche, Tradition* (Hunting, Fishing, Tradition) in the European elections of 1994 to oppose European regulation of hunting that no longer allowed them to shoot the *palombe* (doves), and to which the French government could no longer turn a blind eye, given EU action against the government for nonenforcement.

Thus, these EU-related changes in access and enforcement patterns, although arguably producing greater democratic legitimacy through equality and predictability in the application of the laws, come at the cost of disenfranchising certain groups. The loss of the possibility of accommodating these groups in implementation, by making exceptions to the rules, is particularly problematic in a system where citizens have never had much access to decision-making in policy formulation. And because their only way to be heard now is through confrontation when their concerns are not addressed, the changes represent a threat not just to democratic legitimacy but also to French societal stability.

One procedural solution for France would be to allow greater access to citizens at the policy formulation stage (so that there would no longer be the need to adapt the rules in the implementation) and to encourage greater citizen interest organization and participation in EU policymaking. This would prove useful not only in ensuring that more French societal views are represented at the EU level but it would also provide the French state with partners in the national communicative discourse about policy initiatives in

---

[121] Schmidt (1999*b*).   [122] See Schmidt (2000; 2002a: ch. 6).

Brussels. As it is, French leaders tend to be alone to inform and legitimate EU policies to the national public because in most spheres they do not have strong societal interests able to make the bridge between lobbying in Brussels and communicating with their own national members about the outcome. But not only are such possible solutions with regard to the policy process not easy to accomplish in a country where, despite the real changes in state–society relations, the state still tends to act and society react. It would also further reduce executive autonomy and control—and thereby challenge traditional notions of structural democracy in which the executive, as representative of the French nation, one and indivisible, is expected to be in control over the decision-making process and solely responsible for its outcome. This is in large measure why French leaders' communicative discourse to the general public continues to downplay any EU origins to changes in national policymaking while emphasizing their own leadership in Europe.

Britain

In Britain, statist policymaking processes are not nearly as starkly defined as in France, since traditionally the state has been expected to act only in a very restricted sphere, and society to act on its own. Thus, although in Britain, too, state actors may formulate policies without significant societal input, societal actors have generally had greater access and influence through more open policy networks as well as more freedom in a wide range of domains to regulate themselves through voluntary rules and self-governing arrangements. British flexibility in implementation has thus been grounded not in the French pattern of derogation of the law—which the British would not countenance in any event, given their greater respect for the rule of law—but rather in simply having fewer laws and more societal self-organization. This pattern has changed somewhat over time as societal participation in decision-making has increased while the devolution of power to regulatory agencies has weighted the balance in state–society relations even more toward state (or at least public) actors.

Britain's statist system has never been as sharply demarcated from pluralist or corporatist systems as the French. Britain, especially in the 1960s, was deemed 'pluralist' because of the wide range of economic interests engaged in self-regulation, and the amount of lobbying of parliament.[123] In the 1970s, it was called corporatist because of government attempts at concertation with management and labor.[124] But Britain never quite fit either of these patterns because its pluralism could not account for the autonomy of the government when it chose to act while its 'corporatism' never really worked.[125] It has been statist in the sense that governments have tended to be highly autonomous

---

[123] Beer (1969).   [124] Winkler (1976)   [125] See Cox and Hayward (1983).

and able to make policy absent interest input while the consultation style of its elite civil service has been similar to the French in that, in the words of Hugh Heclo, 'British administrative consultation with outsiders has seemed more often aimed at persuading interest groups than reconciling their positive pressures'.[126] But it has been a much less all-pervasive kind of statism than the French, given how much has been left to society.[127]

This policymaking pattern has its roots not in a revolutionary moment but in an evolutionary history over centuries; and not in a set of principled ideas about an ideal state–society interaction but, rather, in a set of pragmatic ideas that favored limiting the role of the state in favor of a self-regulating society. The long societal struggle beginning at the time of the Magna Carta to ensure the rights of parliament, the courts, and local communities against the claims of the centralizing monarchy ensured that the extension of public activity would be subject to parliamentary—read societal—control.[128] State and society, in other words, developed simultaneously and almost symbiotically, such that the Crown became fused with parliament, and parliamentary sovereignty, understood as the 'Crown in Parliament', became the guarantor of the public interest rather than, as in France, the 'Republican state'. This is why, unlike in France, where the state in many respects came before society and remains an all-important term of reference for all governing activity, maintaining almost mystical qualities for the French,[129] in Britain the term itself is not even part of ordinary usage, with 'government' being the operative word.[130] The 'state', nonetheless, when understood as the executive, has been accorded a great deal of power, so much so that, as Andrew Shonfield noted, in the nineteenth century at the same time that Britain 'pursued with evangelical vigor' the limitation of the sphere of government, it recognized 'the need to maintain the strength of an irreducible hard core of governmental power'.[131] This view of a strong but restricted state has been especially focused on business, because Britain has traditionally had 'an abiding prejudice which sees it as the natural business of government to react—not to act' with regard to business.[132] For the philosophy, we can go back to Adam Smith; for the

---

[126] Heclo (1974: 303).

[127] Note that in Lijphart's categorization (1984), Britain is closest to the pluralist end of the scale rather than the corporatist. But this is because for Lijphart, pluralism is really a measure of noncorporatism as opposed to our definition here, which entails a different kind of relationship with a wider range of interest groups, as discussed in Chapter 5. In Lijphart's discussion, the main focus is on relations with trade unions, which has indeed changed little, remaining decidedly noncorporatist, including under Blair—see Flinders (2004). But the relationship with other interest groups has changed, as argued here, toward more statism of a different kind.

[128] Dyson (1980) and see also Knill (2001: 73–6).

[129] See Burdeau (1970) and the discussion in Schmidt (1996: 337–8).

[130] See Dyson (1980) and Schmidt (1996: 21–2).

[131] Shonfield (1965: 386).

[132] Ibid.

practices, we can go all the way back to the privatization of colonial empire building through the British East India company, and to the largely autonomous role of business and the importance of the City during the years of the British Empire and beyond.

Culture, philosophy, and history have together ensured a very different pattern of state–society relations from France, in particular with regard to business. In France from World War II until the 1980s, the state was expected to lead and business to follow. The response to the weakness of French business in the interwar years and its collaboration with Vichy during World War II was state *dirigisme* through active and effective planning and industrial policy in the postwar period.[133] In Britain, by contrast, business was expected to lead and government to facilitate this, although this did not stop government from intervening (albeit unsuccessfully) when it saw the need, for example, through industrial policies in the sixties and seventies.[134] Thus, unlike in France, where the state made policy for business and then accommodated it where necessary, in Britain, government more often than not left business to make policy for itself within parameters set by the government. This ensured that business would in due course develop significant organizational resources of its own focused on governing itself as well as on influencing government policy toward it—through lobbying.

Although lobbies have traditionally been seen as illegitimate when it comes to the core executive, lobbying of parliament is routine and generally accepted as legitimate. Business has long had well-developed lobbies that sought to influence parliamentary decisions. Big companies even went so far as to put MPs on their payroll while labor unions sponsored MPs. They have also cultivated close ties with civil servants, interacting with them through policy networks which, at least up until the Thatcher years, were characterized by close, cooperative relations. All of this proved great preparation for lobbying the EU.

The British tend to be masters of lobbying at the EU level. They were the first to come to Brussels to lobby, and have done so highly effectively. For British business, the clash of cultures has not been as significant as it has been for the French, not only because of their more extensive lobbying experience as independent agents but also because of their closer collaboration with the national government on EU matters (both in the cabinet office responsible for coordination with the EU and in the ministries). Part of the reason for this has to do with the different ways in which business-government collaboration is organized in Britain by contrast with France. Britain's horizontally integrated policy networks tend to be better suited to representing domestic interests in the multipolar, competitive decision-making structure of the EU than France's more vertical, state-dominated networks. This was illustrated

---

[133] Schmidt (1996).   [134] Hayward (1973) and Schmidt (2002).

in the European negotiations on financial services in the late 1980s and early 1990s, where British business was better able to exploit the multiaccess lobbying system of the EU than French business, which remained more dependent on government representation and less present in Brussels.[135] British businesses' success in the EU, in short, comes in part from the fact that, unable to count on the same kind of national government support as their French counterparts or on the institutionalized routes of their German counterparts, they developed direct lobbying strategies which were also quite effective in the EU policy formulation process.

But although the British clearly do better than the French when it comes to business lobbying, the clash of its overall decision-making culture with that of the EU is no less significant than it is for the French. With the British, for whom decision-making is equally political and centralized at the top, the clash is most evident in the frequent British government demands for 'opt-outs' from EU directives, which reflects their uneasiness with not being able to make a last minute political decision when they do not control the process. Moreover, although the British are less likely to make the same lobbying mistakes of the French, even they have occasionally been caught out in a similar manner, for example, in the sale of Rover to British Aerospace, when the British company, on the advice of government, did not have early enough discussions with the EC.[136]

The British policymaking style is also highly adversarial, making it difficult for British state actors to adapt to the more accommodating and consensual style expected in the EU.[137] They are generally more pragmatic and less adept at 'presenting points of national interest in *communautaire* vocabulary.'[138] There was nothing surprising about Thatcher's uncompromising tone in negotiations in the Council of Ministers, which offended many European partners, since it was 'the genuine voice of British politics where a viewpoint is pressed to either victory or defeat', and was equally the tone of the renegotiation of the terms of British entry by the Labour government of Harold Wilson.[139] We should remember, however, that Thatcher's adversarial tone in her dealings with the EU, combined with the poll tax, is what led to her own party ousting her from power.

Thatcher's adversarial approach was not only disruptive to the EU, but also responsible for altering the traditional relations between state and societal actors in Britain. Societal actors, used to close ties with state actors in policy networks and policy communities, where insider politics

[135] Josselin (1996). On the partial narrowing of the differences between French and British firms, see Fairbrass (2003).
[136] McLaughlin and Jordan (1993: 141–2).
[137] See the discussion in Chapter 4.
[138] Buller and Smith (1998), see also Kassim (2000: 47).
[139] George (1994: 53).

predominated,[140] found themselves left outside in policy area after policy area, as state actors began more aggressively to pursue the government agenda, mostly without significant consultation. For business in particular, up until Thatcher, relations with Whitehall had tended to be close and consensus-seeking, so much so that business had as often as not formed 'private interest' governments to manage its own affairs, with policymaking 'franchised' through the 'private management of public business.'[141] Britain's long decline, in fact, has been ascribed to this close interaction, with the strong 'distributional coalitions' preventing needed change,[142] and the 'gentlemanly' style tending to moderate competitive behavior.[143]

Thatcher changed much of this. She shifted from a consensual to an impositional style of governing, with an elaborate communicative discourse to the general public informed by a neoliberal ideology focused on the rollback of the state and with a very thin coordinative discourse with the most affected interests. Thatcher willingly engaged in the conflictual politics that privatized and deregulated business, and that pitted her government successively against the coal miners, the health service, local government, and education. Reforms following the principles of the 'new public management' involving deregulation, contracting out, 'agencification', and privatization changed the way the state operates. In particular, regulation by independent agency has increasingly taken the place of government administration or self-regulation (as in the financial services sector and the privatized utilities),[144] while market principles and competition have been introduced into sectors where nonmarket principles and cooperation had more often been the norm (as in the health sector). Under John Major, moreover, although the style returned to the more consensual approach of pre-1979 governments—with a softer communicative discourse and more coordinative consultation—the rollback of the state continued, as government continued to set the agenda and initiate policy change.[145]

Under Blair, finally, the style, although perhaps more consensual in appearance because of Blair's discursive manner, was every bit as impositional in policy formulation as that of Thatcher, if not more so. According to a study of the Blair government by Anthony Seldon and Dennis Kavanaugh, whereas Thatcher at least kept up the appearances of cabinet government by holding twice weekly meetings that might last as much as two hours despite the fact that she had already made the decision, Blair barely kept up appearances, with much shorter meetings (sometimes lasting no more than forty minutes) in which the decisions had already been made by Blair on the advice of the

---

[140] See Grant (1989), Jordan and Richardson (1983), Marsh and Rhodes (1992), Rhodes and Marsh (1992) and Richardson (2000).
[141] Richardson (1993) and Richardson and Jordan (1979).
[142] Olson (1982) and Richardson (1994: 181).   [143] Schmidt (2002: ch. 4).
[144] See Moran (2004).   [145] Richardson (1993; 1994: 183–5).

special counselors, and which the ministers simply had to accept.[146] This is a very thin coordinative discourse indeed!

The result of the changes in the content and style of governing since Thatcher has been a change in state–society relations. State actors, for one, have been 'steering' more even as they have expanded societal actors' participation through policy networks. The turn to 'governance' has meant bringing more societal actors into the policy formulation process, whether promoted by the government itself or pushed by the EU. In policy area after policy area, societal interests have been consulted more—even if some groups, such as the trade unions, found this merely 'pro forma' under the Thatcher and Major governments. But although trade unions see the 'New Labour' government as more open to real consultation, they tend to attribute their own increase in influence to their EU level participation. This has been especially with regard to collective negotiations on social and employment issues and to how their resulting specialist insider knowledge has enabled them to exert more influence on government formulation of domestic policy, as in the cases of the EU directives on parental leave and part-time work.[147]

The turn to governance has not thereby reduced state control, though. Much the contrary, it seems to have enabled state actors to maintain if not enhance their control. This has remained true for educational, social, and regional policy, despite the fact that societal interests do have more input.[148] In regional policy, more specifically, EU-mandated pluralist consultation had minimal direct effects, since state actors continued to dominate the consultation process, even if it became somewhat more open in some regions by the late 1990s. This was the case in Yorkshire and Humberside, where regional civil servants created a more collaborative 'partnership' without, however, changing the statist nature of the network.[149] In social policy, moreover, the EU had diffuse effects in some cases: consultation remained statist in the EES but moved toward greater pluralism in the social inclusion OMC through genuine government consultation with antipoverty NGOs and greater government information provision to people experiencing poverty. This was a marked improvement over more statist national antipoverty programs, in which there was barely any consultation or information provision.[150]

But while state actors have thus marginally changed their approach to policymaking, by opening up consultation without giving up control of the process, societal actors have changed their own approach to the policy process much more. Insider groups now expect to be listened to while outsider groups frequently turn to contentious politics so as to be heard. In roads policy, for example, they find 'arenas without rules' in which to introduce new ideas and

---

[146] Kavanaugh and Seldon (1999).   [147] Falkner et al. (2005: 256–7).
[148] Bache (2000, 2003).   [149] Bache (2000).
[150] Armstrong (2005: 302–7) and De la Porte and Pochet (2005: 378–80).

discourse through which to reframe the policy domain.[151] What is more, even the traditional insider groups have increasingly considered direct action as an option where it was deemed useful to gain media attention and the ear of government when it seemed not to be listening, as in the case of the farmers.[152] Thus, we see greater democratization in terms of access even as state control remains significant.

In policy areas now ruled by regulatory agencies, moreover, the state–society relationship has also changed as strong regulators governing *for* the people have replaced weak government administrators governing *with* the people, and have opened up the process to greater public scrutiny and pressure as well as to greater considerations of the public interest rather than only producer interests.[153] However, the new regulatory agencies also retain some of the flexibility of the previous system, since the British regulatory culture is one in which agencies have great discretion to make 'deals' with regulated firms.[154]

In telecommunications, for example, where the EU had no significant effects since deregulation came way before any EU-related reforms, the government set up a central regulator that was able to establish the rules of the game itself and deal with firms as an equal. It thereby exercised stronger public (albeit nongovernmental) leadership than government civil servants had ever exercised in the past at the same time that it was also able to establish relationships of trust and even 'clubbishness' that has echoes of the past, although arguably without its closed and collusive character.[155] This regulatory pattern, together with the government's continued preference for voluntary agreements and codes of conduct whenever possible—and in particular in the realms of corporate governance and social policy as a way of avoiding the possibility of interference from the courts—means that some of the flexibility of the old system has been incorporated into the new, making for greater legitimacy.

In the environmental sector, by contrast, EU-mandated policymaking had very significant direct effects, tranforming national processes, albeit after a long period of inertia. British state actors—both the core executive and the Department of Environment—were 'foot-draggers' early on, resisting change largely because the policies and practices under consideration clashed with its own traditionally more decentralized and voluntary approach.[156] British societal actors were barely involved: Industry interests were for the most part happy to leave it to the state to negotiate for them while most national environmental groups remained nationally focused. By contrast, EU-level environmentalists such as Greenpeace and Friends of the Earth as well as the EU Commission became increasingly proactive in using the opportunities provided by EU directives and the ECJ to press for the enforcement of

---

[151] Dudley and Richardson (1998).   [152] Grant (2001).
[153] Moran (2004).   [154] See Coen (2005).
[155] Coen (2005).   [156] Jordan (2002).

EU-mandated policies in the UK.[157] Only in the 1990s did state actors, in particular the Department of the Environment, embrace change, becoming more proactive, less of a policytaker and more of a policyshaper at the EU level at the same time that at the national level it became more transparent, more focused on prevention, and more statist as the EU forced it to intervene in areas that it had traditionally devolved to frontline agencies and to move to more regulatory or legalistic enforcement.[158]

In the 1980s in particular, Britain resisted complying with EU-mandated policies until forced. In water pollution, it dragged its feet because the directive went against its traditional practices of industry self-regulation—until the government transformed its regulatory system to follow the EU model and the principles of new public management as it privatized the water industry.[159] Throughout, moreover, the government response to the EU's pressure was vocal and negative.[160] In air pollution, similarly, Britain delayed implementation because it had to scupper its century-long tradition of controlling emissions through a decentralized process of informal, voluntary local cooperation in favor of a more statist process with centralizing administrative functions and statutory laws with significant legal sanctions.[161] In waste packaging, where the EU also prescribed relatively high, uniform environmental protection objectives and formal, legalistic patterns of interest intermediation, the 'misfit' with British preferences for self-regulation and low standards as well as opposition from industry did not stop the government from transforming the sector.[162] In environmental auditing, by contrast, where the mandated self-regulatory approach fit British processes well, Britain absorbed the EU-mandated practice.[163]

Beyond these sector-specific, EU-related effects, however, the EU has also had a more general impact on British implementation processes. The EU's regulatory approach complicates Britain's regulatory turn in an unexpected way. While the EU's preference for regulation fits well with British reform initiatives since Thatcher, its preference for legalistic enforcement with statutory laws as opposed to voluntary rules and informal agreements does not. When Margaret Thatcher in her famous speech in Bruges in 1988 declared that: 'We have not successfully rolled back the frontiers of the state in Britain only to see them reimposed at a European level', she was not just voicing her objections to EU initiatives on social policy and the single currency. She was also indicating more generally held British concerns about any Brussels-generated rules that would result in a reduction in the space left open to the private sphere—rules that Britain, at least, would find itself duty-bound to

---

[157] Jordan (2002: ch. 11).   [158] Jordan (2002: 41, 198–200).
[159] Knill and Lenschow (1998), Knill (2001) and Knill and Lehmkul (1999).
[160] Bodyguel (1996: 127) and Buller (1998: 65, 80).
[161] Vogel (1986), Rose (1992) and Duina and Blithe (1999).
[162] Haverland (1999).   [163] Héritier et al. (1996: 207–65).

enforce. This helps explain strong British objections in Fall 1997 to a Commission proposal to institute a law to regulate takeovers largely based on the UK's own City Code on Takeovers and Mergers, on the grounds that it would threaten the UK's nonstatutory system by incorporating it into UK legislation, which would in turn allow nuisance litigation designed to frustrate or kill off bids.[164] It also helps explain the UK's five-year battle against passage of the EIA directive on land-use planning, despite the fact that it merely formalized existing practice in Britain.[165] It especially accounts for the Major government's resistance to all manner of EU social policy directives, in particular the working time directive, on the grounds that such policies limited employers' flexibility and reduced their competitiveness.[166] And it fits with the more general concern over red tape, which British groups tend to bang on about much more than their continental counterparts. Illustrative of this is the January 2005 report of the Financial Services Authority that warned about the risk to British financial services groups from the volume of regulation generated by international, but in particular EU, bodies,[167] or the report for the EC on gender mainstreaming which found that although the UK values such community action, it distances itself from it largely because of a 'fear of red-tape'.[168]

For Britain, the dramatic increase in regulations—in particular those emanating from the EU—which have replaced informal, voluntary arrangements with formal rules and statutory law administered by independent regulatory agencies or enforced by the courts, represents a serious challenge not only to traditional governing practices but also to ideas about procedural democracy. The problem is not the loss of the ability to bend the law in order to accommodate societal interests, as in France, but rather the loss of the ability to have flexible, informal arrangements with which to regulate, or self-regulate, society. The challenge, however, is not only to British societal autonomy, given the expansion of public powers over a wide range of areas traditionally left to private actors, but also to British democracy, which has always been predicated on leaving as much room as possible to the private sphere.

The British have long prided themselves on their civility, that is, their ability to work out problems informally following long-established and long-accepted, but never formalized, rules—the best example of this being the lack of a written Constitution. The formalization that accompanies Brussels directives, and especially its insistence on compulsory rather than voluntary rules, only encourages what the British see as the growing rigidification of a

---

[164] *Financial Times* the, Nov. 21, 1997.   [165] See Jordan (2002: ch. 10).
[166] Falkner et al. (2005: ch. 6).   [167] *Financial Times*, January 19, 2005.
[168] OPTEM, 'Study on Integrating Gender Mainstreaming into Employment Policies: Final Report'. Accessed from http://europa.eu.int/comm/employment_social/employment_strategy/eval/survey/survey_gender_en.pdf on April 20, 2005.

public domain which will only increase the likelihood of legal conflict as it undermines the traditional, informal process of conflict resolution. And unlike for the French, there is no procedural answer to the loss of flexibility for the British on this score, other than perhaps to seek to keep Brussels from enacting more rules and regulations. And this has, in fact, been the focus of much of British political leaders' coordinative discourse in the EU and about the EU to national publics in their communicative discourse, in which they go on and on about too many EU rules and regulation.

Germany

In Germany, unlike in either France or Britain, societal actors are integrated with state actors in corporatist policymaking processes. State actors formulate policies in tandem with certain 'privileged' societal actors, mainly business and labor, and implement them with those self-same actors 'as an integral part of administration'.[169] For corporatist systems generally, the state is at best 'an amorphous complex of agencies with ill-defined boundaries, performing a variety of not very distinctive functions', coequal with the organized interests with which it interacts, and striving for accommodation with an egalitarian style and collegiality in decision-making.[170] Interests, moreover, are organized in peak associations which exercise power over a compliant base and engage in tripartite bargaining between state agencies, business, and labor on a voluntary, informal, and continuous basis.[171] Where the state is unitary, as in the Netherlands and Sweden, the strength of the state actor is such that, where societal actors cannot come to agreement, the state can nevertheless act. This stronger form of corporatism is generally not present in countries with federal or regionalized states, as in Germany. But Germany's weaker corporatism is reinforced by legal instruments. In Germany, public law is an important backup to its corporatist state–society relations, while implementation, where it is not corporatist, is often legalistic.

Germany's policymaking pattern has its roots in an evolutionary history over centuries as well as in a critical juncture at the end of World War II which together contributed to the pragmatic ideals that promoted the cooperative state–society relations of the postwar settlement. Unlike in France or Britain, where revolution or evolution ensured societal counterbalancing of state power, in Germany, a centralized monarchical state power grew up without societal counterbalancing. It thus developed an ideal of the 'common best' that was above societal interests rather than the expression of them, and which was established autonomously by the state.[172] In the absence of democracy but with the need nonetheless to maintain legitimacy, this absolute 'state of

---

[169] Cawson (1986: 37).   [170] Schmitter (1985: 33).
[171] Katzenstein (1985: 32–3).   [172] Grimm (1991: 128–9) and Knill (2001: 62).

authority' (*Obrigkeitsstaat*) to determine the common best came to be seen as appropriately constrained by the rule of law (*Rechststaat*), to protect the private sphere against autocratic state intervention.[173]

In addition to the rule of law, two other principles also developed to counterbalance the authority of the state: federal structures and corporatist policymaking process. Federalism came, as previously discussed, with the establishment of the German nation-state. Corporatism involving state accommodation of corporate societal actors has a longer history, going back to the seventeenth century with the resolution of religious conflicts, and which today involves 'a whole range of intermediary interests that partly assume public functions and party represent private interests', including chambers of commerce, banks, employers' associations, unions, and non-profit organizations active in social service provision.[174] Such accommodation has not, however, as in France, been achieved by derogating the rules but, rather, by ensuring that the rules were constructed and implemented with corporate societal actors. The principles of federalism and corporatism are at the basis of the culture of compromise that characterizes German intrastate and state–society relations, as federal state and Länder have to compromise to ensure the appropriate application of laws and implementation of policies, and this works best when done in concertation with corporate societal actors.

All three principles: legalism, federalism, and corporatism combined in the establishment of the Federal Republic of Germany, at the end of World War II. But here, another crucial ingredient was added: the will to make all three principles work together democratically, which resulted in a culture of consensus that rejected an adversarial past in the interests of a more cooperative future.

This combination of consensus-oriented state–society relations within federal arrangements and a respect for the rule of law has meant that corporatist Germany's decision-making culture comes closer to that of the EU than that of France or Britain, given decisions that are generally arrived at consensually, are much less clearly political, and are rarely arrived at quickly or taken at the top. In the complex process that is German decision-making, where most initiatives require agreement among all relevant actors, the top has little power to impose given the need, depending on the issue, for legislative compromises between the government majority in the lower house, the *Bundestag*, and the opposition often in control of the upper house, the *Bundesrat*; for regionally negotiated collective bargaining agreements between the national peak associations of business and labor; and for coordinated agreements between federal government and the Länder on fiscal and implementation policies. This policymaking process, sometimes referred to as *Politikverflechtung*, a

---

[173] Ellwein (1993*b*: 31), Benz and Goetz (1996*b*: 15) and Knill (2001: 62–3).
[174] Benz and Goetz (1996*b*: 17), see also Knill (2001: 64).

system of political interconnectedness and mutual interdependence in which the different levels interact on an equal basis, can only work effectively where there is consensus reached through compromise.[175] As such, Germany's consensus-generating experience is not so different from the EU's many layered institutional process—where decisions also take a long time to wend their way through an approval process involving many actors at many stages, and where the top, political level (Council of Ministers) is less important for the bulk of everyday issues than the bottom, technical level.

These similarities ensure that in Germany as in the EU, a culture of compromise and cooperation is equally well embedded in central actors' expectations. This makes it easier for German civil servants, used to flexible and collegial ways of cooperating, to negotiate the complex circuits of power in Brussels[176] than, say, for French civil servants used to more hierarchical or authoritative bureaucratic relations. It also makes institutional participation in the EU's vast range of committees, standard-setting, and management bodies a more familiar and therefore easier task for German industry than for French, Italian, or even British industry.

Moreover, Germany's organization of industry in cohesive peak associations, where employers have learned to work cooperatively with one another in setting policies and in bargaining with labor, better matches the EU structure. In fact, although the EU was an initial shock to German big businesses, since they were slow to recognize the strategic importance of lobbying directly and competitively, when they did move to the EU level beginning in the 1990s, they had great strategic advantages. This was due not only to their better fit with the EU cooperative interest intermediation process as a result of their experience of corporatism, but also to their larger size, more diversified portfolios, and international merger activity. Subsequently, they developed a dual lobbying style, with one set of relations at the EU level—where they acted on their own as large firms, as well as part of larger national associations—and another at the national level, where they remained firmly embedded in the national associational networks.[177] Thus, German businesses have been much more multilevel players than either the French or the British. German associations active at the national and EU levels, at 29 percent, way outdistance the French, at 14 percent, and also do appreciably better than the British, at 22 percent.[178]

German firms also have an advantage because they are used to influencing the policy formulation process from the ground up, with highly developed national networks that help form a springboard for EU lobbying as well as for participation in standard setting. German businesses were quick to take advantage of the institutionalized venues like standard-setting committees for

[175] Scharpf (1988).   [176] Wessels and Rometsch (1996).
[177] Coen (1998).   [178] Eising (2004).

which their organization in peak associations and their experience of corporatism prepared them well.[179] Already in the early 1990s, German industry controlled 39 percent of the secretariats of the technical committees of the main standards body, by contrast with Britain's 20 percent, France's 14 percent, and Italy's 8 percent.[180] By March 2005, German industry remained ahead, although its lead had diminished. It controlled 27.6 percent of the secretariats of the technical committees of CEN, the European Committee for Standardization (or 77 out of the 279 technical committees) by contrast with Britain's 19.8 percent (55), France's 18.6 percent (52), and Italy's 10.8 percent (30).[181]

Superior organization is not the only reason German firms do well. Their experience of a consensual style of negotiating together with their responsibility for proposing and not simply responding to policy initiatives also helps. Because consensus and compromise with a multitude of actors in horizontal networks without any clearly recognized authorities are the *modus vivendi* of German political life, adaptation to the EU model is not nearly as difficult as it is for the French, typically used to vertically organized networks with clearly defined governmental authorities who generally make the decision. Moreover, although the British are better used to dealing in such networks, they may offend more, given a policymaking culture in which the signature British politeness is often but a thin veneer, barely hiding a combative and conflictual style. This is not to say, of course, that Germans compromise because they cannot deal with conflict. On the contrary, consensus even in Germany is often achieved only through conflict—but the style has less of the brinkmanship qualities than the British sometimes have. German public as much as private actors, out of necessity, have learned not only how to bargain very hard for what they want but also when to give up and acquiesce—unlike the British before Blair in the EU, who often left rancorous feelings when, in the face of defeat, time and again, they opted out instead of compromising.

Germany also does better in terms of general societal access to supranational decision-making. Because the country has been committed to the 'three "Cs"': consensus, corporatism and cooperative federalism', and because that consensus is institutionalized, both the social partners in the tripartite relationship and the governmental partners in the federal system have had access to supranational decision-making. Business and labor associations have been largely included in deliberations involving major moves forward on European integration (e.g. with conferences held in 1988 on the implications of the Single Act), while the Länder, which play a major role in policy implementation in a great number of areas affected by EU regulation, have been largely

---

[179] Coen (1998).
[180] Egan (1994, 2001).
[181] CEN Technical Committee List, 03/03/2005, http://www.cenorm.be/cenorm/index.htm

brought into the policy formulation process by the federal government.[182] And because the Länder and/or the social partners participate in policy formulation and implementation at both national and European levels, there is much less potential for societal actors to feel disenfranchised by the increasing importance of European level decision-making than in statist regimes. This may help explain why protest related to European integration or Europeanization has been so low in Germany that Rucht proclaimed it 'a myth'—among the 13,201 protest events, only 23 explicitly addressed EU matters.[183] By the same token, however, the participation of the Länder and the social partners in implementation also explains the slower implementation process, and Germany's poor implementation record.[184]

The EU's regulatory approach, moreover, is a better fit for Germans than for the French or British. The German notion of regulation, linked with the concept of 'Rechtsstaat', of rules embodied in public law, is close to that of the EU, since it also assumes universal applicability and no exception to the rules.[185] In fact, because Germany has always codified the law much more than Britain, the increasing legal formalization coming from the EU does not cause the kind of consternation that it does in Britain. This said, German regulatory processes, because they follow the German pattern of regulation in which the rules are embodied in public law, tend to allow for much less flexibility than in the UK, where agencies have much more discretion with regard to setting the rules and making deals with regulated firms.[186] In the case of telecommunications, for example, the more rule-based approach to regulation, together with the fact that multiple authorities—the regulatory agency, the competition authority, and the ministry—all have some say, made the development of an independent and credible regulatory agency difficult if not impossible.[187] Deregulation reproduced the traditionally fragmented patterns of administration with a weak regulator focused as much on establishing its own authority vis-à-vis other authorities as over the businesses it regulated.[188]

Germany has also felt the effects of EU-mandated processes in the environmental sector, but much less than in Britain or France, since its policymaking processes fit better with those mandated by the EU. Germany readily absorbed the 1980 Drinking Water directive, even though the EU's demand for higher water quality standards meant that it took government a long time to negotiate.[189] The equally good fit in waste packaging also did not avoid delays in compliance, because the Länder in the Bundesrat opposed the watering-

---

[182] Bulmer (1992: 66–7).   [183] Rucht (2002: 181).
[184] Wessels and Rometsch (1996), see also the discussion in Chapter 2.
[185] See Dyson (1992).   [186] Dyson (1992).
[187] Coen (2005), see also Thatcher (1999, 2002, 2004).   [188] Coen (2005).
[189] Knill and Lenschow (1998), Knill (2001) and Knill and Lehmkul (1999).

down of the higher German environmental protection targets.[190] By contrast, the environmental auditing directive went against Germany's legalistic and interventionist practices in the area; but transformation in the sector was nevertheless quite easy given the country's corporatist traditions.[191] It is important to note, however, that although Germany has had a reasonably good fit in terms of policymaking processes, actual policy implementation has been slowing in recent years, so much so that Germany has gone from pacesetter in the 1980s to foot-draggers today.[192]

In regional policy, the EU-mandated pluralist consultation process has had even less of a direct effect. It ended in statist forms of consultation, much as in France.[193] Despite a general tradition of joint decision-making, German regional officials were as intent as the French on maintaining their monopoly on representation—with the exception of Bavaria. But although Bavaria did in fact seek to establish corporatist consultation with the social partners, it found it so administratively complicated and time-consuming that it gave up in frustration and sent in its own document, thus effectively also constituting a statist process.[194] In soft-coordination policy areas such as the EES and the Social Inclusion OMC, the EU's suggested policies also had little in the way of diffuse effects. This is because mandates for corporatism in employment policymaking and for pluralism in social policymaking were simply added to ongoing corporatist consultation procedures.[195]

In areas subject to competition policy decisions, such as in the liberalization of electricity and the deregulation of banking, however, Germany has experienced significant EU-related knock-on effects. In the electricity sector, the corporatist community, which went into negotiations with a consensus on minimal liberalization, split apart halfway through the process when federal state actors together with some of the bigger electricity providers changed their minds in favor of extensive liberalization while the municipal and other smaller providers continued to oppose it.[196] The result has been a radical deregulation of the German electricity market and an end to the old corporatist process, or any patterned policymaking process at all, given that the state also lacks the capacity to lead.[197] In the banking sector, the characteristic cooperative, corporatist interfirm relationship also broke down. This happened first when private banks complained to the Competition Directorate that the Landesbanken, the regional public banks, along with the regional savings and loans banks, had an unfair competitive advantage because of regional state guarantees on their loans; and second, when cooperation among the public

---

[190] Haverland (1999).
[191] Benz and Goetz (1996a), Knill and Lenschow (1998), Knill and Lehmkul (1999), and Knill (2001).
[192] Börzel (2002b).
[193] Dupoirier (2004).   [194] Dupoirier (2004).
[195] Büchs and Friedrich (2005).   [196] Eising and Jabko (2002).
[197] See S. Schmidt (2005).

banks themselves collapsed once the two biggest regional banks reorganized their activities in response to the complaint way ahead of the others, thus destroying the united front among public banks.[198] In the case of state aid more generally, in fact, the Competition Directorate's centralized, statist approach to decision-making clashes with Germany's more decentralized, corporatist approach. The misfit helps explain the vulnerability of Germany's corporatist communities to break-up in the face of EU action, in particular by comparison with France.[199]

Beyond these sector-specific effects on national policymaking processes, the EU has had a more general impact on German policymaking processes. Because policy formulation occurs increasingly at the supranational level with a larger group of actors while in area after area new regulatory relationships replace the traditional corporatist accommodations, Germany's traditional corporatist policymaking processes have been under pressure. The balance in business-labor relations may have tipped more toward business because business is generally much more present in policymaking at the EU level than is labor. Moreover, corporatist relations within the national business community may have weakened as a result of the greater access and influence of big business at the EU level. The experience of the TABD is a case in point, since individual lobbying by national firms as opposed to through the national employers' association may have reduced the latter's power and cohesiveness.[200] Rather than a paradigm change or a significant diffuse effect of the EU, however, this may follow from long-standing patterns with regard to foreign trade policies, where the Federation of German Industry (BDI) has never been a monopoly player.[201]

All in all, therefore, the EU has not greatly altered Germany's macrocorporatist pattern even if it has affected micropatterns in a few policy sectors. It has therefore not affected the democratic legitimacy of German governance *with* the people nearly as much as in the cases of France or Britain. This is not only because of better institutional fit but also because of a coordinative discourse among policy actors—state and societal—that ensured agreement among state and societal actors on the content of reform, as well as to use the EU successfully in the communicative discourse to the public to promote acceptance of reform, as in the deregulation of the telecommunications and electricity sectors.[202] But this does not mean that German policymaking does not have legitimacy problems.

Germany's corporatist model of policymaking is not a panacea. Whereas business and unions benefit from direct representation in the formulation and implementation of national policies, other citizen interests must rely more on political party representation, which in some cases ensures almost as much access and influence, as in the case of the environmentalists who have their

---

[198] Grossman (2003: 754–5); see also Grossman 2006.   [199] See Thielemann (2000: 411).
[200] Cowles (2001).   [201] Eising (2003).   [202] Eising and Jabko (2002).

own party, and in other cases not, for example, with consumers, women, or immigrants. In fact, although German nonbusiness interests in general are likely to have greater representation in supranational policymaking than the French, the Italians, or even the British, those citizens with less direct access to policymaking at the EU level are also for the most part those with less at the nation-state level in Germany. The EU, therefore, represents a greater opportunity for German nonbusiness societal interests as well, if they were to take advantage of it. But access is, of course, the problem with EU policymaking for German noneconomic societal actors.

Italy

Italy's traditional policymaking processes are easier to describe by what they are not. Unlike in France, where the state traditionally acted in a wide sphere and society reacted, or Britain, where the state acted in a restricted sphere and society was charged to act on its own, in Italy, the state barely acted in a wide sphere and society often acted on its own around the state—with a pattern of derogation of the rules even greater than in France—or reacted to the state-with an even greater pattern of contestation. What is more, where Italy resembled Germany, with state and societal actors acting together, they did so in a clientelistic rather than corporatist manner. It is only since the 1990s that this pattern has changed for the better, as the state has gained in capacity and societal actors in cooperativeness, and as clientelism has given way to corporatism. Such corporatism remains even weaker than that of Germany, however, since the cooperative orientation of societal actors is of recent vintage, not backed up by public law, and much more dependent on action by a state that remains quite weak, despite changes for the better in the early 1990s.

Italy's policymaking pattern has its roots in evolutionary history as well as in two critical junctures, the first at the end of World War II and the second at the end of the cold war. In Italy, like Germany, the evolutionary history is one of late establishment of a nation-state, with a centralized monarchical state power that grew up without the counterbalancing of society. Here, too, then, the state developed an ideal of the public interest as above societal interests rather than as an expression of them. But this was constrained neither by a philosophy focused on the rule of law nor by strong subnational authorities and corporate societal actors. Moreover, the Italian state, as we have already seen, although formally unitary, was weaker and less capable than the German state because it was confronted with an equally strong but ineffective parliament and less cooperative or competent regions. In addition, Italy's corporate societal actors had neither the organizational strength nor the cooperative interrelations of the Germans. Society itself was highly fragmented, divided as it was between North and South, left and right, Catholics and nonbelievers, big business and small, management and labor, rich and poor, and so on.

Added to this mix was the postwar political settlement commonly known as *partitocrazia*, in which parties dominated the interest articulation process, such that where groups exercised influence in policy formulation, they did so as clients and/or patrons of political parties.[203] This, combined with the corruption linked to the system of *sottogoverno* discussed in Chapter 2, ensured that derogation of the rules was endemic, either as a strategy by state actors to buy cooperation or by societal actors to buy off state actors.[204] Unlike in France, then, where derogation of the rules by elite civil servants was generally assumed democratically legitimate because based on technical considerations when the law did not apply as anticipated, in Italy, derogation by patronage-appointed civil servants was mostly seen as illegitimate because based on partisanship, patronage, or payoffs—unless, of course, one thought of this system as *democracy Italian-style*, as Joseph Lapalombara argued shortly before its collapse.[205]

The regions, moreover, especially following the 1970s regionalization reforms, mostly did what they wanted, such that laws promulgated in Rome ended up with very different patterns of implementation, given differences not only in administrative capacity but also in political orientation. This was a far cry, then, from the coordinated implementation of policy engaged in by the German Länder.

Finally, confrontation on a scale even greater than in France was a regular part of the policymaking pattern, especially for those societal actors cut out of the patronage system who engaged in contestation as a regular form of negotiation—through protests, strikes, and the like.[206] Unionized labor in particular, which was much stronger in numbers but as weak and fragmented in organization as in France, had an even more adversarial relationship with management, with an even higher rate of strikes and job actions. Most importantly, whereas the French government was able to bring labor and management to the table, imposing wage bargains that both labor and management ultimately accepted, the Italian government was rarely able to impose agreements acceptable either to labor or management. Moreover, while labor–management relations got better in the 1980s in France—as the labor markets were radically decentralized following passage of laws on worker–management dialogue, privatization, and state withdrawal from the organization of wage bargaining[207]—in Italy, they got worse. Worker–management dialogue was minimal, privatization was stalled, and repeated attempts at corporatist concertation failed, despite deepening economic crisis, as pensions and wages along with public debt and government deficits skyrocketed out of control.[208]

---

[203] On party politics, see Chapter 4.   [204] Lange and Regini (1989: 254–5).
[205] LaPalombara (1989).   [206] Tarrow (1988) and Stefanizzi and Tarrow (1989).
[207] See Schmidt (2002: ch. 4).   [208] Ferrera and Gualmini (2000, 2004).

This *democracy Italian-style* ended with the end of the cold war and the political renewal tied to the collapse of the old party system in the midst of corruption scandals. These changes, combined with the election of technocratic governments in the early 1990s with great credibility, proved especially beneficial with regard to the relationship with corporate societal actors, and the move toward corporatism. Beginning at this time, labor and management became more willing and able to cooperate with one another as well as to coordinate with the government in corporatist policy concertation, which led to successive, highly successful labor and pension reforms.[209] This also smoothed the way for privatization of public enterprises, including the *services publics* utilities, without nearly the same level of strikes and demonstrations as in France. This was not only because the public utilities did not provide the same high level of service as the French but also because they were not imbued by the public with a set of public service values tied to a 'Republican state'. Moreover, EU-mandated policies were in any case easier to legitimate than in France, since in Italy claiming that the EU was responsible for even unpopular policies ensured public acceptance: thus the headline in the *Corriere della Sera:* 'Privatization? It is imposed by the EC'.[210]

Importantly, however, there were some state and societal actors who had risen above the traditional pattern even prior to the end of the cold war. 'Virtuous circles' of magistrates beginning in the 1980s first pursued the mafia and then politicians and businessmen as the cold war drew to a close, contributing to the demise of the old political class. Moreover, in the vacuum created by the collapse of the old political class and in the absence of administrative elites or even of businesses with a sense of community, networks of academics actively involved in projects for political and economic reform already in the 1980s stepped in the breach in the early 1990s to exercise policy leadership.[211] They did this as advisors to the two main electoral coalitions on the right and the left, providing policy-oriented knowledge through a coordinative discourse that projected largely the same messages with regard to political-institutional and economic reform. Some such advisors were behind the referenda on constitutional and electoral reform that succeeded in establishing a more majoritarian electoral system with two main groups of parties on the center right and center left. Others—in particular those in and around the Bank of Italy and the Treasury—crafted the highly successful macroeconomic discourse based on sound monetary policy that pushed state and societal actors alike to accept the austerity budgets, the one-off EU tax, and the labor and pension reforms necessary to enable the country to accede to EMU.

---

[209] See Ferrera and Gualmini (2004).
[210] *Corriere della Sera* 3 August 1992—cited by Bindi with Cisci (2005).
[211] Radaelli (1998).

Successful reform was spurred by a communicative discourse that argued that government instability combined with in-built permeability to interests impeded internally led structural readjustment, and that therefore the *vincolo esterno*— the external constraint or, better, 'opportunity'—represented by EU pressure was necessary and appropriate to promoting reform.[212] The 'tax for Europe', moreover, as the 'price of the last ticket to Europe', mixing EMU with EU membership, appealed to national solidarity and pride, while messages like 'either Europe or death' served to add passion and emotion.[213] As Romano Prodi, prime minister at time, explained it, 'Nobody would have hidden his or her shame and frustration if our country had been excluded from the euro zone. The choice of explicitly calling the increase in taxation a "tax for Europe" persuaded them to accept what in different circumstances would have been scorned and violently refused.'[214] These discourses, added to the Italian postwar foreign policy goal of not being marginalized in Europe, served as powerful arguments for reform, enhancing the government's efforts to get the unions to agree to pension reforms and the public to accept the EMU tax.[215] And again, the newspapers reinforced this, thus the headline in *La Reppublica*: 'The Twelve ask us for tears and blood.'[216]

The 'Italian miracle', then, was one in which both state and societal actors increased in concentration and cooperation, pushed by crisis and promoted by an effective coordinative discourse of economic reform and a communicative discourse focused on the EU. For all this, however, not all problems have been remedied. Far from it. State administrative capacity, although greatly improved, remains a problem—as evident from the compliance patterns discussed in Chapter 2. It stems not only from the central government's inefficiencies and civil service corruption but also from its difficulties in dealing with the politicized regions.

Moreover, corporatism was on somewhat shakier ground since Berlusconi took over in the late 1990s, since his style was more impositional than cooperative. The result was increasing waves of strikes to oppose new initiatives on pension and labor reform, and little progress in these areas. Attempts at social concertation in social policy, as in the cases of the transposition of the parental leave and part-time work directives, also failed after long periods of negotiation due to lack of agreement between labor and business, leaving the government to proceed without them.[217] Protest also picked up again, although new social movements have changed, with the 'new–new' social movements more pragmatic and less radical in their discourse, more moderate

---

[212] Dyson and Featherstone (1996), Radaelli (1998), and Radaelli (2002).

[213] Radaelli (2002: 225–6).

[214] Prodi (2001: 11).

[215] Radaelli (2002); Sbragia (2001); Ferrera and Gualmini (2004), see also Schmidt (2000).

[216] La Reppublica 5 May 1992—cited by Bindi with Cisci (2005).

[217] Falkner et al. (2005: 258–9).

and less disruptive in their protest activities, and more willing to engage in concertation with state actors.[218]

Societal interests have also had a hard time adapting to the EU's policy formulation process. Italian societal interests, given a long training in clientelism, may have had less to learn than the French with regard to the process of lobbying but they have arguably had more to learn as to its content, to wit, that it is neither a political nor an influence-peddling process. What is more, the clash of decision-making cultures has been as great if not greater for the Italians, given that any political decisions, albeit also emanating from the top, have traditionally been much more clearly political in being party and patronage related.

Like the French, moreover, Italian business has also had some difficulty adapting to the lobbying process, albeit for other reasons, given that business influence has typically been handled under-the-table or as part of the clientelistic process. But leaving this aside—assuming that a new learning process with regard to lobbying has also occurred within Italy since the early 1990s and the corruption trials—one might have expected that Italian businesses, given their greater participation in regionally based economies with horizontally linked networks, would have been better prepared than the French to interact in EU-based networks. This has not been the case, at least as judged by the smaller number of Italian businesses heading the secretariats of the technical committees from the early 1990s to today (as noted above), by comparison with the British, Germans, or French. It is important to note, however, that Italy is always fourth, befitting its fourth place among European countries with respect to GDP, and way ahead of any other member-states in heading committees. In CEN, its 10.8 percent or 30 secretariats of technical committees was many more than the Netherlands' 7.5 percent or 21 secretariats, Belgium's and Sweden's 3.6 percent or 10 each, and Spain's 2.5 percent or 7.[219]

Moreover, big Italian businesses have made their presence felt from the very beginning at the EU level, as prime movers in the 'high politics' forums in Brussels, with Agnelli and Fiat active in the ERT,[220] Olivetti and Pirelli in hi-tech issues. Such businesses have also been at the top of Italy's largely vertical lobbying hierarchies, in which large firms such as Olivetti or Fiat represented small- and medium-sized enterprises (SMEs) and consumer interests. This served a variety of purposes, by consolidating Italian business voice in a situation in which the large number of SMEs had difficulty making themselves heard, given a relatively weak state characterized by patronage.[221] It also served to reinforce big businesses' high level of political autonomy from the Italian

---

[218] Della Porta (2001).
[219] CEN Technical Committee List, 03/03/2005, http://www.cenorm.be/cenorm/index.htm
[220] Cowles (1995).   [221] Coen (1998: 80–1).

government, equally manifest in the dual personality they developed—pushing for EU economic stabilizing measures even as they were benefiting from the large system of state aids.[222]

The EU has also contributed to changing policymaking in a large number of policy sectors. EU-mandated changes have had direct effects in areas such as environmental policymaking. In air pollution, the contrast between Britain and Italy is revealing of differences not only in national processes but also in national administrative capacity. While Britain was slow to implement because it had to scupper its century-long administrative tradition, Italy had nothing to scupper, since it had almost no laws, and what it had was barely enforced, given a lack of administrative capacity. But whereas its inertia was initially due to the lack of strong political constituencies pushing for general pollution control and many against, later, once grassroots movements suddenly emerged in the mid-1980s to late 1980s, inspired by the EU and movements in other member-states, implementation was still stymied, largely because of a continued lack of Italian administrative capacity by state actors at both central and regional levels.[223]

In areas of soft coordination in employment and social policy, the EU's diffuse effects have also been limited because of a lack of political commitment and administrative capacity. In Italy, neither the EES nor the Social Inclusion OMC went even so far as statist consultation. Both processes were mainly administrative exercises, with the social inclusion OMC involving no *ex ante* consultation and only very weak information provision. Both paralleled national antipoverty programs which were plagued by a lack of administrative capacity and condemned through a lack of political commitment.[224] Nonetheless, the Italian discourse focused on the EES was used to help 'win the argument at home', having been used prior to national elections to suggest that it would help promote part-time work and after the elections to claim that it would create employment flexibility.[225]

Even the EU's knock-on effects have been mixed: in road haulage, competition policy decisions led to a reinforcement of the old corporatist patterns.[226] In the public utilities arena, by contrast, the EU's knock-on effects have broken up the old corporatist arrangements. A case in point is telecommunications, where deregulatory reforms mandated by the EU have changed the whole array of players along with their interrelationships.[227] In banking, however, recent scandals—most notably the resignation in December 2005 of Antonio Fazio, governor-for-life of the Central Bank of Italy, who ruled the banking system autocratically, favoring Italian acquirers over foreign banks—suggest that the EU had no diffuse or knock-on effects at least up until then.

---

[222] Coen (1998).   [223] Duina and Blithe (1999).
[224] Ferrera and Sacchi (2005) and De la Porte and Pochet (2005: 378–80).
[225] Visser (2005: 199–200).   [226] Héritier et al. (1996).   [227] Thatcher (1999).

Beyond these sector-specific, EU-related effects on national policymaking processes, the EU has also had a more general impact on the Italian implementation process in much the same way as the French. With its more regulatory and legalistic approach to implementation, the EU no longer allows the kinds of exceptions to the rules that were the stock in trade of the paralyzed state, where state civil servants had the administrative discretion to 'adjust' the laws to reward party loyalty, and societal actors simply ignored the rules in order to make things work around the state. Because state actors are now expected to implement the rules without exceptions, and to ensure that societal actors follow the rules, societal actors who have been traditionally left out of the policy formulation process but used to accommodation or confrontation in implementation have problems as great as similarly situated French societal actors. It should come as no surprise that Italian truck drivers were blocking highways along with their French counterparts to protest deregulatory measures into which they had had no input. Moreover, organized labor, which had been so cooperative in the 1990s with regard to labor and pension reforms in response to the *vincolo esterno*, were much less so under the Berlusconi government. This was not just a reaction to Berlusconi's attempts to impose rather than negotiate reform, or the fact that his was a center-right government and that the unions are largely on the left. It also comes from the need to comply with the external constraints represented by EMU which, now that Italy is fully in, no longer serves quite as persuasively as an argument in the coordinative discourse.

Given Italy's record of implementation of directives, however, the worst is surely yet to come. Italian citizens have yet to feel fully deprived of accommodation in implementation by the requirements of the EU's regulatory or legalistic approach to enforcement. But once EU directives are applied faithfully, the loss of flexibility through making exceptions to the rules is likely to be a source of as much if not more citizen disenfranchisement than in France. When Italy does start implementing the rules, though, it will more likely be the judiciary that ensures it, by contrast with France, where civil servants have already begun to adapt themselves to the new mode of operation.

Italy, in short, has benefited greatly from the EU both in terms of its capacity-enhancing and identity-enhancing effects in policy formulation, with the EU representing the 'rescue of the nation-state'. But Italy faces arguably even greater problems than France with regard to the implementation of policy. Moreover, as in France, political leaders tend to be alone to inform and legitimate EU policies to the national public because they also do not have societal interests strong or organized enough to make the bridge between lobbying in Brussels and communicating with their own national members about the outcome. Italy, however, has at least had more of a permissive consensus, given the general national enthusiasm for Europeanization, and the fact that regionalized Italy does not have the same problems with the impact of the EU as unitary France on structural understandings of democracy. But that permissive consensus may nevertheless be on the wane, as economic Europeanization no longer looks so benign with regard to the economy while administrative Europeanization cuts down on Italy's flexible approach to implementation.

Conclusion

Thus, Italy, France, Britain, and Germany have all undergone significant change in their traditional patterns of policymaking as a result of internal dynamics as well as Europeanization. All have moved toward greater pluralism by way of more societal consultation and regulatory implementation even as they retain basic elements of their traditional patterns. Micro patterns of sectoral policymaking show that all countries are increasingly differentiated in their specific policymaking processes. And yet macro patterns still seem to hold in a wide number of areas. In France, state (or public) actors largely remain in control of policymaking even though consultation has indeed grown in policy formulation while regulatory and legalistic implementation has increasingly replaced the administrative discretion of the past. In Britain, similarly, state (or at least public) actors have retained control in policy formulation even though societal access has increased at the same time that they have gained greater control in policy implementation as the self-regulation of the past has given way to more regulatory and legalistic enforcement. Germany has remained largely corporatist, even if some sectors have become more pluralist as a result of knock-on effects and others more regulatory and legalistic. Italy, finally, is a mix, arguably more corporatist than clientelist today, but with some sectors more pluralist, others more regulatory and legalistic—with state capacity the real problem. But for all four countries, Europeanization has affected the procedural bases for democracy. And here, again, Britain has been more concerned than France, but both have been more concerned than Germany, which has itself been more concerned than Italy.

4

The European Union and National Politics

When the French voted 'no' by a clear majority of 55 percent in the referendum on the Constitutional Treaty on May 29, 2005, and the Dutch followed suit by an even larger negative majority of 63 percent three days later, they were stating loud and clear that they were less interested in solving the problems of the EU than in protesting its impact on their own countries. The vote itself, together with the accompanying debates, showed vividly the pressures on national politics that have come with EU-related changes in national policies and practices. The referenda revealed an increasing gulf between the elites, overwhelmingly in favor of European integration, and the people, much more skeptical for reasons ranging from concerns on the right about the EU's impact on sovereignty and identity to concerns on the left about its impact on the economy and the welfare state. But it also showed an alarming rise of the extremes on both the right and the left, along with a split right down the middle even within mainstream parties on the EU's current and future development. Equally importantly, the referenda were just the latest, and most dramatic, signs of new political difficulties centered around increasing European integration and Europeanization. The problem for national politicians today is that the EU has had a significant impact not only on national institutional structures and policymaking processes, as we have already seen, but also on national politics.

There is no name for the EU's system of representative politics. Representation in the EU has little in common with either national majoritarian or even proportional systems, and politics is focused more on interest-based compromise than on party-based competition. As such, the EU level taken on its own is not democratic in the sense of governance *by* and *of* the people via a directly-elected government, although it can be democratically legitimated in other ways, by its combination of governance *with* the people through semipluralist interest representation and governance *for* the people through effective policies generated by and administered through its quasi-federal institutional structures. But this makes for *policy without politics* at the EU level, as policies are made without the kind of debate along a left–right divide normally found at the national level.

By setting this system on top of those of its member-states, the EU has 'de-politicized' national politics by marginalizing national partisan politics at the EU level while Europeanizing more and more policies, thereby removing them from the national political arena. This makes for *politics without policy* at the national level. National party politics have become more divisive on the issue of European integration as a result, while electoral politics have become more volatile, risking the twin problems of growing voter disaffection and political extremism in response to Europeanization. Complicating this general set of effects, however, has been the EU's differential impact on member-states' representative politics depending on where they sit along a continuum between majoritarian and proportional representation systems. Overall, the EU has put more of a damper on the competitive, polarized politics of majoritarian systems than on the more compromise-based, consensus-oriented politics of proportional representation systems.

The chapter begins with a brief sketch of the EU's representative politics in comparison with national politics. It then examines the EU's effects on national politics generally as well as differentially between majoritarian and proportional representation systems in terms of questions related to party politics and electoral participation, referenda and citizen activism, trust in government, identity and class between majoritarian and proportional representation systems. The chapter follows, as usual, with a more detailed consideration of the EU's effects on each of our four country cases, France, Britain, Germany, and Italy. Again, we see further differentiations: While Europeanization has been equally problematic for the polarized, majoritarian politics of France and Britain, Britain has been more politically polarized for much longer around the issue of Europe than France, despite the fact that it has shielded itself more from EU encroachments on national policies. Europeanization has been least disruptive to Germany's consensus-oriented, proportional representation system and most salutary to Italy's more conflictual, mixed system of representation. Although both countries are much less politically polarized on the issue of Europe than either Britain or France, Germany has been less enthusiastic about Europeanization when it has felt EU policy encroachments than Italy, which remains enthusiastic regardless of the encroachments. Finally, in leaders' legitimating discourse about Europe, while the French tout their leadership in the EU as sovereignty and rights-enhancing, the British either decry the loss of sovereignty and rights or tout the economic benefits, the Germans welcome membership in the EU as enhancing national identity, and the Italians also welcome it as a boon for national pride.

The EU's 'Policy without Politics'

Whereas EU institutional structures and policymaking processes have much in common with national structures and processes, EU politics has little in common with national politics. Although the EU bears some institutional resemblance to the federal structures of the US and much to its policy making processes, it bears none at all to its representative politics. The EU lacks a directly-elected president, a strong legislature, and vigorous political parties in a competitive, majoritarian electoral system. What is more, unlike the United States, where politics and partisan competition is ever-present, in the EU, partisan differences and political contestation have been submerged by the general quest for consensus and compromise. Such a lack of resemblance also applies to the EU's own member-states with majoritarian electoral systems, like France, Britain, and Italy (from 1994, given its mixed, predominantly majoritarian system), where first-past-the-post electoral arrangements make for the polarization of party competition into two main parties or multiparty coalitions. With this winner-take-all system, the majority in government is better able to impose its political program. Only member-states with proportional electoral systems, like Germany, the Netherlands, Belgium, and Italy prior to 1994, come closer to the EU in their more consensus-oriented multiparty politics. In these systems, political actors need to compromise, or face immobility. But even here, partisanship is present in a way it is not in the EU (see Table 4.1).

If we were to picture the EU's member-states on a continuum from majoritarian to proportional representation systems, then Britain and France would

Table 4.1. Representative politics of simple and compound polities

	Electoral system	Parliamentary interaction orientation	Political style	Party politics	Partisan politics
Simple polities (UK, Fr)	Majoritarian	Competition	Conflictual	Highly polarized	Yes
Compound polities (US, It post-1994)	Majoritarian	Competition	Conflictual	Highly polarized	Yes
Compound polities (Ger, It pre-1994)	Proportional	Compromise	Consensus-oriented	Somewhat polarized	Yes
Highly compound polity (EU)	Indirect and proportional	Compromise	Consensual	Not polarized	Interest-based (national, public, or organized interest)

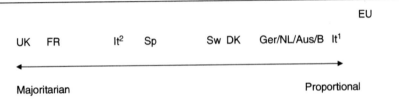

Figure 4.1. Simple and Compound Polities along a continuum between majoritarian and proportional electoral systems (It[1] prior to 1994; It[2] post-1994)

sit at one end, and Italy post-1994 closer to the middle, whereas Germany, Belgium, the Netherlands, and Italy prior to 1994 would be at the other end.[1] The EU would be much farther along the proportional end of the continuum, except that it does not sit on the continuum at all, given that its politics does not elect a government (see Figure 4.1).

Most importantly, however, EU politics is not really politics in any traditional sense of party and partisanship, since it is mainly about interests, whether the national interests projected by the member-states in the Council of Ministers, the European Council, and the IGC; the public interests defended by national representatives in the EP; or the organized interests mediated by European Commission officials as well as, increasingly, by members of the EP. Partisan politics is marginalized in this interest-based politics because political parties at the European level are weak and not very cohesive; the Commission's consensus-oriented, technical approach to policy initiation and development avoids left–right divides; and issues decided in codecision procedures with the Council are voted mostly by supermajorities in Parliament (where the Parliament amends or blocks). Most importantly, there is no EU *government* with the political authority and legitimacy derived from EU-wide elections. Rather, there is EU *governance* in which nationally elected executives in the Council provide for strong but indirect national representation and the nationally elected members of the EP provide for very weak but direct representation. The EP, although the most legitimate institutional body with respect to political participation *by* and citizen representation *of* the people in the EU, remains the weakest of representative institutions with the weakest of partisan politics by comparison with national political institutions and partisan politics.

In the Council of Ministers, of course, politics does come into play. But national leaders have difficulty projecting their political preferences in the

---

[1] Lijphart's quantitative approach puts this more precisely using indicators such as single party government with minimal winning coalitions between 1945 and 1999—where the United Kingdom (with a score of 96.7%) followed by France (62.5%) sit at one end while Germany (with a score of 36.2%), the Netherlands (25.3%) and Italy (10.9%) sit at the other—and disproportionality in legislative elections between 1945 and 1996—where France (with a score of 21.08%) followed by the UK (10.33%) sit at one end while Italy (3.25%), Germany (2.52%), and the Netherlands (1.30%) sit at the other (Lijphart 1999: 183, 334)—as elaborated by Della Porta (2003: 16, 19).

Council, since they come up against the realities of EU policymaking, in which the Commission has control over initiatives, the Council's voting rules demand supermajorities (with QMV) or unanimity, the EP has increasing say as a result of codecision, and everything takes a long time. Even when the Council in the late 1990s had a clear center-left majority concerned primarily about unemployment, it nevertheless failed in its attempt to set up an 'economic government' that would have forced the ECB to add unemployment to its calculations when deciding on monetary policy. The center-right majority since 2004 has done no better in imposing a more neoliberal agenda.

For the most part, the preferences projected by national executives in the policy formulation process in the Council involve 'national interests', defined broadly as consisting of whatever nations are interested in and, concomitantly, of what is in their interest—more liberalization and deregulation (Britain), more environmental protection (Germany and the Scandinavian countries), special regimes for *services publics* or general interest services (France), promoting a larger trade area through eastward enlargement (Britain), attempting to reduce their contribution (Germany), or protecting their full share of EU funding (the CAP for the French, the structural funds for the Italians, maintaining the rebate for the British). In policy implementation, it goes without saying that national interest is also the focus, although politics may also enter, for example, when the UK under the Conservatives dragged its feet on enforcement of social and environmental policy directives and France under right-wing governments refused to limit state aid.[2] But this is another matter.

Only in the EP could one talk about party politics. The EP is itself organized on the basis of political parties with ties to the national parties, and MEPs are themselves elected on political platforms in national elections.[3] The problems with this, however, are manifold. First, the national elections to the EP themselves do not provide for any clear European political mandate because they are nationally based rather than Europe-wide and have been largely second-order national elections at that.[4] Such elections suffer from disappointing turnouts by voters[5]—who have tended to cast their ballots more in response to domestic politics than to European dynamics, often as referenda on national governments' performance (especially when they occur in the middle of a government's term in office).[6] This said, there is evidence to suggest that a certain amount of 'creeping Europeanization' of EP elections

---

[2] See Chapter 2.
[3] See Ladrech (2002).
[4] Reif and Schmitt (1980) and Reif (1997).
[5] Turnout in EP election declined from 70% in 1984 to 59% in 1994, 49% in 1999, and 45% in 2004—Hix (2005: 194).
[6] van der Eijk and Franklin (1996), Gabel (2001), and Mair (2001). See also the discussion in Chapter 1.

may have been occurring, with voters increasingly expressing opinions on purely European issues. But this is not necessarily good news, since it may reflect national electorates' increasing dissatisfaction with the course of EU integration.[7]

Second, parties are underdeveloped at the EU level. They have weak party discipline and cohesion, given the amalgam of different national parties in any given European party grouping with differing agendas, different voting instructions from their national parties, and even different ideologies.[8] But cohesion and discipline have been improving, in particular since the early 1990s,[9] along with the growing consolidation of parties along a left–right divide, as evident from party manifestos and roll-call votes.[10] The consolidation has speeded up since 1999, moreover, once EP leaders decided that the 'grand coalition' approach in the 1994–9 term was in part to blame for continued high abstention rates in the 1999 vote, despite the EP's demonstration of muscle in the Santer affair.[11]

Complicating matters is the growing split along lines of support for or opposition to further European integration. This institutional division between pro-integration 'supranationalism' and anti-integration 'sovereignty' has to be added to the ideological division between a more pro-market, socially conservative right and a more pro-regulation, and socially progressive left.[12] The cross-cutting cleavages along the institutional integration and/or sovereignty dimension and the socioeconomic left-right dimension make for great unpredictability with regard to where any one party grouping, and within that any one of its members, may stand on any given issue, despite growing party consolidation. With regard to EP elections, this institutional integration and/or sovereignty cleavage has long been a 'sleeping giant', because national electorates have been more oriented to the left and/or right party dimension.[13] But this may well be changing—the 2004 EP elections were a foretaste of this, while the fallout from the referenda on the Constitutional Treaty in France and the Netherlands, where major parties were split internally over how to vote, may very well have a snowball effect. Soon, we may see lasting internal national party divisions or even splits based on the integration and/or sovereignty dimension when fighting national elections, and not just EP elections.

Third, much of the legislation that goes through the EP does not lend itself to left/right political divides, given how technical the content. But even when

---

[7] See Manow (2005).
[8] Klingemann (2005).
[9] Hix and Lord (1997), Hix (2005: 187–92), and Hix et al. (2005).
[10] Gabel and Hix (2002), Hix and Lord (1997), and Klingemann (2005).
[11] Kreppel and Hix (2003).
[12] Gabel and Andersen (2002), Marks and Wilson (2000), Hooghe and Marks (1999), and Hix and Lord (1997).
[13] van der Eijk and Franklin (2004: 47).

legislation does lend itself to partisan considerations, the voting rules work against passage of politically charged legislation because second readings of proposed amendments in the codecision procedure require an absolute majority of all MEPs, which really means 67 percent, or a two-thirds majority since attendance is generally no more than 75 percent. This makes for grand coalitions and compromise, since only supermajorities can amend or block Council legislation. Moreover, because the Commission initiates and the Council deliberates before the EP gets even to look at legislation, EP parties are forced to seek the political in legislation that will have been 'depoliticized' in its drafting by the Commission.

But while party politics in the Parliament remains weak, another kind of politics has been quite strong: the politics of the public interest. In the early years, EU 'politics' was almost exclusively concerned with the public interest vs. 'private interests', as the Parliament was the focus of public interest groups unable to gain access to Commission or Council decision-making on issues related to the environment, consumer protection, and human rights concerns.[14] Members of Parliament responded in kind not so much because they were all necessarily sympathetic to such issues but because these issues generally had a broader public appeal, were less well represented in the Commission, and therefore served to increase MEPs' political weight and to gain public attention.[15] More recently, as the Commission has itself become more open to a fuller range of interests, as private interests have also increasingly been lobbying the Parliament, and as partisan politics has been on the rise, the focus in the EP could be restated as one of promoting the 'European interest', that is, the public interest of all European citizens, above the national interest which is the focus of the Council.[16]

However, when it comes to issues of particular importance to their home country, naturally MEPs, pressured by their national governments, revert to the politics of national interest. Political ideology, moreover, does play a role in MEPs' openness to different interest groups, as conservatives and liberals tend to be more friendly to producer interests, Social Democrats and Greens to environmental and social interests, while all pay attention to consumer interests. But national origin also plays a role, as MEPS tend to divide along North–South lines, related to their differing levels of familiarity with lobbying.[17]

The members of the Commission are also divided along many of the same lines as MEPs, whether in terms of national origins, political ideology, competences, or even their view of role for the Commission itself—to serve

---

[14] On the environment and biotechnology, see: Judge et al. (1994).
[15] Kohler-Koch (1997: 85–6).
[16] At least in the view of German MEP Elmar Brok. Conversation with author, Cambridge, MA, December 9, 2004
[17] European Parliament (2003).

intergovernmental interests or to be a supranational power.[18] The one kind of division which is not supposed to affect the Commission, however, is the political—whether the politics of party, the politics of national interest, or even the politics of the public interest. Rather, it is supposed to be a neutral body, a nonmajoritarian, nonpoliticized body, avoiding the politics of national interest, eschewing party politics, being open to all organized interests. And yet, of course, EU Commissioners do have political affiliations, which they are not supposed to bring to their job performance, and they do come from individual member-states, although they are not to represent national interests.

Lately, however, an element of party politics has crept in with the latest nomination of the president of the Commission, where the political 'color' of the president reflected that of the majority in the newly elected 2004 EP. This is something that the proposed Constitutional Treaty would make official by mandating that the European Council take the EP elections into account when nominating a candidate (Article I–26). It introduces the notion that political orientation in appointment is acceptable even though party politics within the Commission must be avoided. The Commission could become even more political than this without becoming politicized if, as Paul Magnette has suggested, it were to provide alternative policy options with ideologically different bases for deliberation by EU political actors, meaning representatives of the member-states and members of parliament. This would contribute to a politically clear public deliberation that therefore does not deny politics or suppress it.[19] Another way of introducing more politics into the EU as a whole, as Simon Hix argues, would be to reverse the current process of appointment of the Commission president, by allowing a majority in the EP to nominate, a qualified majority in the Council to approve. This would not, however, mean that the Commission would become the equivalent of a national-level multi-party coalition government, since the Commission president would not have the same independence to form or change the 'government ministers'.[20] But although more politics might address the problem of the 'democratic deficit' with regard to, participatory democracy, it could undermine the' 'output' legitimacy of the EU's *'policy without politics'*.

For the moment, in any event, 'political' politics largely remains outside the Commission. As for the politics of the public interest, it is much less pronounced in the Commission than in the Parliament. If there is any politics in the Commission to speak of, it is the politics of organized interests, as elaborated in the previous chapter. This is because the Commission's main focus in terms of ensuring its own political legitimacy has been through the expansion of interest consultation *with the people*, in particular, by expanding participation by 'civil society' in policy formulation and expert opinion in rule-making.

---

[18] Hooghe (2001: ch. 4).   [19] Magnette (2001).   [20] Hix (2005: 204–5).

The EU's Impact on Politics in Majoritarian and Proportional Systems

Politics in the EU, in short, does not look much like the politics of its member-states, whether majoritarian or proportional in electoral system, given that it is mainly about the politics of interest rather than about the politics of party. National partisan politics is marginalized at the EU level. First, the national interest politics of the Council means that national ministers speak in the Council in the interest of the nation as a whole rather than as the representative of the governmental majority. Second, the public interest politics of the EP means that members of the EP speak for the 'European' public interest rather than as representatives of electoral majorities. Third, the organized interest politics of the Commission results in citizens exercising voice more effectively when lobbying in Brussels than when voting or protesting in national capitals. The upshot is that the EU carries on making policies without much politics, while at the national level politics continues, but without much sway over EU policies. This has a variety of destabilizing effects on national politics.

The EU's Impact: National 'Politics without Policy'

This lack of traditional representative politics at the EU level puts tremendous pressure on the national politics of all the member-states, with both direct and indirect effects.[21] The direct effects resulting from the lack of EU politics are responsible for the increasing divisiveness of national party politics in EP and national elections, whether over EU policies or the very fact of integration. The indirect effects are related to the Europeanization of policies which, already depoliticized at the EU level, are further depoliticized at the national because taken out of the national political arena. There are also diffuse effects from the experience of the EU's lack of politics, as citizens may lose interest in national politics as a result of becoming accustomed to being governed by institutions that are neither politically representative nor electorally accountable in the traditional way.[22] But the knock-on effects from all the above are even more serious, with EU-related depoliticization serving to demobilize some voters and radicalize others while pushing yet others into alternative forms of participation.

But whether direct, indirect, diffuse, or knock-on in effect, simple polities with majoritarian representation systems are likely to feel the effects of EU-level politics more than compound polities with proportional systems. This is because the EU's compromise-oriented, interest-based politics better fits with the compromise-oriented, party-based politics of proportional representation

---

[21] On this distinction, see also Mair (2006).
[22] See Mair (2006).

systems. In majoritarian systems, by contrast, governments have not generally needed to compromise on their political commitments, given the weakness of the opposition in the winner-take-all electoral system, unless they are in a federal system when one of the two chambers is controlled by the opposition (as in the United States). The subordination of national partisan politics to EU interest-based politics may therefore lead to greater disaffection on the part of the electorates of majoritarian systems, which have come to expect more clearly politically demarcated policies and positions, or, alternatively, more confrontation. The effects are likely to be muted for the electorates of proportional systems, which are used to more ambiguous policies and positions based on compromise, and therefore less likely to find cause for disaffection or confrontation.

These general patterns do not always hold, however. Countries may be oriented toward consensus and compromise even in majoritarian representation systems or toward conflict and contestation even in proportional representation systems.[23] Although majoritarian systems tend to be more polarized and confrontational, in particular, when they occur in unitary states, there are examples of consensus-oriented politics—Britain in the early postwar years until at least 1964, when 'Butskellism' described the pattern of consensus politics between Conservatives and Labour;[24] France in periods of cohabitation, in particular, between Mitterrand and Balladur in 1993–5 (but not Chirac 1986–8) and arguably between Chirac and Jospin in 1997–2002.[25] Moreover, some majoritarian systems may tend to be more confrontational, with citizens regularly protesting in the streets, as in France, others less, waiting for elections to sanction the government, the case of Britain. Similar kinds of distinctions apply to proportional representation systems. Although proportional representation systems are more likely to be infused with a spirit of compromise and a desire to achieve consensus, they can be highly conflictual once in a while, as in the Netherlands in the 1970s, or even most of the time, the case of Italy for the entire postwar period until 1994, when it switched to an electoral system more weighted toward majoritarianism.

History and culture, however, also make a big difference to how different countries respond politically to the EU. Experiences of war, attachment to principles of sovereignty, conceptions of political rights, and constructions of national identity, all color national attitudes toward the EU as well as affect national voting patterns and public opinion. Interests, economic as well as political, needless to say, add to the mix of factors, as do events. All of this together lends insight into why one needs to use caution when using statistical

---

[23] See also discussion by Pasquino (2003).
[24] 'Butskellism' as a term derived from mixing the names of the two principal architects of consensus, Conservative R. A. Butler and Labourite Hugh Gaitskell.
[25] See Elgie (2002).

analyses of elections and opinion polls to help explain the EU's differential effects on its member-states' political systems. But they are nevertheless useful in pointing to differing patterns of member-states' responses to the the EU.

The EU's Direct Effects on National Politics

The EU's direct effects are for the moment very weak, given the lack of the kind of strong, partisan party politics at the EU level which is found at the national level. Multilevel party politics is certainly growing, but party politics is still highly nationalized.[26] It will be a long time before we see the 'supranationalization' of politics at the EU level that would be the equivalent of the 'nationalization' of politics that occurred over the course of the last two centuries in European countries.[27] But as noted above, European elections have already complicated national electoral politics by acting as referenda on government performance and by adding another source of cleavage to national party politics, with the integration and/or sovereignty dimension further complicating the left–right divide. And if the 'sleeping giant' were to arouse itself fully, the politicization of national politics along the integration and/or sovereignty dimension could make it harder for national representative politics to work effectively.

The problems for national politics, moreover, are likely to be greater in majoritarian electoral systems, where political competition is largely organized around the left–right divide, and winning requires the coalescing of forces on either side of that divide. Any cross-cutting cleavages in a two-party system could seriously damage a party's chances of having a broad enough appeal, while in a multiparty system it could affect a coalition's ability to form a large enough coalition with a broad enough appeal. An example of such a problem is what happened to the British Labour Party in the early 1980s, where the internal divisions between those for and against staying in Europe helped produce the schism which led to the creation of a small Social Democratic Party (SDP) and an unelectable Labour Party. But France has experienced more recent problems. The presidential candidate of the left in the 2002 elections, Lionel Jospin, lost in the first round to the extreme right wing candidate Le Pen in part because of the candidacy of Jean-Pierre Chevènement, who had defected from the Socialist Party mainly because of his anti-integration, prosovereignty stance. And then of course there was the French referendum on the Constitutional Treaty, which tore apart the left, but which also did not spare the right.

By contrast, proportional representation systems, in which governmental coalitions may encompass a number of parties with varying agendas, including ones that do not fit the traditional left–right divide, are likely to be better

---

[26] Mair (2004) and van der Eijk and Franklin (2004).
[27] For the nationalization of politics, see Caramani (2004).

able to accommodate yet another party based on yet another cleavage—although too much issue-based fragmentation may be damaging here too. The potential problems are nevertheless more limited because the presence of one or more party with pro- or anti-European flavor does not necessarily directly affect the election, only the formation of a government afterward. And although the resulting government might not perform very well if the cross-cutting cleavages are too strong, it nevertheless has the advantage of a system which pushes parties toward compromise. Governmental coalitions in Denmark and the Netherlands in the early 2000s are examples of this. However, the experience of Italy's mixed majoritarian system, where the Berlusconi government of 2001–6 contained the anti-European Northern League (LN) and the pro-European National Alliance (AN), suggests that it is possible to accommodate extremes within the ruling coalition—but then, Italy has had the experience of half a century of proportional representations systems behind it.

The EU's Indirect Effects on National Politics

The EU's indirect effects are of much greater concern for national politics than the direct effects. This is because, however problematic the direct effects may be to national politics, they are minimal for the moment and in any case promote more, not less, politics. Although these direct effects may be disruptive to existing party politics, they can nevertheless be seen as part of the reinvigoration of representative politics, by intensifying intraparty and interparty competition while contributing to the rise of new third party movements in majoritarian systems and flash parties in multiparty systems.

By contrast, the EU's indirect effects 'depoliticize' national politics through the Europeanization of more and more policy sectors, which effectively removes them from the national political arena. Because the policy content has been settled in Brussels, with little room for national maneuver, most policies will not become a focus of political mobilization or even a topic of political debate. They are likely to be treated in the national legislative arena as merely technical matters, to be passed through national parliaments without debate and administered by national administrations. This is depoliticizing to the extent that it reduces political parties' policy options by limiting the policy space available to competing parties in transposing EU-related policies; the policy instruments, in particular, where authority has been delegated to EU level, nonmajoritarian institutions; and the policy repertoire, where market-making through deregulation and liberalization has preference over market-correcting through industrial policy and state aid. All of this together in turn hollows out party competition and devalues national electoral competition.[28]

---

[28] See Mair (2004, 2006).

What is more, it impoverishes national political debate because once these Europeanized policy sectors are taken off the national political agenda, they are no longer the focus of national leaders' communicative discourse. National leaders, for obvious reasons, do not tend to talk about that over which they do not have much control. Thus, we have not been hearing much about monetary policy in eurozone countries since the single currency came into circulation in 2002 except when governments fail to meet the criteria of the Stability and Growth Pact (SGP); or industrial policy, except when governments fall foul of state aid rules; or even environmental policy, except when governments fail to comply; and so on. These issues have been moved into the Europeanized, coord-inative discourse of policy construction, where they may in fact be part of a highly elaborate EU deliberative process; but the national communicative dis-course with the general public tends to be largely absent. Instead, the public does hear a lot about social policy, education, pensions, public service reform, health services, and the whole range of purely national issues over which national leaders have focused their political agendas, without much reference to Europe. Moreover, where they cannot ignore a Europeanized policy, they are likely to talk about such policies as if the EU has little or nothing to do with them.

Studies that test for the Europeanization of the public sphere by considering reports on European actors and issues in the national media confirm this. The Europub survey of quality newspapers across a range of EU countries between 1990 and 2002 found relatively low (although increasing) levels of European-ization via reference to EU actors or issues across most policy areas. There was a lot of discussion of EU actors in the area of monetary policy in the run-up to EMU (up from 10% to 31%), as to be expected, and of European integration, given enlargement and the constitutional issues (up from 24% to 34%). But in all other issues areas, whether pensions, education, or troop deployment, Europeanization tended to be negligible, while immigration actually declined (from an already low 7% in 1990 to 5% in 2002).[29] Asylum policy in the 1990s illustrates the paradox, since political leaders in several European countries carried the ideas developed in EU summits—such as 'safe third countries'—to their constituents without ever acknowledging their EU source.[30] With regard to newspaper references to EU actors in our four country cases specifically, the UK, predictably, remained lowest (going from 5% in 1990 to 8% in 2002), followed by France (11–13%) and Germany (8–13%), with Italy the highest (7–17%). Consideration of EU issues between 1990 and 2000—regardless of whether the references were to EU or national actors—follows a slightly dif-ferent pattern: The UK remains lowest (up from 11% to 18%); Italy (up from 8% to 26% in 2000) is on a par with Germany (up from 14% to 26%), whereas France shows the greatest Europeanization (up from 19% to 34%), suggesting

---

[29] Europub results—Koopmans (2004: 22–4, 39–45).
[30] Europub results—Koopmans (2004: 5).

that while France may not give credit to EU actors, it at least considers the issues important.[31]

Generally speaking, then, the EU does not receive much attention in the member-states. This is confirmed by Eurobarometer data on knowledge and understanding of the EU, in which when asked how much they know, one in five respondents (19%) admitted to having no knowledge or almost none (scores 1 to 2) and one in two (51%) admitted to having a limited knowledge (scores of 3 to 5 on a scale of 10) as opposed to only one in four (27%) claiming reasonable knowledge (scores 6 to 8) and only 2 percent, great knowledge.[32] This is corroborated by tests of that knowledge, in one of which only 29 percent knew that it was false to say that the last EP election was in June 2002—presumably, the only ones who had voted in the elections in June 2004!

Only where an EU policy is controversial does the issue become politicized at the national level. But this does not do much for national politics. Since EU-related policies, once agreed in the supranational context, are ordinarily not open to reversal, regardless of national leaders' complaints and citizens' protests, the resulting message is mostly depoliticizing. It suggests to the general public that national politics does not matter, even if on occasion the protesters are bought off—as in the case of the farmers in France during the Uruguay round, those in Britain at the time of BSE.

The EU's Knock-On Effects on National Politics

The knock-on effects of all of this can be significant. For one, citizens may turn away from traditional representative politics, demoralized by the lack of national politics and consequently demobilized electorally. This can be seen in the lower rates of participation in national as well as EU voting. Studies of participation in national legislative elections from the mid-1980s to the early 2000s show a significant rise in levels of abstentionism across EU member-states. Interestingly enough, moreover, abstentionism increased more in our two majoritarian systems, France and the UK (up by 14% and 16% respectively from reasonably high levels of 22% and 25%) than our proportional and mixed systems, Germany and Italy (both up by around 7% from relatively low levels of around 11%).[33] Note that countries with proportional representation systems like Belgium, Denmark, Luxemburg, Austria, and the Netherlands exhibit patterns similar to those of Italy and Germany, whereas countries with majoritarian systems like Ireland exhibit patterns similar to France and the UK (see Table 4.2).

Instead of demobilization, however, citizens may instead be mobilized to vote for the political extremes. The rise in populist extremist parties on the

[31] Europub results—Koopmans (2004: 22–4, 39–45).
[32] Eurobarometer 63 (2005).
[33] Idea Data Base, discussed in Bréchon (2002: 103).

Table **4.2.** Evolution of abstention rates in national legislative elections from the 1980s to the 2000s in the EU (in percentages)

	1980s Year	Abstention rate	Late 1990s, early 2000s Year	Abstention rate
Belgium*	1987	6.6	1999	9.6
Denmark,	1988	16.0	2001	12.9
Luxembourg*	1989	12.6	1999	13.5
Germany	1983	10.9	1998	17.8
Sweden	1985	10.1	1998	18.6
Italy	1987	11.1	2001	18.6
Austria	1986	9.5	1999	19.6
Netherlands	1986	15.5	2002	22.0
Greece*	1989	14.2	2000	25.0
Spain	1989	30.0	2000	31.3
Ireland	1987	26.7	1997	33.9
Finland	1987	27.9	1999	34.7
France	1986	21.5	2000	35.6
Portugal	1987	27.4	1999	39.0
UK	1987	24.6	2001	40.6

* Country where voting is obligatory.

Source: Idea Data Base—presented in Bréchon (2002: 103).

Note: Countries are classed by ascending order of abstention rate in the previous election.

right in particular are testimony to this,[34] whether new third party movements in majoritarian systems such as the extreme right National Front in France[35] or flash parties in multiparty systems such as Pym Fortyn's radical right party in the Netherlands. Here, differences in majoritarian and proportional representation systems are apparent not in the fact of extremism—which has little to do with electoral system—but in how it affects electoral politics. So far, only in proportional or mixed representation systems do extreme right parties get to participate in government—for example, Austria (Jörg Haider's party). In majoritarian systems, they tend to affect the first round where there are two-round elections. The clearest example of this was the French presidential election of 2002, when the extreme right candidate Jean-Marie Le Pen knocked out the front-running Socialist candidate, Prime Minister Jospin, who came in third, mainly because his constituency voted for a slew of candidates on the extreme left, in addition to the 3 percent for Chevènement.

There is, however, yet another alternative. Rather than becoming demobilized or radicalized with regard to voting, citizens may instead turn to interest-based politics or to other forms of nonparty-based activism, whether conventional interest group politics, advocacy politics, or social movements. But in all cases, they will be leaving the sphere of representative politics behind to focus on the policymaking process, at regional, national, or EU levels, or even the legal system, via appeal through the national courts to the ECJ. In

---

[34] Betz (1994). [35] Mayer (1999).

compound polities where proportional representation often combines with corporatist processes, whether in unitary, regionalized, or federal states, the temptation to circumvent the political process may be great, since the policy-making process normally links national- to EU-level policymaking. For simple polities, especially where majoritarian politics combines with statist processes and unitary states, the turn to the policymaking process may be easier for some groups, those with the resources to take their case to Brussels, than for others, which may instead take their case to the streets. Confrontation, as we have already seen, is more of a risk for simple polities with statist policymaking processes, and majoritarian politics only accentuates this.[36]

When citizens turn away from electoral politics to the policymaking process, then, representative democracy is diminished in all systems, even though procedural democracy—through the EU's policymaking processes or legal system—may be enhanced. This is not necessarily such a bad thing. In increasingly complex and fragmented societies, where people have less and less time to do more and more, participation *by* the people through voting is a blunt-edged instrument, little able to parse through the complicated questions arising from decisions that have become more and more technical. In this sense, the rise of governance *with* the people—if truly open in access and transparent in process—is a necessary corrective to the vagaries of government *by* and *of* the people through voting. But it may still not be a very satisfying or accepted corrective, in particular, in majoritarian systems, again, where governing with the people is seen as illegitimate.

This is why we have also seen increasing demands for more direct democracy through more citizen participation and control over decision-making, which is to add to government *by* and *of* the people by providing more venues for political participation with more immediate effects. The vehicles have been referenda and citizen initiatives on ballots, mass demonstrations, 'advocacy democracy', grassroots mobilization, and social movements.[37]

In Europe, referenda have spread: the UK had its first in 1975, Sweden adopted the referendum in 1980, Finland in 1987.[38] But countries which have seen the most precipitous losses in government confidence have also seen some of the highest increases in referenda, as in Italy in the 1990s, where citizens were asked to decide such questions as television ownership rules, store opening hours, labour union reform, and residency rules for members of the Mafia (in 1995).[39] The problem with referenda is that at the same time that they increase citizen access, they add to an electoral marketplace that is already experiencing a glut through the proliferation of elections—national,

---

[36] See discussion in Chapter 3.
[37] Dalton, Buerkin, and Drummond (2001).
[38] Dalton, Scarrow, and Cain (2003: 10).
[39] Dalton and Gray (2003: 37).

EU, local, and regional. This can result in voter fatigue and, therefore, less rather than more participation.[40] Moreover, on EU referenda, one gets national answers to European questions.

Citizen activism has also been on the rise.[41] Interestingly enough, in our four country cases, associational membership largely went down between 1990 and 1999 while protest activities—including signing petitions, participating in boycotts or in an authorized demonstration, engaging in a wildcat strike, or occupying buildings—went up. Membership in two or more associations dropped in France from 19 percent to 14 percent, in Britain from 28 percent to 15 percent, in Germany from 38 percent to 22 percent, although in Italy it actually went up from 14 percent to 18 percent. By contrast, participation in at least two acts of protest went up in France from 24 percent to 39 percent, in Britain from 16 percent to 24 percent, in Germany from 12 percent to 25 percent, and in Italy from 17 percent to 30 percent.[42] It is clear that protest activity is not only on the upswing, it is more prevalent than associational activity. But these figures also suggest that we cannot make any generalizations with regard to differences in majoritarian and proportional representation systems.

The problem for the EU is that neither citizen activism nor referenda work in areas subject to Europeanization effects, since direct democracy cannot address the issues that have already been removed from the national political arena. For citizen activism to make a difference, it would need to move to the EU level. But as we have already seen, the obstacles to this are great, just as they are with regard to organizing interest representation at the EU level for most nationally-based groups. Moreover, where direct democracy has been used to address the EU, that is, national referenda on treaties, the results have been mixed—we need mention only the very close vote in the French referendum on the Maastricht Treaty and the negative first vote in Denmark, the negative first vote in the Irish referendum on the Treaty of Nice, not to mention the negative votes in the latest referenda on the Constitutional Treaty in France and the Netherlands. And these results only add to the crisis of representative democracy in the EU.

The EU's Effects on Representative Democracy

Representative democracy has been in a crisis for quite a while now, and not just in the EU. Europeanization is not responsible for the crisis, although it further contributes to it by increasing the pressures on EU member-states

---

[40] Dalton and Gray (2003).
[41] See Ingelhart (1997), Dalton (2003: Chap. 4), Norris (2002: ch. 10) and Dalton, Scarrow, Cain (2003).
[42] Bréchon (2002: 105–6).

through its direct effects on party politics, its indirect effects on political competition and debate, and its knock-on effects on political participation. Indications of the general crisis of representative democracy are found in the surveys, opinion polls, and electoral studies that show that political participation is down while public skepticism of politicians and politics is up, both of which are closely linked to the widespread erosion of citizen confidence in public institutions.[43]

The loss of trust has been generated by national performance problems resulting from external forces such as international economic interdependence[44] and from internal sources such as political corruption.[45] The reasons for loss of trust show as great a variation among EU member-states as among non-EU countries;[46] and here, again, the kind of electoral system does not make much difference. The World Values Survey (WVS) shows that all countries lost confidence in political institutions between the early 1980s and early 1990s, although there was no generalizable downward pattern. Our four country cases actually showed some of the least change in average percentage of confidence between 1980–1 and 1990–1 from a sample of seventeen advanced industrialized democracies. France slipped from 57 percent to 56 percent, Britain from a higher 64 percent to 60 percent, Germany from 55 percent to 53 percent, and Italy from a much much lower 44 percent to 41 percent.[47]

By the 1990s, however, attitudes became much more negative. Eurobarometer polls on citizens' trust in government from 1994 to 2003 show a major drop for all countries. The EU15 began at 44 percent in 1994 and ended at 31 percent in Fall 2003; France began at 46 percent in 1995 and fell to 30 percent in Fall 2003; Germany went from 49 percent in 1994 to 24 percent in Fall 2003; Britain went from 46 percent in 1994 to 24 percent in Fall 2003, and Italy went from 34 percent to 27 percent.[48] (Given the results, it is small wonder that the Eurobarometer eliminated this question altogether from subsequent surveys.) The Eurobarometer polls on citizens' satisfaction with national democracy from 1993 to 2004 give a much better impression, as all are on the rise, with the basic levels higher than in the citizens' trust polls, with the one exception of Italy (see Figure 4.2). This suggests that one can have limited trust in one's government of the moment (meaning the party in power) but can still be satisfied with one's democratic institutions—unless, of course, those

---

[43] Klingemann and Fuchs (1995), Hayward (1995), Klingemann (1999), Dalton (1999), Dalton (2003), Pharr and Putnam (2000), Norris (1999a), Newton and Norris (2000), and Gray and Caul (2000).
[44] Scharpf (2000b).
[45] Della Porta, Donatella (2000).
[46] Dalton (1999: 63), Newton and Norris (2000), and Bréchon (2002).
[47] World Values Surveys (1981–4, 1990–3).
[48] Eurobarometer (1994–2003).

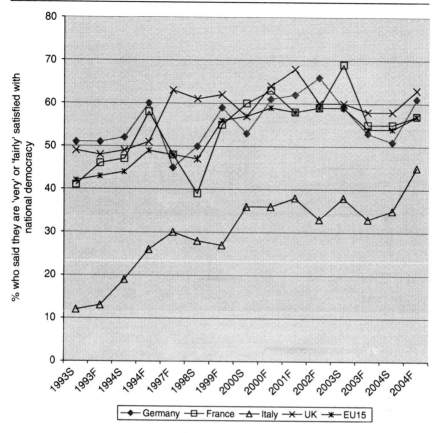

Figure 4.2. Percentage of people who said they were 'very' or 'fairly' satisfied with national democracy

Source: Eurobarometer Results, 1993–2004. Question reads: 'On the whole, are you very satisfied, fairly satisfied, not very satisfied or not at all satisfied with the way democracy works in (OUR COUNTRY)?'

institutions continue to be unsatisfactory but the government is not so bad, certainly the case of Italy during this period. The results of the Eurobarometer polls on citizens' trust in the EU between 1997 and 2003 complete this story. The EU fared only a little better on trust than its member-states on average, at 43 percent for the EU15, with Germany at 36.7 percent and France at 43.1 percent, by contrast with the UK, which trusted the EU much much less than its national government, at 24.3 percent on average, and with Italy, which trusted the EU much much more than its national government, at 56.7 percent on average (see Figure 4.3).[49]

[49] This survey was also dropped in favor of a question regarding satisfaction with EU democracy.

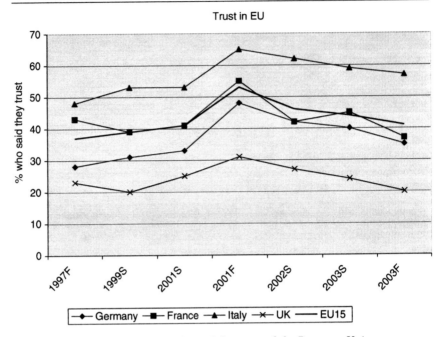

Figure 4.3. Percentage of people who said they trusted the European Union

Source: Eurobarometer Results (1997–2003). Question reads: I would like to ask you a question about how much trust you have in certain institutions. For each of the following institutions, please tell me if you tend to trust it or tend not to trust it?

These differentials in country patterns of support for the EU, with Britain very low, Italy very high, and Germany and France somewhere in between, are reproduced across a wide range of questions. Most telling, perhaps, are the polls asking whether membership in the EU is a 'good thing'. In 1973, the UK was lowest at 31 percent, Italy highest at 69 percent, while France at 61 percent and Germany at 63 percent were paired. In 1981, Italy was even higher at 73 percent, the UK even lower at 24 percent, while Germany at 50 percent was again paired with France at 49 percent, but both now over 10 points lower than the previous decade.[50] Between 1992 and 2004, moreover, the British remained consistently least favorable to the EU, at an average of 35 percent, by contrast with the Italians, who were most favorable, scoring 30 percentage points higher on average. The Germans and the French remained squarely in between, at averages of 47 percent and 49 percent respectively, but often traded places with regard to who was more or less enthusiastic depending upon the moment (see Figure 4.4).

---

[50] Eurobarometers (1973, 1981).

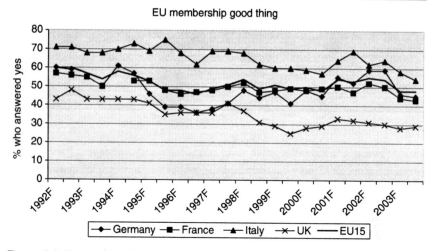

Figure 4.4. Percentage of people who feel their country's membership in the EU is a 'good thing'.

Source: Eurobarometer Results (1992–2004). Question reads: 'Generally speaking, do you think that (OUR COUNTRY'S) membership of the European Union is [A good thing, a bad thing, neither good nor bad, don't know]?'

Eurobarometer polls on feelings of citizenship and identity show a slightly different set of results for Germany and France. The Eurobarometer poll of 1982 showed Germans thinking of themselves as citizens of Europe at a very high rate, 75 percent, by comparison with the French at 61 percent, the Italians at 55 percent, and the British as usual the lowest, at 27 percent. By 1992, the last time this question was asked, the polls showed a staggering decline of feelings of European citizenship among Germans, down to 37 percent, a drop of 38 points, compared to the French who held much steadier, at 54 percent, the Italians at 57 percent, or even the British at 33 percent.[51] The national identity question that substituted for the one on citizenship, asking whether respondents saw themselves in the future as only their own nationality or also European shows the Germans with a composite identity at about the same low level in 1996 (35%) but climbing to end up at the EU average of 46 percent in 2004, while the British with a composite identity hovered around a low 30 percent, the Italians remained near to or above a high 60 percent, and the French near to or above an average 50 percent (see Figure 4.5). Why the collapse in identification with Europe for the Germans in the 1980s and the 1990s as opposed to the French? Leaving aside German unification that may have increased feelings of being mainly 'German' in the 1990s,[52] concern over Eurosclerosis and financial

---

[51] Eurobarometers 17 (1982), 37 (1992).
[52] See Minkenberg (2005).

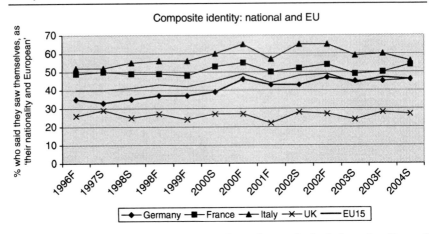

Figure 4.5. Percentage of people who see themselves as both their nationality and European

Source: Eurobarometer Results (1996–2004). Question reads: 'In the near future do you see yourself as (NATIONALITY) only, (NAT.) and European, European and (NAT.), European only, don't know?'

squabbling in the 1980s, and in particular over losing the Deutschmark to the euro in the 1990s, made Germans feel that European integration would only contribute to their problems. This was in contrast to the French, who remained convinced that European integration would help solve their problems.[53] Evidence for this appears in the response to the Eurobarometer question: 'Would you say that your country has on balance benefited or not from being a member of the EU'? Here, Germany remained significantly lower from the mid-1990s on than the EU15 average as well as France and Italy, and even worse than Euroskeptic Britain between 1995 and 1998 (see Figure 4.6).

The contrast between Britain and Italy with regard to feelings of national identity is equally significant, as British scores for those who saw themselves as British alone averaged 63 percent by contrast with the Italians, who averaged 27 percent.[54] Views of how much the country benefits and whether the EU is a 'good thing' also clearly have an effect on the scores, suggesting that identity grows with perceptions of the EU's efficacy in solving problems.[55] But lest one assume that strong national identity correlates with Euroskepticism and that weak national identity correlates with Euro-enthusiasm, we need only cite France, with both a strong identity and strong support for Europe. The explanation: France's perceived leadership role in Europe. More generally, in fact, the strength of national identity may be positively or

---

[53] Schild (2001).   [54] Eurobarometer 1996–2004.   [55] See Kritzinger (2005).

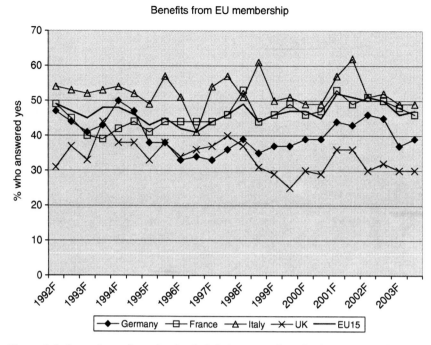

Figure 4.6. Percentage of people who feel their country benefits from EU membership

Source: Eurobarometer Results (1992–2004). Question reads: 'Taking everything into consideration, would you say that (OUR COUNTRY) has on balance benefited or not from being a member of the European Union?' [Benefited, not benefited, don't know.]

negatively correlated with support for the EU depending on perceptions of whether European integration strengthens or weakens national identity[56] or national institutions.[57]

Class also matters. Elites, regardless of country, have tended to be more supportive of European integration as reported in Eurobarometer polls than the masses: in France 93 percent versus 46 percent, Britain 86 percent versus 36 percent, Germany 98 percent versus 39 percent, and Italy 97 percent versus 68 percent.[58] Confirmation for this comes from the Europub study, which finds support for the integration process in articles in the quality newspapers much stronger among state and party actors (+.26 across the seven European countries studied) than among civil society actors, whether economic interest groups (+.12), the media (+.13), or other civil society groups (+.13). Within groups, moreover, among state and party actors support is highest

[56] Schild (2001).
[57] Van Keesbergen (2000).
[58] Eurobarometer no. 46 Autumn 1996.

for the most powerful, that is, governmental actors (+.34), lower for the legislative actors (+.24) and political parties (+.02) which can be held politically accountable. Among economic groups, the stronger economic interests, employers and business organisations, are more supportive (+.20) than the trade unions (+.12). Transnational civil society actors are barely present. Finally, the debates themselves are elite dominated, with state and party actors the main voice to be heard in the communicative discourse in all the issue fields, but in particular European integration, with 81 percent of all speakers, by contrast with transnational civil society actors, which are barely there.[59]

Whatever the differentials in patterns of responses in public opinion polls and the press, however, we should not forget that support of European integration has generally gone down, switching from a permissive consensus to a 'constraining dissensus'.[60] The erosion in support is related to the EU's direct, politicizing effects which have introduced EU-related political cleavages into national politics, to its indirect depoliticizing effects which have removed policies from the national political arena, and to its knock-on effects which have demobilized some voters, radicalized others, and led yet others to alternative forms of activism. As European integration has progressed, Europeanizing not only national policies but also national institutional structures and policymaking processes, national politics has taken the heat, and the public has been responding accordingly.

The EU's Impact on Representative Politics in France, Britain, Germany, and Italy

EU member-states' political responses to Europeanization have common sources in the lack of politics at the EU level and the EU's depoliticization of an ever-expanding number of policies in the national political arena. This has led to increasing polarization on the issue of European integration across member-states along with decreasing political participation and rising extremism. But they manifest themselves in different ways. The way member-states have engaged with Europe is not just a question of *being*, that is, the result of differences in history, culture, and politics, as reflected in deeply rooted national conceptions of citizenship with different understandings of sovereignty, political rights, and identity. It is also a question of *doing*,[61] involving how member-states have engaged in Europe—France as leader through much of the EU's history, Germany as willing partner, Italy as enthusiastic follower,

---

[59] Europub results—Koopmans (2004: 28).
[60] Hix (1999), Hooghe and Marks (1999), van der Eijk and Franklin (1996), and Niedermayer and Sinnott (eds) (1995).
[61] See discussion in Chapter 1.

and Britain, the awkward partner. However, it is equally importantly a question of *saying*, which affects how actors perceive what they are *doing* and transforms their *being*. To legitimate engaging in Europe, the French communicative discourse has emphasized the country's gains in interests and identity through leadership that brings *grandeur* and promotes universal political rights while ignoring the losses to 'Republican state' sovereignty—the concern of the anti-Europeans. The British discourse has focused on the gains in economic interest while remaining silent on the losses to parliamentary sovereignty and the historically established rights of Englishmen—the concern of the Euroskeptics. The German and Italian discourses have been much less concerned with questions of sovereignty and rights than of identity. And here, while German discourse has portrayed EU membership as enhancing a new German-as-European national identity, Italian discourse has presented an Italian-as-European identity as a source of national pride as well.

France

France's Fourth Republic, which went from the end of World War II to 1958, was characterized by great governmental instability. This resulted from a highly proportional system of electoral representation combined with institutional structures that left the central executive weak in the face of a strong but ineffective parliament riven by conflictual party politics. The Fifth Republic that replaced it, in reaction against the parliamentary paralysis of the Fourth Republic, left nothing to chance: It created a first-past-the-post majoritarian electoral system which forced the fractious parties of the left and the right to divide into competing coalitions in order to win elections—something which proved easier for the right than the left until 1981.[62] The result has been a highly competitive and polarized politics in which elected governments have had the capacity to impose policies and the opposition little voice, let alone power to obstruct, except in periods of cohabitation from the mid-1980s on.

The conception of representative democracy infusing this political system has strong roots in the French Revolution. It reflects the Rousseauian view prevalent at the time of the Revolution that democracy presupposes an indivisible general will which ought not be broken apart—not structurally through federalism, not procedurally through the 'particularism' of interests, and not even politically through proportional representation (for the Fifth Republic at least). But it also takes much from the Jacobin notion of the 'one-and-indivisible' Republican state, in which the executive is to carry out the 'sovereign' will of the 'nation' constituted by the French people, by acting as the guarantor of national unity, as the protector of citizens' universal 'rights of man', and as the carrier of universal revolutionary values.[63] Republican citizenship, moreover, is

---

[62] Hoffmann (1959), Williams (1966), Duverger (1996), Schmidt (1996: ch. 1).
[63] See Bellamy (2004: 15), Laborde (2004), and Jenkins and Copsey (1996).

constituted by membership in the nation. But such membership is established not so much by birth as by socialization into a shared political community, constituted by culture, language, and a way of life, with commitment to patriotism as a civic virtue and a basic belief in the superiority of French civic culture.[64] French identity, moreover, is all bound up in this civic nationality, such that feelings of identity and citizenship tend to fuse.

Any form of supranational institution, and not just the EU, necessarily challenges these basic premises of French democracy, since it reduces state autonomy while undermining national identity constructions based on French civic nationality. How then to build the EU without challenging state autonomy or national identity?

President Charles de Gaulle's solution was to claim to maintain national sovereignty and state autonomy by exercising a strong French leadership in Europe which would serve to promote both French interests and identity, by bringing back French grandeur, the greatness that had been France, as it projected France's universalist values onto the rest of Europe. This approach to European integration provoked relatively little dissension in the right-wing governing coalition that remained in power between 1958 and 1981, while on the left, only the Communists (PCF) were opposed, suspicious of European integration because they saw it as a capitalist plot that would expose workers to the dangers of market liberalism.[65] Business played little role, taking a wait-and-see attitude, while French intellectuals sought to defend more universalistic causes, and were little interested in Europe,[66] with the notable exception of Edgar Morin.[67]

De Gaulle's approach to Europe fit well with his renewal of French nationalism and his emphasis on grandeur and *indépendance* in foreign policy. European integration was to enable France to increase its own power in the world through Europe, since Europe was a *multiplicateur de puissance* (multiplier of power). But no need to worry about sovereignty or identity issues. The state could not be subsumed by Europe, de Gaulle insisted, because it was there to defend republican values, because it was sovereign *pour la nation et par la nation* (for the nation and by the nation). Instead of a federal Europe, there was to be a 'Europe of states' (*une Europe des états*) which would serve French national interest, in which France would have a leading role as first among equals, Germany would be contained, and Britain, with its alien 'Anglo-Saxon' approach, would be kept out.[68] The 'empty chair' crisis in 1965 underlined de Gaulle's opposition to any increase in the EU's supranational powers. But neither this, nor his subsequent veto of British membership, was acceptable to the pro-Europeans in the governmental coalition, not only in the UDF but

---

[64] Weil (1991: 472), Brubaker (1992: 10), and Laborde (2004: 51–3).
[65] See Cole (1996).
[66] Frank (1998).
[67] Morin (1987).
[68] See: Cole (2001), Risse (2001), and Larsen (1997: 97).

even among Gaullists. De Gaulle's successor as president, Georges Pompidou, let Britain in, concerned that continued opposition to its membership would isolate France in Europe. President Giscard d'Estaing, leader of the centrist, liberal party, the UDF (Union pour la Démocratie française) gave new impetus to the EU with all manner of institutional reform, in addition to the launch of the EMS.[69] But despite the greater deepening and widening of European integration that took France beyond where de Gaulle might have wished, the Gaullist paradigm—of France having a leadership role in Europe as the dominant partner in an unequal relationship with Germany in order to have a special and leading role at the international level—prevailed.[70]

On the left, the major change in discourse and policy with regard to Europe came with the Socialist government's great U-turn in economic policy in 1983. This is when President François Mitterrand began to modify the Gaullist paradigm, by accepting a greater loss of national autonomy in policymaking through the Single Market Act and EMU. In his discourse, he sought to construct a new vision of France and Europe which conjoined the future of the French nation with that of European integration, as a modernization of the Republican tradition and as a way of ensuring the continued grandeur of France in a globalizing world in which it had little power on its own. This new vision was one in which France in a more federal Europe was to be the country's future, France's grandeur was to be that of Europe, and France's sovereignty was to be extended within the context of a larger European sovereignty.[71] Thus, Mitterrand presented Europe as a necessity for France, in particular, to fend off le déclin (economic decline). But France was also to be a necessity for Europe, with France as a leader of Europe.[72]

For the most part, Mitterrand's new vision predominated, largely unchallenged politically until the debates preceding the referendum on the Maastricht Treaty in 1992. Through the 1980s, the left showed little resistance, with the exception of Jean-Pierre Chevènement, who defended the unitary, Republican state against all loss of sovereignty to Europe, and the Communist Party (PCF-Parti Communiste français), more concerned about economic issues. On the right, the divisions ran deeper. In the center right, there was a split. There were those who chose to embrace Mitterrand's new vision, whether as the only route to future grandeur—mainly Gaullists like Jacques Chirac—or as an appropriate move toward more federalism—summed up by the head of the UDF in 1999, François Bayrou, who insisted that, 'when confronted with the old Jacobin spirit, we are the Girondins of France and the Girondins of Europe'.[73] And there were those who remained faithful to de Gaulle's vision of Europe, with a strong state

[69] Parsons (2003); and see discussion in Chapter 2.
[70] Cole (2001: 58–9).
[71] Risse (2001) and Larsen (1997).
[72] Mitterrand (1986: 15, 104).
[73] Speech by François Bayrou to the Conseil National de l'UDF (Feb. 7, 1999)—cited in Zollner (1999).

and Republican values in a Europe of nations—left-wing Gaullists such as Philippe Séguin and right-wing ones such as Charles Pasqua. On the extreme right, Le Pen's National Front was obsessed about issues related to immigration and sovereignty, while on the far right, Philippe de Villier's *Mouvement pour la France*, was intent on preserving traditional values.

The confrontation between pro-European and anti-European positions came to a head in the televised debate between Mitterrand and Philippe Séguin. Before the debate, Mitterrand had already been engaged in a legitimating discourse by reference to history, about the need to avoid 'the risk of reversion to the destructive rivalries of the past'; to the present, given France's 'eminent vocation to play a determinant role in Europe;' and to the future since 'France is our fatherland, but Europe is our future'.[74] In the debate, Séguin argued that to ratify the Maastricht Treaty was to give up national sovereignty and democracy for an undesirable federal system in which French interests would be subordinated to those of foreign interests. Mitterrand responded that neither national sovereignty nor democracy would be jeopardized; there was no necessary transition to a desired (for Mitterrand) federal system; and neither French interests nor French preferences were in any danger of foreign domination, even if certain competences had naturally and necessarily been transferred over the previous thirty-five years to the European level.[75] Mitterrand won the debate—ensuring the passage of the referendum, albeit by the thinnest of margins (50.8–49.2%).

The Maastricht referendum seemed to settle the matter politically until the legislative elections of 1997. During that time period, there was a virtual taboo among mainstream parties against criticism of EMU, characterized by those opposed to monetary union as a *pensée unique* that refused to contemplate any economic problems with regard to it, let alone ones related to a loss of sovereignty.[76] In the interim, however, concern was growing with regard to the impact of EU policies that now seemed to conflict with French perceptions of identity and sovereignty, in particular, as a result of pressures to rationalize the welfare state related to EMU and to deregulate the *services publics*. Only in the run-up to the 1997 elections, however, did these concerns come to the surface and find expression in divisions over European integration within the right and the left, as the *souverainistes* on the far right, Charles Pasqua in particular, split from the mainstream right to create his own party and Chevènement split from the Socialists to do the same. The debate on Europe, however, showed no clear-cut cleavages between mainstream parties, with both sides largely pro-European, including the PCF.[77] The main issue here is

---

[74] *Politique Étrangère* (December 1991: 151–2, February 1992: 164, June 1992: 122)—cited in Banchoff (1999).

[75] 'Dialogue' (1992).

[76] See, for example, Todd.

[77] See Evans (2003).

that all leaders, once in power, are forced by the reality of the EU to come round to embracing it. It took François Mitterrand two years, Jacques Chirac six months, and Lionel Jospin two weeks!

When the left took power after the surprise win in the legislative elections—inaugurating cohabitation with the right-wing president—there were only subtle changes with regard to the discourse on Europe. President Chirac largely continued to resist conceptualizing Europe as federal or France as anything other than unitary while reiterating Mitterrand's (and de Gaulle's) vision of France's leadership role in Europe. Illustrative is a speech to the European Parliament in 2002, in which he declared that: 'To build and perfect Europe in the twenty-first century is to pursue France's great adventure . . . to make the great voice of France heard: it will spread afar these high standards and these republican values to which our compatriots are so deeply attached . . .'[78] Prime Minister Lionel Jospin, while maintaining the same basic approach, sought to project a somewhat more realistic and less heroic vision, by talking of the costs and benefits of Europe, and by speaking of Europe as a 'federation of nation-states' for which he was willing to trade sovereignty for subsidiarity.[79] On the left at the time, only Chevènement was categorically against any constitutional future, insisting that the German proposal for a federal Europe reflecting its own structures suggested that the country still had not recovered from its Nazi past.[80]

Public opinion over this time period, for all this increasing divisiveness in the political debate, remained largely favorable to the European enterprise. A majority of French in Eurobarometer polls had for a long time continued to see membership as a 'good thing', even though there had been a dip below 50 percent beginning in 2002 (see Figure 4.4). A French IPSOS poll in 2001, moreover, found that a very large majority of respondents, when asked if Europe was mostly a good or bad thing, said that it was good 'for people like them' (73%) and for France in general (78%).[81] Equally significantly, the French remained largely positive about EU level control of policymaking in a wide range of areas. Foreign policy was seen as appropriately the domain of the EU, with 70–80 percent in favor, currency policy fluctuated more, but remained within a 60–80 percent band, while immigration and defense policy fluctuated from 50 percent to above 60 percent, and areas that one would naturally assume to be the national domain, were, the cases of culture, justice, and health and welfare (see Figure 4.7).

Similarly, moreover, a larger majority saw little threat to national identity from the EU. Sofres polls from 1992 to 2001 show that only around 40 percent

---

[78] Jacques Chirac. Speech in Strasbourg to the European Parliament (6 March 2002).
[79] Cited in Cole and Drake (2000).
[80] Comments on May 21, 2000 on France 2—*Le Monde* (May 22, 2000).
[81] IPSOS (December 2001).

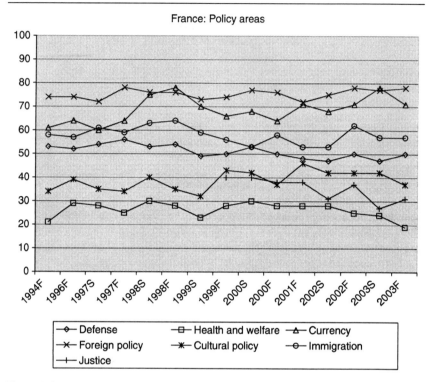

Figure 4.7. Percentage of French respondents who said that decision-making should be at the EU level in a range of policy areas

Source: Eurobarometer Results (1994–2003). Question reads: 'For each of the following areas, do you think that decisions should be made by the (NATIONALITY) government, or made jointly within the European Union?'

of respondents felt that European construction would end by destroying French identity and values, whereas those who saw no menace averaged around 54 percent.[82] It is also interesting to note, however, that although a majority of French retained a composite identity, feeling French and European in Eurobarometer polls (see Figure 4.5), when asked in an IPSOS poll in 2001 to rank by order of importance the territorial level to which they felt most attached: first came France (44 percent), then their region (34%), then their city (33%), and in fourth place only, a majority came in for Europe (53%).[83] Thus, although the French may indeed feel a composite identity, European identity remains very far behind the French.

[82] Sofres (1992, 1994, 1999, 2000, 2001).
[83] IPSOS (December 2001).

Public debate over the EU also reflects the lack of significant concern with the EU. We have already seen that quality newspapers did not engage in much discussion of the EU in the 1990s and early 2000s, and that even in the areas of greatest Europeanization, monetary policy and integration, it remained comparatively low. By 2003, however, interest in the EU had picked up, in particular as a result of increasingly heated public debates about the future institutional configuration of Europe in the run-up to the Constitutional Treaty, on enlargement to the East, and, to a lesser extent, France's failure to live up to the terms of the SGP with regard to its deficit. My own sampling of editorials in quality newspapers found discussions about whether the Constitution should mention God; how enlargement, in particular, with regard to Turkey, would affect the EU; and whether France should conform to the SGP. EU-related identity questions were largely absent, with only the very occasional concern about EU encroachments on French daily life or about what would happen to the 'language of Molière in the future Babel' of Europe.[84] By contrast, there were significant debates about the nature of French 'Republican' citizenship that had been going on since the 1980s and 1990s. These were grounded in a revival of the Third Republic's notion of citizenship, in which *laïcité,* or secularism, had been added to the revolutionary values of *liberté, égalité, fraternité.*[85] The discussions mainly focused on questions of assimilation, 'exclusion', and immigration, in particular, of North African Muslims, and especially with regard to the issue of girls wearing head scarves to school. But these debates have been very *franco-français,* meaning that this was a French issue considered in very French terms. Europe barely figured.[86]

By the summer and fall of 2003, once the Constitutional Convention had reported out, the discussion shifted to what structure the EU should have, whether to hold a referendum, whether the Socialists would vote 'no' to make Chirac look bad, and whether the issue of Turkish membership would muddy the waters in any referendum. Since 2002, moreover, increasing numbers of small books and pamphlets had been coming out on the issue of a 'federal' Europe and on a constitution for Europe, which became a virtual flood of books by late 2004 and early 2005, in the run-up to the referendum.[87] But the discussion of Europe became a major focus of public attention, as seen through TV coverage as well as in individuals' conversations, only beginning in the fall of 2004—as a result of contentious debates by the Socialists over the party position on the referendum and by the Parliament over Turkish membership in the EU—and then again in the spring of 2005, building up from February through to the May referendum campaign, when the EU became the

---

[84] Lexis-Nexis search with the keyword 'Europe' in headline or caption for editorials and op-eds in *Le Figaro* and *Le Monde* the for the year, 2003.
[85] Schnapper (1994), Colas (2000). See also the discussion in Laborde 2004.
[86] Notable exceptions are Balibar (2001) and Ferry (2002).
[87] See, for example, Guetta and Labarde (2002) and Badinter (2002).

primary focus of news attention—number three in March, number two in April, and number one in May.[88]

In the year preceding the referendum, most thought that there would be little problem with passage. Opinion polls on the Constitutional Treaty itself showed that close to two-thirds of French respondents (62%) felt that the EU should have a constitution in spring 2004—although this was lower than Germany's 68 percent and Italy's 78 percent but much higher than Britain's 42 percent (see Figure 4.7). It is important to note that six months after the failure of the referendum, over two-thirds of French respondents still felt that the EU should have a constitution, with 69 percent feeling that it should be renegotiated.[89] The problem was that whereas people felt that the EU should have *a* constitution, was it *this* constitution? Once people began reading the Constitutional Treaty, which had been widely distributed, they began asking whether this 'Treaty establishing a *Constitution* for Europe', as it was entitled, and which began with '. . . his Majesty the King of the Belgians,' was appropriate. Moreover, by this time, a more general mood of pessimism had taken over the country, with growing levels of dissatisfaction with the government—mostly focused on the president. The dislike of Chirac was so high, in fact, that at one point the left-wing newspaper *Libération* suggested that if Chirac really wanted the referendum to succeed, he should promise to resign in response to a favorable vote.

The failure of the French referendum occurred for a variety of reasons.[90] First, in the debates, people spoke past one another. While those in favor discussed the Constitutional Treaty, those against focused mainly on the problems of France, which they now blamed on EU policies. Philippe de Villiers, on the extreme right, said it all in his campaign posters against the Constitutional Treaty when he claimed that: 'We all have a good reason to vote no'. For those on the extreme right, in particular, the Constitutional Treaty raised worries about sovereignty and identity. But they engaged in little active campaigning, since their constituency was already well primed. It was on the left that the 'no' campaign was most vibrant not just on the extremes but even among the moderates—especially once former Socialist Prime Minister Laurent Fabius gave legitimacy to the no by arguing against the neoliberalism of the EU and claiming that voting 'no' was really a 'yes' for Europe, since the Treaty could and should be renegotiated as a more 'social' Europe.

The resulting flood of activism has not been seen since May 1968. Some focused on the simple fact of the 'Constitution', like José Bové, who argued that it would 'fix' for all time the neoliberalism that was threatening the quality of French life. Others focused on Part II, on the Charter of Fundamental Human Rights, to claim, for example, that the Charter's mention of the right to life meant that abortions would be outlawed; that its guarantee of

[88] Piar and Gerstlé (2005: 54–6).
[89] Eurobarometer 64 (2005).
[90] See Laurent and Sauger (2005).

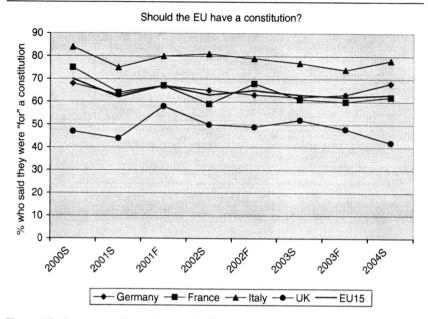

Figure 4.8. Percentage of people who think the EU should have a constitution

Source: Eurobarometer Results (2000–4). Question reads: 'What is your opinion on the following statement? Please tell me whether you are for it or against it: A constitution for the European Union.' [For, against, don't know.]

the right to work was a retreat from the French Constitution's right to have work; and that to talk of services in the 'general interest' meant that France's public services would ultimately be destroyed. Most of the detailed criticism was focused on Part III, however, which merely reiterated past treaties. But this became the opportunity to question the free market basis of the EU since the Treaty of Rome and the economic changes since the 1980s, in which the EU was portrayed as the Trojan Horse bringing in the forces of globalization, destroying French *services publics*, and undermining the welfare state.

The proratification camp did not know how to respond. Having started campaigning late, and on the defensive, supporters of the yes had very little sense about what to say, and they lacked the grassroots organizing, the internet connections, or the mobilizing ability of those against ratification. Most importantly, however, they did not seem able to find a discourse with new ideas that worked. Even Socialist posters that should have helped the 'yes', such as 'Say yes' to 'Social Europe', instead helped the no, given widespread assumptions about the EU's negative affects on the welfare state.[91] To say that the Constitutional Treaty was not about the impact of EU policies on France but rather about the EU as a polity seemed to beg the question. Moreover, even

[91] Duhamel (2005).

speaking to the EU Constitutional Treaty was not easy, since the best one could do is to say that it did not change much other than ameliorate the institutional workings of the EU and constitutionalize the Charter of Fundamental Human Rights, thus responding to the citizens' concerns about an EU level democratic deficit.

President Chirac, in his televised appearances, only made things worse. He basically said that 'you cannot vote no' because, he argued, using the usual time-worn discourse, that a yes vote would enable him to go to the EU to defend French national interests and values, and that Europe was the guarantor of peace and prosperity—despite the fact that peace was now a given, prosperity was not so good, and his leadership was in question. Most notably, on the issue of whether the EU was 'too liberal', rather than challenging the basis presupposition—that liberalism was something imposed by Brussels and bad for France—Chirac claimed that he would protect France by fighting in the EU against 'Anglo-Saxon ultra-neo-liberalism'. Thus, he reinforced the assumption that France was in fact threatened by globalization brought in via Europe rather than telling the truth, that since the mid-1980s France had been liberalizing, privatizing, deregulating, and modernizing the economy in ways that had ensured its continued world competitiveness. It did not help that the services directive had come up in mid-March, just before the referendum campaign, with visions of 'Polish plumbers' who were going to invade France, taking good jobs away from French plumbers while undermining the French welfare state with their lower 'home country' social benefits.

Studies of TV news on European issues show that coverage of the 2005 referendum was on a par with the 1992 referendum (300 + minutes on prime-time news TF1 and France 2), but also that the linkage with social issues was much greater for the later referendum. Whereas in 1992, news coverage about social issues involved only 4.5 percent of the discussion, in 2005 they took up a much larger 24 percent of the discussion.[92] The negative consequences of this linkage can be found in opinion polls on voting intentions in the referendum in mid-April and mid-May 2005. Concerns about the EU's effects on standard of living, unemployment, or social rights (welfare) were as key for those voting 'no' in the referendum as were concerns about the EU's effects on identity (attachment to the EU) and sovereignty (whether to reinforce the EU's powers or to maintain national sovereignty) (see Table 4.3). Interestingly, the greatest shifts in votes from April to May (of at least + 5) were by those who worried about the effects of the EU on their standard of living (in particular the no votes, which went up 15.7 points to 74.7 percent); those who did not think that the EU Constitution guaranteed social rights (the yes votes went down 7.4 points to 19.3 percent while the no votes went up by the same number of points to 80.7 percent); and those who were very or somewhat attached to the

---

[92] Piar and Gerstlé (2005: 71).

Table **4.3.** Voting intentions in the French Referendum on the EU Constitutional Treaty related to social concerns and attitudes toward European integration

	Survey in mid-April 2005 (%)		Survey in mid-May 2005 (%)	
	Yes(%)	No(%)	Yes(%)	No(%)
Confident in evolution of *standard of living*	69.7	30.3	72.9	27.1
Worried about evolution in *standard of living*	41	59	35.3	74.7
Fear effects of adoption of Constitutional Treaty on unemployment rates in France	41.9	58.1	38.9	61.1
Don't fear effects of adoption of Treaty on unemployment rates in France	83.9	16.1	81	19
Agree that with the European Constitution the *social rights* of European citizens are *guaranteed*	81.2	18.8	82	18
Disagree that with the European Constitution the *social rights* of European citizens are *guaranteed*	26.7	73.3	19.3	80.7
Very or Somewhat Attached to the *EU*	72.6	27.4	62	38
Little or Not at All Attached to the *EU*	12.8	87.2	15.9	84.1
In order to respond to the big issues, it is necessary to reinforce the powers of Europe	74.7	25.3	70	30
In order to respond to the big issues, it is necessary to maintain the sovereignty of the country	35.5	64.5	36.9	63.1

Source: CEVIPOF—Brouard and Sauger (2005).

EU (yes votes down 10.6 points to 62 percent, no votes up 10.6 points to 38 percent). This suggests that those already worried about the EU's negative effects on income and welfare were most swayed by the 'no' campaign while a full third of those who identified with the EU nonetheless intended to vote against the Treaty, with over a fifth having shifted between April and May. Interestingly, views on the EU's role in unemployment and on sovereignty issues changed little (under 5 percent for yes and no votes), suggesting that people had made up their minds on these issues long before. By contrast, neither party affiliation nor attitude toward Turkey mattered much.[93]

Finally, the vote showed a major cleavage between elites and masses, as well as elites and masses, with a large majority of people with high incomes (€3,000 a month) in favor while those with low incomes (under €1,000 a month) against, with 79 percent of blue collar workers, 67 percent of employees, and even 53 percent of the middle class against.[94] Among public employees, the 'no' vote was equally high, as it was for the French farmers, despite being the principle beneficiaries of EU subsidies through the CAP. This time around, there was no Mitterrand who in 1992, to the farmer in tears claiming that Brussels was killing him, responded that he would have been dead twenty years before had it not been for Brussels.

The failure of the referendum was no accident. The immediate causes were the combination of an unpopular government, economic and social pessimism,

[93] Piar and Gerstlé (2005: 123–8, 132).
[94] IPSOS poll (May 30, 2005).

and fear of the 'other'—meaning immigrants as much as the EU.[95] It was also a safe way to express one's concerns, because this was not about electing a government, only expressing an opinion in a referendum. And the French have generally been unpredictable in referenda—De Gaulle's defeat in the 1969 referendum on the reform of the Senate—which led to his resignation—is a case in point.

The deeper reasons have to do with the fact that the French have not come to terms with the Europe that they themselves have played a central role in building. As Kalypso Nicolaïdis has put it, the French need to change their *EUtopia*, but a large majority have not yet engaged in the 'Copernican revolution' which would, in Dominique David's terms, take them out of their *hexagonie*, that is, French narrowness of focus on itself.[96] De Gaulle's vision of French leadership of a Europe that enhances French while having little negative impact on French identity while state sovereignty and autonomy remains at the core of political leaders' communicative discourse about the EU and its relationship to France fifty years on. But France now no longer leads Europe, French identity is in crisis, French sovereignty is increasingly pooled, and state autonomy has been replaced by a sharing of supranational authority and control. Equally importantly, the referendum is a sign that the voting public has finally become interested politically in Europe, and wants greater input into EU decisions.[97] In short, they want to bring 'politics' back in, and especially into those Europeanized areas removed from the national political arena, like monetary policy and immigration policy. To respond, French leaders will need not only to devise new discourses that address the normative appropriateness of Europe but also find new ways to bring the public more into the decision-making process with regard to Europe.

Britain

Britain's political system is, if anything, more polarized and competitive than that of France's Fifth Republic, but even more stable, given a first-past-the-post, two-party majoritarian electoral system. Although both systems concentrate tremendous power in the executive—France's Fifth Republic has been called a 'presidential monarchy,'[98] Britain's democracy, an 'elective dictatorship'—Britain's one-party governments have even more power to lead than French multiparty governments. But the British parliament, despite the executive's greater concentration of power, nonetheless has much more

---

[95] Perrineau (2005).
[96] Nicolaïdis (2005: 499–500). The 'hexagon' stands for the shape of the country's national territory.
[97] Dehousse (2005).
[98] Viansson-Ponté (1963).

influence than the French because it has much more 'voice'. Although both parliaments are 'arena' legislatures rather than 'transformative' ones, that is, more 'talking shops' than 'working' parliaments, Britain's talking shop is the focus of real public attention, with much public resonance as a result of the debates on contested issues. Britain's 'Westminster system' is an adversarial one in which government proposes and opposition opposes on such a regular basis that, as Bernard Crick has suggested, parliamentary activities resemble a continuous election campaign.[99] The weekly debates in the prime minister's question time between government and opposition, with prime minister and cabinet on one side, opposition leader and 'shadow' cabinet on the other, represent highly elaborate communicative discourses to the public on the issue of the day.

The conception of representative democracy infusing the British political system comes not from a revolutionary moment, as it does for the French. Rather, for the British it comes from an evolutionary process going back to the Magna Carta, the execution of Charles I in 1642, and the 'Glorious Revolution' of 1689 which established the undivided sovereignty of Parliament, in which the slowly developing rules of democracy are part of their 'unwritten Constitution'. Parliamentary sovereignty itself has been a powerful emotive concept combining a sense of power, authority, influence, independence, and individualism, plus a sense of national self-determination, at the same time that it has been a symbol of 'liberty' and 'Britishness'.[100] Notions of political rights are also bound up in the concept. Thus, whereas French notions of political rights are justified philosophically, by reference to the universal rights of man as declared at the time of the French revolution, the British notion of political rights as embodied in parliamentary sovereignty is justified by reference to history and the traditional liberties of Englishmen.[101] Finally, whereas French Republican citizenship and identity are bound together in a civic nation-state identity, in Britain identity remains separate from citizenship—with identity containing a larger component of ethnicity and territoriality, given the strong sense of being Scottish, Welsh, Irish (of Northern Ireland), and even English, as opposed to 'British', which rallies very few people. Citizenship, instead, is bound up in a sense of rights, duties, and participation.

Any form of supranationalism, and not just the EU, challenges these basic premises of British democracy, just as it does the French. But the EU's consensus-based culture of negotiation is at odds even more with the British political culture than the French—at least since Thatcher. Moreover, European integration clashes with British notions of sovereignty, in particular with the de jure interpretation which assumes a zero-sum trade-off—the Euroskeptic view—by contrast with the de facto intepretation. This latter interpretation takes a more

---

[99] Crick (1970)—cited in Bogdanor (2005: 697).
[100] Peterson (1999) and Baker (2001: 277).
[101] Gamble (1985: 73). See also the discussion in Larsen (1997: 38–9).

flexible perspective, by considering limits to state autonomy as a result of the larger political, economic, and security context, for which Europeanization serves to enhance, rather than diminish, the practical exercise of sovereign authority.[102]

British concerns about the encroachments of the EU go beyond the question of executive autonomy and its implications for parliamentary sovereignty, however, to tap into more deep-seated notions of political rights that also make European integration more difficult to countenance. While European integration for the French can represent an enhancement of their universally established rights, for the British it is more likely to be seen as a threat to their nationally, historically established rights. And because the defense of these rights has often also been perceived as a struggle against the continent and not only the crown, invocation of parliamentary sovereignty is imbued with deep, historical meaning that can be seen as fundamentally anti (continental) European.[103]

The experience of war with the European continent, and in particular, World War II, has also reinforced British identity and pride in citizenship in such a way as to make European integration more problematic for the British. At the end of World War II, while French, German, and Italian leaders in continental Europe, whether Robert Schuman, Konrad Adenauer, or Alcide De Gasperi, saw European unity through supranationalism as the only response to the failures of the nation-state arising from the dangers of nationalism, the British saw only the successes of their own nation-state, and therefore, no need to submerge it through supranationalism. European unity was fine for the 'Europeans', as Winston Churchill made clear, but not for the British, who had been saved by their patriotism, and defended their 'island' in their 'finest hour'.[104] Giving this up was difficult also because of the history of Empire, and the sense, as Anthony Eden put it, that 'Britain's story and her interests lie far beyond the continent of Europe'.[105]

For most of the postwar period, British leaders' communicative discourse to the public about the EU has been cast in terms of gains and losses or problems and opportunities, has tended to be economistic, has typically expressed an overriding concern with the issue of sovereignty, and has preferred intergovernmentalism to any talk of a move toward a federal system.[106] The common view was reflected in Churchill's statement in 1953 that 'we are with Europe but not of it. We are linked but not comprised. We are interested and associated but not absorbed.'[107] And this attitude, rather than pushing the British

---

[102] Wallace (1986) and Lynch (1999: 82–3). See also Patten (2005: 83–7).
[103] Wallace (1986: 383).
[104] Bogdanor (2005: 691).
[105] Cited in Bogdanor (2005: 692).
[106] Preston (1994: ch. 7).
[107] Quoted in Cash (1992: 15).

toward Europe in the early postwar period, oriented them more toward the transatlantic relationship with the United States. For the British at this time, 'Europe' was not to be a unique project but part of the project of the 'West' involved in defending freedom, democracy, and the rights of man, and therefore not to be separated from the Atlantic Alliance.[108] Reluctance with regard to European integration, however, focused not only on the transatlantic relationship but also on the Commonwealth, at least for a while.[109] Moreover, most did not think European integration had much future. Notable in this regard was the British response at the Messina conference which led to the ECSC, when the British representative, Russell Bretherton, is alleged to have declared—in a statement some suggest was drafted by Anthony Eden—that 'you are trying to negotiate something you will never be able to negotiate. But if negotiated, it will not be ratified. And if ratified, it will not work.'[110]

When the British finally did join the EEC, the government gave reasons that were more pragmatic or instrumental than anything else while those opposed invoked national sovereignty and identity. In the first application for membership in 1961, Conservative Prime Minister Harold Macmillan presented membership as necessary for commercial reasons, to protect national economic interest.[111] The view of those opposed was perhaps best expressed by Labour leader Hugh Gaitskell, who rejected membership on the grounds that it would be the end of 'a thousand years of history' and the end of the Commonwealth.[112] But interest won out then, as it did in the later successful application. Labour Prime Minister Harold Wilson's discourse in the renegotiations on entry—which was meant to maintain party unity in a situation in which the majority of party members was hostile but an influential minority of the party leadership was in favor—was one which presented membership as 'defending the national interest against interfering foreigners.'[113] Few at the time saw joining as a potential threat to national sovereignty or identity,[114] except for those on the right wing of the Tory Party such as Enoch Powell and the left wing of the Labour Party. But the difference between the anti-integrationists and the pragmatists (by contrast with the many fewer genuinely pro-integrationists) was less in their understanding of the relationship of Britain to Europe than in their gut-feelings that colored their assessment of the practical benefits and of the dangers to national sovereignty.[115]

For Margaret Thatcher as well, the EU was primarily to be embraced for its economic value, and have little effect on national sovereignty. By sovereignty,

[108] Larsen (1997: 57)
[109] Gowland and Turner (2000).
[110] Quoted in Young (1998: 93).
[111] George (1994: 55, 59).
[112] Quoted in Featherstone (1988: 54).
[113] Barker (1973)—cited in George (1994: 55).
[114] Lord (1992).
[115] Marquand (1979).

Thatcher variously meant Parliament's constitutional supremacy, the executive's independent policymaking capacity, the expression of democratic consent, and nationhood and self-governance. She variously invoked it to oppose EU-related policy.[116] But the language of interest was the focal point of government discourse, which consistently depicted its actions as ones focused on 'standing up for our interests' and 'safeguarding our interests'[117] and to 'fight tenaciously for British interests within' the European Community.[118] Instead of seeing Europe as part of a larger 'grand design' in which the country was to play a pivotal role, as did the Mitterrand government, the Thatcher government saw its role in Europe as one of a sobering influence, of offsetting the grand designs by not 'letting ourselves be distracted by Utopian goals'.[119]

Although Thatcher did much to bring Britain more into Europe, she was always rather wary of Europe since, as she often said, Britain's problems have always come from Europe, the solutions from the United States. During her period in office, the Tory Party itself became increasingly split between pro-Europeans such as Kenneth Clark and Euroskeptics like Nigel Lawson. In the early 1980s, Labour was across the board much more hostile to Europe. But instead of wanting to promote a multiracial Commonwealth, as in the early postwar years, it was intent on making Britain truly socialist, and had pledged in its party Manifesto of 1983 to get out of the European Community if elected—which is part of the reason for the exit of pro-Europeans to the newly formed SDP. Only the Liberals had a consistently pro-European line which went beyond the language of interest to espouse more idealistic support of integration, and which dismissed sovereignty concerns.[120]

Thatcher herself, moreover, actually moved between two different discourses: one which presented integration as a zero-sum game with regard to indivisible, 'crown-in-parliament' sovereignty, the other which saw a close and cooperative relationship as furthering British interests within a larger sovereignty.[121] She used the first primarily in her early years (1979–84), as epitomized by her speech declaring 'I want my money back' with regard to the EC budget. The second came in the middle period (1984–88) when she used a more *communautaire* language as she sought to lead Europe toward greater market liberalism. At this time, she even accepted qualified majority voting because she saw it as serving to move Europe toward economic liberalization, and seemingly overlooked the fact that giving up the unanimity rule represented arguably the most significant loss of national sovereignty yet for Britain. But Thatcher moved back to the first discourse and concerns with national

---

[116] Lynch (1999: 80).
[117] *Conservative Manifesto* (1983)—cited in Larsen (1997: 55–6).
[118] Thatcher's speech to the Conservative Party conference in Blackpool (Oct. 14, 1983).
[119] Thatcher, Bruges Speech (Sept. 20, 1988).
[120] Larsen (1997: 59).
[121] Larsen (1997: 66–8).

sovereignty in her last years (1988–90). In her Bruges speech of September 1988, although Thatcher insisted that Britain's destiny was in Europe, she made much of the differences with regard to national identity and attachment to freedom. Thus, she insisted that: 'We have not successfully rolled back the frontiers of the state in Britain only to see them re-imposed at a European level, with a European super-State exercising a new dominance from Brussels.'

It is in her last years in office that her more strident rhetoric on Europe became too much for many in the Tory Party. Cabinet members by this time were split. Some supported her view, like Nicholas Ridley, who in July 1990, likened giving up sovereignty in the context of the debate over European monetary integration to giving it to Adolf Hitler (and had to resign over the remark).[122] For others, by contrast, such as Geoffrey Howe, sovereignty was a 'resource to be traded rather than guarded'.[123] And this is the position that won the day. Thatcher was deposed as prime minister because her increasing stridency made ongoing negotiations on EMU with other EC member-states difficult; and the Conservatives, as the party of industry and finance, were not willing to be left out of EMU.[124]

The discourse of Thatcher's successor, John Major, proved initially to be much more conciliatory and cooperative. Major saw EU membership as in the national interest, and did not have the deep beliefs about identity, national pride, and sovereignty that stirred Thatcher and the Euroskeptics.[125] But he was restrained by his party both on the social chapter, which the party would not have accepted, and on Monetary Union, for which he had to negotiate an opt-out. This was in large measure because of Thatcher who had 'captured the mood of Conservative party culture with her strident nationalism and her spirited rejection of "'socialism by the back door'"'. And Major was unable to overcome this.[126] His more positive view of Europe did not stop him, however, from carrying on an increasingly negative discourse about the dangers of European integration as his majority in Parliament became more and more narrow. This is when he played on the nationalism that Thatcher had nurtured, in particular with the BSE (mad cow) scare. Subsequently, moreover, once the Conservative Party had lost governmental power and the Euroskeptics had gained control of the party, they became increasingly focused on the political dimensions of the EU, and the fear that it would undermine the institutional bases of traditional executive autonomy.[127] Now came the repetitive discourse about the dangers of a federal 'superstate', although no Tory leader actually ever pledged to leave Europe.

---

[122] Watkins (1992); and discussion in Pilkington (1995: 99).
[123] Howe (1990: 678).
[124] See George (1994: 60).
[125] See Seldon (1998).
[126] George (1994: 61) and Patten (2005: 98–102).
[127] Buller (2000).

By the time 'New Labour' came to power in 1997 under the leadership of Prime Minister Tony Blair, the Labour Party had become much more convinced that British interests were compatible with those of Europe, and it was much more supportive of most EU initiatives than the Tories.[128] In the 1997 electoral discourse about the EU, however, the main difference was that 'New Labour' did not raise any sovereignty or institutional issues with regard to further integration. Prime Minister Blair's discourse on Europe was much more like Thatcher's second, more moderate discourse, which argued for close cooperation to further British economic interests. The most noticeable difference is that whereas Thatcher's primary discourse came down very hard on protecting sovereignty and identity, Blair largely remained silent on these issues when he addressed the question of Europe. But, in fact, he publicly addressed the question of Europe comparatively little in his many years in office. Most notable is the fact that most of his most important speeches about Europe were delivered outside the UK, and that in his election campaigns Europe was largely absent. What came out most clearly is that he saw the EU primarily as an intergovernmental, economic community, despite recognizing its growing political dimension in areas of foreign and security policy. Overall, the assessment of his two terms in office has been one of 'missed opportunities', with the first term characterized by some leadership initiatives—on security and defense policy as well as on enlargement—the second not even that.[129]

On EMU, Blair's argument was much like that of his predecessors, presenting entry as a purely economic issue, promising a referendum if a Labour cabinet recommended it and Parliament agreed.[130] Subsequently, while the Tories ruled out British membership in the single currency for at least two parliamentary terms, Blair's government committed itself in principle to join 'if the economic conditions are met' because 'it is the national interest that will always come first'.[131] But as the 2001 election approached, national interest seemed to be replaced by more narrow political interest, with the commitment of the Blair government to a decision on EMU further delayed. The new defense initiative with regard to Europe appeared to be Blair's way of counterbalancing the backpeddling on EMU, to demonstrate that Britain could still play a central role in Europe. But even here, the minute the media questioned the potential impact of a European army on national sovereignty and the transatlantic relationship, Blair backed off to the point of denying the Europeanness of the project, insisting it was instead all about NATO revival.[132] And

---

[128] Gamble and Kelly (2000).
[129] Smith (2005).
[130] Daniels (1998: 72–96).
[131] Tony Blair, Statement to the House of Commons (February 23, 1999).
[132] Howorth (2002).

once the Iraq war kicked off, Blair focused more on the transatlantic relationship; and had in any event expended all his political capital on the Iraq war.[133]

By 2004, the referendum on the euro had become moot because Blair had promised to hold a referendum on the Constitutional Treaty instead. The pledge of a Constitutional referendum was driven by the desire to keep the issue off the agenda of the 2004 EP elections as well as to keep it out of the 2005 general election. It was also assumed that it would be easier to sell the Constitutional Treaty, where the UK hovered around 50 percent in support at the time Blair decided to go for a referendum (see Figure 4.8), than the euro, where support fluctuated between 20 percent and 30 percent (see Figure 4.9). Blair's expected strategy, to cast it as Britain in or out of Europe, fit well with opinion polls that found across time that a majority tended to favor staying in Europe but out of the euro. According to Mori polls, 53 percent of British favored staying in Europe in 1977, 55 percent in 1987, 58 percent in November 1997, a high of 62 percent in June 2000, and down to 54 percent in June 2003.[134] A Eurobarometer poll of January 2005 shows that this level of support continued, with six in ten (60%) respondents agreeing that UK membership of the EU is a good thing while only 35 percent disagreed. Even more notably, seven in ten (72%) agreed that UK membership was a good thing for all other European countries (vs. 22 percent who disagree).[135] By contrast, Mori showed even larger majorities than Eurobarometer polls in favor of staying out of the euro—62 percent in 1991, 74 percent in November 1996, 71 percent in June 2000, 64 percent in May 2003 (see Figure 4.10).[136]

The referendum on the Constitutional Treaty would have been very hard to win, however, even were Blair to have been able to frame it as a question of Britain in or out of Europe, and successfully pitch it as pitting current economic interests against outdated political values. This is because the pro-European Labour leaders, just as the pro-European Tory leaders (of which there are now in any case very few), had not prepared the public. Public opinion was on its way down, and the press was extremely negative, with erroneous claims—as minister for Europe, Dennis MacShane, complained in a speech to the Birmingham business community—such as: 'the Queen would be replaced, we would be forced to join the euro, Germany would take control of our nuclear weapons, and Brussels would take charge of our North Sea Oil. We would even be forced to drive on the right.'[137] The press also expressed concerns that the Constitutional Treaty would increase social regulation coming from Brussels, stifling British capitalism, while the right to strike in the

---

[133] Garton Ash (2004, 1).

[134] Mori polls (1977–2003).

[135] Flash Eurobarometer 'The United Kingdom and the European Union' (January 2005).

[136] Mori polls (1991–2003).

[137] Dennis MacShane, minister for Europe, Speech to the Joint business Breakfast, Birmingham and Coventry & Warwickshire Chambers of Commerce, West Midlands, 13/08/04.

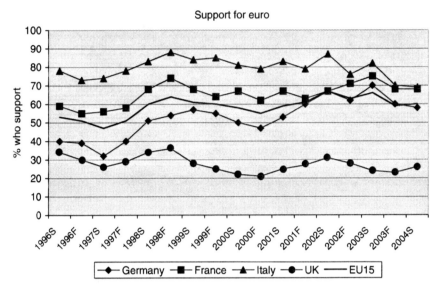

Figure 4.9. Percentage of people who support the euro

Source: Eurobarometer Results (1996–2004). Question reads: 'What is your opinion on the following statement? Please tell me whether you are for it or against it: A European Monetary Union with one single currency, the Euro.' [For, against, don't know.]

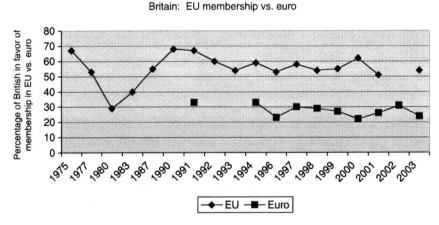

Figure 4.10. British favorable responses on membership in the EU and in the euro

Source: Mori various years. Question on membership in the EU: If there were a referendum now on whether Britain should stay in or get out of the European Union, how would you vote? Question on membership in the Euro: If there were a referendum now on whether Britain should be part of a Single European Currency, how would you vote?

Charter of Fundamental Human Rights would bring back the bad old days. Thus, as Timothy Garton Ash has remarked, we have the paradox of the British voting 'no' for the very reasons that the French might have voted 'yes', and vice versa, since what the French saw as Anglo-Saxon economic neoliberalism, the British saw as French (and German) social overprotectionism.[138]

Once the Constitutional Treaty was put in mothballs following the negative votes in referenda in France and the Netherlands, Blair was off the hook. And certainly, there was no way Blair could have held a referendum in the UK after the French 'no'. A Mori poll on June 1, 2005, a day after the vote, showed a 'no' vote winning by a margin of 72 to 28 percent, and 67 percent wanting a referendum to be held so that they would have the chance to vote 'no'.[139] Blair's speech on June 23 to the EP at the inception of the British presidency interpreted the negative votes on the Constitutional Treaty as a 'vehicle for the people to register a wider and deeper discontent with the state of affairs of Europe' that constitutes 'not a crisis of political institutions' but 'a crisis of political leadership', and then suggested policy directions in which to 'modernize', including rethinking the budget which spent 40 percent on the CAP. The speech was well-received, and raised expectations about British leadership in rethinking the EU.[140] But these expectations were disappointed by the end of the British presidency, which was seen as having done little positive, and descended, once again, into budgetary wrangling to keep its rebate.

Why such a potent degree of euroskepticism in Britain? Beyond issues of history and identity constructions are two other highly salient factors: party politics and discourse. First, the way in which the political parties have divided on Europe has made for much greater EU-related cleavage in Britain than in France. Although the number of Euroskeptics as a share of the vote in parliamentary elections is actually quite close (30.4% in France, 34.5% in the UK, as opposed to the EU average of 15.37%), they manifest themselves quite differently. In the UK, they dominate the right of the left/right cleavage in a two-party majoritarian system, and are largely 'soft sceptics', with 32.4 percent in the Conversative Party vs. the 'hard skeptics' of the tiny UK Independence Party. In France, by contrast, they are marginalized on the right and left extremes of a multiparty majoritarian system, and are predominantly the 'hard skeptics' of the National Front and related groups, at 26.7 percent vs. 3.7 percent of 'soft skeptics' including breakaway parties on the right (around de Villiers and Pasqua) and left (around Chevènement).[141] This makes for much stronger effects in the UK, where the Euroskeptics have been able to

---

[138] *Le Monde* (29–30, May 2005).
[139] Mori (2005).
[140] Tony Blair, speech to the EU Parliament (23 June 2005).
[141] Taggart and Szczerbiak (2002) and Stratham and Guiraudon (2003).

take over an entire party, than in France, where they are effectively kept out of regular politics.

But the second, even more significant factor has to do with the close to twenty years of negative discourse on the EU that created the Euroskeptics in the first place. As Chris Patten describes it, although the de jure view of sovereignty which saw the country giving itself away piece by piece, 'drifting ever closer to its own destruction' in the words of a Conservative Party pamphlet of 2000, had been going on for years, it is Margaret Thatcher who 'gave this drift to destruction its greatest momentum'. With her speech in Bruges in 1988, she 'destroyed at a stroke the traditional British relationship with Europe.... Suddenly, the Conservative Party was dominated by a nightmare vision of Europe—the imminent arrival of the superstate—that still prevails in the party today.'[142] The emphasis on sovereignty and identity, a leitmotif throughout her tenure in office, became a rallying cry against Europe. But Blair can also be blamed for his failure to even try to make a sustained case for Europe and the euro, despite large majorities in Parliament. His claim early on that he could turn public opinion around within three months of deciding to go for the euro, and therefore need not address the topic before then, was a bit of hubris that he was lucky enough not to have had tested. Public opinion can be changed, but this generally takes time, and requires good arguments—since saying what the country has been doing can alter peoples' sense of being—in a positive or negative direction.

Blair's silence on the EU left Fleet street and the Euroskeptics largely unchallenged with regard to their discourse about the deleterious impact of the EU on national sovereignty and identity. Although Blair and his ministers have occasionally inaugurated information campaigns on Europe to dispel the falsehoods, they have been few and far between, and have not been sustained. By contrast, the newspapers have waged a nonstop anti-Europe campaign, when they speak of Europe at all. No need for any sample of the news to confirm this. If anything is printed about the EU—which is rare, as evident in the extremely low rate of news coverage of EU issues and actors—it is likely to be negative, in particular, from tabloids like the *Sun*, but even from seemingly respectable newspapers like *The Times* and the *Independent*. Only the *Guardian* and the *Financial Times* tend to be somewhat pro-European.

All of this has had its effect in terms of public hostility to the EU. The impact of the negative communicative discourse on public opinion can be seen across policy areas across time. A large majority of British tend to be against EU-level control of most areas: these include defense, currency policy, health and welfare, immigration, justice, or cultural policy. Interestingly enough, the only area over which a majority of the British would be willing to have EU

---

[142] Patten (2005: 87, 93).

level control is foreign policy (see Figure 4.11). More generally, in a Eurobarometer poll of 2005, 69 percent agreed that too many decisions that concern the UK are being taken at the European level (vs. 27% who disagree).[143] And yet, when asked about specific policies by the EU in particular policy areas, the British tend to be highly favorable. Thus, for example, 67 percent say that EU rules on safety in the workplace has benefited workers, 59 percent that the EU has contributed in a positive way to the environment, 58 percent that consumers have been protected, and 56 percent that food quality has improved as a result of membership.[144]

Britain's relationship with Europe, in sum, has had a very different political trajectory from that of France. French political elites have had a positive vision of France in Europe which, by emphasizing gains in French leadership, interest, and values while minimizing public awareness of the impact of European integration on sovereignty and identity, has promoted cross-party agreement and public support for a very long time, although it now causes real problems. By contrast, British political elites have had no vision of Britain in Europe at all

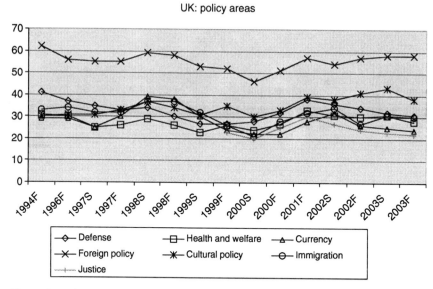

Figure 4.11. Percentage of British respondents who said that decision-making should be at the EU level in a range of policy areas

Source: Eurobarometer Results (1994–2003). Question reads: 'For each of the following areas, do you think that decisions should be made by the (NATIONALITY) government, or made jointly within the European Union?'

[143] Flash Eurobarometer 'The United Kingdom and the European Union' (January 2005).
[144] Ibid.

and, by emphasizing only gains in interest while maximizing public awareness of the impact of European integration on questions of sovereignty, identity, values, and leadership, has provoked EU-related, cross-party cleavages and public disapproval which have only grown over time.

Germany

Germany's political system has been characterized by great governmental stability throughout the postwar period. This has resulted from a proportional system of electoral representation complicated by federal institutions in which periodic national elections that decide the governmental majority in the Bundestag are complemented by frequent regional elections for the Bundesrat (16 *Land* elections held at different times over four years) which affect the composition of the upper house and are fought over federal issues. As a result, coalition governments in control of the lower house can find themselves at any point in their term in office confronted with an opposition-controlled upper chamber. This demands compromise between government and opposition on top of that already required among parties within any government coalition. Such compromises are generally forthcoming. Although elections are highly competitive, and the left–right divide significant, the political cleavages are not so great as to rule out agreements across that divide or even 'grand coalitions' of parties of the left and the right. This has been assured by the culture of consensus and cooperation that developed in the aftermath of World War II as a rejection of the conflictual political culture of the past and in the context of institutions based on legalism, federalism, and corporatism.

The conception of representative democracy that infuses this system is one that operates with notions of 'compounded representation' similar to those of the EU, thus ensuring it fewer problems with European integration than France or Britain, which operate with more 'simple' notions of representation and executive responsibility.[145] Because no one institutional actor has control over the decision-making process and different bodies share responsibility for its outcome, it is likely to adjust more readily to having an added level of shared decision-making with no clear lines of responsibility (once all such bodies have accepted the legitimacy of that added level, of course). Its culture of consensus-building also fits well with the EU. In addition, because Germany's institutional structures ensure that the German state is only 'semi-sovereign', it does not have the same level of problems with regard to questions of sovereignty as France or Britain.

Germany's lack of a full sense of national sovereignty can be explained by reference not only to its federal, semi-sovereign state but also its national identity constructions. For the Germans, Europe was neither what

---

[145] On compounded representation, see Brzinski et al. (1999).

the British saw as the 'other', as a threat to sovereignty and identity, nor what the French saw as a furthering of national identity and an extension of sovereignty. Rather, Europe *is* Germany's national identity, and sovereignty is subsumed under the larger Europe, if it is considered at all. 'Europeanness' as 'Germanness' was the way in which German national identity was reconstructed in the early postwar period—although 'Atlanticist' was also a component of that identity. This was a deliberate effort both to reject the previous German national identity associated with a militarist and authoritarian nationalism and to ensure that Germany would have a peaceful future as part of a more federal Europe.[146] Integration was to ensure, in Hans-Deitrich Genscher's reiteration of Thomas Mann's famous phrase, 'not a German Europe, but a European Germany'.

Importantly, however, elements of the past nevertheless color the present understandings of citizenship and identity. National identity in Germany developed without the 'statist' component of France or Britain, given the absence of a bounded territory under a single monarch. Because of the multiplicity of smaller territories without any single overarching authority, eighteenth century conceptions of nationhood made culture rather than politics its central identifier. In the nineteenth century ethnicity (*jus sanguinis*), rather than territory (*jus soli*), was added to the cultural as the basis for membership in the German 'nation', since the German nation-state, unified by Otto von Bismarck in 1871, did not include all the Germans.[147] Citizenship, thus, remained separate from German identity, which was linked much more to 'ethnic nationality' than French identity, in which ethnic difference was irrelevant. As Renan famously put the distinction, the French 'civic nation' was founded on a 'daily plebiscite' by its citizens, the German 'ethnic nation' was based on inherited characteristics.[148] This understanding of German identity was embedded in the German Basic Law, which established the Federal Republic as the legitimate political expression of Germans bound by culture and ancestry, including those in East Germany.[149] Because this ethnic identity was not fused with a sense of citizenship tied to a state, as in France, where nation-state and national identity could be seen as one and the same, German national identity in terms of ethnicity could more readily allow for Europeanness fused with Germanness to become a substitute nation-state identity. This was also possible because the Federal Republic was an incomplete nation-state in the process of working out an identity.[150]

The subsuming of nation-state identity under EU identity worked so well not only because of an ethnicity-based understanding of national identity and

---

[146] See Banchoff (1999) and Risse (2001).
[147] Preuss (2004), Brubaker (1992), and Minkenberg (2005).
[148] Renan (1947).
[149] Preuss (2004), Banchoff (1999), and Brubaker (1992).
[150] See Zimmer (1999).

a weak conception of sovereignty but also because German national interest was reconstructed as European interest. This included not only foreign policy interests but also, importantly, economic interest. Close economic linkage with the rest of Europe was not only economically advantageous, given Germany's large, export-oriented industrial sector, it was politically advantageous because it demonstrated Germany's commitment to economic and political integration.[151] Equally importantly, Germany's willingness to be the paymaster for Europe—to expiate its guilt because of the war as well as to make Europe work through side payments to ensure agreement by reluctant member-states—put Germany at the center of Europe. But although in the center, it did not lead, having what has sometimes been called a 'leadership avoidance reflex'.[152] And it could not, given federal structures that, as we have already seen, made it hard for it to decide what its preference were, let alone project them to the EU level.[153] Rather, it pursued its interests not unilaterally but in partnership with others, mostly France, and it achieved its interests indirectly, through the generalization of its own institutional patterns in the EU, whether with regard to monetary integration, standard-setting, or regional inclusion in decision-making.[154]

Much of this conceptual reconstruction of sovereignty, identity, and interest was set in the early postwar period. Chancellor Konrad Adenauer is the leader who brought Germany into the ECSC, cementing the country's support for Europe by presenting it as the only way to ensure Germany's survival and that of its neighbors, because survival could 'only be maintained within a community that transcends national borders' and that Germans had a particular obligation 'after we—great numbers of us—assumed tremendous guilt through this war, to place all our spiritual, moral and economic powers in the service of this Europe, so that it becomes a force for peace in the world'.[155] He also, however, sealed the deal with NATO. At the time, the Social Democratic Party (SPD) in opposition offered a muted response to Germany's membership in the ECSC, since it was not opposed to European integration, only the form that it was taking. Party Chairman Kurt Schumacher, with a vision of German unification as first priority, rejected the ECSC on the grounds that this 'French project' would undercut German sovereignty (what little there was of it) and make the Federal German Republic (FRG) economically dependent. Adenauer's general response was that only through integration in the ECSC and other supranational institutions could Germany slowly regain its sovereignty and, ultimately, its unity.[156] Adenauer's 'Rhineland' vision of integrating Germany and Western Europe became the founding vision upon

---

[151] Paterson (1996: 168) and Maurer (2001).
[152] Jeffery and Paterson (2003: 61).
[153] See the discussion in Chapter 2.
[154] Jeffery and Paterson (2003: 61–2).
[155] Schwartz (1975)—cited in Banchoff (1999: 188).
[156] Banchoff (1999: 188–9).

which his successors would have to build,[157] in much the same way that De Gaulle's became for subsequent French leaders.

By the 1960s, the SPD had given up its opposition to the form that European integration took in the 1950s. And from then on, the German position on European integration became a matter of consensus for political parties on the right and the left, having survived changes in government and, most significantly, changes in territory as a result of German unification. Succeeding Chancellors may have had additional visions, Ludwig Erhard with the 'social market economy' and Willy Brandt with *Ostpolitik*, aiming to normalize relations with Central and Eastern Europe, but these had little effect on the overarching paradigm except for their impact on the Atlanticist–Europeanist axis.[158] In the early 1980s, we still find Chancellor Helmut Kohl discussing the importance of European integration in terms similar to those of Adenauer's Rhineland vision, as rooted in historical memory and with Germany unity and European unity as 'two sides of the same coin'.[159] In 1984, in answer to the basic question 'why we should say yes to Europe', Kohl argued that it was 'because we have learned from history', '. . . because we want to reunite Germany', '. . . because we want to defend freedom and democracy', and '. . . because we want to realize welfare and social justice'.[160] After 1989, Kohl's discourse expanded the Rhineland vision to accommodate unification while using the creation of a united Germany as a major legitimizing argument for a push toward even deeper European integration.[161] In the Maastricht ratification debate in 1991, Kohl invoked the danger of the war to push EMU and eastern enlargement of the EU, insisting that 'the united Germany wants no return to the Europe of yesterday', reiterating that 'old rivalries and nationalisms should not be allowed to revive', and, like Mitterrand, intoning that 'Germany is our fatherland' and 'Europe our future'.[162] Unlike in the 1950s with regard to the ECSC, the opposition SPD was fully behind the Treaty, as was the Christian-Democratic Union (CDU) as a whole and its coalition partner, the liberal Free Democratic Party (FDP). Only the CDU's Bavarian coalition partner, the Christian–Socialist Union (CSU), and a small wing of the FDP showed some skepticism.

Since unification, however, differences among policy elites have developed with regard to how Germany should act in Europe,[163] while European integration itself has become more contested as its effects have been felt on national policies and the economy. From 1998, moreover, with the Schröder government, a new approach to Europe was articulated. In it, although

---

[157] Paterson (1998: 20–1).
[158] Paterson (1998: 22–3).
[159] See discussion in Banchoff (1999: 64–6).
[160] Hedetoft (1998: 5).
[161] Paterson (1998: 27–8).
[162] *Bulletin* (1991: 72–3)—cited in Banchoff (1999: 192).
[163] See Bach (1999).

Germany was to remain a 'tamed power',[164] some wanted it to be freer to pursue its national interests and others wanted it to free itself from some of the 'burdened' aspects of its identity. The first view was epitomized by Schröder, as he attempted to further German interests by reducing German contributions to the EU budget at the time of his EU presidency in the first half of 1999. This he justified by stating that it was time for Germany to regard itself as a normal country and for others to do likewise, since 'every partner may clearly defend their national interests, only we Germans apparently may not'.[165] Earlier, he had already argued that 'my generation and those following are Europeans because we want to be, not because we have to be. That makes us freer in dealing with others' including 'Germany standing up for its national interests'.[166]

Foreign Minister Joschka Fischer exemplified the second view of Germany's role in Europe, which involved shedding some of Germany's burdened identity. This was most apparent in Fischer's response to Chevénement on the Constitutional Treaty, when he insisted that the '"German question" is no longer open' more than fifty years after Hitler.[167] His initiative to move the EU forward in a more federal direction, by launching the constitutional debates, was more in keeping with Kohl's supranational vision than Schröder's more national interest based approach.[168] Equally important, however, for both Germany and the EU, was his advocacy role in changing German government policy and public opinion with regard to committing troops in offensive military operations against a sovereign state, in the case of the Kosovo campaign.[169]

With both views, German leaders began mapping out a more assertive role for Germany in Europe, albeit still very far from a French role. It will be interesting to see how Chancellor Angela Merkel builds on either of these views. However, she has the possibility of adding a third view, increasingly prevalent in Germany, in particular among conservatives. This is the view pushed primarily by Edmond Stoiber, head of the CSU in Bavaria, who has championed subsidiarity, and has been intent on ensuring that the EU does not encroach on national and, in particular, regional level competences—read Bavaria.[170] Already in 1993, he had argued that Kohl's vision of Germany in Europe was outdated, that the country should focus more on national interest in EU negotiations, and that the leadership should pay more attention to majority public opinion on the EU—read EMU.[171]

---

[164] Katzenstein (1997*a*).
[165] *Welt am Sontag* (Feb. 27, 1999).
[166] *Financial Times* (Nov. 10, 1998); see discussion in Hyde-Price and Jeffery (2001: 700–1).
[167] 'France vs. Germany: What Kind of Europe?' Debate between Jean-Pierre Chevènement and Joschka Fischer, published in Le Monde and Die Zeit, *Prospect* (August–September 2000).
[168] Jeffery and Paterson (2003: 71–2).
[169] Hyde-Price and Jeffery (2001: 704–5).
[170] Hyde-Price and Jeffery (2001).
[171] Paterson (1998: 31–2).

This last view has elements of 'soft' Euroskepticism, meaning greater criticism of EU policies without questioning membership.[172] But other soft Euroskeptic views have been developing to the left of the SPD, with the PDS—the East German former Communists—and its pan-German successor led by Oskar Lafontaine, much more critical of EU-driven macroeconomic policy, as well as in parts of all three mainstream parties. There are, however, very few 'hard' Euroskeptics on the order of the French FN or the British UKIP and a sizable chunk of the Conservative Party, and those that exist are so small as to have no parliamentary representation, although they are occasionally elected to municipal or even regional bodies.[173]

Even as policy elites have become more assertive with regard to Germany's position in Europe, the general public has become less uncritical of the EU, in particular with regard to its impact in policy areas that raise questions of identity and sovereignty such as the currency, immigration, and the social market economy. However, whereas public opinion polls show a slide in support for the EU, public debate about the EU remains largely pro-European, with rarely any signs of Euroskepticism—in great contrast to the UK. Most of the discussion in a sampling of editorials in quality newspapers in 2003 was constructive in tone when considering Europe's common identity and values, in particular on the issue of reference to Christianity in the Constitution, or about institutional reform, in particular in view of enlargement to the east, with Turkey a central issue, and on maintaining regional and local autonomy.[174]

Giving up the Deutschmark in favor of the euro has arguably been the hardest for Germans to accept, both as a symbol of national sovereignty and as a sign of economic strength and stability. In the run-up to EMU, growing concerns that the euro would be less stable than the DM came in warnings from academics and the media while the public opinion polls were negative at the time of the overwhelming Bundestag vote in favor.[175] The Eurobarometer polls on citizens' support for the euro between 1996 and 2004 show that the Germans were significantly less supportive than the French and especially the Italians in the beginning, with less than one in three respondents in favor (32%) in spring 1997 by contrast with France's over one in two (56%) and Italy's three out of four (74%) in favor—Britain was for obvious reasons even lower than Germany, at just over one in four respondents (26%), but then it did not join. Germany only came up to the EU15 average in 2002, once the euro came into regular use (see Figure 4.9). Note that German polls paint an

---

[172] See Taggart and Szczerbiak (2001).

[173] Lees (2002).

[174] Lexis-Nexis search with the keyword 'Europe' in headline or caption for editorials and op-eds in the Frankfurter Allgemeine and the Suddeutsche Zeitung for the year, 2003.

[175] Thiel and Schröder (1998: 115).

even grimmer picture, with a low of one in five for the euro (19%, with 57% against) in 1995, still close to one in three (30%) in 2001, but a jump to close to two out of three in 2002 (61%, with those against down to 19%).[176]

Immigration policy and enlargement to the east have also been at issue. On enlargement, although in the early 1990s Germany was the first to call for quick integration of the Eastern European countries—much to the concern of Mitterrand at the time—it has been much more cautious on future enlargements, in particular, with regard to Turkey. Much of this has to do with its concerns about the effects of immigration, not only on jobs, given high-unemployment rates, but also on identity. This can be demonstrated in citizen attitudes toward which level should control immigration policy, the EU or the national. This is the only major policy area other than the currency where Germany does not follow the general trends. On immigration, Germany has moved to substantially lower levels of support for EU-level control of policy-making than all the member-states other than the UK (which is not a member of Schengen). Otherwise, a majority, and sometimes even a large majority, of Germans tends to be in favor of EU-level control of the areas that one might expect (see Figure 4.12). These include not only defense and foreign policy but also currency policy, despite the lower level of support for the euro—in fall of 2003, for example, whereas support for the euro was at 60 percent, support for EU-level control of currency policy was at 71 percent. One can be disappointed in practice with EU level control without opposing it in principle. By contrast, no more than between 30 and 40 percent were willing to give up control over health and welfare, cultural policy, and justice to the EU level.

For Germany, as for France, the more important questions about identity are ones internal to the country. Beginning in the 1980s, this involved questions of how to deal with German history, and in particular, the Nazi past.[177] Beginning in the 1990s and continuing today, the main issue has been the split between West and East Germany. The split itself is not apparent in the opinion polls on Europe, where the levels of confidence are reasonably close across Germany. But they come out in polls on confidence in democracy, with West Germans highly confident that 'with democracy, we can solve the problems we have in the Federal Republic'—at 65 percent in 1991 and 60 percent in 2001 whereas in the East, only 41 percent responded positively in 1991, 39 percent in 2001.[178]

The main question for Germany in Europe today is how its national construction of identity as 'German as European' will fare as European integration continues. This is less a question of political institutional adaptation, however, than one of economic adjustment. Because Germany's economic organization

---

[176] Allensbacher Jahrebuch (1994–2002).
[177] Knichewski (1996).
[178] Allensbacher Jahrebuch (1991, 2001).

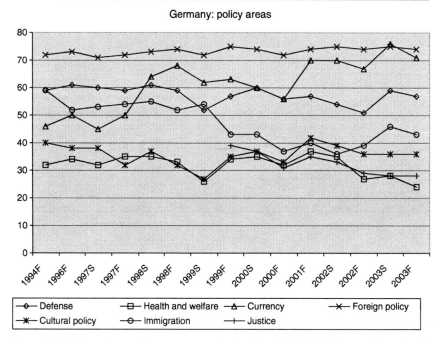

Figure 4.12. Percentage of German respondents who said that decision-making should be at the EU level in a range of policy areas

Source: Eurobarometer Results (1994–2003). Question reads: 'For each of the following areas, do you think that decisions should be made by the (NATIONALITY) government, or made jointly within the European Union?'

is inseparable from the political, with the social market economy reinforced by federal structures (given the Länders' powers in industrial policy) and corporatist processes (given the role of the social partners), the question for Germany is whether the Europe-led neoliberal reforms will ultimately challenge the governance foundations of Germany's social market economy, and whether the euro will be stable and strong enough to replace the Deutschmark to the satisfaction of the citizenry.

Italy

Italian politics in the postwar period has long been treated as something of a joke by outsiders. Governmental instability was rife, with governments lasting on average 12.3 months between 1945 and 1988.[179] And yet there was an underlying stability in the governing process, as the same names and faces appeared and reappeared as ministers in Christian Democratic coalition

---

[179] Fabbrini and Donà (2003: 33).

governments. This anomaly was the result of a highly proportional system of electoral representation combined with institutional structures that left the central executive very weak in the face of a strong but highly inefficient parliament.[180] Parliament itself was controlled by political parties or, rather, by one central party, the Christian–Democrats (DC), which formed coalitions and alliances. Italy's 'First Republic' was a system much like the French Fourth Republic, then, although even more clientelistic;[181] and it was not replaced by a Fifth Republic in the late 1950s. It had to wait until the early 1990s for any major shift in electoral system. But even then, the electoral reforms did not provide the fully majoritarian system or the structural reforms strengthening the executive that have given so much power to the French executive.

The postwar political settlement, moreover, in consequence of the cold war, was largely focused on keeping the Communist Party (PCI) out of government and the Christian Democrats in—with large infusions of money from the United States (read CIA) to help. The Christian Democrats' gratitude was expressed by such total compliance with Washington's wishes in foreign policy that Italy was often described in the media as 'the Bulgaria of the West'.[182] Internally, moreover, the Christian Democrats held the PCI at bay not so much through mass party politics as through clientelism—by maintaining power through localistic ties, the trading of favors, and corruption, with strong support from the Catholic Church and conservative social forces—not to mention the Mafia in the South.[183] In Parliament, politics proceeded by deal-making and logrolling, with lowest common denominator policies the rule. The result was the postwar system known as *partitocrazia* in which political parties dominated every aspect of political and administrative life—controlling the interest articulation process and contributing to the corruption of the civil service.

Underlying this system were vast cleavages: politically between right and left, territorially between north and south, and religiously between practicing Catholics and nonbelievers or non-practicing Catholics. These many sources of cleavages coalesced into one big divide between Catholics and Communists, with political allegiances organizing society by way of subcultures sustained through associations, networks, and activities around either the Christian Democrats or the Communists. These divisions were also territorial, with the Communists dominant in the 'red belt' regions of Emilia Romagna, Tuscany, and Umbria in the north central area while the Christian Democrats controlled the 'white belt' regions of the north east as well as the South. Clientelism and corruption was endemic, although more in the South than the North, and much more among the Christian Democrats

---

[180] See Hine (1993) and Morlino (1998).
[181] See Warner (2001).
[182] Mancini (2000: 26).
[183] Allum (1997), Warner (2001), and Hopkin (2004).

and their coalition partners than among the Communists.[184] In fact, the red belt regions increasingly became models of democratic practice that also fueled economic modernization in what became known as the 'third Italy' of regional production systems.[185]

The result of this political system was immobilism, state incapacity, and yet a flourishing economy and a vibrant society, largely because both economy and society managed to operate around the state. European integration, in this context, represented the 'rescue of the nation-state', by helping to overcome state incapacity and parliamentary inefficiency with reforms that, without the EU, could not have passed.

Europe, however, was not only welcomed for promoting government effectiveness *for* the people. Equally importantly, Europe offered a great escape from the burdens of the recent past. In the early postwar years, European integration for Italy, as for Germany, was a way to recover from defeat—in Italy's case, as an ally of Germany in World War II until 1943 as well as two decades of fascism under Mussolini. Much like Germany, Italy wanted to put the war behind it, by constructing not only a new Italy based on democratic precepts but also a new identity of which it could be proud. But whereas for Germany, the new German-as-European identity was to substitute for a German identity, forgetting the political past almost entirely, the Italian-as-European served to reinforce Italian identity, to be the contemporary pillar ensuring a bridge to the past greatness of Rome, of the Italian city-states of the Renaissance, and of the *Risorgimento* (the unification of Italy in the mid-1800s to late 1800s), as well as to the Italian Resistance.[186]

Another explanation for Italy's enthusiasm for European integration is that Italians' nation-state identity has been quite frail at least by comparison with other nation-states, the result of the absence of strong national allegiance and the preservation of traditions of localism, federalism, and social partnership.[187] But the lack of a nation-state identity did not preclude having a strong sense of identity as a 'nation'. That developed in the postwar years from the clash between the two dominant political cultures, the Catholic and the Communist, with a collective identity emerging from the transformation of 'private hate' into 'public friendship'.[188] A sense of national identity without the state, however, predates the postwar period, and provides yet another explanation for Italians' easy acceptance of European integration—although

---

[184] Graziano (1980) and Della Porta (1996).

[185] Putnam (1993) and Locke (1995).

[186] On the complexities of the debate on Italian identity and its relationship to citizenship, which is generally seen to bring together the liberal patriotism of the Risorgimento, moderate Catholicism, nationalism, and the republican tradition, see: Cerutti (1996), Rosati (2000), and Galli della Loggia (1996).

[187] Mancini (2000).

[188] Pizzorno (1993: 193–4).

the experience of two centuries of war, culminating in World War II, is arguably explanation enough, and not just for the Italians.[189] According to Pier Ferdinando Casini, President of the Chamber of Deputies from 2001 through 2006, the Italians' 'sense that the country was a single entity in terms of culture, civilization, language, and history... perhaps explains our willingness to shed much national sovereignty in the interests of European construction'.[190] But sovereignty was also not an issue for the Italians because of its institutional structures, much as for the Germans, given a weak but centralized state.

National pride also mattered with regard to European integration, and was intimately linked to the identity issues. While Germany found itself at the heart of Europe, not only economically and geographically but also as a central motivating factor, Italy was more on the margins, and very afraid of not belonging to the club. Wanting to be part of Europe was in fact a mix of many things, not just the desire to put the past behind them or to counter immobility but also to overcome a sense of inferiority. This was nicely expressed by Luigi Spaventa as the complex in which 'small brown people cannot afford not to associate with tall, fair people'.[191]

Italy, in short, embraced European integration without the reservations of France and Britain with regard to sovereignty and even more enthusiastically than Germany, given that national identity as European was joined by the pride to be European. The Eurobarometer polls on citizens' pride in country between 1999 and 2003 offers an interesting side note to this, especially with regard to the contrast between Italy and Germany. Whereas pride in country—especially as enhanced by membership in the EU—was a sentiment that the Italians could and did have, it was not a concept that the Germans had much of since the end of World War II. Of our four countries, Germany has the lowest scores on national pride in Eurobarometer polls, at an average of 18 percent of citizens saying they were 'very proud' of nationality, by contrast with Britain, with the highest, at 58.5 percent, with Italy at an average of 41 percent and France 37 percent.[192] Significantly, when the responses for 'fairly proud' of country are added to the 'very proud', the same ratios largely apply, although Germany jumps to the 60th percentile (to be fairly proud of one's country presumably does not bring back bad memories the way to be very proud does), Britain to the 90th. Most notably here, though, Italy can be seen to climb from a level below that of France to just above Britain in 2002 (see Figure. 4.13).

[189] See Cerutti (1996).

[190] Pier Ferdinando Casini, President of the Chamber of Deputies, speech in Berlin, 11 January, 2002 (author's translation).

[191] He calls this the 'Toni Kroeger complex'. La Reppublica (August 2, 1978)—cited in McCarthy (1995: 51).

[192] Eurobarometer (1999–2003).

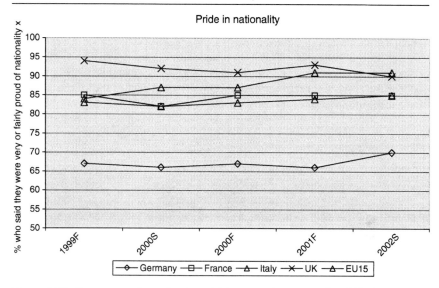

Figure 4.13. Percentage of people who said they were 'very proud' and 'fairly proud' of their nationality

Source: Eurobarometer Results (1999–2003). Question reads: 'Would you say you are very proud, fairly proud, not very proud, not at all proud to be (NATIONALITY AS SPECIÆED IN QUESTION I OF QUESTIONNAIRE)?'

But Italy's approach to Europe is not solely based on its capacity, identity, and pride-enhancing features. Even though Italy's approach has tended from the very beginning to be characterized by 'rhetorical fervor', in the words of Sergio Romano, it was accompanied, as he went on to note, by 'indifference, craftiness, and lots of quiet reservations' plus, of course, self-interest.[193]

Alcide De Gasperi, the architect of Italy's postwar recovery, is the leader who brought Italy into the ECSC, cementing the country's support for Europe by equating European integration with progress and with democracy, as the way to bring Italy into the circle of advanced countries and to put it squarely in the center of Western Europe. De Gasperi's was a political decision, based on strong support for supranationalism, as a way of eliminating conflicts among Europeans. But it was not a bipartisan position: the Italian left-wing opposition voted against ratification of the ECSC Treaty as well as the Treaty of Rome, while the PCI also voted against the EMS and the Socialists abstained in 1979.[194] The PCI was initially opposed for ideological reasons, seeing the EU as locking Italy into the West and keeping it from rapprochement with the Soviet Union. By the 1970s, however, the PCI had changed its position. By the 1980s,

---

[193] Romano (1997). [194] See Romano (1997).

all parties were agreed that European integration was a good thing. Such agreement did not, however, do much to stop Italy from the downward spiral in its public finances in the 1980s, despite membership in the EMS, or to promote better transposition or enforcement of EU directives. This had to wait for the collapse of the 'First Republic' with the end to the cold war.

In the early 1990s, political renewal came with the disintegration of the old political parties—the Christian Democrats literally disappeared as a party while the PCI recreated itself as the Democratic Party of the Left (PDS)—and with the demise of the system of *partitocrazia* that had been responsible for government 'immobilism'. This was precipitated not only by the external political changes related to the collapse of the Soviet Union but also by internal dynamics, in particular by the *tangentopoli* (bribe-city) and *mani pulite* (clean hands) investigations that exposed the old system of political corruption and deal-making at the basis of the old clientelistic relationships. Moreover, the state gained greater capacity and a new set of political parties and politicians as a result of reforms that produced more of a two party system by moving to a mixed but largely majoritarian electoral system, with 75 percent of seats first-past-the-post, 25 percent proportional.[195] In 1994, 71 percent of the members of the Chamber of Deputies were elected for the first time, in 1996, 46 percent, by contrast with 28.2 percent in 1987.[196] Although more thorough-going constitutional reforms were not passed, the electoral changes were nevertheless sufficient to alter the way in which government operated, giving it clearer responsibility and greater independent authority. Elections now led to loose coalitions forming ahead of the vote, giving voters a clear choice for prime minister, by contrast with the past, where coalition governments were formed and the prime minister chosen after the fact. The Italian system as a result gained greater capacity to act. The most notable example of this was accession to membership in the EMU, which succeeded not only because of electoral reforms but also, as we have already seen, of the use of the EU in the communicative discourse to promote the economic reforms necessary for membership and appropriate to safeguard Italian national pride.[197]

But although the Italian political system got better, instability has remained and the proliferation of parties continues, with 49 parties by 2006. There is some evidence to suggest that a stable system of political alliances on the center-left and the center-right has been consolidating itself, however.[198] And although there were seven changes of prime minister between 1992 and 2000, the eighth, Berlusconi, has had remarkable longevity, having been in office from 2001 through 2006.[199] But the failure to consolidate mass parties, a

---

[195] See Cotta and Isernia (1996), Pasquino (1997), and D'Alimonte and Bartolini (1997).
[196] Fabbrini (2000: 176).
[197] See discussion in Chapter 3.
[198] Bartolini et al. (2004: 16).
[199] Andreatta (2001: 58).

characteristic of the 'First Republic', continues to have serious consequences for stable party politics in the Second,[200] as does the lack of constitutional reform. Political divisiveness has also been a problem, especially after 1998.[201] The Berlusconi government in particular has sought to bring back the old left-right cleavages, with a rhetoric that unremittedly equates all of the left with the PCI of the pre-Berlin Wall era. Thus, the kick-off to the general election campaign in February 2006 was Berlusconi's speech to a Forza Italia rally in which he said that Churchill liberated us from the Nazis, Silvio Berlusconi will liberate US from the communists'.[202] This came after he claimed that 'only Napoleon did more' than he had and, when asked whether he was really comparing himself to Napoleon, responded: 'I am certainly taller'.[203]

Regional, political, and religious differences also continue to be significant. The rise of the populist, extreme-right *Lega Nord* (Northern League), with its pledge in the mid 1990s to secede from Italy in order to create the new state of Padania, vaguely bordered by the banks of the river Po to the south and the Alps to the north, is just one example of the mixing of regional issues with politics. But another even more telling one is the example of graffiti on a wall in Florence on May 26, 2005, with the message *Grazie Liverpool*, thanking the soccer team for having beaten *AC Milan*, the team owned by Silvio Berlusconi! This is a tribute to political and regional rivalries.[204] Religion also remains divisive, as the Catholic vote remains significant on social issues related to rights for cohabiting couples, euthanasia, the abortion pill, and human bio-engineering in the 2005 referendum.[205]

Political divisions have been developing even over the EU, in part as the center-left and center-right coalitions seek to differentiate themselves from one another and as parties within coalitions seek the same. In the center-right coalition (CDL), in fact, a greater note of Euroskepticism has emerged since Berlusconi became prime minister. But while Berlusconi's Forza Italia has taken a moderate Euroskeptic tone, as Berlusconi blamed the Euro for having increased inflation and stymied his attempt to bring about a second economic miracle,[206] the postfascist National Alliance (AN) has become decidedly pro-European, in particular once its leader GianFranco Fini became Italy's representative to the Constitutional Convention. In its 2002 mission statement, the AN's aim was to achieve more unity among the nation-states of Europe and proposed establishing a confederation of nation-states.[207] By contrast, the

---

[200] Hopkin (2004).
[201] Fabbrini and Donà (2003: 33).
[202] Financial Times (13 February 2006).
[203] New York Times (14 February 2006).
[204] Noted by Stella Tillyard, Prospect (January 2006: 8).
[205] Ibid.
[206] La Reppubblica (23 January, 2004)—cited in Albertazzi and McDonnell (2005: 965).
[207] Albertazzi and McDonnell (2005: 966).

Northern League (LN) has become an increasingly stridently Euroskeptic voice, especially after Italy's entering the EMU dashed its hopes of a great political future were Italy to fail to quality.[208] After this, it turned to 'la devolution', increasing regional power, but unlike many regional autonomy movements, it became antiglobalization and antiEuropeanization, presenting itself as defender of the North against both, claiming that Italy had paid too high a price due to Eurogenerated inflation, and took increasingly protectionist (China is now one of its targets) and xenophobic positions.[209] It reserved its venom primarily for the junior members of its own CDL coalition, however, seeing the AN and the small Christian Democratic party as old First Republic politicians, prosouth, propublic sector, and, lately, pro-immigration.[210] It attacked the AN in particular for its more moderate stance on immigrants—Fini even proposed that immigrants vote in local elections—in part because of what this would do to the Lega's own narrow views of Italian citizenship and identity.

Even so, the overall attitude toward Europe remains positive, and there is no serious debate in Italy over the EU of the kind found in Britain or France. In the media, the press discourse on the EU since the early 1990s continues to encompass the same two different pro-European discourses. The first has been a discourse about the primacy of the EU, which subordinates Italy's position to that of the EU, and which emphasizes Italy's need to comply, with Italy's interest presented as identical to that of the EU. The second has been a more critical discourse, focused on Italy's national interest and emphasizing Italy's independent political will and socioeconomic interests. Although this second discourse first appeared in 1993, it was reinforced in 1999, and has become increasingly predominant in the Berlusconi years.[211] Importantly, however, the Italians, like everyone else, do not pay that much attention to the EU on a day-to-day basis, as evident from the low level of coverage in quality newspapers. The actual issues considered, however, when considered, were pretty similar to those in other countries. In a sampling of editorials in quality newpapers between 2002 and 2004,[212] I found that the topics encompassed EU constitutional reform, the importance of the SGP—with a criticism of France and Germany for 'behaving like Italians' in not abiding by it;[213] the EU's need for immigration and better EU-level policy to stem illegal immigration; enlargement—but not about Turkey; and identity, primarily on the issue of Christianity but also on the benefit of European integration for Italy. Very little Euroskepticism here, much like Germany.

[208] Cento Bull and Gilbert (2001: 106–9) and Albertazzi and McDonnell (2005: 955).
[209] Betz (2002) and Albertazzi and McDonnell (2005).
[210] Diamanti (2005) and Albertazzi and McDonnell (2005: 956).
[211] Triandafyllidou (2005).
[212] Lexis–Nexis search with the keyword 'Europe' in headline or caption for editorials and op-eds in La Stampa and Corriere della Sera from May 2002 to May 2004.
[213] La Stampa (April 8, 2004).

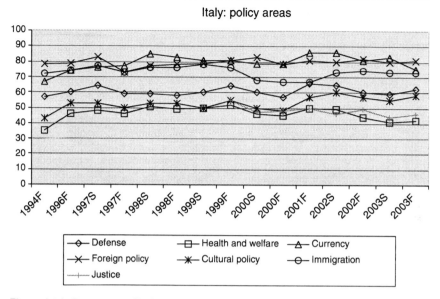

Figure 4.14. Percentage of Italian respondents who said that decision-making should be at the EU level in a range of policy areas

Source: Eurobarometer results (1994–2003). Question reads: 'For each of the following areas, do you think that decisions should be made by the (NATIONALITY) government, or made jointly within the European Union?'

In fact, citizens' attitudes tend to be much more skeptical toward Italian politics and democracy than toward the EU. Although satisfaction with democracy in Italy has improved since its low point of 12 percent in 1993 (see Figure 4.2), it has remained way below the average of the EU15 or of our other three country cases. Even if we were to discount the incredibly low figures in the mid-1990s, following the collapse of 'First Republic', the average from 1997 to 2004 still leaves a differential of nineteen points or more between it and our other three cases as well as the average of the EU15. It is not very surprising, therefore, that the Italians showed the highest level of support for the EU by comparison with our other three cases, as evident in their higher composite identity (see Figure 4.5), in their much greater trust in the EU than in their own government (see Figure 4.3), and in their greater dissatisfaction with their national democracy (see Figure 4.2). It is also telling that the Italians were the most enthusiastic in terms of seeing membership in the EU as a good thing (see Figure 4.4), in feeling that they benefited from the EU (see Figure 4.6), in wanting the euro (see Figure 4.9), and in supporting the constitution (see Figure 4.8). In addition, in all the major policy areas, without exception, Italians scored highest in terms of wanting the EU level to be in charge (see Figure 4.14). Most amazing, in fact, is the level of preference for EU-level control even for areas like cultural policy, justice policy, or health and welfare (close to or sometimes even above the 50% mark) in great contrast with all the other member-states.

Italy, in short, has continued to express enthusiasm for European integration, but it is no longer entirely unquestioning. It is likely to become even more critical, however, as compliance questions become political issues, and if political cleavages with regard to integration and/or sovereignty come to divide the left as much as the right. For the moment, however, the postwar Italian vision of Europe remains largely intact, and continues to serve as an antidote to state paralysis. The real issue for Italy, however, remains one of state capacity. With Berlusconi having changed the electoral system back to proportional representation for the 2006 election, the new Prodi government does not have the large, solid majority that would have likely guaranteed the political capacity to govern effectively. In Italy, governing effectively *for* the people, having been enhanced by the EU, is likely to be undermined by Italy's latest reform to 'democratic' governing *by* and *of* the people. As a result, only in Italy may the EU's *policy* without *politics* be a welcome development, given the hyperpoliticization of all issues at the national level.

Conclusion

The political spillovers from Europeanization have affected all four of our countries, although in different ways to differing degrees. The EU's *policy without politics* has put tremendous pressure on national politics, in particular in France, as dramatized by the referendum. Funnily enough, however, while the outcome of the referendum may have been bad for the EU, it may have been good for French feelings about democracy in the EU. In a survey of whether respondents felt that their voice counts in the EU, of our four countries, over half of the French agreed (58%) as opposed to only slightly over a third of Germans (37%) and Italians (36%) and only a quarter of the British (26%).[214] Politics may be part of the problem for democracy in Europe, in particular, as political parties on the left as well as the right become politicized along integration/sovereignty lines, and as voters become demobilized or radicalized as a result of national *politics without policy* on EU-related issues. But politics is also part of the solution—only, however, if national leaders come up with new legitimating ideas and discourse for Europe and new ways of bringing politics back into policymaking.

---

[214] Eurobarometer 63 (Fall 2005).

5

Theorizing Democracy in Europe

Theorizing about the development of the EU has tended to divide into four main questions: First, how did the nation-state members manage to build cooperation through the process of European integration? Second, how did the resulting cooperative institutions function in the EU? Third, how did the policies they produce alter member-states' policies through the process of Europeanization? Fourth, how have the supranational institutions themselves affected member-states' institutions and democracy through that self-same process of Europeanization?

In this book, I have focused on the last of these questions, although not to the exclusion of the others. The first three questions have been investigated, debated, and theorized in depth and at length by EU scholars. The theoretical debates related to the process of European integration have divided over the drivers of the process—whether the member-states through 'intergovernmental' cooperation or EU institutional actors through 'neofunctional spillover' and supranational decision-making.[1] The debates about the EU's institutional design have disputed what the EU *is*—whether something of a federal system or something never seen before; who is in charge; and how to remedy the EU's 'democratic deficit'.[2] The debates about the Europeanization of policies have sought to define Europeanization itself—whether as a top-down process, a bottom-up process, or both;[3] and to identify the mediating factors, mechanisms, and decision-rules that influence policy outcomes.[4]

[1] Intergovernmentalists include Hoffmann (1966), Moravcsik (1998), and Milward (1992). Neofunctionalists include Haas (1958), Lindberg (1963), and Schmitter (1970). Supranationalists include Sandholtz (1996), Sandholtz and Stone Sweet (1998).

[2] On what the EU is, see Scharpf (1988), Sbragia (1993), Ruggie (1993), and Schmidt (2004a). On who is in charge, see Scharpf (2000), Tsibelis (1995), and Pollack (1997). On the democratic deficit, see Habermas (1996), Weiler (1999), Scharpf (2000, 2002), Moravcsik (2002), Majone (1998), and Lord and Magnette (2002).

[3] On the debates about Europeanization, see Olsen (2001), and Radaelli (2003). On Europeanization as a top-down process see: Ladrech (1994), Kohler-Koch (1997), Héritier et al. (2001), Radaelli (2000, 2003), Börzel and Risse (2000), and Schmidt (2002a). As a bottom-up process see: Caporaso and Jupille (1999). As both, see Cowles, Caporaso, and Risse (2001), and Rometsch and Wessels (1996). For an excellent overview of the topic, see Börzel and Risse (2006).

[4] See Héritier, Knill, and Minger (1996), Héritier et al. (2001), Knill and Lehmkuhl (1999), Knill and Lenschow (2001), Börzel (1999), Schmidt (2001a), and Schmidt (2002a), Chapter 2.

But while the three questions related to the *drivers* and *design* of European integration and to the *policies* resulting from Europeanization have largely been theorized, the fourth question related to the Europeanization of national *polities* has not. There have of course already been significant theoretical studies of the impact of particular EU institutions on those of particular countries—whether institutional structures; policymaking processes; or representative politics.[5] However, there have been relatively few studies that attempt to theorize across institutions and countries about the impact of EU institutions on national institutions and democracy more generally.[6] The reasons for this are clear: it is only now that we have enough information about the particular polity impacts to move to the more general. But the need for such theorizing is great. For Europe itself, understanding the *polity* impact of the EU is a first step in reconciling national democracies to the new realities, especially important in light of the debacle with the Constitutional Treaty.

But how, then, to theorize about the impact of the EU on national polities? In order to begin to elaborate on this fourth question, we need to go back momentarily to the second, to consider the institutional design of the EU. Only with a clearer idea of what the EU is can we assess its impact. This is why the book began with a discussion of the EU as a whole before going on to examine its impact on national polities through the Europeanization of national institutional structures, policymaking processes, and representative politics. In this chapter, I provide a brief recap of my argument about the EU as a regional state and the general question of its democratic legitimacy before considering, in turn, theories about the EU's impact on national institutions, ideas, and discourse.

The European Union as Regional State: Democratic Legitimacy in Question?

In defining the EU, drawing parallels with established forms of political and economic organization mainly based on the nation-state can be misleading, although they are nonetheless useful in highlighting what makes the EU different. Unlike most economically advanced, democratic countries such as the United States, Japan, or even the EU's own member-states, which have finality as nation-states, the EU is best considered as in the process of development into a *regional state*. As such, it is characterized by shared rather than indivisible sovereignty, variable rather than fixed boundaries, composite

---

[5] On institutional structures, see Norton (1996a), Tapio and Hix (2001), Stone Sweet (2000), and Conant (2002). On processes, see Kohler-Koch and Eising (1999) and Falkner (1998). On politics, see Mair (2001), Gabel (2001), and van der Eijk and Franklin (1996).

[6] A notable exception is Wessels' 'fusion' theory on integration.

Table 5.1. Institutions in the nation-state and the European Union regional state

International form	Sovereignty	Boundaries	Identity	Governance	Democracy
Nation-State (US)	Indivisible	Fixed	Coherent	Simple or compound	*by, of, for,* and *with* EU level: *for* and *with*
Regional State (EU)	Shared	Variable	Composite	Highly compound	National: *by* and *of*

rather than coherent identity, highly compound governance rather than simple or compound government, and fragmented rather than cohesive democracy (see Table 5.1).[7]

In this regional state, EU governance—not government—is much more compound than that of any nation-state, given great diffusion of activity through multiple authorities at different levels, in different centers, with different forms of governing. Compared to the United States, arguably its closest counterpart in global size and weight, the EU shows both significant similarities and striking differences going beyond the contrasts in international form between nation-state and regional state to encompass questions of institutional configuration (see Table 5.2). The EU's vertical division of powers between the center and constituent members is more tipped in favor of the periphery than in the United States while its horizontal separation of powers between executive, legislative, and judiciary branches involves much more overlap in institutional roles and responsibilities, leading to a greater confusion of powers than in the United States (or any other federal state). Moreover, even though the EU's dominant policymaking process is most akin to the pluralist policy formulation and regulatory implementation of the United States, it is less open, less political, and more cooperative in policy formulation while its regulatory implementation is less transparent, less open, more delegated and, in consequence, less uniform in application. Finally, the EU's representative politics is very far from that of any nation-state—and especially that of the United States, where direct elections for the president by a majoritarian representation system are highly polarized. Not only are there no EU-wide elections for an EU leader in a depoliticized, consensus-oriented system, but representation mixes a weak EP directly elected by a proportional system with a stronger Council 'indirectly elected' because made up of nationally elected ministers, with interest-based politics in place of partisanship.

---

[7] We could add to this list a highly differentiated rather than fully integrated economy. But there is no room here to elaborate on this aspect of the 'regional state'. For more detail on the nature of the EU economy, see Schmidt (2002a).

In this system, democracy is more fragmented than that of any nation-state. In national polities, democracy tends to be based on some mix of four main democratic legitimizing mechanisms: government *by* the people through political participation (or 'input democracy'), *of* the people through citizen representation, *for* the people through effective government (or 'output democracy'), and what I call, adding a preposition to the traditional formulation, government *with* the people through interest consultation (legitimized in the United States as pluralism). In the EU, only two of these four legitimizing mechanisms are very prominent at the supranational level, effective governance *for* the people and interest consultation *with* the people, while government *by* and *of* the people is left largely to the member-states.[8]

Currently, there is no consensus to increase democratic legitimacy by shifting government *by* and *of* the people to the EU level through the direct election of EU leaders or EU-wide parliamentary elections—nor would this necessarily help democratize the EU, given the lack of a collective identity and will. But this means that democratic reforms of the EU still focus mainly on improving governance *for* the people, through greater accountability and transparency, and *with* the people, through more interest-based access and a greater opening to 'civil society'. This does little to decrease the fragmentation of EU democracy as a whole.

All of this together makes for big questions with regard to democratic legitimacy if the point of comparison is the nation-state. However, when considered as a regional state, in which democracy is seen more as an amalgam of the national and the supranational, the EU manages to pass most of the tests for democratic legitimacy also applied to nation-states. Its 'federal' checks and balances, its voting rules ensuring supermajorities, its elaborate interest

Table 5.2. Institutional comparisons between United States and EU

	Federal structures vertical	Federal structures horizontal	Pluralist formulation	Regulatory implementation	Representative politics
USA	Tipped in favor of center	Separation of powers	Open, political, competitive	Rule-making somewhat open, uniform application	Politicized, direct elections for president
EU	Tipped in favor of subfederal units	Dynamic confusion of powers	Less open, technical and apolitical, cooperative	Rule-making less transparent, less open, application more delegated, less uniform	Depoliticized, consensus-oriented, elections proportional & indirect, no president

[8] See Schmidt (2004).

intermediation process *with* the people, and its consensus politics go very far toward guaranteeing good governance *for* the people.

By the same token, however, these very same elements can undermine the bases of national level government *by* and *of* the people upon which EU-level governance depends for 'input' legitimacy. The lack of any significant EU-level government *by* and *of* the people leaves the general electorate frustrated because unable to make their views heard directly on policies that affect them directly. The EU, in short, has engendered a split-level democracy in which the EU level consists largely of *'policies without politics'* while the national level consists of *'politics without policies'*—at least when it comes to those growing numbers of policies decided at the EU level that are removed from the national.

This absence of EU-level politics puts tremendous pressure on national politics, the real locus of the 'democratic deficit'. Because citizens not only exercise their votes at the national level but as members of 'civil society' also mostly express their voice at that level through interest representation as well as protest, national politicians find themselves the focus of citizen discontent. They are held to blame for policies which they may not have made, do not like, but can do nothing to change. Until citizens learn to organize, pressure, and protest at the EU level, national politics will continue to suffer from the lack of politics at the EU level. But any such interest-based politics *with* the people at the EU level cannot in any event solve the political problems at the national level, which come from the very presence of EU-level institutions, their impact on national institutions, and the challenge to national ideas about democracy in the absence of any new legitimating discourse or new democratic practices.

The EU's Impact on National Institutions

Differences in national institutional design are just as important to understanding the EU's experience of regional integration as is the EU's own institutional design. National architectures have significant implications not just for our fourth question about the Europeanization of national polities but even for the first question about the process of European integration itself. It is something, however, that has received little attention from both sides of the debates about European integration.

For the intergovernmentalists, on the one side, the member-states represent unitary actors, collectively responsible for European integration through the treaties and the Council, driving integration as the principals for whom the other EU institutional actors are the delegated agents. Here, intergovernmental cooperation trumps the supranational. For the neofunctional supranationalists, on the other side, the process is more complex because of the priority of EU institutions and the 'multilevel' governance system through which a wide range of state and societal actors from EU, national, and subnational levels have access. Here, supranational decision-making trumps the intergovernmental. But while intergovernmentalists and supranationalists differ over whether the key actors are unitary or multiple, imposing or imposed upon, constraining or constrained, they both tend to assume that their generalizations apply uniformly across the member-states.

This is a mistake. The member-states are not only unitary and not just multilevel but also multiform, with some imposing and others imposed upon, some constraining and others constrained to differing degrees in various ways in different arenas at different times. How this plays itself out in any given case depends on a variety of factors but, most importantly for our purposes, whether member-states are *simple* or *compound* in institutional design.

Theorizing Institutional Interrelationships in Simple and Compound Polities

Although much of political science divides into studies of institutions and their structural interrelationships, studies of public policy and policymaking processes, or studies of the politics of representation and contestation, the three subjects are inextricably linked. While institutional structures give shape to the policymaking processes which breathe life into institutional structures, politics makes them matter by adding ideas, values, interests, and cleavages to policymaking processes and institutional structures.

To explain the interrelationships, we first of all need to put state and societal structures together—to see how structures influence policymaking processes. This is best conceptualized by considering state and societal structures in terms of their levels of concentration or fragmentation. With regard to state structures, unitary states tend to be characterized by more concentrated power and authority, federal and regionalized states by more diffuse power and authority. With regard to societal structures, by which I mean the organization of interests, key dividing lines consist of either concentration through vertically connected peak associations or dispersion through more horizontally structured, less interconnected interest groups.

Putting state and societal structures together in a fourfold table shows some revealing patterns (see Table 5.3). In cases where state and societal structures are both concentrated, in unitary states with highly organized interests, we find the strong form of corporatism typical of countries like the Netherlands and Sweden. This is where the state acts as a coequal with certain ' 'privileged' interests', generally business and labor, in policy formulation and implementation. In cases where societal structures are concentrated but the states are fragmented, as highly organized interests confront federal or regionalized state structures, we get the weaker corporatist processes of Germany and Italy (since 1992), although clientelism is another possibility (as in the case of Italy). Here,

Table 5.3. Policymaking processes related to state and societal structures

	Concentrated societal structures	Fragmented societal structures
Concentrated state structures (unitary state)	Strong corporatist (Sweden/Netherlands)	Statist (France/UK)
Fragmented state structures (federal or regionalized state)	Weaker corporatist (Germany/Italy) or clientelist (Italy)	Pluralist (USA/EU)

societal actors play a stronger role than the more fragmented state in policy formulation and implementation. By contrast, where state structures are concentrated but societal ones are fragmented, in cases where a unitary state faces disorganized interests, we get statist processes, as in France and the UK. Here, the state generally formulates policy alone, without interest involvement, but implements policy flexibly through accommodation with interests. Finally, where both state and societal structures are fragmented, as federal or regionalized states engage with disorganized interests, we get pluralism, as in the United States and, even more so, the EU. Here, policy formulation is open to a wide range of organized interests but closed in implementation, which tends to be regulatory or legalistic in form, as the policies are applied without exception.

This kind of fourfold table, however, does not do justice to the changing degrees of concentration or fragmentation of state and society in different countries and sectors at different times. It may therefore be more useful to consider the same relationship along two axes, one going from state concentration to fragmentation, the other from societal concentration to fragmentation. This would also allow us to see changes over time as a result of changing structures and relationships due to a range of other factors, such as increasing state concentration, decreasing societal fragmentation, changes in patterns of state and societal cooperation or competition, and the like (see Figure 5.1).

For example, Italy which has long been characterized by fragmented state and fragmented societal structures, which puts it on the line between pluralist and weak corporatist policymaking processes, experienced an increase in the concentration of its state and societal structures in the 1990s. This came in response to electoral reforms that instituted a more majoritarian representation system and to greater corporatist cooperation between business and labor—although both have lately been threatened, corporatism by Berlusconi's policymaking style, majoritarianism by a last minute electoral return to proportional representation. By contrast, in Sweden, long characterized by concentrated state and societal structures that ensured a strong version of corporatism, the breakdown in cooperative relations between employers and unions in national level corporatism in the early 1980s weakened the

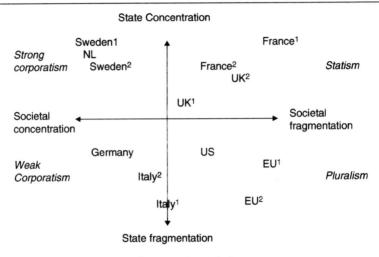

Figure 5.1. Changing patterns of state–society relations.

corporatist relationship, although it still continues at a sectoral level.[9] The Netherlands, by way of comparison, has changed little with regard to state-society relations, while Germany has moved only marginally toward even weaker corporatism.

France and the UK, however, have been moving in different directions, the former toward greater societal concentration, the latter toward greater state concentration. In France in recent years, although the vision of state action unsullied by interest interaction remains, societal concentration has been increasing as societal actors have become better organized and more mobilized. Moreover, the state has become more open to involving them, for example, in corporatist-like negotiations between business and labor 'in the shadow of the state' with the 35-hour work week.[10] In the UK, the state concentration which had been offset by policy networks in policy formulation and self-regulation in policy implementation has now been increasing as the policy networks have been breaking apart and as self-regulation is being replaced by the regulatory agencies and legalistic controls of the 'steering state'.

The EU has also changed, moving from greater state concentration in the early years, with comparatively little input from highly fragmented societal actors, to greater state fragmentation and somewhat greater societal concentration. Interests have coalesced in the process of gaining access and influence in EU policymaking while more and more state actors have entered as a result of successive enlargements.

---

[9] See Scharpf and Schmidt (2000).
[10] See Schmidt (2002), chapter 2.

There is yet another level of complication to the interaction of state and societal structures, however, which comes from politics. Electoral systems also have an influence on state and societal interaction. When majoritarian representation systems combine with a unitary state structure, as in the UK or France, they tend to reinforce the concentration of power in the executive whereas when proportional systems are found in unitary states, as in the Netherlands, they diffuse that power. This is also the case for regionalized states that are still formally unitary, as in Italy, which had highly diffused executive power when it had proportional representation prior to 1994, and had had greater concentration of power in the executive following the electoral reforms of the early 1990s that introduced a mixed majoritarianism. In federal states, majoritarian systems tend to concentrate power a bit more, as in the United States, whereas proportional systems diffuse it even further, as in Germany or even the EU.

More significant, however, is how electoral representation systems can influence the style of interaction. Majoritarian systems which concentrate power in the majority party or coalition of parties, as in Britain and France, tend to polarize state actors along partisan political lines as well as to promote greater competition more generally among societal actors. By contrast, proportional systems which tend to diffuse power among a wider range of parties, as in corporatist Germany and Italy, tend to promote compromise among state actors and to depend on cooperation with societal actors. The most interesting contrast in this regard is that between the United States and the EU. The United States' majoritarian politics ensures that pluralist policymaking is infused by polarized and politicized interactions among state actors and competitive interactions among societal actors. The EU's indirect, proportional politics instead ensures a pluralist policymaking process that is more compromise-oriented and depoliticized with regard to state actors, and more cooperative among societal actors (see Figure 5.2). This said, majoritarian systems can be quite consensual—the case of the UK in the early postwar years until at least 1964, when 'Butskellism' was the preferred style—and proportional systems, highly conflictual—Italy in the postwar years until at least 1976 exemplified this.[11]

Putting the politics together with structures and processes yields what I have called *simple* polities when majoritarian representation systems combine with statist policymaking processes and unitary states to channel governing activity through a single authority and *compound* polities when proportional representation systems combine with corporatist policymaking processes and federal or regionalized states to disperse power through multiple authorities. This can be pictured by situating the EU and its member-states along a continuum from

[11] See Pasquino (2003).

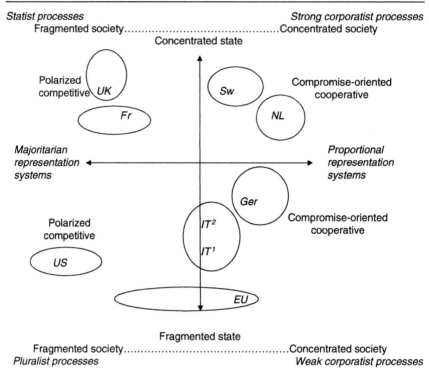

Statist processes
Fragmented society..Concentrated society
Strong corporatist processes

Concentrated state

Polarized competitive UK

Sw

Compromise-oriented cooperative

Fr

NL

Majoritarian representation systems

Proportional representation systems

Ger

Polarized competitive

IT²

Compromise-oriented cooperative

IT¹

US

EU

Fragmented state
Fragmented society...Concentrated society
Pluralist processes
Weak corporatist processes

Figure 5.2. Interaction orientations resulting from political representation systems combining with state and societal structures (country name indicates where country sits with regard to politics, circles approximate how countries fit with structures and processes)

simple polities to compound polities—which essentially adds together the three continua outlined in the three previous chapters encompassing unitary-regionalized-federal structures, statist-pluralist-corporatist policy-making processes, and majoritarian-proportional representation systems (see Figure 5.3).

It is important to note that although this distinction has much in common with Lijphart's dichotomy of 'majoritarian' and 'consensus' democracies, it differs in important ways. First, my approach focuses on three dimensions—structures, processes, and politics—instead of Lijphart's two—federal-unitary and executive-parties.[12] Lijphart's first dimension of federal-unitary category omits one of the three categories of institutional structures, the in-between category of 'regionalized' state; his second dimension of executive-parties

[12] Lijphart (1984, 1999).

Figure 5.3. EU and member-states on a continuum between simple and compound polity

collapses into one category, my two categories of 'representative politics' and 'policymaking processes'. Instead of his two processes, pluralist and corporatist, I again have three—pluralist, corporatist, and statist. As for politics, which for Lijphart encompasses the overall dichotomy between majoritarian and consensus democracy, I instead subsume it under my larger dichotomy of simple vs. compound polity—politics is a separate dimension with two categories, majoritarian and proportional representation systems. This is important because by making an overall differentiation of majoritarian and consensus democracy, Lijphart's dichotomy implies that majoritarian democracies will always have confrontation and consensus ones the opposite. But in real life, this is not the case.[13] It might be a bit more complicated to quantify these indicators, but we would be likely to get better results. And after all, we still do have continua, three different ones that combine into one overarching continuum of simple to compound polities.

At one end of the continuum are countries such as Britain, France, and Ireland to a lesser extent. These are more simple polities characterized by unitary states in which power and authority have traditionally been concentrated in the executive; by statist processes in which the executive has had a monopoly on policy formulation but accommodates interests through more flexible policy implementation; and by majoritarian representation systems where voting and voice are polarized along partisan lines. As a result, simple polities tend to have great capacity to impose change subject, however, to the sanctions of elections or protest.

At the other end of the continuum are countries such as Germany, Italy, Spain, or Belgium. These are compound polities characterized by federal or regionalized institutional structures with a high diffusion of power through multiple authorities; by corporatist processes with a moderate level of interest access and influence, in which certain 'privileged' interests are involved in policy formulation and implementation; and by proportional systems of representation with an emphasis on consensus or compromise-oriented politics, despite partisan patterns of voting and exercising voice. As a result, compound

[13] See Pasquino (2003).

polities have little capacity to impose change and tend instead to negotiate it among a wide range of policy actors. Whether they succeed or not, here, depends first and foremost on whether they reach agreement, with sanctions from elections or protest coming secondary.

In between are a range of other countries that often cannot be situated institutionally as neatly at any one place on the continuum, as one or another institutional element may be more simple even though the polity as a whole functions in a more compound manner, or vice versa. Thus, for example, while the Netherlands and Sweden are both closer to the compound end of the continuum, given corporatist policymaking processes and consensus-oriented politics, they also exhibit characteristics of more simple polities, since both are unitary states while Sweden also has more majoritarian politics. This enables both countries to act like more simple polities and impose change when corporatist processes break down and/or they cannot arrive at consensus, as in the case of the reform of welfare policies in the 1990s.[14] The United States is the quintessential mix, since although it is a compound polity, given federal structures and pluralist processes, its majoritarian representation system polarizes politics while introducing a competitive element into state and societal interactions. Even in polities that are closer to the simple end of the continuum, however, certain sectors may in fact operate in a more compound manner. This has been the case of agricultural policy and certain areas of labor policy in France, and of particular aspects of environmental policy in Britain and France. But by the same token, even the most compound of polities act like more simple ones in such sectors as monetary policy, competition policy, and defense and security, where power tends to be concentrated in a single authority.

Above this national continuum sits the EU, at the very extreme of the compound end. While in international relations terms, the EU can best be characterized as a regional state, in comparative institutionalist terms it is better defined as a *highly compound* regional polity.[15] As such, the EU has a high degree of diffusion of power and authority through quasi-federal institutional structures, allows for a high level of interest access and influence through semipluralist policy formulation processes, ensures the uniform application of the rules through regulatory implementation processes, and

[14] Scharpf and Schmidt (2000).
[15] The term is used by others as well. Leslie (2001: 217) defines 'compound polity' as an entity that is relatively highly institutionalized, which makes authoritative decisions at different levels with clearly demarcated boundaries, but which is generally in chronic conflict. I use the term in a somewhat looser manner, without demanding clearly demarcated boundaries or assuming, ex ante, chronic conflict. Rather, I would suggest constant negotiation which may be conflictual but may also be consensual (see below). Fabbrini's (2004) discussion of 'compound democracy' is closest is to my own. For the EU as a 'compounded government', see Kincaid (1999).

emphasizes consensus-oriented politics through largely nonpartisan patterns of voting and exercising voice in a weak proportional representation system.

Given these differences in institutional design between the EU and its member-states, the next question is: What can we expect when the highly compound EU meets simple or compound member-states in the process of Europeanization?

Europeanization of Simple and Compound Polities: A Question of 'Institutional Fit'

Europeanization has been defined in a great many ways.[16] It has been presented as a top-down process,[17] a bottom-up process,[18] or both.[19] For our purposes, Europeanization is best understood as the top-down process of member-state adaptation to the EU to distinguish it from European integration as the bottom-up process of projecting influence and the top-level process of building the EU.[20] Elsewhere, I have illustrated this by picturing European integration with vertical arrows going up from the member states to the EU, along with horizontal arrows at the EU level representing EU policy and polity development, followed by vertical arrows going down to the EU member-states, with a feedback loop at the bottom level into the vertical arrows going up, as member-state experiences of Europeanization affect their further projections of influence on the EU (see Figure 5.4).[21] What this means is that although it is useful to separate analytically Europeanization from European integration to focus on the impact of the EU on national polities, these two processes are in fact intertwined. Any full explanation of member-state responses to the EU requires seeing how the two processes interact, especially over time,[22] rather than taking only a bottom-up or top-down perspective.[23]

THE NATURE OF 'INSTITUTIONAL FIT'

Europeanization has meant that the EU has had a major impact on all its member-states' governing activities. It has 'federalized' national institutional structures by shifting the focus of governmental power upward from national to EU authorities. It has 'pluralized' national policy formulation processes by

---

[16] See Olsen (2001), Radaelli (2000), and Featherstone (2003).
[17] Ladrech (1994), Héritier et al. (2001), Radaelli (2000, 2003), and Börzel and Risse (2000).
[18] Caporaso and Jupille (1999).
[19] Cowles, Caporaso, and Risse (2001), and Rometsch and Wessels (1996).
[20] Schmidt (2002a), chapter 1).
[21] See Schmidt (2002a: 43).
[22] See Dyson (2002).
[23] On the problems that result from limiting one's perspective, see Schmidt and Radaelli (2004: 189–92).

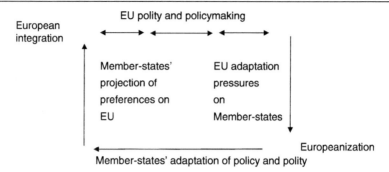

Figure 5.4. Europeanization vs. European integration

moving the locus of interest access and influence from national capitals to Brussels. It has 'juridified' national policy implementation processes by promoting more regulatory and legalistic modes of enforcement. And it has 'de-politicized' national representative politics by removing policies from the national political arena while subordinating national partisan politics to the consensus-oriented, interest-based politics of the EU, whether the national interest politics of the Council, the public interest politics of the parliament, or the organized interest politics of the Commission.

The EU as a highly compound polity has consequently served to move all EU member-states' governance practices farther along the continuum toward the compound end. Europeanization, however, is not the only reason for this. Such changes also result from the general evolutionary patterns of mature democracies. These include the rise of decentralization and devolution of subnational governmental units; the increase in forms of more direct democracy and the growth of civil society; the development of transnational global as well as European networks based on physical or 'virtual' (Internet-based) coordination; and the growing emphasis on the 'rule of law' in all societies. But while all advanced democracies have experienced these kinds of changes, the EU has gone one step further by adding another layer of governance. And it has thereby been instrumental in pushing EU member-states even farther along the continuum toward the compound end than might otherwise have occurred.

In so doing, however, the EU has had a comparatively greater impact on countries toward the simple end of the continuum, with unitary structures, statist policymaking processes, and/or majoritarian representation systems, than on countries toward the more compound end, with federal or regionalized structures, corporatist policymaking processes, and/or proportional representation systems. This is mainly because of a lack of 'fit' in institutional structures, policymaking processes, and representative politics (see Table 5.4).

Table 5.4. Governance practices in simple and compound polities and the impact of the highly compound EU

	Institutional structures	Policymaking processes		Representative politics	Impact of EU institutions on member-states
		Formulate	Implement		
Simple polity	Concentrated	Low	Flexible	Polarized and politicised	Disrupts thru greater diffusion of authority, opens up interest access, reduces flexibility, de-politicizes
France, UK	unitary	statist	derogation or self-regulation	majoritarian representation	
Compound polity	Diffuse	Moderate	Flexible or Rigid	Consensus-oriented and politicised	Complements thru greater diffusion, adds to interest access, allows flexibility or maintains uniformity, reinforces consensus
Germany, Italy	federal, regionalized	corporatist	corporatist or legalistic	proportional representation	
Supranational compound polity	Highly diffuse	High	Rigid	Highly consensus-oriented and depoliticised	
European Union	quasi-federal	semi-pluralist	regulatory and legalistic	weak direct proportional	

The EU's quasi-federal institutional structures tend to be more disruptive to simple polities by diffusing the executive's traditional concentration of power in unitary states (as in France and Britain) than to compound polities where the traditional balance of power has largely been maintained in federal states (as in Germany, Belgium, and Austria) or where the executive may have gained in power even as other authorities have gained in independence in regionalized states (as in Italy and Spain). Moreover, the EU's semipluralist policy formulation and regulatory implementation processes tend to impinge more on simple polities (like France and Britain) by introducing interests into statist formulation processes from which they were formerly excluded and by excluding interests from flexible implementation processes in which they were formerly included. By contrast, in compound polities the EU has mostly only further opened up interest access in corporatist formulation processes while reinforcing corporatist or legalistic implementation processes (as in Germany, Austria, Belgium, and Italy) and denying clientelistic processes (in Italy and Belgium). Finally, the EU's depoliticized, consensus-oriented politics tends to clash more with simple polities (like France, Britain, and Ireland) by subordinating the polarized partisan politics of their majoritarian representation systems to the search for consensus than with compound polities (like Germany, Denmark, and Italy), where it tends to reinforce the already consensus-oriented—albeit partisan—politics of their proportional representation systems.

THE LIMITS OF ARGUMENTS RELATED TO 'INSTITUTIONAL FIT'

Isomorphism, or the question of institutional 'fit', however, is a double-edged sword. It is mainly a problem for countries toward the 'simple' end of the continuum when we consider the Europeanization of national polities, as the top-down impact of the EU's governance practices on those of its member-states. European integration, as the bottom-up process of generating European policies, in which member-states project their national policy preferences onto the EU, is another matter entirely. For simple polities, the same institutional arrangements that make for disadvantages with regard to adapting national practices to the EU make for advantages with regard to projecting state (although not societal) preferences on the EU and enforcing EU-related decisions. By contrast, for compound polities, the same institutional arrangements that make for advantages with regard to adapting national practices make for disadvantages with regard to projecting state (although not societal) preferences and enforcing EU-related decisions (see Table 5.5).

Whereas in the process of Europeanization, fit between EU and national governance practices helps account for member-state's ease of adaptation, in the process of European integration, 'misfit' may instead be the key to national executives having fewer problems and greater clout. Simple polities such as Britain and France, in which governing activity is more concentrated in the executive, are often better able to project national preferences onto the European stage than compound polities such as Germany and Italy in which

Table 5.5. Different challenges depending on polity type

	Instit'l Fit with EU	Europeanization adaptation	European Integration preference projection		Europeanization compliance	
		↓ Top down; Member-state adapts national practices to EU practices	↑ Bottom up; Member-state projects national policy preferences on EU		↓ Top down Member-state's capacity to comply with EU policies	
			State actors	Societal actors	State actors	Societal actors
Compound polity	High	Easier	Harder	Easier	Harder	Harder
Simple polity	Low	Harder	Easier	Harder	Easier	n/a

governing is more dispersed through multiple authorities. Other factors are of course also at work, such as relative size and economic weight (with bigger countries naturally having greater sway than smaller), strategic position (e.g. when a country has the presidency of the European Council), or good ideas and innovative practices (e.g. Germany with regard to EMU, with all that that entailed in terms of monetary stability and independent central banks). But there can be little question that countries where the executive has hierarchical control of its ministries and regions is more effective in Brussels because it is able to speak in one voice than those where ministries and regions have greater measures of independence.

By the same token, however, in the process of European integration simple polities' societal actors may have greater difficulty projecting their own preferences onto the national or EU stage. Statist policymaking processes may be a greater handicap to societal actors acting at the EU level because they are often less schooled in the art of exercising influence in policymaking as well as less well-organized to do so than societal actors in compound polities (with the exception of the British). Statist societal actors thus are likely to have a steeper learning curve with regard to the EU policy formulation process, but they also have a lot to gain as a result of their potential empowerment from EU-level access and influence (as in the case of business in France). On this score, whereas corporatist societal actors generally may have less to learn with regard to EU processes, those without EU-level access have potentially a lot to lose if decision-making moves up to the EU level (e.g. labor in Germany).

Institutional architecture also generally ensures simple polities an easier time in applying EU policies, since executives need not negotiate compliance with subnational regions or corporatist interests, as in many compound polities, in particular Germany and Spain. But while this explains well the stellar compliance rates of unitary Britain and the rather bad ones of federal Germany, they do not explain unitary France's even poorer record, let alone that of regionalized Italy. Compliance is equally a matter of state administrative capacity—the explanation for why Italy has had such a bad compliance record—as well as a question of political will—the explanation for France's only marginally better record.[24] Moreover, although compound polities may have a harder time complying because they have to negotiate reforms rather than simply impose them, where they manage to reach agreement, the negotiated policy outcomes may work better and to the satisfaction of all. However, where agreement cannot be reached in a given set of negotiations, the outcome could be a lot worse than in simple polities where the state can better control the results. In fact, in compound polities where agreement fails, the corporatist system in the given sector could simply burst apart (as was the case for deregulation of electricity and

[24] For one study which serves to demonstrate this, see Falkner et al. (2005).

transport in Germany)[25] while the regionalized center-periphery relations could lead to major delays in implementation (as was initially the case for environmental policy in Spain).[26]

THE LIMITS OF CROSS-COUNTRY GENERALIZATIONS ABOUT 'INSTITUTIONAL FIT'

Generalizations about the more disruptive impact of the EU on simple polities than on compound polities, in short, apply to top-down Europeanization but not to the bottom-up projection of preferences or to the application of EU rules. But even this does not tell the whole story. Once we take a closer look at particular country cases, we also butt up against the limits of any cross-national country comparisons. This is because cross-national country comparisons that are accurate depictions of the comparative impact of the EU on different countries do not tell us about where such countries ultimately end up institutionally. Outcomes must be differentiated from impact.

Simple polities, however much more disruptive the impact of the EU, still channel governing activities more through a single governing authority than in compound polities, which continue to have greater dispersion of governing activities through multiple authorities. Moreover, even though adaptation to the EU may not have altered the institutional arrangements as much in compound polities than simple ones, it may have forced institutional actors in compound polities to do more to maintain their institutional arrangements than simple polities when adjusting to EU-mandated change.

For example, even though the EU's quasi-federal institutional structures that may have had a greater impact on the institutional balance of unitary states, federal, and regionalized states have actually had to work harder and to change more in terms of the internal workings of national institutions to reestablish their preexisting balance—as was the case for the Länder in Germany and the regions in both Spain and Italy. Moreover, the independence of the regions of unitary states is still negligible by comparison with that of the regions of federal or regionalized states—Scotland has nothing like the powers of Bavaria, to say nothing of regular British or French regions compared to Italian or German regions. In addition, the courts in France and the UK remain more protective of executive prerogatives and less likely to refer cases to the ECJ.

Similarly, despite the fact that the EU's semipluralist policymaking processes may have impinged more on statist policymaking, by bringing societal actors into consultation for the first time, state and societal actors in corporatist settings may have had to renegotiate more in order to maintain their cooperative interrelationships—the case of telecommunications in Germany—and have sometimes failed—the case of electricity and banking in Germany. Moreover,

---

[25] S. Schmidt (2004); see Chapter 3 for the full discussion.
[26] Börzel (2002).

demands for regulatory implementation only further reinforce public (even if not state) control in statist systems—in particular in Britain, where the state has increased its 'steering' capacity—whereas in regionalized and federal systems, it tends to fragment executive control even further—the difference between British and German telecommunication agencies is a case in point.

Finally, with regard to electoral politics, although the EU may have had a greater demobilizing effect on national citizens in majoritarian systems, because more disenchanted by the depoliticization of policies and by politicians unable to keep political commitments, the electorates of majoritarian systems may still be better able to make their displeasure known more clearly through the ballot box.

Most importantly, though, it should be noted that Europeanization generally comes a far second to national dynamics of change, as national executives have themselves granted increasing powers to subnational authorities; as national parliaments have increasingly made themselves heard even beyond their growing powers of oversight through the exercise of voice; as national administrations have modernized and become more efficient; as regulatory agencies have been established; and as national courts have benefited from increasing independence, whether the result of national reform processes, EU empowerment, or self-empowerment. Thus, sorting out the external, EU-related changes from the internally generated changes in institutions is not easy. This helps explain why quantitative studies like that of Jeffrey Anderson have found few specifically identifiable effects of Europeanization on the internal workings of member-states' democracies.[27] Where everything is a moving target moving at different speeds in various directions, more subtle qualitative analysis is necessary to see which EU-related institutional changes make a difference. This is why it has been essential to add to the generalized comparisons and contrasts detailed examinations of the different country cases.

Theorizing the Europeanization of Sectoral Policymaking Processes

These differential national patterns of institutional fit with the EU are only part of the story, however. The macro patterns of adjustment to the EU, in particular with regard to national policymaking processes, are complicated by the micro patterns of policymaking in any given policy sector, which may differ from the macro pattern at EU or national level.

To capture the complexity of policymaking within different policy arenas, the more sectorally focused policy literature has long since moved away from discussions of statist, corporatist, and pluralist patterns which were the primary analytic framework of the postwar period through the 1980s.[28] The sectoral

---

[27] Anderson (2002).   [28] See the discussion in Schmidt (1996).

Table 5.6. State and societal actors in statist, pluralist, and corporatist sectoral policymaking

	Statist issues networks	Pluralist issues networks	Pluralist policy communities	Corporatist policy communities
State Actors	State leadership with low societal consultation	State leadership with high societal consultation	State's decisions shaped by high societal consultation	Joint decision-making with equal or greater societal leadership
Societal Actors	Unstable, competitive membership with low participation thru lobbying	Unstable, competitive membership with high participation thru lobbying	Stable, cooperative membership with maximal participation in decision-shaping	Stable, cooperative membership with restricted participation in joint decision-making

literature has tended to identify a continuum in interactions among state and societal actors from closed policy communities with stable membership and cooperative participation in joint decision-making to more open, more loosely constituted policy communities with members involved in cooperative decision-shaping, to even looser and more open issues networks with more unstable membership, competition among interests, and consultation through lobbying.[29] Although this literature brings us closer to understanding sector-specific processes of state—society interaction, it does little to set this into national institutional context, or to link the micro patterns with the macro patterns. We can, however, building on the work of Gerda Falkner,[30] put the micro and macro together, using these micro categories not as a substitute for the macro national patterns but as a helpful, added level of detail. These provide further detail to the continuum between statist, pluralist, and corporatist processes, where we can label the closed policy communities of the policy literature 'corporatist policy communities'; the more open ones, 'pluralist policy communities'; the open issues networks, 'pluralist issues networks'; and the less open issues networks more controlled by state actors, 'statist issues networks'[31] (see Table 5.6). This combination of national patterns with the policy literature can be visualized as intersecting, concave and convex vectors in which pluralist policymaking fills the intersection of the two vectors; statist policymaking sits on the left side of the axis below the intersecting vectors, and corporatist policymaking, on the right side. The y-axis goes from low societal participation (where societal actors participate little, with little stability over time) to high societal participation (where societal actors participate a lot, often shaping decisions); and the x-axis, from high state autonomy (where

[29] See, for example, Jordan and Richardson (1983), Marsh and Rhodes (1992), Rhodes and Marsh (1992), Marin and Mayntz (1991), Richardson (2000), Marsh and Smith (2002), and the discussion in Falkner (2001).

[30] Falkner (2001).

[31] Although Falkner also has a category of 'statist cluster', in which state actors do not consult, I prefer to subsume this under statist issues network, since the state generally engages in formal consultation by informing societal actors of its plans, even when it doesn't listen to their responses or allow lobbying.

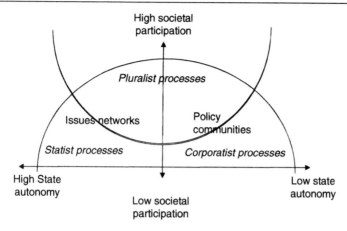

Figure 5.5. Spatial relationship between statist, pluralist, and corporatist processes together with issues networks and policy communities

state actors lead the policymaking process) to low state autonomy (where state actors are involved in joint decision-making) (see Figure 5.5).

This range of patterns can be found at both the EU and national levels. The question is: how does any one pattern at the EU level potentially affect another pattern at the national level? Here, I hypothesize (following Falkner) that when there is stronger EU 'state' leadership, less interest participation, and more interest competition, national joint decision processes, societal participation, and cooperation are at risk whereas when there are strong EU joint decision processes, much participation, and significant cooperation, national state leadership, and societal competition are likely to be reduced. Finally, where the EU pattern matches the national pattern, there will be no significant change. It is perhaps easier to gain a sense of this by plotting out potential responses in terms of pluses and minuses related to increasing or decreasing state leadership and societal participation, with 0 for no change (see Table 5.7). What is interesting here is not so much the detailed interaction of statist, pluralist, and corporatist policy issues and networks—which, although useful for sector-focused analysis, tends to muddy the waters for our purposes—as the more general interaction effects. These show that where the EU is more pluralist or corporatist in policymaking, it is potentially more empowering to interests in national statist policymaking—pulling traditional statist patterns toward pluralism or corporatism—while where it is more pluralist or statist, it can be disruptive of national corporatist policymaking—pulling the traditional pattern more toward pluralism or statism.

This kind of analysis is limited, however, by the fact that it speaks only to potential impact, without considering a further range of factors which might account for actual impact. These factors are identified in the Europeanization

Table 5.7. Potential impact of EU sectoral processes on national sectoral processes in terms of state leadership and societal participation

		EU statist issues network	EU pluralist issues network	EU pluralist policy community	EU corporatist policy community
Statist Issues Networks	State leadership	0	−	− −	− − −
	Societal participation	0	+	+ + +	+ +
Pluralist Issues Network	State leadership	+	0	−	− −
	Societal participation	−	0	+	+
Pluralist Policy Community	State leadership	+ +	+	0	0
	Societal participation	− − −	− −	0	−
Corporatist Policy Community	State leadership	+ + +	+ +	0	0
	Societal participation	− −	−	+	0

Note: 0 equals no change; − equals change on the decrease; + equals change on the increase.

literature concerned with the impact of EU policies on national ones. They consist of the EU-related adjustment pressures, adjustment mechanisms, and interaction effects as well as the national mediating factors that influence policy outcomes in different policy sectors in different countries.[32] Although this literature has tended to deal only tangentially with the impact of the EU on national policymaking processes, it can nevertheless be usefully adapted to our purposes—to explain the underlying dynamics to the micro patterns discussed in Chapter 3.

Europeanization has different potential effects on its member-states depending upon the kinds of pressures for adjustment and the mechanisms of adjustment to such pressures.[33] EU-related pressures encompass the policymaking processes that the EU may mandate in any given sector; the policymaking processes that the EU may suggest for any given sector or the learning experiences that state and societal actors may glean through participation in EU processes; and the incentives provided by EU policies that may tempt state and/or societal actors to break with existing national processes. Certain adjustment mechanisms tend to be linked to these pressures, with imposition

[32] See Héritier, Knill, and Minger (1996), Radaelli (2000), Héritier et al. (2001), Knill and Lehmkuhl (1999), Knill and Lenschow (2001), Börzel (1999), Schmidt (2001a), and Schmidt (2002a), Chapter 2.
[33] See Knill and Lehmkuhl (1999) and Radaelli (2000).

Table 5.8. Factors affecting the impact of Europeanization on sectoral policy processes

EU Pressures	Potential Adjustment Mechanisms	Potential Interaction Effects	Examples
EU-mandated processes	Imposition	Direct	Environmental policy mandates for pluralist consultation or legalistic enforcement; regional policy mandates for pluralist consultation; competition policy mandates for regulatory agencies and legalistic enforcement
Learning experiences from EU processes	Diffusion	Diffuse	National Action Plans in European Employment Strategy suggesting corporatist consultation and in Social Inclusion OMC suggesting pluralist consultation; pluralist business lobbying; gender mainstreaming
Incentives from EU policies	Competition	Knock-on	Competition policy related to banking, electricity, transport policy, agricultural policy

the mechanism by which national policymaking tends to adjust to EU-mandated processes, since national actors are obligated to change their processes; diffusion the way in which national policymaking adjusts to EU-related learning experiences and suggested rules, as national actors may change their processes in response to the new ideas represented by those experiences or suggestions; and competition the mechanism for adjustment to EU-related incentives, as national actors may break with national processes in response to perceived advantages from new policies. This said, these mechanisms may also be paired with other pressures, since EU mandates can also lead to the diffusion of ideas, while both EU-related learning experiences and incentives can promote competition among national actors or imposition of a given process by the proponents of change.

These pressures and mechanisms, in turn, have different potential interaction effects on national policymaking (Table 5.8). They may have a direct effect where EU-mandated processes impose change in national policymaking processes, as in EU mandates for pluralist consultation of societal interests in regional policy and some areas of environmental policy and pluralist consultation or legalistic enforcement in environmental policy.[34] They may have a diffuse effect where EU-related learning experiences or suggested rules lead to the diffusion of new ideas, as in lobbying or in the open method of

---

[34] There is no room here to go into greater detail on the different kinds of mandates, which may be 'hard' because they specify a set of rules to follow, as in the Maastricht critieria for European Monetary Union, or softer because the rules are less specified, as when the EU requires that regulatory agencies be set up, but leaves to member-states the decision as to the form (see Schmidt [2002*b*]), or when 'conditionality' with regard to EU enlargement presses prospective EU members to adjust (Schimmelfennig and Sedelmeier [2004]).

coordination (OMC), with EU recommendations for corporatist consultation in the European Employment Strategy (EES) or for pluralist consultation in the Social Inclusion OMC. But they may instead have a 'knock-on' effect in cases where EU policies act as incentives for state and/or societal actors to break the policymaking rules, as for example in competition policy decisions in banking, electricity and transport.

All of the above speaks to the potential impact of the EU on national policymaking processes. The actual outcomes can be very different, given the range of factors identified in the Europeanization literature which also may affect national responses. While fit or misfit with policymaking legacies set the stage, policymaking preferences dictate whether misfit is seen as a problem or an opportunity, policymaking capacity affects whether state and societal actors can respond effectively, and discourse enhances capacity to respond by altering perceptions of legacies and influencing preferences.[35] As a result, while in some sectors, the interaction effects of the EU and national policymaking processes may be significant, entailing the transformation of national processes, in others the EU may have only a minor impact with the absorption by national processes of any EU-related changes, and in yet others the EU may have almost no impact at all, as national processes show inertia with regard to the EU.[36]

In short, adjustment here depends not only upon the nature of EU pressures for change—whether by EU-related mandate, learning, or incentive—the mechanisms of adaptation—whether by imposition, diffusion, or competition—and the interaction effects—whether direct, diffuse, or knock-on. It also depends upon the nature of member-state responses, which may entail transformation, absorption, or inertia depending upon a variety of national mediating factors, including policymaking legacies, preferences, capacity, and discourse. Given all of this, we might ask whether we can still talk about Europeanization in terms of macro patterns of national policymaking. The answer is yes. For although national patterns are indeed less distinctive than in the past, they nevertheless remain distinguishable along a continuum from statist through corporatist. Pluralism, however, has become a new default option in between the two.

All of this discussion of macro and micro patterns of policymaking, together with the previous discussion of the adaptation in responses to better or worse institutional fit, speaks to the fact that traditional national practices have changed—although more in some areas than in others, and more dramatically in simple polities than in compound polities. But this analysis, which focused on institutions, is not sufficient to enable us to explain why national practices changed (or not) in the way they have. For this, we need to turn to the role of ideas and discourse in institutional change—which will also fill out the picture with regard to politics.

---

[35] As adapted from Schmidt (2001a, 2002a, chapter 2.
[36] As adapted from Héritier (1996, 2001).

The EU's Challenge to National Ideas About Democracy

The EU's institutional impact on its member-states represents a challenge not only to national practices but also to national ideas about the organizing principles of democracy. This is because ideas about democracy, just like the institutions that underpin democracy, themselves differ significantly in simple and compound polities. In simple polities, democratic legitimacy tends to be focused on a single authority, the executive, whereas in compound polities, legitimacy rides on the functioning of the system as a whole.

The foundational principles of simple polities such as France and Britain reflect the belief that institutional structures ought to concentrate power in the executive in order to enable it to govern effectively *for* the people; that policy formulation ought to be closed to interests via government *with* the people so as to safeguard majority government *by* the people against abuse by minorities; that policy implementation should be open to interest consultation *with* the people so as to accommodate minority interests; and that representative politics needs to be focused on the executive elected *by* the people and representative *of* the people for it to be able to express the *will* of (a majority of) the people. In compound polities such as Germany and Italy, by contrast, the organizing principles reflect the belief that institutional structures ought to diffuse power through a multiplicity authorities to safeguard minorities against the abuses of majority government *by* the people; that policy formulation and implementation processes ought to be open to interest consultation via government *with* the people so as to ensure the most effective government *for* the people; and that representative politics needs to be diffused in multiple authorities elected *by* the people and representative *of* the people so as to ensure that they express the *will* of *all* of the people.

In consequence, the EU's emphasis on governance *for* the people and *with* the people clashes more with the foundational organizing principles of simple polities than of compound polities. For simple polities such as Britain and France—where political legitimacy *by* and *of* the people is focused on the executive who is alone to govern *for* the people and not *with* the people—the EU diffuses the executive's power, introduces interests into a policy formulation process from which they were formerly excluded, eliminates interests from a policy implementation process in which they were traditionally accommodated, and forces compromise on an executive expected to express the majority will. In France, for example, EU-related institutional change clashes with ideas about the 'one-and-indivisible' Republican state, as embodied by the executive which represents the governmental majority elected *by* the people and charged to carry out its 'sovereign' will without compromise or obligation to any other authorities, to formulate policy without consultation *with* organized interests, but to accommodate such interests through derogation in policy implementation. In Britain, moreover, EU-related institutional change clashes with notions of 'parliamentary sovereignty', as embodied by the executive which represents the governmental majority elected *by* the people and charged to carry out its will, again, without obligation to other authorities or intermediation *with* other interests, but to accommodate such interests through self-regulation in policy implementation.

For compound polities such as Germany and Italy—where political legitimacy *by* and *of* the people rests on a multiplicity of authorities who consult *with* the people as they govern *for* the people—the EU only adds more authorities to an already diffuse institutional structure, more interests to an open policy formulation process, and more compromise to a consensus-oriented political process. For Germany, EU-related changes complement a 'semi-sovereign' state in which the Basic Law explicitly allows sovereignty to be shared with supranational authorities and in which decision-making is assumed rightfully to be the result of political compromise among a profusion of consensus-oriented governmental as well as nongovernmental (corporatist) actors at multiple levels of government. The only potential problem for legitimacy would come were the further dispersion of authority in the EU to be seen as dissipation. For Italy, EU-related change is not just complementary but democracy-enhancing, because it contributes to greater governing effectiveness *for* the people, helping to rescue the nation-state from the governmental paralysis produced by the long-standing dissipation of power and authority.

Institutional design alone, therefore, lends insight into why simple polities have greater problems of legitimacy than compound polities with regard to the Europeanization of the national polity. It also helps explain member-states' approaches to building legitimacy into the EU polity in the process of European integration. Compound polities with federal states are more likely to promote a more federal vision of the EU and to propose increasing the powers of the Commission and the Parliament in order to enhance supranational legitimacy—in line with their own multiple branches and levels of authority. Simple polities with unitary states, by contrast, are likely to promote a more intergovernmental vision of the EU and to resist increasing the power of any supranational authorities other than the Council. This largely explains initial positions in response to Fischer's proposals for a new 'Constitution' for the EU. However, top-down fit with national institutions does not always match bottom-up preferences for supranational institutions, as smaller compound polities with unitary states sometimes prefer federalist supranational arrangements, for example, the Netherlands. Moreover, unitary Britain has consistently promoted a vision of a supranational economic community in which legitimacy follows even more from market-related effectiveness than from intergovernmental control—which helps explain its willingness to sacrifice national sovereignty in the Single Market Act.[37]

---

[37] See Rittberger (2003).

It goes without saying that other questions of democratic legitimacy also can and do come up, however. These are related to changes in governance practices or policies that may clash with more nationally specific political, social, and economic values, for example, about the appropriate balance of power between given institutional authorities, about the inviolability of long-established political rights, about the bases of citizenship, identity and community, about the grounds for social justice and the equitable distribution of social goods, or about the just distribution of economic goods and the organization of the economy. With these kinds of questions, the lack of fit with the EU may be as great for compound polities as for simple ones.

In explaining responses to Europeanization, such historically and culturally grounded values are often difficult to separate except analytically from the institutionally grounded organizing principles of democracy, since they serve to inform them and, indeed, may also be informed by them. However, sorting the two out serves a heuristic function, by helping to explain why the clash with ideas about organizing principles does not in and of itself determine national responses to Europeanization. Put another way, where one's independent variables are the institutional organizing principles of democracy, these culturally and historically based political, social, and economic values act as intervening variables in the explanation of national responses to the process of Europeanization (see Figure 5.6).

In simple polities, for example, these political, social, and economic values lend insight into how countries mediate (or not) the clash with their democratic organizing principles—for example, why the French, with their ideas about grandeur and the universal rights of man, have embraced European integration despite its potential impact on the unitary identity of the 'Republican state' whereas the British, with their attachment to parliamentary sovereignty and ideas about the 'historically-established rights of Englishmen' have kept Europe more at arms' length. In compound polities, other ideas show how the fit with democratic organizing principles was enhanced by social and political values, with the Germans embracing Europe as a way to submerge nation-state identity in a larger whole, the Italians, as a way to rescue national pride along with the nation-state, and the Spaniards, as a way to reinforce democracy—the same reason as the Greeks, despite their more simple polity.

Policy issues that have particular resonance with national values can also help explain responses to EU initiatives. Thus, Sweden and Denmark resisted joining the euro because of concerns about its impact on social justice in the social-democratic welfare state while Germany largely embraced it because it fit with notions of economic order and stability, despite the German public's qualms with regard to giving up the Deutschmark. Similarly, moreover, although the French and the Germans have both on the whole been pro-European, when EU policies threaten Germany's economic order through

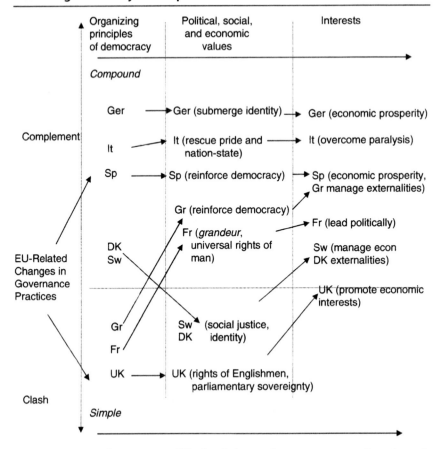

Figure 5.6. National responses to EU-related changes in governance practices, depending upon organizing principles of democracy, mediated by other democratic values and interests

decisions against the lending practices of the regional banks or the French state's social service mission through liberalization of public utilities, the responses are as negative as the British or the Swedes on the euro. What is more, the French no vote in the referendum on the Constitutional Treaty made clear that policy issues related to the euro's impact on the welfare state and liberalization of the *services publics* go to the heart of the left's concerns about social justice while the impact of enlargement and immigration on national identity was the major concern on the right—as it was for the Dutch no vote on the right and the left, although the euro's alleged inflationary impact was also an issue.

Interests also matter, of course. One cannot understand the general push for European integration without recognizing the economic, political, and social interests that enabled countries to overcome ideational obstacles to change—the French desire to lead politically in Europe; the German interest in serving its economic and social purposes; the British willingness to go with economic interest, despite political reticence; the Italian hope to overcome the economic, political, and social costs of state paralysis; or the need for small states such as Denmark, Sweden, and Austria to be part of a larger political entity so as better to manage economic externalities.

Experiences of European integration or Europeanization may also have an effect on perceptions of the Europeanization of governance practices. Thus, for example, success in projecting national preferences onto the EU can help offset concerns about the impact of the EU on national democracy—the case of France, where leadership in the EU has until recently served to obscure the state's real loss of autonomy, with national leaders presenting France's role in building Europe as its 'great adventure'.[38] By contrast, success in policy implementation may only increase concerns about the impact of the EU—as in Britain, where its stellar compliance record has meant that it has only felt the effects of Europeanization more, thereby adding to the clash with national historically and culturally grounded ideas. Finally, Britain's experience of better economic performance outside the eurozone than that of France, Germany, or Italy within it, added to its clash in values, helps explain its continued reticence to join the EMU.

Thus, although Europeanization has had a greater impact on simple polities than on compound polities due to matters of institutional fit, national responses to the EU depend not only on how Europeanization fits with institutionally grounded ideas about democracy but also on how it fits with culturally and historically grounded political, social, and economic values, with political, social, and economic interests, as well as with experiences of European integration and policy implementation. What is more, such national responses are clearly not fixed, since ideas, values, and interests all change over time as a matter not only of experience but also of social construction. Time-lags of course are natural with regard to things changing, since recognizing that things have changed, let alone adjusting ones' ideas to the changes, takes time.[39] But the problem for the EU's member-states is that they have not as yet come to recognize how such changes have affected national democracy, let alone devise new ways to adjust to such changes.

All of this, however, demands yet another kind of analysis. So far, our explanatory tools have included interests, institutions, culture, and ideas. There is one analytic tool not yet explored but which is also key for the explanation of the dynamics of national adaption: discourse.

---

[38] Jacques Chirac. Speech in Strasbourg to the European Parliament 6 March 2002. See discussion in Chapter 2.
[39] My thanks to Stefano Bartolini for raising the problem of time-lags in recognizing and adjusting to change.

Discourse and EU Democracy

Democracy is not just a matter of *interests*—based on people getting much of what they want and need; of *institutions*—consisting of the rules and procedures that shape the way people get what they want and need; of *culture*—encompassing the customs and mores that frame what people want and need; or of *ideas*—reflecting the principles underpinning what people believe that they have a right to want and the government an obligation to provide. It is also about *discourse*—about how the principles, customs, and rules related to what people want and need are constructed and how they are communicated by and to the people. Democracy, in other words, is not only driven by interests, shaped by institutions, and framed by culture; it is informed by ideas that are conveyed through discourse.

Discourse and the Foundations of Democracy

Public discourse at its most general level encompasses a set of ideas about public action and a set of communicative interactions between public actors and society focused on generating and legitimizing those ideas in the public sphere. Such discourse is a key component for understanding democratic politics, and central to the explanation of the dynamics of change as well as continuity in democratic polities.

Ideas and discourse are at the very foundations of democracy, enabling citizens not only to reason through difficulties and debate differences but also to construct new interpretations of political life, to give voice to public concerns, to gain a sense of joint purpose and meaning, and all in all to legitimize national policies, practices, and purposes.[40] Discourse does all of this through the use of a common language that conveys ideas which make sense of current events in terms of broader considerations of contemporary political life, generally by providing a coherent vision of the present and its natural progression into the future.

Generally speaking, in contemporary studies of democracy, political scientists focus primarily on institutions. They consider the degree of openness and freedom in elections, government responsiveness to interest representation and civil society, the viability and independence of judicial systems, the vibrancy of parties and their alternation in office, the powers of legislatures and their ability to counterbalance the executive, the amount of autonomy and decentralization of subnational units, and so on. But the essence of democracy is not here.

Strip away all of the modern-day structures, processes, and politics, and you can still have democracy as long as there is discourse and a common public

---

[40] See: March and Olsen (1995: 84–5) and Dryzek (1990).

space within which to carry it out. Early Greek democracy was primarily based on this assumption—that the 'demos' or citizenry was to deliberate and decide, and that all that was institutionally necessary was the 'agora', or place of assembly, for a 'polis' to be constituted. Greek tragedy was largely focused on what could go wrong in such a direct democracy, without institutionally consecrated rules to ensure, among other things, that individual or minority rights were protected against the vagaries of majority opinion, fed by majority interest.[41] Plato wrote the *Republic* to define what kinds of institutional rules were necessary to ensure that the right kinds or castes of individuals would constitute the polis (and, thereby, avoid the dangers of discourse endemic to politics based on narrow self-interest). And much of the history of political philosophy provides a slow march of ideas for the range of institutions that would be needed to limit the possible excesses that come from undisciplined discourse, let alone unfettered interest, in polities that were becoming more and more complex—from Hobbes to Locke to Montesquieu to Hegel.

In modern political philosophy, democratic discourse as a central preoccupation appears in Rousseau, for whom discourse was at the foundations of his 'general will' society (and which has sometimes itself been seen as a precursor to the undemocratic discourse of totalitarianism, albeit unfairly).[42] In contemporary philosophy, on the Anglo-American side it appears in the work of John Rawls and in the vast number of political theorists now focusing on 'deliberative democracy' or 'discursive democracy'.[43] In continental philosophy, it shows up primarily in phenomenology and critical theory, and is most developed as political theory in the work of Jürgen Habermas on 'communicative action'.[44] But Habermas's focus on discursive democracy, as that of philosophers more generally, is more prescriptive, focusing on the normative requirements of a noncoercive public discourse that would ensure an ideal democratic state, than it is descriptive of the empirical role of discourse in contemporary democracy, which is the focus of the framework for analysis I use herein.

Discourse as Framework for Analysis

'Discursive Institutionalism' is the name I give this framework for analysis,[45] because discourse must be set in context. It cannot be separated (except analytically) from the interests to which it gives expression, the institutions by which it is shaped, the culture which frames it; and the ideas which it serves to generate and convey. Methodologically, this approach constitutes a fourth

---

[41] On the role of Greek tragedy, see Farrar (1992).
[42] See Popper (1957).
[43] For example, Elster (1988), and Dryzek (1990).
[44] See, for example, Habermas (1996).
[45] Schmidt (2002a), see also Campbell (2004).

'new institutionalism' which has the same epistemological status as the three older new institutionalisms—rational choice, historical, and sociological institutionalism[46]—as a framework for analysis within which one can describe and analyze phenomena as well as develop and test theories.

Although interests certainly help explain political action in democracies, as rational choice institutionalists insist, they do not operate in a vacuum. Institutions constrain such action and serve as the context within which interests are formed, expressed, and routinized over time, as historical institutionalists contend. Moreover, cultures define the rules by which such interests and institutions are constituted, as sociological institutionalists maintain. But how are interests mobilized for positive, communal action? How are the constraints that institutions impose overcome? And how are interests reinterpreted or institutions reconstituted within any given culture? Little within the rational choice, historical institutionalist, or sociological institutionalist literatures adequately explains this. Only an approach, which takes into account the communicative aspects of human interaction through discourse, helps us with this.

What makes discursive institutionalism particularly useful in studies of institutional change is that it builds on the evidence of all three other approaches—using it as background information—at the same time that it overcomes their static structural bias through the dynamics of discourse.[47] The dynamics comes from the fact that at the same time discursive institutionalism takes interests, institutions, and culture as constitutive of ideas, it sees ideas as reconstitutive of interests, institutions, and culture. This is because discourse serves to redefine interests and reconfigure interest-based coordination; to reshape structures and follow new historical paths; and to reframe rules and create new norms. Most importantly, however, discursive institutionalism shows the dynamics not only through the changes (or continuity) of ideas but also in the discursive interactions among policy actors, political actors, and publics—that is, who speaks to whom about what, when, how, and where.

This very dynamics, however, also ensures that we could never claim discourse as *the* independent variable in the explanation of change, since it is very difficult to separate it from the other variables related to interests, institutions, or culture. We thus never ask when is it the cause but, rather, when is discourse *a* cause, enabling change by reconceptualizing interests, reshaping institutions, and reframing culture or constraining change as it reflects interests, follows institutional paths, and reifies cultural norms.[48]

Empirically, the causal influence of discourse can be demonstrated in a variety of ways. The causal influence itself can be captured through focused

---

[46] See the discussion in Hall and Taylor (1996).
[47] See Schmidt (2005b).
[48] Schmidt (2002a: 250–6) and Schmidt and Radaelli (2004).

studies that engage in process-tracing of ideas held by different actors to show how they led to different policy choices;[49] studies that show how speakers 'entrap' their publics through 'rhetorical action', such that even where actors have not changed their preferences, they are obliged to follow the policy implications of the discourses they accepted in the past;[50] and studies that take matched pairs of cases where everything is controlled for but the discourse.[51] Evidence can be found in the pronouncements, speeches, party platforms, and debates of political elites; in newspaper editorials, media commentary, and public debates; in the statements of opposition leaders, opinion leaders, community leaders, and activists; through interviews, participant-observation, and elite-tracing; and through opinion polls, surveys, election results, protest movements, strikes, and demonstrations.

But how do we establish the causal influence of discourse theoretically? More specifically, how do we establish when a polity, whether simple, compound, or the highly compound regional EU, has a transformative discourse? The problem is that people always talk. So when does it matter? And when does it not? To determine this requires three steps. First, we need to outline the ideational criteria for a good discourse in terms of the substantive content of ideas, that is, 'what you say' cognitively and normatively. Second, to be able to assess whether it is transformative, we have to consider the discourse in terms of its interactive processes, that is, 'who says what to whom'. And third, to be able to pinpoint the influence, we need to ask about the institutional context.

DISCOURSE AS IDEAS

In terms of substantive content, discourse may contain two different kinds of arguments, cognitive and normative. Cognitive arguments depend for success on their ability to define the problems to be solved, to propose adequate policy solutions to those problems, and/or to develop a public philosophy that provides the key to both problems and solutions.[52] They tend to be supported by reference to the techniques and principles of scientific disciplines, and justified in terms of the 'logic of necessity'. Truthfulness is not so much at issue here as is the cognitive interpretation of the 'facts', only some of which may be in question at any given time,[53] with truth in this context better understood as a question of the relevance and applicability of the ideas.[54] Cognitive arguments abound in the justification of European integration, in particular, the linking of economic interdependence to ensuring lasting peace,

---

[49] For example, Berman (1998), and Blyth (2002).
[50] Schimmelfennig (2001).
[51] For example, Schmidt (2002d, 2003).
[52] There is a vast literature on this. See, for example, Mehta (2004), Campbell (2004).
[53] See Radaelli and Schmidt (2004: 366–8).
[54] For a discussion of the cognitive criteria for success based on the philosophy of science, see Schmidt (2002a: 217–20).

the refrain of all leaders in the early postwar period, whether by de Gaulle, Churchill, Adenauer, or De Gasperi, that came on top of nationally specific reasons related to the necessity of economic integration and how it served national interests—political as well as economic.

A 'good' normative argument, by contrast, is not so much concerned with demonstrating the truth or applicability of the ideas in question as with their appropriateness. Thus, it tends to make appeal to the norms and principles of public life, with its success dependent upon to what extent it resonates with values, whether newly emerging or long-standing ones in the societal repertoire.[55] This normative side of discourse, in short, legitimates its ideas in terms of a logic of appropriateness. For all leaders in the postwar period, integration was not just necessary, it was also appropriate to end war and promote a brighter future for all. Here, too, of course, there were nationally specific arguments which appealed to different, culturally and historically derived normative values.

Both cognitive and normative arguments are key to understanding when discourse has transformative power, and when it does not. For Germany, the transformative power of the postwar discourse came from its cognitive justification of European integration in terms of gains in foreign policy and economic interests together with its normative legitimization for superimposing a European identity onto the German in terms of past guilt and future promise. In Italy, the transformative power of discourse was evident in the successful push toward EMU, when cognitive arguments about the necessity of fiscal and pension reforms combined with normative arguments appealing to Italian national pride if it were left out of EMU and 'intergenerational solidarity' for pension reform. One set of arguments without the other makes for a weaker discourse. This has been the case of the UK, where pro-European leaders' cognitive arguments about the economic benefits of European integration lacked any normative component, leaving to the Euroskeptics the appeals to deeper values of parliamentary sovereignty and the historically established rights of Englishmen. In France, by contrast, cognitive arguments about French leadership ensuring its interests combined with normative arguments about how such leadership enhances French *grandeur* and projects its universalistic values served as a powerful enough cocktail to enable French political leaders to ignore another set of normative issues—the impact on national sovereignty and identity. As time has gone on, however, the Gaullist paradigm has created increasing 'cognitive dissonance', mainly because the French no longer lead Europe, and sovereignty and identity have not been recast in ways capable of legitimizing Europeanization effects in France—as the referendum on the Constitutional Treaty demonstrated.

---

[55] See Schmidt (2000, 2002: 220–2).

But this points to the importance of other criteria, such as coherence and consistency in message. If we consider the most successful of discourses with regard to Europe, de Gaulle's discourse of leadership, for example, or Adenauer 'Rhineland' vision, they tended to provide a set of arguments that held together at the time as well as over time, so much so that they constrained future discourse. De Gaulle's discourse has been the paradigm at the core of French leaders' discourse up until today, Adenauer's for German leaders. Both may now have been stretched beyond their limits, France because of the effects of Europeanization, Germany because unification has at the very least made it a very different space from what it was at the end of World War II. For Britain, where coherence and consistency in message comes only from the euroskeptics, national leaders have a very long way to go to construct a new discourse that could coherently and consistently make the normative case for Europe. For Britain, it would require a recasting of the discourse of national identity. But a new discourse for France might have to do so as well. Only Italy for the moment seems to be able to continue with its postwar discourse coherently and consistently.

This said, although we generally think of a good discourse as coherent and consistent, sometimes vagueness or ambiguity makes for discursive success. Most importantly for the EU as a whole, the ambiguity of the phrase: 'federal union of nation-states' has allowed all countries to see themselves in the formula—with Germany and Italy emphasizing the 'federal,' France and Britain the 'union of nation-states', even though this still may not be ambiguous enough for those British worried about a federal 'superstate'.

DISCOURSE AS INTERACTIONS

How to determine whether a discourse is good—by being cognitively justified and normatively legitimated—requires a further consideration of how it is communicated. And this depends on who talks to whom in the process of policy construction—the sphere of the 'coordinative discourse'—and political communication—the sphere of the 'communicative discourse' (see Figure 5.7).

In the coordinative discourse, the main interlocutors are policy actors—experts, organized interests, civil servants, elected officials, and public figures—who coordinate the construction of policy often using ideas conveyed by policy 'entrepreneurs' and/or developed in discursive communities—whether 'policy networks' based on the exchange of ideas; 'epistemic communities' united on the basis of shared ideas; 'advocacy coalitions' which share both ideas and access to policymaking; or 'strong publics' that critically deliberate about policies, such as the EP.[56] In the EU, the coordinative discourse encompasses most discursive interactions—whether among ministers in the

---

[56] Kohler Koch (2002), Haas (1992), Sabatier (1996), and Eriksen and Fossum (2002).

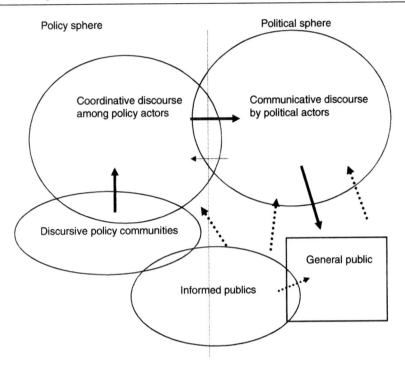

Figure 5.7. The flow of ideas and discourse among actors in the policy process

Note: Solid arrows show direction of ideas and discourse, dotted arrows show feedback, overlap shows where some actors may operate in both spheres.

Council, among Commissioners and civil servants in the Commission, among MEPs in the parliament, between members of the EP and the Commission, between members of the Commission and the Council, not to mention among all members of EU institutions and civil society, whether through arenas, 'forums', comitology committees, public hearings, and more. In the EU, moreover, because the deliberative process is one in which making good arguments is the primary road to success, the politics of interests is less significant here than expertise and scientific justification, and 'arguing' therefore takes precedence over 'bargaining', at the very least in the Commission, where the process has been seen as contributing to 'deliberative supranationalism'[57] or 'directly deliberative polyarchy'.[58] This kind of discourse is often closed to public view, as policy actors in the coordinative discourse talk mainly to one another.

In the political sphere, the domain of the communicative discourse, the key interlocutors are political actors—politicians, spin doctors, campaign

[57] Joerges and Neyer (1997).
[58] Gerstenberg and Sabel (2000).

managers, government spokespersons, party activists—who *communicate* the ideas developed in the context of the coordinative discourse to the public. These include both the general or 'weak' public of citizens and the 'informed publics' of 'organized private persons' or policy forums made up of community leaders, activists, experts, organized interests, the media—for discussion, deliberation and, ideally, modification.[59] Here, it is most important to note that although the communicative discourse can appear to be hierarchical, as leaders speak to national publics or to the media, deliberation is inherent in the subsequent give-and-take with regard to public reactions, whether immediately in the news media by journalists and opinion leaders, or later, in election campaigns and election results. The original ideas in the discourse, moreover, may also come from the public. Most interesting in this regard are the social movements that eschew the coordinative discourse with state actors through established channels of consultation and target instead the communicative discourse to the general public, whether through public pronouncements or targeted actions of 'contestation' designed to attract media attention.[60]

It is important to note that both coordinative and communicative discourses address both cognitive and normative issues, but with different emphases. The coordinative discourse tends to be more focused on the cognitive arguments— as policy actors debate policies' relative technical and scientific merits, such as the most suitable criteria to use for European monetary integration, the best way to privatize, or how to rationalize social services. The normative arguments about such policies' appropriateness, although also important, are not necessarily articulated in this sphere unless they appeal to newly emerging values or clash with long-standing ones, since if they resonate with existing values their normative legitimacy is often simply assumed. The normative mainly comes up explicitly where policy actors disagree on the fundamentals, for example, on whether to adhere to the agreed-upon criteria for monetary integration, whether to privatize at all, or who is to bear the brunt of cuts in social service. But this is naturally also when the debates spill over into the political sphere, and the issues are taken up in the communicative discourse.

In the communicative discourse, the cognitive arguments may get shorter shrift, since political actors often assume the cognitive adequacy of the policy—especially if it fits with long-established scientific 'truths'—as they seek to show the policy's normative resonance with the underlying values of the polity. This is where government and opposition generally air their reasons for seeking to pass or to block particular policies, legitimating their arguments on the basis of differing political positions which often also differ in the values of the polity to which they appeal. Right/left divides are the most obvious

---

[59] Eriksen and Fossum (2002), Habermas (1989), and Rein and Schoen (1994).
[60] Sommier (2003), Birchfield (2004).

bases for such divisions, but they can also be based on religious beliefs, lifestyle issues, and ethnic diversity among others. Often, of course, the normative divisions also bring with them alternative cognitive arguments about a policy's adequacy. Thus, for example, in Britain although the Euroskeptics opposed to EMU did make cognitive arguments about the policy's deleterious effects on the economy, they reserved most of their powder for normative arguments about its impact on sovereignty and identity. Moreover, whereas in the debates in the Constituent Assembly on the Constitutional Treaty, the coordinative discourse was largely cognitive, focused on how to reform the institutions, in the debates in the referenda on the Treaty, the communicative discourse was mainly normative, with those opposed citing the impact of immigration on national identity or the effects of the EU's neoliberalism on the welfare state, and those in favor insisting that institutional reform would serve to democratize the EU.

The communicative process is often complicated by the fact that political actors must speak not just to the merits of any given policy—as do policy actors—but also to how it fits into a larger policy program that spans a number of policy sectors—say, economic policy, which may bring together monetary policy, financial markets, policies toward business, telecommunications, energy policy, and so forth—and which must also mesh with policy programs in other areas—say, with labor and social policy. Here, the communicative discourse clearly requires political actors to make cognitive arguments at a more general level about the technical adequacy of the policy program(s)— arguments which are also taken from the coordinative sphere and translated into more publicly accessible language. But it is the normative that takes center stage in this sphere (see Figure 5.8). Political actors, after all, need to win elections on the basis of political programs that they can argue persuasively are not just technically sound in terms of policies but also that are considered just, fair, and right in terms of the polity.[61] And they have to win such elections against politicians from rival parties with communicative discourses about alternative political programs that may muster different cognitive and normative arguments. Election outcomes depend at least in part on the ability of the 'master' politicians—presidential and prime ministerial candidates—to communicate a 'master' discourse to the public by weaving together the coordinative ideas about a wide range of policy programs into a (at least seemingly) coherent political program that provides a 'vision' of where the polity is, where it is going, and where it ought to go.[62] Some political leaders have been true masters at this, in the UK, Churchill, Thatcher, and

---

[61] Here, one could also, following Easton, differentiate between the 'specific' support of interests for particular policies and the 'diffuse' support based on beliefs about the legitimacy of the policy in terms of the political system. See the discussion in Jachtenfuchs et al. (1998: 412).

[62] For more on the 'master' discourse, see: Schmidt (2002), chapter 5.

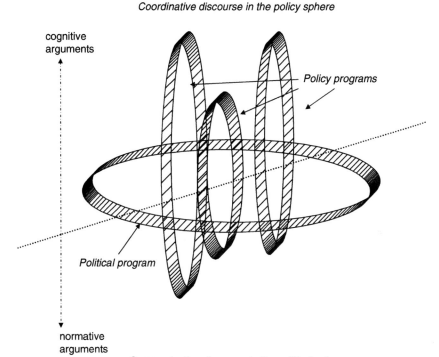

Coordinative discourse in the policy sphere

cognitive
arguments

Policy programs

Political program

normative
arguments

Communicative discourse in the political sphere

Figure 5.8. Policy programs and political program in coordinative and communicative discourse

Blair; in France both de Gaulle and Mitterrand—but not Chirac; in Germany, certainly Adenauer, possibly Kohl, but not Schröder; in Italy, De Gasperi, but certainly not Berlusconi.[63]

Other factors also play a role. Most importantly, success comes often not just because of the ideas in the discourse and how leaders project them, that is, the psychological imponderables. It also involves their ability to control the medium of delivery as well as the 'spin', and whether they ensure a coherent message, by ensuring that members of their government also project the same one. Contrast Blair, who has exercised effective control over his ministers, with Schroeder who, when first elected, was not the only 'master' of the discourse, given that party chairman Oscar Lafontaine provided a rival, more left-leaning discourse.[64]

---

[63] See Schmidt (2002*a*), chapter 6.
[64] Schmidt (2002*a*), chapter 6.

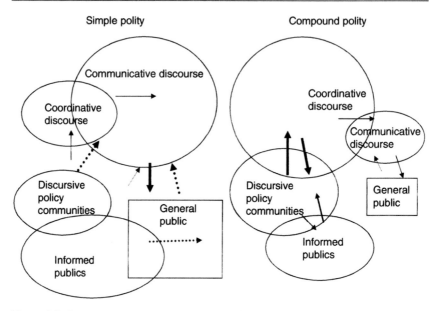

Figure 5.9. Discourse interactions in simple and compound national polities

Put into the terms of democratic theory, because political leaders must be elected *by* the people as representatives *of* the people, they need to convince the public that they are able to govern effectively *for* the people on the basis of policies developed or implemented *with* the people. And for this, both coordinative and communicative discourses are crucial. But, importantly, institutional arrangements make for differences in the discursive process.

DISCOURSE IN 'SIMPLE' AND 'COMPOUND' POLITIES

Discourse is not just about what you say, or to whom your say it, but also 'where you say it'. And this speaks to the question of institutional context. Although all polities have both coordinative and communicative discourses, some polities emphasize the one, some the other. Countries' differential responses to Europeanization are related not only to the focus of their ideas but also to the locus of their discourse—both the coordinative discourse among policy actors, which tends to be more developed in compound polities, and the communicative discourse to the general public, which tends to be much more elaborate in simple polities (see Figure 5.9).

In simple polities such as Britain, France, and to a lesser extent Ireland, the coordinative discourse tends to be quite thin, the communicative discourse highly elaborate. The concentration of power in the executive, the restricted nature of interest representation, and the polarization of politics means that political actors are naturally focused on communicating to the public decisions taken behind closed doors by a restricted policy elite, rather than on coordinating policy construction with other policy actors, interests, or political agents. Here, the transformative power of discourse is therefore most likely to be evidenced in public responses to the communicative discourse—through quiescence or protest, positive or negative election results, and opinion polls and surveys.[65] In Britain, the discourse itself comes out not just in speeches by political leaders but in the weekly sessions of the Prime Minister's questions, in which the British parliament carries the communicative 'voice' as the government presents its programs while the opposition plays the role of constant critic. This ensures a highly contentious communicative discourse to the general public, in which both sides are heard. In France, where the weak parliament has little voice, and is not necessarily heard, the communicative discourse is often one between political leaders and the street—although intellectuals have also traditionally played the role of critics.

The problem with the thinness of the coordinative discourse within simple polities is that it tends to leave to the public little option other than protest where it disagrees with government initiatives, whether through polemics in the press, strikes, demonstrations, or elections. Depending upon the intensity of the public reaction, the government may decide to persist with the discourse and the policy unchanged in the face of confrontation—in which case the policy's soundness and appropriateness is in doubt—or withdraw it—in which case the problems remain unsolved. In either case, democratic legitimacy is in question.[66]

Legitimacy can be enhanced in simple polities, however, in two ways. The first is by increasing government openness and citizen participation in the communicative discourse. Indeed, most conceptions of deliberative democracy are predicated on this, that is, on the assumption that the more participants in the discourse the better—as Habermas[67] would argue. But it is important to note that in practice occasionally less is better, where the public airing of certain issues agreed among policy actors may lead to less than 'ideal' results—as in cases of immigration policy where public debates have become highly politicized and subject to populist exploitation.[68]

The second way is to increase openness and participation at the coordinative stage of discourse, before the state acts and society has nothing left to do but to react. One way to do this is to replace the traditionally limited, government-controlled information-imparting process with more open deliberative processes—the case of Sweden in the social policy arena in the early 1990s when, in the absence of coordination with the social partners, the government

---

[65] See Schmidt (2002a, Chapter 5, 2003b).
[66] See Schmidt (2002a, Chapter 5).
[67] Habermas (1989).
[68] Guiraudon (1997).

organized an elaborate consultation process with the public.[69] Another approach is to delegate policy construction to committees of sages charged to produce a policy recommendation on the basis of widespread interest consultation and public deliberation, which creates a semicoordinative discourse within the communicative sphere through media attention and public exposure. This has been the frequent solution of French governments for controversial issues (e.g. on citizenship and on *laïcité*—on head scarves in schools) as well as of British governments (although admittedly all governments do this to some extent). Governments can also devolve their powers to societal interests in certain spheres, for example, by creating a coordinative discourse between social partners in the shadow of the state—the case in France with regard to the 35-hour work week. Deregulation is probably the most far-reaching of such remedies, since it shifts the locus of the discursive interaction from government to independent regulatory agencies which are required by law to hear all sides and make decisions in a transparent manner—without the arbitrariness that comes when civil servants use their administrative discretion to make exceptions to the rules, as traditionally in France or in Italy.

In compound national polities such as Germany, Italy, Belgium, Austria, Denmark, and the Netherlands, by contrast, the coordinative discourse tends to be more elaborate and the communicative discourse thinner. The diffusion of power in multiple authorities, the wide interest consultation, and the consensus-oriented politics ensures that policy actors will be more focused on coordinating agreement among themselves and legitimizing any such agreements through 'subdiscourses' to their constituencies in terms of their own particular cognitive and normative criteria. The communicative discourse is therefore left to the government, which has the task of communicating agreements to the general public in more vague terms. This is because any detailed communication could risk unravelling compromises reached in private by violating ideas and/or values contained in the different groups' subdiscourses.[70] It follows therefore that the transformative power of discourse is more likely to be evidenced in the outcomes of the coordinative discourse, that is, whether or not there is any agreement on contested issues.[71]

The problem with the thinness of the communicative discourse within compound national polities is that it tends to leave the public with little significant orienting or legitimizing information beyond what it may have obtained as members of constituent groups (and thus as an informed public). The very structure of the discursive process, thus, may seem to violate Habermas's democratic ideals based on public deliberation and 'communicative action',[72] given

---

[69] See Schmidt (2003*a*).
[70] See Schmidt (2002*a*, chapter 5).
[71] Schmidt (2001, 2002*a*) and Schmidt and Radaelli (2004).
[72] Habermas (1989).

that public deliberation will necessarily be uninformed and have little effect upon decisions already made on the basis of private deliberations behind closed doors. That Habermas developed his political philosophy in compound Germany should come as no surprise. For Germany, expanding participation in the communicative discourse could be the key to increasing legitimacy, to ensure greater deliberation with the general public. This might have helped with regard to the sagging levels of favorable public opinion with regard to entrance in the euro. But the case of Italy shows that more communication is not always the solution. Because there are so many different political actors communicating their own conflicting views to the general public, political polarization means that Italians listen attentively only to their own preferred leaders, and the cacophony of voices does nothing for overall legitimacy.

Legitimacy can be enhanced in compound polities also by ensuring that the coordinative discourse is inclusive—by covering most relevant groups in society; transparent—because made public through open meetings reported in the news; and responsive—because open to modification in the light of criticism. Problems occur mainly where the coordinative discourse marginalizes certain groups—immigrants, the unemployed, and women; where policy elites do not communicate enough with constituent members; and where it occurs behind closed doors that do not leak, leaving the public in the dark about agreements. These latter dynamics go some way toward explaining the success of the leader of the extreme right, Jörg Haider in Austria in the 1990s, whose communicative discourse resonated not so much because of his thinly disguised Nazi references but because, in the absence of any real communicative discourse from the government, his talk represented a 'breath of fresh air' while his normative defense of 'family values' resonated at a time when welfare state reforms threatened to undermine the male-breadwinner model.[73]

However, the success just a few years later of Pym Fortyn in the Netherlands, which has long had a highly inclusive, transparent, and responsive coordinative discourse, suggests that the structure of discourse in compound polities alone—by minimizing the communicative sphere—is a problem. This certainly also helps explain the dismal failure of Dutch leaders to develop a persuasive communicative discourse in the referendum on the Constitutional Treaty—made worse by the fact that this was their first referendum ever. But the problems may not only result from institutional structure but also from a lack of political imagination. In the 2002 election, Dutch mainstream politicians failed to address the politically sensitive issues concerning the public, such as the question of immigration, foreigners, and law and order, which left the field open to exploitation by the extreme right.[74] In the 2005 referendum on the Constitutional Treaty, the government, in addition to being unpopular,

---

[73] See Schmidt (2000a, 2003).
[74] See Schmidt (2003a).

did not have a clue as to how to talk about Europe. And this, of course, has equally been a problem for simple polities such as France. In the 2005 referendum, the mainstream leaders on the left as much the right were equally devoid of ideas about how to speak about Europe.

Only in two cases does the communicative discourse naturally come to the fore in such compound polities: in election periods—when its adversarial tone may undermine the cooperative demands of the coordinative discourse—and when the coordinative discourse breaks down.[75] In this latter instance, the communicative discourse may offer a solution, by providing a new frame within which key policy actors can reconstruct the coordinative discourse as it exhorts all parties to the debate to come to the table. But for this, one needs to have good 'communicators' with good ideas and policy actors willing to come back to the table. This is not such an easy task, however, given the large numbers of actors able to speak with authority, but who are likely to have very different messages for the public. The potential result is that many good ideas communicated to the public may get drowned in a sea of conflicting messages, and that it will in any case take time for any clear voices to be heard through the din, let alone come to agreement on what is to be done. This has certainly been the problem for German Chancellor Schröder, as evidenced by his diffi-culties in liberalizing the 'social market economy' and reforming pension systems in the face of stalemate between business and unions. But such success is not impossible, witness the successful efforts by Italian prime ministers in the 1990s (with the exception of Berlusconi) to institute pension reforms and enable Italy to qualify for EMU.[76] However, the difficulties of constructing a strong communicative discourse in compound polities is even more poten-tially a problem in the highly compound EU.

Discourse in the EU and Its Impact on Simple and Compound National Polities

The EU, as the most compound of governance systems, has the most elaborate of coordinative discourses, the thinnest possible of communicative discourses (see Figure 5.10). The multiple authorities open to a wide range of interests and focused on reaching a consensus ensures a vast coordinative discourse in which EU officials, national government representatives, experts and interests in 'policy networks', epistemic communities, 'advocacy coalitions', 'strong publics', and the like coordinate agreement on policies and communicate those agreements to their own constituencies. But the relative paucity of EU-level political actors, combined with the absence of a European public and all that goes with it in terms of a common language, media, politics, and so on, makes for a meager communicative discourse. When scholars criticize the lack

---

[75] For more detail, see Schmidt (2000*a*, 2002*a*, chapter 5).
[76] Schmidt (2000*a*, 2002*a*).

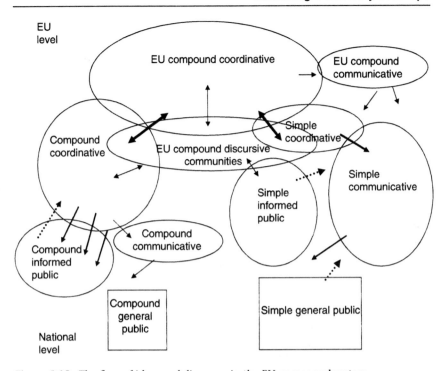

Figure 5.10. The flow of ideas and discourse in the EU compound system

Solid arrows show direction of ideas and discourse, dotted arrows show feedback, overlap show where some actors may operate in both spheres.

of a 'European public sphere', they are in fact referring to the poverty of the communicative discourse in what we would refer to as the EU's political sphere, not the EU's policy sphere in which the coordinative discourse is vast and in the process of continuing expansion.

At least for the moment, much of what passes for EU communicative discourse is filtered through national leaders and policy actors, with the exception of sensational moments (e.g. Commission President Prodi's criticism of the SGP criteria as 'stupid'). Only in those areas of exclusive EU competence, in international trade, in competition policy, in the ECB, or the ECJ, does one find an authoritative communicative discourse expressed through one voice—and even here, there are problems, as evidenced by the communicative difficulties of the first head of the ECB, Wim Duisenberg. Otherwise, the number of different voices speaking with authority makes for great difficulty in getting any clear messages out.

The EU, however, under increasing attack since the early 1990s for its perceived democratic deficit, has been seeking to increase its legitimacy by developing a more robust communicative discourse focused on polity as well as policy issues. On polity issues, national leaders have been the clearest voices with regard to the issue of the EU's democratic future, starting with Joschka Fischer's push for a federal Europe in 2000 and continuing with the Constitutional Convention and the Constitutional Treaty.[77] The recommendations to name a nonrotating President of the European Council as well as a Foreign Affairs Minister are both responses to the perceived need for a stronger European voice, capable of communicating directly to the European public. The EU Commission, moreover, in addition to issuing a white paper on governance addressing polity issues of transparency and accountability, has sought to build a communicative component into its coordinative pronouncements and texts on new policy initiatives. In EU agricultural policy, for example, these communicative elements play a dual role: at the same time they serve to reassure the public about the impartiality and transparency of the policy process itself—and as such can be seen as discourse directed more at polity issues—they also are intended to appeal directly to national publics on the policy issues, and thereby to exert pressure on national leaders.[78] But the main thrust of the EU Commission's policy discourse remains in the coordinative realm, addressed to the networks of governmental and nongovernmental actors involved in policy construction at the EU level, even as many of these self-same actors are also part of another set of coordinative and/or communicative interactions at the national level, deliberating about how to respond to EU-level policy formulation or how to implement nationally the EU policies already decided.

The very nature of the EU-level discursive interactions has generalizable effects on the discursive processes within all national polities. Generally speaking, the extensive European level coordinative discourses among policy actors add to the national ones in increasing numbers of policy sectors while the minimal European communicative discourse to the general public largely leaves to national actors the communicative discourse to the public. But again, Europeanization has a differential impact on simple and compound polities.

Compound polities tend to be less affected by the EU's elaborate coordinative discourse, mainly because the EU simply adds new, nongovernmental voices to an already rich array involved in national policy construction. Because all such voices are able to speak directly to their own diverse interest constituencies about the new policies they helped deliberatively construct, they can ease acceptance of EU-related changes. Such was the case of many of the deregulatory policies in the public utilities sector in both Germany and Italy, whether in telecommunications or electricity. But it has also been the case for environmental and social policy in Germany.

By contrast, in simple polities the EU adds nongovernmental voices to a policy construction process in which they have generally had little direct role, given their traditional lack of input or standing in national policymaking. The problem here is that while these nongovernmental voices may contribute to

[77] See the discussions in Chapter 2.   [78] See Fouilleux (2004).

EU-level policy construction, they are not likely to be able to do at the national level what those in compound polities can readily do, that is, legitimize EU-related policies to national constituencies, since they are often weak intermediaries at the national level. As a result, political actors in simple polities may find themselves much more alone when communicating to the general public on EU-related policies. Moreover, where national organized interests are not present at the EU level and policies go against their wishes, the discursive legitimization problems for political leaders' communicative discourse are even greater. This was the case of public services workers in France and the truck-drivers in France as well as in Italy—suggesting that problems will also occur in compound polities where groups are cut out of EU level-policy formulation.

By the same token, however, simple polities could do better with the EU's thin communicative discourse. This is mainly because national politicians are better able to speak clearly and in a single voice to the public about the implications for the polity of the changes in policies and practices, were they to so choose. The problem is that they have for the most part not chosen to do so, whether in France, where political leaders try to ignore the impact of Europeanization on the polity, or in the UK, where they tend mainly to complain about it. This a major problem for democratic legitimization, given that simple polities have been harder hit by Europeanization in terms of their foundational organizing principles of democracy. Compound polities, less affected in terms of organizing principles, given their greater institutional fit with the EU, may nevertheless have an even harder time where nationally specific values of democracy are challenged—the social market economy in Germany; derogation of rules in Italy—mainly because of the potential cacophony of voices speaking to the issue, and communicating conflicting messages to the general public.

Thus, although simple polities face a greater ideational challenge from EU-related changes in governance practices than compound polities, given the much greater clash with foundational democratic organizing principles, in practice they could have an easier time in speaking to the changes because of their stronger communicative voice. Discursive misfit, in short, much as institutional misfit, can work to the simple polity's advantage. It is a good thing that compound polities have a better institutional fit with regard to Europeanization, because its discursive fit with the EU makes for a weak communicative discourse to speak to any change.

Conclusion

European integration is at risk, then, not so much because of the institutional changes related to Europeanization but because of the lack of new ideas and discourse that address those changes at the national level. Although the EU has had a greater impact on simple polities than on compound ones, both kinds of polities have nevertheless had to deal with EU-related changes in governance practices and challenges to traditional ideas about democracy. Moreover, even though simple polities may have an advantage with regard to addressing the issues through the communicative discourse, they have not used that ability to the fullest. Neither simple nor compound polities have sought to generate new ideas, let alone new national practices, to make up for the EU-related changes. The EU itself can be no use here. There is no EU-level solution to the democratic deficit at the national level, especially since the EU itself suffers from the lack of a strong, central voice able to communicate directly to the general public. Because European integration affects each country differently, given differences in institutions, interests, culture, and history, each country has to find its own way with regard to the reevaluation of national democracy in light of Europeanization.

Conclusion: The Prospects for Democracy in Europe

Before discussing the prospects for democracy in Europe, we need to ask ourselves one last question: How has the EU managed to get so far, given a system that is so contingent in sovereignty, uncertain in boundaries, unclear in identity, complicated in governance, and fragmented in democracy? The answer is: It has come as far as it has because of these very attributes. These attributes are an expression of the creative tension between the EU and its member-states, propelling them at one at the same time into ever-increasing regional integration and continuing national differentiation.

In the past, the EU's dynamism has been promoted by not clearly articulating its end-point or institutional goals, leaving some to hope for a federal nation-state equivalent, others to fear anything beyond the nation-state, and most happy for something in between. Although such ambiguity was the formula for progress in the past, it is counterproductive today. The EU has moved so far so fast in the past two decades—from the Single Market Act through European Monetary Integration to enlargement to the east, not to mention the beginnings of a common foreign and security policy, integration of justice and policing, elimination of frontiers, and more—that it is natural that national citizens want to know, need to know, what it really is and where it is going. Not talking about it feeds fears about how far it might go—both in policies and territory—and provides fodder for those opposed to further integration.

Europe today requires, above all, greater clarity of purpose and better understanding on the part of its citizens. I have argued that it is not a nation-state 'in waiting' but a *regional state*. Thinking of the EU as a regional state is useful as a way of breaking preconceived notions of what the EU ought to become while emphasizing the state-like qualities of the EU, although other concepts can have a similar effect—whether postnational international form, neomedieval empire, condominio, and so on. The important thing here is to recognize that the EU is a new form of supranational cum intergovernmental order which is already democratic, just not in the same way as a nation-state, given the split in democratic legitimizing mechanisms between governance *for* and *with* the people at the EU level and government *by* and *of* the people at the national level. The resulting strains, which make for *policies without politics* at the EU level and *politics without policies* at the national, are at the basis of the problems for democracy not just in the EU taken as a whole but also for each and every member-state, with simple polities more affected than compound.

The prospects for democracy in the EU are nevertheless good so long as national leaders and national publics face up to the problems. But facing up to the problems will not be easy. For the EU level, it requires recognizing that for the time being at least reinforcing democracy cannot mean creating more governing *by* and *of* the people through any directly elected government. And yet more 'democracy' is clearly required. The difficulty is that doing more with regard to democracy butts up against the contradictions inherent in the fragmented basis of EU democracy.

First of all, more 'democracy' most certainly entails devising more avenues for interest consultation *with* the people—beyond where the Commission has gotten with its *White Paper on Governance*—as well as continued efforts to increase transparency and accountability in governing *for* the people. Nationally based organized interests and social movements that are primarily focused at the national level need to learn to organize, pressure, and protest at the EU level—and national governments need to do more to help them do so. Expanding the access of 'civil society' at the EU level is also a way of increasing the EU's legitimacy in governing *for* the people, by devising policies that are more reflective of the concerns of all the people. This, combined with more measures to increase awareness of the EU and EU responsiveness to citizens' concerns—for example, through things like the provision in the Constitutional Treaty to allow petitions carrying the signatures of one million citizens to trigger a Commission review (Article 46, clause 4)—helps increase the EU's democratic legitimacy. But although bringing more groups into EU-level pluralist policymaking processes and providing for more EU-focused 'direct democracy' may have a positive impact on EU-level legitimacy, it can also have a deleterious effect on national representative politics generally, by channeling citizens' energy and attention away from action *qua* voters to action *qua* interests. Moreover, it is likely to have more of a negative impact on simple polities, where citizens are considered primarily as political actors, than in compound ones, where they are also involved as corporate actors.

The only way out of this dilemma is to invent new ways to repoliticize the EU level other than in the traditional nation-state manner through direct elections of a governing body. Some suggestions about how to repoliticize the EU already appear here and there in the book. National political interests also need to organize, pressure, and protest more directly in Brussels, not only through the 'virtual' parties of the 'virtual' parliament but more directly through national governments in the Council and through political representations to the Commission. For this to work appropriately, however, political ideas need to be reintroduced into the policy debate itself. One way would be to have the Commission frame proposed legislation in terms of 'political' alternatives rather than as purely technocratic, to allow proper debate. This would ensure, for example, that directives focused on liberalization and deregulation of markets would not just be the outcome of the struggle between 'technocratic' best practice and organized interests in the Commission, national interests based on national practice in the Council, and European public interest in the Parliament. Instead, the choices would be framed explicitly from the very beginning in political terms by the Commission, with the different possible normative orientations made clear alongside the cognitive in the coordinative discourse. It could then be debated publicly in the Council and the Parliament to bring politics back into policymaking through an EU level communicative discourse. This, of course, is easier said than done. To be workable, repoliticization would require further EU-level institutional changes.

The EU itself would need to develop a more communicative voice to the European public. This might be improved in a small way by reforms proposed in the Constitutional Treaty with regard to a foreign minister as well as a nonrotating president, to provide a single voice through which to speak to EU policies. But to make the EU a truly deliberative sphere it would be necessary also to have public debates in the Council on the issues themselves. This, however, would mean lifting the veil of secrecy from the Council, a recommendation proposed by the Constitutional Convention and dropped from the Constitutional Treaty—which is something the Council could agree to do on its own, since it is not written into the treaties. The debates in the Council could then be supplemented by public debates with the Parliament, a bit like the British parliament's prime minister's 'Question Time', when the government makes its case and the opposition gives its response. In this case, the ministers responsible for a given issue could meet with the parliamentary committee or the Parliament as a whole in public session, aired on national television programs equivalent to C-Span (with interpretations into the national language, easy since the EU already provides this for the MEPs themselves), and reported in the national news media if and when an issue captures public attention. With these kinds of debates, deliberative democracy in a European public sphere could begin to take shape as national leaders speak as Europeans to European issues. It would also make it more difficult for them to say one thing in meetings with EU leaders and another to national publics.

One very important caveat, however. Although such transparency could contribute to creating a European deliberative sphere, it would also certainly make it more difficult for the Council to reach any agreements at all! The EU has been built on bargains made behind closed doors, based on compromises that do not make for good legitimizing discourses to the general public. Council members might have second-thoughts about agreeing to any number of policies were they to have to legitimate them after the fact in public debate. But even leaving aside the problems of discourse 'in the shadow of transparency', just getting to agreement would be made more difficult by the reintroduction of left-right orientation to the policies themselves. Left-right policy deliberations may make policymaking more recognizable and relevant to the public, but it also introduces yet another source of division into member-state deliberations, already burdened by considerations of national, public, and special interests. The phenomenal progress in terms of EU policies has largely been due to the removal of politics from the decision-making process. Reintroducing it could slow or even stop forward movement, already made more difficult by the enlargement of the EU, with 25 member-states now considering national interest in the Council. Thus, repoliticizing may be good in terms of governance *by* and *of* the people, but it could prove a disaster for governance *for* the people, that is, for the EU to move forward in an efficient and effective way. And of course, if it is not able to move forward, the greater deliberative democracy would be an exercise in frustration, and a bigger turn-off to European citizens than even the current system.

Thus, repoliticizing the EU level could effectively destroy the EU's 'policy without politics' at the same time that, in the end, it could also further depoliticize citizens, worsening the problems of national 'politics without policy'. The one way out of this dilemma is to give up the goal of repoliticizing the EU entirely. Or at most to open up Council meetings only very selectively, where public deliberation could be useful as a unifying device. Foreign policy issues such as the run-up to the Iraq war, where the EU would have benefited from Blair, Schröder, and Chirac talking to each rather than at one another, would be a case in point. Otherwise, best would be to accept the fragmented nature of EU democracy and recognize that the only possible remedy for the 'democratic deficit' at the EU level is to further increase governance *for* and *with* the people at that level. But what then to do about the resulting national level problems? Reconcile national publics to the fragmented nature of EU democracy and do more to bring national publics into EU decision-making, whether by encouraging more direct EU-level access via interest groups or more indirect access by way of national governments. More difficult but still possible would be to try to reclaim the policies removed from the national political arena by ensuring national parliaments a greater role in EU-related decisions. This will be facilitated if and when the Constitutional Treaty's protocol comes into force that requires that parliaments have much more information about Council legislation and deliberation, about Commission consultation documents and legislative program and planning as well as about EU finances from the Court of Auditors.

But regardless of whether national leaders prefer repoliticizing the EU level or reconciling national publics to its lack of politics, they need to take action at the national level. National leaders, first and foremost, need to stop blame-shifting and credit-taking as per their convenience in their communicative discourses to the public. The referenda made clear how deleterious this has been to the EU, as have opinion polls that show the eroding support for the EU among national publics everywhere. Since national leaders are the main communicators about Europe, they need to use some of their scarce political resources to explain the EU as it really is. This would mean that they would need to stop talking about national choices as if Europeanization did not exist—which leads to frustration and, ultimately, demobilization or radicalization at the national level—and about European choices as if national preferences could be the determining influence on them—which leads to deadlock and lowest-common-denominator solutions at the EU level. Instead, they would do best to speak realistically about the benefits of the EU, the constraints the country should therefore be willing to accept, and the choices that are still open and can be realistically pursued at the national level.

A continuing communicative discourse about the EU would serve not only as a tool for improved understanding—if only so that national leaders themselves are no longer held exclusively to account by national electorates for EU policies for which they are not responsible, cannot control, and may not be committed to politically. It could also serve as an activation device—to encourage citizens to make their voices heard directly in Brussels—whether as interest-based or political actors. The tragedy of the French referendum in particular is that much of French 'civil society'—including social movements such as ATTAC as well as political parties and interest groups—spent an incredible amount of time and energy on mobilizing at the national level against the Constitutional Treaty. None of that energy has subsequently been translated into positive action at the EU level.

But discourse alone encouraging civil society to become active in Brussels is not enough where national citizens lack the capacity to go to the EU level directly. In such instances, national governments would also need to provide national routes to EU influence. This could involve bringing national citizens into the national EU-related policy formulation process, or encouraging more citizen recourse through the courts. But this is of course again more difficult for simple polities than compound ones, since they would have to overcome built-in institutional as well as ideational obstacles, given unitary states where the courts are not expected to exercise independent powers and statist processes where the executive is expected to have exclusive powers of formulation. By the same token, however, simple polities might find it easier than in compound polities to get the message across about the EU, given its ability to speak in a single voice. All of this, however, assumes that there is any such message.

The problem for all member-states is that the postwar visions of their countries in Europe, with all that that means in terms of ideas about democracy as well as sovereignty and identity, no longer adequately account for the new realities. New communicative discourses that reexamine national ideas about democracy, sovereignty, and identity in relation to Europe are needed. But this is no easy task. Such discourses cannot just be the creation of national leaders 'spitting in the wind,' but need to be the result of extended national deliberation among informed publics, including intellectuals and opinion leaders in business and civil society, in addition to the media. Coming up with new legitimating ideas is arguably more of challenge for simple polities like France and Britain than compound polities like Germany and Italy, given that Europeanization itself alters national governance practices more in simple polities than compound ones and that national discourses have been more at odds with the realities of Europeanization. A good way to illustrate the ideational problems for simple as opposed to compound polities is by analogy to polytheistic and monotheistic religions. Where you already have a number of gods, a few more is not a major problem—as when the Greeks incorporated Roman gods once conquered by the Romans. However, when you believe in only one God—read the French Republic state and British parliamentary sovereignty—the inclusion of any others is an attack on the very fundamentals of one's faith—as it was for the Christians when forced to accept the Roman gods.[1]

This said, it is not easy for any country to reevaluate their visions of Europe. The French need to rethink their vision of leadership in Europe which ensures economic gains and no losses in sovereignty and identity, given that they know that France no longer leads Europe, are in crisis over national identity, and increasingly blame EU 'neoliberalism' for their economic problems. The British need to develop a vision of Britain in Europe, given that the discourse of economic interest does not respond to growing concerns about sovereignty and identity, while the idea of British separateness in Europe could very well lead to the reality of British separation from Europe in the event of a referendum on Britain 'in or out of Europe'. The Germans need to update their vision of 'German-as-European' in light of the changes related to unification and fading memories of World War II, especially since they increasingly question the benefits of membership and worry about the EU's impact on the social market economy. The Italians, finally, need to concern themselves not so much with their vision of Italy in Europe as with their implementation of European rules in Italy, since their pride in being European is likely to suffer as a result of the fact that the EU 'rescue of the nation-state' is no longer enough to rescue the nation-state.

Once the member-states begin to rethink their national understandings and reevaluate their national visions of Europe, it may be possible to return to the Constitutional Treaty and the constitutional 'settlement'. But it should already be clear in light of the above discussions that the institutional proposals in the Treaty actually seem quite reasonable even as they now stand.

[1] Schmidt (1999a).

Any solution short of instituting a truly federal system, which was not in any event in the cards, would have been likely to create significant problems of legitimacy or accountability of one sort or another. For example, any radical increase in the powers of the EP would serve to decrease member-state power as represented in the Council of Ministers (and especially those of the smaller countries, which have greater voice through the Council than through the Parliament, given differences in population size). This would undermine the traditional intergovernmental bases of EU legitimacy unless the powers of the Council were also increased. If on top of this the Commission were to be directly elected, or even only elected by Parliament from among its members, the resulting setup would even further reduce the powers of the Council of Ministers and the traditional grounds of legitimacy while politicizing the policy-formulation process. This might be acceptable, of course, if the EP concomitantly gained in representative legitimacy, that is, if it were to be elected by European citizens on the basis of pan-European parties that expressed the collective will of the citizenry. But in the absence of any such collective will, such elections would be problematic and the politicization of the Commission counterproductive. The solution of the Constitutional Convention, to increase the powers of all branches of the EU without significantly altering the balance of powers among them, was therefore probably the only solution possible or appropriate.

But whatever the solution, any increase in the powers of the EU's institutions necessarily encroaches on those of its member-states. We have already seen that Europeanization has moved all member-states farther along the continuum toward more federal institutional relationships, with greater disruption to the traditional balance of powers in unitary than regionalized or federal states; has introduced greater pluralism in policy formulation and regulatory enforcement in policy implementation, with greater disruption to statist systems than corporatist ones; and has subordinated partisan politics to its depoliticized consensus-oriented, interest-based politics, and more so in majoritarian systems than in proportional ones. Member-states need to take on board all of these changes, along with the equally if not more important ones following from internal dynamics of change. This means coming up with new ideas that take stock of the new 'democratic' governing practices already in place, with each member-state making sense of these in terms of national ideas and values and, where necessary, devising new practices that make up for their own particular democratic deficits.

In brief, the prospects for democracy in the EU are not so bad, since new practices are already in place, as is the blueprint for EU institutional redesign. But for democracy in the EU to cease being a problem, national leaders and publics need to talk and think more clearly about who they are and where they are going, together in the EU as well as individually within each member-state. This will not be easy. But no one ever said that building Europe would be easy.

References

Aalberts, T. E. (2004). 'The Future of Sovereignty in Multilevel Governance Europe—A Constructivist Reading', *Journal of Common Market Studies*, 42(1): 23–46.

Abdelal, R. (2007). *Capital Rules: The Construction of Global Finance*. Cambridge, MA: Harvard University Press. (forthcoming).

Agranoff, R. (1996). 'Federal Evolution in Spain', *International Political Science Review*, 17(4): 385–401.

Albertazzi, D. and McDonnell, D. (2005). 'The Lega Nord in the Second Berlusconi Government: In a League of Its Own', *West European Politics*, 28(5): 952–72.

Alliès, P. (2003). 'Constitution post-libérale', *Le Monde* July 3: 16.

Allum, P. (1973). *Italy: Republic Without a Government?* New York: Norton.

—— (1997). 'From Two into One': The Faces of the Italian Christian Democratic Party', *Party Politics*, 3: 23–52.

Alter, K. (1998). 'Who Are the "Masters of the Treaty"?: European Governments and the European Court of Justice', *International Organization*, 52(1): 121–47.

Anderson, B. (1983). *Imagined Communities*. London: Verso.

Anderson, J. (1996). 'Germany and the Structural Funds: Reunification Leads to Bifurcation', in L. Hooghe (ed.), *Cohesion Policy and European Integration: Building Multi-Level Governance*. Oxford: Oxford University Press.

—— (2002). 'Europeanization and the Transformation of the Democratic Polity 1945–2000', *Journal of Common Market Studies*, 40(5): 793–822.

—— (2005). 'Germany and Europe: Centrality in the East', in S. Bulmer and C. Lequesne (eds.), *The Member-States of the European Union*. Oxford: Oxford University Press.

Andreatta, F. (2001). 'Italy at a Crossroads', *Daedalus*, 130(2): 45–65.

Armstrong, K. A. (2005). 'How Open Is the United Kingdom to the OMC Process on Social Inclusion?', in J. Zeitlin and P. Pochet with L. Magnusson. (eds.), *The Open Method of Co-ordination in Action: The European Employment and Social Inclusion Strategies*. Brussels: Peter Lang.

Artis, M. J. (1998). 'The United Kingdom', in J. Forder and A. Menon (eds.), *The European Union and National Macroeconomic Policy*. London: Routledge.

Aspinwall, M. (1998). 'Collective Attraction—The New Political Game in Brussels', in J. Greenwood and M. Aspinwall (eds.), *Collective Action in the European Union: Interests and the New Politics of Associability*. London: Routledge.

Bach, J. P. G. (1999). *Between Sovereignty and Integration: German Foreign Policy and National Identity after 1989*. New York: St Martin's Press.

Bache, I. (1998). *The Politics of European Union Regional Policy*. Sheffield, UK: Sheffield Academic Press.

—— (2000). 'Government Within Governance: Steering Economic Regeneration Policy Networks in Yorkshire and Humberside', *Public Administration*, 78(3): 575–92.

—— (2003). 'Governing Through Governance: Education Policy Control Under New Labour', *Political Studies*, 51: 300–14.

—— George, S. and Rhodes, R. A. W. (1996). 'The European Union, Cohesion Policy, and Subnational Authorities in the United Kingdom', in L. Hooghe (ed.), *Cohesion Policy and European Integration: Building Multi-Level Governance*. Oxford: Oxford University Press.

Badinter, R. (2002). *Une Constitution Européenne*. Paris: Fayard.

Baker, D. (2001). 'Britan and Europe: The Argument Continues', *Parliamentary Affairs*, 54: 276–88.

Balibar, É. (2001). *Nous, Citoyens d'Europe?* Paris: La Découverte.

Balme, R. and Jouve, B. (1996). 'Building the Regional State: Europe and Territorial Organization in France', in L. Hooghe (ed.), *Cohesion Policy and European Integration: Building Multi-Level Governance*. Oxford: Oxford University Press.

Banchoff, T. (1999a). 'German Policy Toward the European Union: The Effects of Historical Memory', *German Politics*, 6(1): 60–76.

—— (1999b). 'National Identity and EU Legitimacy in France and Germany', in T. Banchoff and M. P. Smith (eds.), *Legitimacy and the European Union: The Contested Polity*. London and New York: Routledge.

Barbier, J-C. (2005). 'Has the European Social Model a distinctive activation "touch"?', in M. Jepsen and A. S. Pascual (eds.), *The European Social Model*. (forthcoming).

Barker, E. (1973). *The Common Market*. London: Hove

Bartolini, S. (2002). Paper prepared for Willfried Spohn (ed.), *Europeanisation and the Nation-State—Cross Disciplinary Approaches and Case Studies*.

—— (2005). *Re-Structuring Europe: Centre Formation, System Building and Political Structuring Between the Nation State and the European Union*. Oxford: Oxford University Press.

Bauby, P. and Toledo, A. (2002). 'L'Interaction acteurs-règles dan le secteur électrique', in J. P. Faugère, S. Ferrand-Nagel, M.-A. Barthe, F. Rochelandet, and F. Legros (eds.), *Politiques Publiques Européennes*. Paris: Economica.

Beer, S. (1969). *British Politics in the Collectivist Age*, Revised edition. New York: Random House.

Beetham, D. and Lord, C. (1998). *Legitimacy and the EU*. New York: Longman.

Bellamy, R. (2004). 'Introduction: Modern Citizenship', in R. Bellamy, D. Castiglione, and E. Santoro (eds.), *Lineages of European Citizenship: Rights, Belonging and Participation in Eleven Nation-States*. Basingstoke, UK: Palgrave Macmillan.

—— and Castiglione, D. (2000). 'The Uses of Democracy: Further Reflections on the Democratic Deficit in Europe', in Eriksen and Fossum (eds.), *Integration Through Deliberation?*

Bellier, I. (1994). 'Une culture de la Commission Européenne? De la rencontre des cultures et du multilinguisme des fonctionnaires', in Y. Mény, P. Muller, and J.-L. Quermonne (eds.), *Politiques Publiques en France*. Paris: Harmattan, pp. 49–60.

Benz, A. and Eberlein, B. (1999). 'The Europeanization of Regional Policies: Pattterns of Multi-Level Governance', *Journal of European Public Policy*, 6: 329–48.

—— and Goetz, K. H. (1996a). *A New German Public Sector? Reform, Adaptation and Stability*. Aldershot, UK: Dartmouth.

—— —— (1996b). 'The German Public Sector: National Priorities and the International Reform Agenda', in *A New German Public Sector? Reform, Adaptation and Stability*. Aldershot: Dartmouth.

References

Bereni, L. and Lépinard, E. (2004). 'Les Femmes ne sont pas une Catégorie: Les Stratégies de Légitimation de la Parité en France', *Revue Française de Science Politique*, 51(1): 71–98.

Betz, H. G. (1994). *Radical Right-Wing Populism in Europe*. New York: St Martin's Press.

—— (2002). 'Exclusionary Populism in Austria, Italy and Switzerland, "Rechtpopulismus in Europa" ', International Workshop, Renner Institute, Vienna, http://www.extremismus.com/texte/eurex3.pdf

Biancarelli, J. (1991). 'La communauté Européenne et les Collectivités Locales: Une double dialectique compexe', *Revue Française d'Administration Publique*, no. 60: 515–28.

Biersteker, T. J. (1999). 'Locating the Emerging European Polity: Beyond States or State?', in J. Anderson (ed.), *Regional Integration and Democracy: Expanding on the European Experience*. Lanham, MD: Rowman & Littlefield.

Bindi C. F. and Grassi, S. (2001). "The Parliament of Italy: From Benevolent Observer to Active Player" in *National Parliaments on their Ways to Europe: Losers or Latecomers?* Eds. Andreas Maurer and Wolfgang Wessels. Baden-Baden, Germany: Nomos.

—— and Cisci, M. (2005). 'Italy and Spain: A Tale of Contrasting Effectiveness in the EU', in S. Bulmer and C. Lequesne (eds.), *The Member States of the European Union*. Oxford: Oxford University Press.

Birchfield, V. (2004). 'Institutionalized Power and Anti-Establishment Politics in France: The Case of Attac', Paper prepared for delivery to the conference: Interest Groups in the 21st Century in France and Europe: An Interdisciplinary Perspective—IEP/Cevipof, Paris (24–25 September).

Bodyguel, M. (1996). *La qualité des eaux dans l'Union Européenne: Pratique d'une reglementation commune*. Paris: L'Harmattan.

Bogdanor, V. (2005). 'Footfalls Echoing in Memory: Britain and Europe: The Historical Perspective', *International Affairs*, 81(4): 689–702.

Bognetti, G. (1982). 'Direct Application and Indirect Impact of the Constitution in the Italian Legal System', in *Italian National Reports to the XIth International Congress of Comparative Law, Caracas*. Milano: Giuffrè.

Bomberg, E., Cram, L., and Martin, D. (2003). 'The EU's Institutions', in E. Bomberg and A. Stubb (eds.), *The European Union: How Does It work?* New York: Oxford University Press.

Börzel, T. (2001). 'Non-Compliance in the European Union. Pathology or Statistical Artefact?', *Journal of European Public Policy*, 8(5): 803–24.

—— (2002a). *States and Regions in the European Union: Institutional Adaptation in Germany and Spain*. Cambridge: Cambridge University Press.

—— (2002b). 'Pace-Setting, Foot-Dragging, and Fence-Sitting: Member State Responses to Europeanizaton', *Journal of Common Market Studies*, 40(2): 193–214.

—— and Risse, T. (2000). 'When Europe Hits Home: Europeanization and Domestic Change', *European Integration Online Papers (EIOP)*, 4: 15; http://eiop.or.at/eiop/texte/2001-006a.htm

—— (2006) 'Europeanization: The Domestic Impact of EU Policies' in *Handbook of European Politics* K. E. Jorgensen, M. Pollack and B. Rosamund (eds.). London: Sage.

Bourblanc, M. (2005). 'The European Integration of Water Issues: Popular Consultation and Circular Integration', Paper prepared for presentation at the *European Identity and Political Systems* conference of EPSnet, Sciences Po, Paris, 17–18 June.

Bréchon, P. (2002). 'Des valeurs politiques entre pérénnité et changement', *Futuribles*, 277: 92–128.

Breton, R. (1995). 'Identification in Transnational Political Communities', in K. Knop et al. (eds.), *Rethinking Federalism: Citizens, Markets, and Governments in a Changing World*. Vancouver: University of British Columbia Press.

Brewin, C. (2000). 'European Identity', in J. Andrew, M. Crook and M. Waller (eds.), *Why Europe? Problems of Culture and Identity*. New York: St Martin's Press.

Broscheid, A. and Coen, D. (2004). 'Lobbying Systems in the European Union: A Quantitative Study', Paper prepared for presentation at the 14th Conference of Europeanists, Chicago, IL: March 11–13).

Brouard, S. and Sauger, N. (2005). 'Comprende la Victoire du 'Non': Proximité Partisane, Conjoncture et Attitude à l'Égard de l'Europe', in A. Laurent and N. Sauger (eds.), *Le Référendum de Ratification du Traité Constitutionnel Européen du 29 Mai 2005: Comprendre le 'Non' Français*, Cahiers du Cevipof no. 42: 121–42.

Brubaker, R. (1992). *Citizenship and Nationality in France and Germany*. Cambridge, MA: Harvard University Press.

Brunazzo, M. and Piattoni, S. (2004). 'Negotiating the Regulation of the Structural Funds: Italian Actors in Regional Policymaking', *Modern Italy*, 9(2): 159–72.

Brzinski, J., Lancaster, T. D., and Tuschhoff, C. (1999). 'Introduction', in *Federalism and Compounded Representation in Western Europe*.

Büchs, M. and Friedrich, D. (2005). 'Surface Integration: The National Action Plans for Employment and Social Inclusion in Germany', in J. Zeitlin and P. Pochet with L. Magnusson (eds.), *The Open Method of Co-ordination in Action: The European Employment and Social Inclusion Strategies*. Brussels: Peter Lang.

Buller, H. (1996). 'Privatization and Europeanization: The Changing Context of Water Supply in Britain and France', *Journal of Environmental Planning and Management*, 39(4): 461–82.

—— (1998). 'Reflections Across the Channel: Britain, France and the Europeanisation of National Environmental Policy', in P. Lowe and S. Ward (eds.), *British Environmental Policy and Europe*. London: Routledge.

Buller, J. (2000). 'Understanding Contemporary Conservative Euro-Skepticism: Statecraft and the Problem of Governing Autonomy', *Political Quarterly*, 71: 319–27.

—— and Smith, M. J. (1998). 'Civil Service Attitudes Towards the European Union', in D. Baker and D. Seawright (eds.), *Britain for and Against Europe*. Oxford: Clarendon Press.

Bulmer, S. (1986). *The Domestic Structure of European Policy-Making in West Germany*. New York and London: Garland.

—— (1992). 'Completing the European Community's Internal Market: The Regulatory Implications for the Federal Republic of Germany', in K. Dyson (ed.), *The Politics of German Regulation*. Aldershot, UK: Dartmouth.

—— (1997). 'Shaping the Rules? The Constitutive Politics of the European Union and German Power', in P. Katzenstein (ed.), *Tamed Power, Germany in Europe*. Ithaca, NY: Cornell.

—— and Burch, M. (1998). 'Organizing for Europe: Whitehall, the British State and European Union', *Public Administration*, 76(4): 601–28.

—— Maurer, A., and Paterson, W. (2001). 'The European Policy-Making Machinery in the Berlin Republic: Hindrance of Handmaiden?', *German Politics*, 10(1).

Burdeau, G. (1970). *L'État*. Paris: Seuil.

References

Burley, A.-M. and Mattli, W. (1993). 'Europe Before the Court: A Political Theory of Legal Integration', *International Organization*, 47: 41–76.

Burnham, J. and Maor, M. (1995). 'Converging Administrative Systems: Recruitment, Training and Role Perceptions', *Journal of European Public Policy*, 2(2): 185–204.

Bush, E. and Simi, P. (2001). 'European Farmers and Their Protests', in Imig and Tarrow (eds.), *Contentious Europeans*.

Campbell, J. L. (2004). *Institutional Change and Globalization*. Princeton, NJ: Princeton University Press.

Caporaso, J. and Jupille, J. (1999). 'Institutionalism and the EU: Beyond IR and Comparative Politics', *Annual Review of Political Science*.

—— —— (2001). 'The Europeanization of Gender Equality Policy and Domestic Structural Change', in M. G. Cowles, J. Caporaso, and T. Risse. (eds.), *Transforming Europe*. Ithaca, NJ: Cornell University Press.

Caramani, D. (2004). *The Nationalization of Politics: The Formation of National Electorates and Party Systems in Western Europe*. Cambridge: Cambridge University Press.

Cash, W. (1992). *Europe: The Crunch*. London: Duckworth.

Cassese, S. (2003). 'The Age of Administrative Reform', in J. Hayward and A. Menon. (ed.), *Governing Europe*. Oxford: Oxford University Press.

Cento Bull, A. and Gilbert, M. (2001). *The Lega Nord and the Northern Question in Italian Politics*. Basingstoke, UK: Palgrave Macmillan.

Cerutti, F. (1996). 'Identità e Politica', in Furio Cerutti (ed.), *Identità e Politica*. Roma, Italy: Laterza.

—— (2003). 'A Political Identity of the Europeans?' *Thesis Eleven*, 72: 26–45.

—— (2005). 'Europe's Deep Gisis' *European Review*, 13(4): 525–540.

Chayes, A. and Chayes Handler, A. (1995). *The New Sovereignty: Compliance with International Regulatory Agreements*. Cambridge, MA: Harvard University Press.

Cini, M. (1996). *The European Commission: Leadership, Organisation, and Culture in the Commission*. Manchester, UK: Manchester University Press.

Coen, D. (1997). 'The Evolution of the Large Firm as a Political Actor in the European Union', *Journal of European Public Policy*, 4(1): 91–108.

—— (1998). 'The European Business Interest and the Nation-State: Large-Firm Lobbying in the European Union and Member States', *Journal of Public Policy*, 18(1): 75–100.

—— (2005). 'Managing the Political Life Cycle of Regulation in the UK and German Telecommunication Sectors', *Annals of Public and Cooperative Economics*, 76(1): 59–84.

—— and Héritier, A. (2005). *Redefining Regulatory Regimes: Utilities in Europe*. Cheltenham, UK: Edward Elgar.

—— and Thatcher, M. (2005). 'The New Governance of Markets and Non-Majoritarian Regulators', *Governance*, 25(3): 329–346.

Cohen, J. and Rogers, J. (1992). 'Secondary Associations and Democratic Governance', *Politics and Society*, 20(4): 391–472.

Cohen, M. D. March, J. D., and Olsen, J. P. (1972). 'A Garbage Can Model of Organizational Choice', *Administrative Science Quarterly*, 17: 1–25.

Colas, D. (2000). *Citoyenneté et Nationalité*. Paris: Gallimard.

Cole, A. (1996). 'The French Socialists', in J. Gaffney (ed.), *Political Parties and the European Union*. London: Routledge.

—— (2001). *Franco-German Relations*. London: Longman.

—— and Drake, H. (2000). 'The Europeanization of the French Polity', *Journal of European Public Policy*, 7(1): 26–43.

Coleman, W. D. and Chiasson, C. (2002). 'State Power, Transformative Capacity and Adapting to Globalization: An Analysis of French Agricultural Policy, 1960–2000', *Journal of European Public Policy*, 9(2): 168–85.

Collignon, Stefan (2004). *Vive la République Européenne*. Paris: Edition de la Martinière.

Conant, L. (2001). 'Contested Legal Boundaries and Institutional Adaptations: The Europeanization of the Law in France, Germany, and the United Kingdom', in Cowles, Caporaso, Risse (eds.), *Transforming Europe: Europeanization and Domestic Change*. Ithaca, NY: Cornell University Press.

—— (2002). *Justice Contained: Law and Politics in the European Union*. Ithaca, NY: Cornell University Press.

Cotta, M. and Isernia, P. (1996). *Il gigante con i piedi di argilla*. Bologna, Italy: Il Mulino.

Cowles, M. G. (1995). 'Setting the Agenda for a New Europe: The ERT and EC 1992', *Journal of Common Market Studies*, 33(4): 501–26.

—— (2001). 'The TransAtlantic Business Dialogue', in M. G. Cowles, J. Caporaso, and T. Risse (eds.), *Transforming Europe*. Ithaca, NY: Cornell University Press.

—— Caporaso, J., and Risse, T. (2001). *Transforming Europe: Europeanization and Domestic Change*. Ithaca, NY: Cornell University Press.

Cox, A. and Hayward, J. (1983). 'The Inapplicability of the Corporatist Model to Britain and France: The Case of Labor', *International Political Science Review*, 77.

Craig, P. and de Búrca, G. (1998). *EU Law: Text, Cases, and Materials*, 2nd edn. Oxford: Oxford University Press.

Cram, L. (1993). 'Calling the Tune Without Paying the Piper? Social Policy Regulation: The Role of the Commission in European Community Social Policy', *Policy and Politics*, 21: 23.

—— (1998). 'The EU Institutions and Collective Action: Constructing a European Interest?', in J. Greenwood and M. Aspinwall (eds.), *Collective Action in the European Union: Interests and the New Politics of Associability*. London: Routledge.

Curtin, D. (1998). 'Civil Society and the European Union: Opening Spaces for Deliberative Democracy', *Collected Courses of the Academy of European Law*.

—— (2003). 'Private Interest Representation or Civil Society Deliberation? A Contemporary Dilemma for European Union Governance', *Social and Legal Studies*, 12(1): 55–75.

D'Alimonte, R. and Bartolini, S. (1997). ' "Electoral Transition" and Party System Change in Italy', *West European Politics*, 20(1): 110–34.

Dalton, R. (1999). 'Political Support in Advanced Industrial Countries', in P. Norris (ed.), *Critical Citizens: Global Support for Democratic Government*. Oxford: Oxford University Press.

—— (2003). *Democratic Challenges, Democratic Choices: The Decline in Political Support in Advanced Industrial Democracies*. Oxford: Oxford University Press.

—— and Gray, M. (2003). 'Expanding the Electoral Marketplace', in B. E. Cain, R. Dalton, and S. E. Scarrow (eds.), *Democracy Transformed? Expanding Political Opportunities in Advanced Industrial Democracies*. Oxford: Oxford University Press.

—— Buerkin, W., and Drummond, A. (2001). 'Public Attitudes Toward Direct Democracy', *Journal of Democracy*, 12: 141–53.

Dalton, R., Scarrow, S. E., and Cain, B. E. (2003). 'New Forms of Democracy? Reform and Transformation of Democratic Institutions', in B. E. Cain, R. Dalton, and S. E. Scarrow (eds.), *Democracy Transformed? Expanding Political Opportunities in Advanced Industrial Democracies*. Oxford: Oxford University Press.

Daniels, P. (1998). 'From Hostility to "Constructive Engagement:" The Europeanization of the Labor Party', *West European Politics*, 21(1): 72–96.

De Búrca, G. and Scott, J. (eds.) (2000). *Constitutional Change in the EU. From Uniformity to Flexibility?* Oxford: Hart Publishing.

De Gaulle, C. (1970). *Mémoires d'Espoir: Le Renouveau, 1958–1962*. Paris: Plon.

De la Porte, C. and Pochet, P. (eds.) (2002). *Building Social Europe Through the Open Method of Coordination*. Brussels: P.I.E.—Peter Lang.

—— —— (2005). 'Participation in the Open Method of Co-ordination: The Cases of Employment and Social Inclusion', in J. Zeitlin and P. Pochet with L. Magnusson (eds.), *The Open Method of Co-ordination in Action: The European Employment and Social Inclusion Strategies*. Brussels: Peter Lang.

Deeg, R. (1995). 'Germany's Länder and the Federalization of the European Union', in C. Rhodes and S. Mazey (eds.), *The State of the European Union vol. 3: Building a European Policy?* Boulder, CO: Lynne Rienner.

Dehousse, R. (2003). 'Beyond Representative Democracy: Constitutionalism in a Poly-centric Polity', in J. H. H. Weiler and M. Wind (eds.), *European Constitutionalism Beyond the Nation-State*. Cambridge: Cambridge University Press.

Dehousse, R. (2005). *La Fin de l'Europe*. Paris: Flammarion.

Della Cananea, G. (2000). 'Italy', in H. Kassim, G. Peters, and V. Wright (eds.), *The National Co-ordination of EU Policy Making: The Domestic Level*. Oxford: Oxford University Press.

Della Cananea, G. (2001). 'Italy', in H. Kassim, A. Menon, B. G. Peters, and V. Wright (eds.), *The National Co-ordination of EU Policy Making: The European Level*. Oxford: Oxford University Press.

Della Porta, D. (1996). 'Political Parties and Corruption: Reflections on the Italian Case', *Modern Italy*, 1(1): 97–114.

—— (2000). 'Social Capital, Beliefs in Government, and Political Corruption', in S. Pharr and R. Putnam (eds.), *Disaffected Democracies*. Princeton, NJ: Princeton University Press.

—— (2001). 'Social Movements and New Challenges to Representative Democracy: A Perspective from Italy', *Politique Européenne*, (4): 73–104.

—— (2003). 'Dimensions of Political Opportunities and the Europeanisation of Public Spheres: Report for the Europub project. http://europub.wz-berlin.de

—— and Kriesi, H.-P. (1999). 'Social Movements in a Globalizing World: An Introduction', in *Social Movements in a Globalizing World*. Basingstoke, UK: Palgrave.

Della Sala, V. (2004). 'The Italian Model of Capitalism: On the Road Between Globalization and Europeanization', *Journal of European Public Policy*, 11(6): 1041–1057.

Dente, B. and Regonini, G. (1989). 'Politics and Policies in Italy', in P. Lange and M. Regini (eds.), *State, Market, and Social Regulation: New Perspectives on Italy*. Cambridge: Cambridge University Press.

Derlien, H-U. (2000). 'Germany: Failing Successfully?', in H. Kassim, G. Peters, and V. Wright (eds.), *The National Co-ordination of EU Policy Making: The Domestic Level*. Oxford: Oxford University Press.

Desideri, C. (1995). 'Italian Regions and the European Community', in B. Jones and M. Keating (eds.), *The European Union and the Regions*. Oxford: Clarendon Press.

'Dialogue du Président de la République avec M. Philippe Séguin' (1992). *La Politique Etrangère de la France: Textes et Documents, septembre-octobre 1992*, Ministère des Affaires Etrangères. Direction de la Presse, de l'Information et de la Communication.

Diamanti, I. (2005). 'Ma la Lega ha bisogno di Bossi?', *La Reppublica*, January 9, 2005.

Dimitrakopoulos, D. (1997). *Beyond Transposition: A Comparative Inquiry into the Implementation of European Public Policy*, Ph.D. theses, University of Hull.

—— (2001). 'Incrementalism and Path Dependence: European Integration and Institutional Change in National Parliaments', *Journal of Common Market Studies*, 39: 3: 405–22.

DiPalma, G. (1977). *Surviving Without Governing: Italian Parties in Parliament*. Berkeley, CA: University of California Press.

Donà, A. (2003). 'L'europeizzazione del sistema di governo: il caso della legge comunitaria', in S. Fabbrini (ed.), *L'Europeizzazione dell'Italia: L'impatto dell'Unione Europea sulle istituzioni e le politiche italiane*. Rome: Laterza.

Dryzek, J. (1990). *Discursive Democracy: Politics, Policy, and Political Science*. Cambridge: Cambridge University Press.

du Granrut, C. (1994). *Europe, Le Temps des Régions*. Paris: LGDJ.

Dudley, G. and Richardson, J. (1998). 'Arenas Without Rules and the Policy Change Process: Outsider Groups and British Roads Policy', *Political Studies*, 46: 727–47.

Duhamel, O. (2005). *Pour L'Europe*. Paris: Senil.

Duina, F. and Blithe, F. (1999). 'Nation-States and Common Markets: The Institutional Conditions for Acceptance', *Review of International Political Economy*, 6: 4: 494–530.

—— and Oliver, M. J. (2004). 'National Parliaments in the European Union: Are There Any Benefits to Integration?', Paper prepared for presentation for the American Political Science Association National Meetings, Chicago, Sept. 1–5.

Dupoirier, E. (2004). 'Les Groupes d'Intéret Économiques comme Acteurs des Politiques Régionales de Développement Territorial Financées par les Fonds Structurels Européens', Paper prepared for the conference 'Les Groupes d'Intéret au XXIeme Siècle', Sciences Po, Paris, Sept. 24–25.

Duverger, M. (1996). *Le Système Politique Français*. Paris: Presses Universitaire de France.

Dyson, K. (1980). *The State Tradition in Western Europe*. New York: Oxford University Press.

—— (1992). 'Theories of Regulation and the Case of Germany: A Model of Regulatory Change', in K. Dyson (ed.), *The Politics of German Regulation*. Dartmouth: Aldershot/ Brookfield, pp. 1–28.

—— (2002). 'Introduction' in *European States and the Euro: Europeanization, Variation, and Convergence*, K. Dyson (ed.). Oxford: Oxford University Press.

Eberlein, B. (2004). 'Formal and Informal Governance in Single Market Regulation', in T. Christiansen and S. Piattoni (eds.), *Informal Governance in the EU*. Cheltenham, UK: Edward Elgar.

References

Egan, M. (2001). *Constructing a European Market: Trade Barriers, Regulatory Strategies and Corporate Responses*. Oxford: Oxford University Press.

—— and Wolf, D. (1999). 'Regulatory Oversight in Europe: The Case of Comitology', in C. Joerges, and E. Vos (eds.), *EU Committees: Social Regulation, Law, and Politics*. Oxford: Hart Publishing, pp. 239–58.

Eising, R. (2003). 'Interest Groups: Opportunity Structures and Governance Capacity', in K. Dyson and K. Goetz (eds.), *Germany, Europe and the Politics of Constraint*. Oxford: Oxford University Press.

—— (2004). 'Multilevel Governance and Business Interests in the European Union', *Governance*, 17(2): 211–45.

—— and Jabko, N. (2001). 'Moving Targets: Institutional Embeddedness and Domestic Politics in the Liberalization of EU Electricity Markets', *Comparative Political Studies*, 34(7): 742–67.

Elazar, D. (2001). 'Federalism Without Constitutionalism: Europe's *Sonderweg*', in K. Nicolaïdis and R. Howse (eds.), *The Federal Vision: Legitimacy and Levels of Governance in the United States and the European Union*. Oxford: Oxford University Press.

Elgie, R. (2002). 'La Cohabitation de Longue Durée: Studying the 1997–2002 Experience', *Modern and Contemporary France*, 10(3): 297–311.

Ellwein, T. (1993). 'Tradition—Anpassung—Reform' in W. Seibel, A. Benz, and H. Maeding (eds.), *Verwaltungsreform und Verwaltungspolitik im Prozess der deutschen Einigung*. Baden-Baden, Germany: Nomos.

Elster, J. (1988). *Deliberative Democracy*. New York: Cambridge University Press.

Erhel, C., Mandin, L., and Palier, B. (2005). 'The Leverage Effect: The Open Method of Co-ordination in France', in J. Zeitlin and P. Pochet with L. Magnusson (eds.), *The Open Method of Co-ordination in Action: The European Employment and Social Inclusion Strategies*. Brussels: Peter Lang.

Eriksen, E. O. and Fossum, J. E. (2002). 'Democracy Through Strong Publics in the European Union'?, *Journal of Common Market Studies*, 40(3): 401–24.

European Commission (2001). *European Governance: A White Paper*. COM (2001) 428.

Evans, J. (ed.) (2003). 'Europe and the French Party System', in *The French Party System*. Manchester, UK: Manchester University Press.

Fabbrini, S. (2000). 'Political Change Without Institutional Transformation: What Can We Learn from the Italian Crisis of the 1990s?', *International Political Science Review*, 21:2: 173–96.

—— (2003). *L'Europeizzazione dell'Italia: L'impatto dell'Unione Europea sulle istituzioni e le politiche italiane*. Rome: Laterza.

—— (2004a). 'Madison in Brussels: EU and US as Compound Democracies', Paper prepared for presentation at the panel on '*The United States of Europe? American and European Models of the EU*' at the American Political Science Association National Meetings, Chicago: Sept. 2–5, 2004.

—— (2004b). 'Transatlantic Constitutionalism: Comparing the United States and the European Union', *European Journal of Political Research*, 43(4): 547–69.

Falkner, G. (1998). *EU Social Policy in the 1990s: Towards a Corporatist Policy Community*. London: Routledge.

—— (2001). 'Policy Networks in a Multi-Level System: Convergence Towards Moderate Diversity?', in K. H. Goetz and S. Hix (eds.), *Europeanised Politics? European Integration and National Political Systems*. London: Frank Cass.

—— Wolfgang, C. M., Eder, M., Hiller, K., Steiner, G., and Trattnigg, R. (1999). 'The Impact of EU Membership on Policy Networks in Austria: Creeping Change Beneath the Surface', *Journal of European Public Policy*, 6(3): 496–516.

—— Treib, O., Harlapp, M., and Leiber, S. (2005). *Complying with Europe: EU Harmonisation and Soft Law in the Member-States*. Cambridge: Cambridge University Press.

Farrar, C. (1992). 'Ancient Greek Political Theory as a Response to Democracy', in J. Dunn (ed.) *Democracy: The Unfinished Journey, 508 BC to AD 1993* Oxford: Oxford University Press.

Featherstone, K. (1988). *Socialist Parties and European Integration*. Manchester, UK: Manchester University Press.

—— (1988). ' "Europeanization" and the Centre Periphery: The Case of Greece in the 1990s', *South European Society and Politics*, 3(1): 23–39.

—— (2003). 'Introduction: In the Name of "Europe",' in K. Featherstone and C. Radaelli (eds.), *The Politics of Europeanization*. Oxford: Oxford University Press.

—— and Radaelli, C. (eds.) (2003). *The Politics of Europeanization*. Oxford: Oxford University Press.

Ferrera, M. and Gualmini, E. (2004). *Rescued by Europe?: Social and Labour Market Reforms in Italy from Maastricht to Berlusconi*. Amsterdam: Amsterdam University Press.

—— and Sacchi, S. (2005). 'The Open Method of Coordination and National Institutional Capabilities: The Italian Experience', in (eds.), J. Zeitlin and P. Pochet with L. Magnusson *The Open Method of Co-ordination in Action: The European Employment and Social Inclusion Strategies*. Brussels: Peter Lang.

—— Rhodes, M., and Hemerijck, A. (2000). 'What Role for EU Social Policy', in *The Future of Social Europe: Recasting Work and Welfare in the New Economy*. Portugal: Celta.

Ferry, J.-M. (2002). 'La Référence Républicaine au Défi de l'Europe', *Pouvoirs*, (100): 137–52.

Flinders, M. (2005). 'Majoritarian Democracy in Britain', *West European Politics*, 28(1): 61–93.

Forbes, I. (2004). 'Making a Crisis out of a Drama: The Political Analysis of BSE Policy-Making in the UK', *Political Studies*, 53: 342–57.

Fouilleux, E. (2004). 'Reforms and Multilateral Trade Negotiations: Another View on Discourse Efficiency', *West European Politics*, 27(2): 235–55.

Fourcans, A. (1993). *L'Entreprise et l'Europe*. Paris: Interédition.

Franchini, C. (1994). *Amministrazione Italiana e Amministrazione Comunitaria. La Coamministrazione nei Settori di Interesse Comunitario*. Padova, Italy: CEDAM.

Frank, R. (1998). 'Les Contretemps de l'Aventure Européenne', *Vingtième Siècle*, 60: 82–101.

Fraser, N. (1992). 'Rethinking the Public Sphere: A Contribution to the Critique of Actually Existing Democracy', in C. Calhoun (ed.), *Habermas and the Public Sphere*. Cambridge, MA: MIT Press, pp. 109–42.

Frears, J. R. (1975). 'The French Parliament and the European Community', *Journal of Common Market Studies*, 12: 140–58.

Furlong, P. (1996). 'The Italian Parliament and European Integration', in P. Norton (ed.), *National Parliaments and the European Union*. London: Frank Cass.

Gabel, M. (2001). 'European Integration, Voters, and National Politics', in D. Imig and S. Tarrow (eds.), *Contentious European: Protest and Politics in an Emerging Polity*. Lanham, MD: Rowman & Littlefield.

Gabel, M. and Christopher, J. A. (2002). 'The Structure of Citizen Attitudes and the European Political Space', *Comparative Political Studies*, 35: 893–913.

—— and Simon, H. (2002). 'Defining the EU Political Space. An Empirical Study of the European Election Manifestos, 1979–1999', *Comparative Political Studies*, 35: 934–64.

Galli della Loggia, E. (1996). *La Morte della Patria: La Crisi dell'Idea di Nazione tra Resistenza, Antifascismo, e Repubblica*. Roma: Laterza.

Gallo, F. and Hanny, B. (2003). 'Italy: Progress Behind Complexity', in W. Wessels, A. Maurer, and J. Mittag (eds.), *Fifteen into One? The European Union and Its Member-States*. Manchester, UK: University of Manchester Press.

Gamble A. and Kelly, G. (2000). 'The British Labour Party and Monetary Union', *West European Politics*, 23: 1–25.

Gamble, A. (1985). *Britain in Decline: Economic Policy, Political Strategy, and the British State*. London: Macmillan.

Garret, G. and Weingast, B. R. (1993). 'Ideas, Interests, and Institutions: Constructing the European Community's Internal Market', in J. Goldstein and R. O. Keohane (eds.), *Ideas and Foreign Policy: Beliefs, Institutions, and Political Change*. Ithaca, NY: Cornell University Press, pp. 195–6.

Garrett, G. and Tsebelis, G. (1996). 'An Institutional Critique of Intergovernmentalism', *International Organization*, 50(2): 269–90.

Garton Ash, T. (2004). *Free World: America, Europe, and the Surprising Future of the West*. New York: Random House.

Geddes, A. and Guiraudon, V. (2004). 'Britain, France, and EU Anti-discrimination Policy: The Emergence of a EU Paradigm', *West European Politics*, 27(2): 334–53.

Gellner, E. (1964). *Thought and Change*. London: Weidenfeld Nicholson.

George, S. (1990). *An Awkward Partner: Britain in the European Community*. Oxford: Oxford University Press.

—— (1994). 'Cultural Diversity and European Integration: The British Political Parties', in S. Zetterholm (ed.), *National Cultures and European Integration: Exploratory Essays on Cultural Diversity and Common Policies*. Oxford: Berg.

Gerstenberg, O. and Sable, C. (2000). 'Directly Deliberative Polyarchy: An Institutional Ideal for Europe? http://www.law.columbia.edu/sable/papers/gerst-sable1029.doc

Giuliani, M. (1996). 'Italy', in D. Rometsch and W. Wessels, (eds.), *The European Union and Member-States: Toward Institutional Fusion*. Manchester, UK: Manchester University Press.

—— (2001). 'Europeanization and Italy: A Bottom-Up Process?', in K. Featherstone and G. Kazamias (eds.), *Europeanization and the Southern Periphery*. London: Frank Cass.

—— and Piattoni, S. (2003). 'Italy: Both Leader and Laggard', in E. E. Zeff and E. B. Pirro (eds.), *The European Union and the Member-States*. Boulder, CO: Lynne Rienner.

Göetz, K. (1994). 'National Governance and European Integration: Intergovernmental Relations in Germany', *Journal of Common Market Studies*, 33: 91–116.

Gowland, D. and Turner, A. (2000). *Reluctant Europeans: Britain and European Integration, 1945–1998*. Harlow, Essex: Longman.

Grande, E. (1996). 'The State and Interest Groups in a Framework of Multi-Level Decision-Making: The Case of the European Union', *Journal of European Public Policy*, 3(3): 318–38.

Grant, C. (1994). *Delors: Inside the House that Jacques Built*. London: Nicholas Brealey.

Grant, W. (1989). *Pressure Group Politics and Democracy in Britain*. Hemel Hempstead, UK: Philip Allan.

—— (2001). 'Pressure Politics: From "Insider Politics to Direct Action"?', *Parliamentary Affairs*, 54: 337–48.

Gray, M. and Caul, M. (2000). 'Declining Voter Turnout in Advanced Industrialized Democracies: 1950–1997', *Comparative Political Studies*, 33: 1091–122.

Graziano, L. (1980). *Clientelismo e Sistema Politico—Il Caso dell'Italia*. Milan: Franco Angeli.

Graziano, P. (2003). 'La nuova politica regionale italiana: il ruolo dell'europeizzazione', in S. Fabbrini (ed.), *L'Europeizzazione dell'Italia: L'impatto dell'Unione Europea sulle istituzioni e le politiche italiane*. Rome: Laterza.

Greenwood (n/a). '*Organized Civil Society and Democratic Legitimacy in the EU*'. Manuscript.

Greenwood, J. (2003). *Interest Representation in the European Union*. Basingstoke, UK: Palgrave/Macmillan.

—— and Aspinwall, M. (eds.) (1998). *Collective Action in the European Union: Interests and the New Politics of Associability*. London: Routledge.

Greven, M. (2000). 'Can the European Union Finally Become a Democracy?', in M. Greven and L. W. Pauly (eds.), *Democracy Beyond the State? The European Dilemma and the Emerging Global Order*. Lanham, MD: Rowman & Littlefield.

—— and Pauly, L. W. (eds.) (2000). *Democracy Beyond the State? The European Dilemma and the Emerging Global Order*. Lanham, MD: Rowman & Littlefield.

Grimm, D. (1991). 'The Modern State: Continental Traditions', in F.-X. Kaufmann (ed.), *The Public Sector—Challenge for Coordination and Learning*. Berlin: de Gruyter.

—— (1997). 'Does Europe Need a Constitution?', in P. Gowan and P. Anderson (eds.), *The Question of Europe*. London: Verso.

Grossman, E. (2003). 'Les Groupes d'intéret économiques face à l'Intégration Européenne: le cas du secteur bancaire', *Revue Francaise de Science Politique*, 53(5).

—— (2006). 'Europeanization as an Interactive Process: German Public Banks meet EU State Aid Policy', *Journal of Common Market Studies*, 44(2): 325–48.

Gualini, E. (2003). 'Challenges to Multi-Level Governance: Contradictions and Conflicts in the Europeanization of Italian Regional Policy', *Journal of European Public Policy*, 10:4: 616–36.

Guédon, M-J. (1991). *Les Autorités Administratives Indépendantes*. Paris: LGDJ.

Guetta, B. and Labarde, P. (2002). *L'Europe Fédérale Pour & Contre*. Paris: Grasset.

Guiraudon, V. (2001). 'Weak Weapons of the Weak? Transnational Mobilization Around Migration in the European Union', in D. Imig and S. Tarrow (eds.), *Contentious European: Protest and Politics in an Emerging Polity*. Lanham, MD: Rowman & Littlefield.

—— (2003). 'The Constitution of a European Immigration Policy Domain: A Political Sociology Approach', *Journal of European Public Policy*, 10(2): 263–82.

Gunlicks, A. B. (ed.) (1989). 'Federalism and Intergovernmental Relations in West Germany: A Fortieth Year Appraisal', *Publius*, 19.

References

Haas, E. (1958). *The Uniting of Europe.* Stanford, CA: Stanford University Press.

Haas, P. M. (1992). 'Introduction: Epistemic Communities and International Policy Coordination', *International Organization,* 46: 1–35.

Habermas, J. (1989). *The Structural Transformation of the Public Sphere* (trans. T. Burger and F. Lawrence). Cambridge, MA: MIT Press.

—— (1996). *Between Facts and Norms: Contributions to a Discourse Theory.* Polity Press.

Haverland, M. (1999). 'National Adaptation to European Integration: The Importance of Institutional Veto Points', *Journal of Public Policy,* 20(1): 83–103.

Hayward, J. (1973). 'National Aptitudes for Planning in Britain, France, and Italy', *Government and Opposition,* 9(4).

—— (1986). *The State and the Market Economy.* New York: New York University Press.

—— (1995). 'Organized Interests and Public Policies', in J. Hayward and E. C. Page (eds.), *Governing the New Europe.* Cambridge: Polity Press.

Heclo, H. (1974). *Modern Social Politics in Britain and Sweden.* New Haven, CT: Yale University Press.

Hedetoft, U. (1998). 'Germany's National and European Identity: Normalisation by Other Means', in C. Lankowski (ed.), *Break Out, Break Down or Break In? Germany and the European Union after Amsterdam.* Washington, DC: AICGS Research Report no. 8.

Helfferich, B. and Kolb, F. (2001). 'Multilevel Coordination in "European Contentious Politics": The Case of the European Women's Lobby', in I. Doug and S. Tarrow (eds.), *Contentious Europeans.* Lanham, MD: Rowman & Littlefield.

Héritier, A. (1999). 'Elements of Democratic Legitimation in Europe: An Alternative Perspective', *Journal of European Public Policy,* 6(2): 269–82.

—— Knill, C., and Mingers, S. (1996). *Ringing the Changes: Regulatory Competition and the Transformation of the State.* Berlin: De Gruyter.

—— et al. (eds.) (2001). *Differential Europe: European Union Impact on National Policy-Making.* Boulder, CO: Rowman & Littlefield.

Hine, D. (1993). *Governing Italy: The Politics of Bargained Pluralism.* Oxford: Clarendon Press.

—— (2001). 'Europeanization and the Machinery of the Italian Government', in K. Featherstone and G. Kazamias, (eds.), *Europeanization and the Southern Periphery.* London: Frank Cass.

—— (2004). 'Explaining Italian Preferences at the Constitutional Convention', *Comparative European Politics,* 2(3): 302–19.

Hirst, P. (1994). *Associative Democracy.* Cambridge: Polity Press.

Hix, S. (2005). *The Political System of the European Union.* Basingstoke, UK: Palgrave Macmillan.

—— and Lord, C. (1997). *Political Parties in the European Union.* London: Macmillan.

—— Noury, A., and Roland, G. (2005). 'Power to the Parties: Cohesion and Competition in the European Parliament, 1979–2001', *British Journal of Political Science,* 35(2).

Hobsbawn, E. and Ranger, T. (1983). *The Invention of Tradition.* Cambridge: Cambridge University Press.

Hoffmann, S. (1959). 'The French Constitution of 1958: The Final Text and its Prospects', *American Political Science Review.*

—— (1966). 'Obstinate or Obsolete? The Fate of the Nation State and the Case of Western Europe', *Daedalus,* 95: 892–908.

—— (1989). 'The European Community and 1992', *Foreign Affairs*, 68(Fall): 41.

Hölscheidt, S. (2001). 'The German Bundestag: From Benevolent "Weakness" Towards Supportive Scrutiny', in A. Maurer and W. Wessels (eds.), *National Parliaments on Their Ways to Europe: Losers or Latecomers?* Baden-Baden, Germany: Nomos.

Hooghe, L. (ed.) (1996). *Cohesion Policy and European Integration: Building Multi-Level Governance*. Oxford: Oxford University Press.

—— (2001). *The European Commission and the Integration of Europe*. Cambridge: Cambridge University Press.

—— and Marks, G. (1999). 'The Making of a Polity: The Struggle over European Integration', in H. Kitschelt, P. Lange, G. Marks, and J. Stephens (eds.), *Continuity and Change in Contemporary Capitalism*, Cambridge: Cambridge University Press, pp. 70–97.

Hopkin, J. (2004). 'Paying for Party Response: Parties of the Centre-Right in Postwar Italy', in K. Lawson and L. Poguntke (eds.), *How Parties Respond*. London: Routledge.

Howe, G. (1990). 'Sovereignty and Interdependence: Britain's Place in the World', *International Affairs*, 66(4): 675–95.

Howorth, J. (1996). 'France and Gaullist Euroscepticism: Re-Reading the French Blueprint for a United Europe', in M. Adcock, E. Chester, and J. Whiteman (eds.), *Revolution, Society and the Politics of Memory*. Melbourne: University of Melbourne.

—— (2000). 'Being and Doing in Europe Since 1945: Contrasting Dichotomies of Identity and Efficiency', in J. Andrew, M. Crook, and M. Waller (eds.), *Why Europe? Problems of Culture and Identity*. New York: St Martin's Press.

—— (2002). 'ESDP and NATO: Joint Future or Deadlock?', Paper prepared for the Bertelsman Foundation/Venusberg Group Conference *Evaluating Nato's Future and the Consequences for European Security*, Netherlands Institute of International Relations, Clingendael, The Hague, December 4–5.

—— (2004). 'The European Draft Constitutional Treaty and the Future of the European Defense Initiative: A Question of Flexibility', *European Foreign Affairs Review*, 9(4): 483–508.

Hull, R. (1993). 'Lobbying Brussels: A View from Within', in S. Mazey and J. Richardson (eds.), *Lobbying in the European Community*. Oxford: Oxford University Press.

Imig, D. and Tarrow, S. (eds.) (2001a). *Contentious Europeans*. Lanham, MD: Rowman & Littlefield.

—— —— (2001b). 'Political Contention in a Europeanising Polity', in K. Goetz and S. Hix (eds.), *Europeanised Politics? European Integration and National Political Systems*. London: Frank Cass.

Inglehart, R. (1997). *Modernization and Postmodernization: Cultural, Economic and Political Change in 43 Societies*. Princeton: Princeton University Press.

Jachtenfuchs, M. and Kohler-Koch, B. (1995). 'Regieren im dynamischen Mehrebenensystem', in M. Jachtenfuchs and B. Kohler-Koch (eds.), *Europaeishes Integration*. Opladen, Prussia: Leske und Budrich, pp. 15–44.

—— Dietz, T., and Jung, S. (1998). 'Which Europe? Conflicting Models of a Legitimate European Political Order', *European Journal of International Relations*, 4(4): 409–45.

Jacobsson, K. (2004). 'The Methodology of the European Employment Strategy: Achievement and Problems', SCORE, Stockholm University, mimeo.

Jeffery, C. (1994). 'The Länder Strike Back: Structures and Procedures of European Integration Policy-Making in the German Federal System', Paper presented at the ESRC

Research Seminar on State Autonomy in the European Community, Christ Church, Oxford.

—— (ed.) (1996). *The Regional Dimension of the European Union: Towards a Third Level in Europe*. London: Frank Cass.

—— (1999). *Recasting German Federalism*. London: Pinter.

—— and Paterson, W. (2003). 'German and European Integration: A Shifting of Tectonic Plates', *West European Politics*, 26(4): 59–78

Jenkins, B. (2000). 'From Nation-Building to the Construction of Europe: The Case of France', in J. Andrew, M. Crook, and M. Waller, (eds.), *Why Europe? Problems of Culture and Identity*. New York: St Martin's Press.

Jobert, B. (1992). 'Représentations sociales. Controverses et débats dans la conduite des politiques publiques', *Revue française de science politique*, 42(2): 219–34.

Joerges, C. (1999). ' "Good Governance" Through Comitology?', in C. Joerges and E. Vos (eds.), *EU Committees: Social Regulation, Law, and Politics*. Oxford: Hart Publishing, pp. 311–38.

Johnson, N. (1998). 'The Judicial Dimension in British Politics', *West European Politics*, 21(1): 148–66.

Jones, B. and Keating, M. (eds.) (1994). *The European Union and the Regions*. Oxford: Clarendon Press.

Jordan, A. G. and Richardson, J. J. (1983). 'Policy Communities: The British and European Policy Style', *Policy Studies Journal*, 11.

Jordan, A. (ed.) (2002*a*). *Environmental Policy in the European Union: Actors, Institutions and Processes*. London: Earthscan.

—— (2002*b*). *The Europeanization of British Environmental Policy—A Departmental Perspective*. Basingstoke, UK: Palgrave.

Josselin, D. (1996). 'Domestic Policy Networks and European Negotiations: Evidence from British and French Financial Services', *Journal of European Public Policy*, 3(3): 297–317.

Jouve, E. (1967). *Le Général de Gaulle et la Construction de l'Europe*, vol. II. Paris: LGDJ.

Judge, D., Earnshaw, D. and Cowan, N. (1994). 'Ripples or Waves: The European Parliament in the European Community Policy Process', *Journal of European Public Policy*, 1(1): 28–51.

Kagan, R. (2003). *Of Paradise and Power*. New York: Knopf.

Kandermans, B., de Weerd, M., Sabucedo, J. M., and Rodriguez, M. (2001). 'Framing Contention: Dutch and Spanish Farmers Confront the EU', in D. Imig and S. Tarrow (eds.), *Contentious European: Protest and Politics in an Emerging Polity*. Lanham, MD: Rowman & Littlefield.

Kassim, H. (1998). 'The European Union and National Policy Making: The Case of Air Transport', Paper prepared for presentation at the annual meetings of American Political Science Association Boston, MA, September 3–6.

Kassim, H. (2000). 'The United Kingdom', in H. Kassim, A. Menon, G. Peters, and V. Wright (eds.), *The National Co-ordination of EU Policy Making: The Domestic Level*. Oxford: Oxford University Press.

—— (2003*a*). 'The European Administration: Between Europeanization and Domestication', in J. Hayward and A. Menon (eds.), *Governing Europe*. Oxford: Oxford University Press.

—— (2003b). 'Meeting the Demands of EU Membership: The Europeanization of National Administrative Systems', in K. Featherstone and C. Radaelli (eds.), *The Politics of Europeanization*. Oxford: Oxford University Press.

—— (2005). 'The Europeanization of Member-State Institutions', in S. Bulmer and C. Lequesne (eds.), *The Member States of the European Union*. Oxford: Oxford University Press.

—— Menon, A., Peters, G., and Wright, V. (eds.) (2000). *The National Co-ordination of EU Policy Making: The Domestic Level*. Oxford: Oxford University Press.

—— —— —— —— (eds.) (2001). *The National Co-ordination of EU Policy Making: The EU Level*. Oxford: Oxford University Press.

Katzenstein, P. (1985). *Small States in World Markets*. Ithaca, NY: Cornell University Press.

—— (1989). 'Conclusion', in P. Katzenstein (ed.), *Industry and Politics in West Germany: Toward the Third Republic*. Ithaca, NY: Cornell University Press.

—— (ed.) (1997a). *Tamed Power, Germany in Europe*. Ithaca, NY: Cornell.

—— (1997b). 'United Germany in an Integrating Europe', in P. Katzenstein (ed.), *Tamed Power, Germany in Europe*. Ithaca, NY: Cornell.

Kavanaugh, D. and Seldon, A. (1999). *The Powers Behind the Prime Minister: The Hidden Influence of Number Ten*. London: HarperCollins.

Keating, M. (1988). *State and Regional Nationalism: Territorial Politics and the European State*. Hempel Hempstead, UK: Harvesster Wheatsheaf.

—— (1998). *The New Regionalism in Western Europe*. Cheltenham, UK: Edward Elgar.

—— and Jones, B. (1995). *The European Union and the Regions*. Oxford: Oxford University Press.

Keeler, J. (1987). *The Politics of Neocorporatism in France: Farmers, the State, and Agricultural Policymaking in the Fifth Republic*. New York: Oxford University Press.

Keohane, R. O. and Hoffmann, S. (1991). 'Introduction', in R. O. Keohane and S. Hoffmann (eds.), *The New European Community: Decision-Making and Institutional Change*. Boulder, CO: Westview.

Kerremans, B. (1996). 'Non-Institutionalism, Neo-Institutionaism, and the Logic of Common Decision-Making in the European Union', *Governance*, 9(2): 217–40.

Kielmansegg, P. G. (1996). 'Integration und Demokratie', in M. Jachtenfuchs and B. Kohler-Koch (eds.), *Europaische Integration*. Opladen, Prussia: Leske and Budrich, pp. 47–71.

King, P. (1982). *Federalism and Federation*. London: Croom Helm.

Klingemann, H-D. (1999). 'Mapping Political Support in the 1990s: A Global Analysis', in P. Norris (ed.), *Critical Citizens: Global Support for Democratic Government*. Oxford: Oxford University Press.

—— (2005). 'A Policy Supply Perspective on Social Democratic Parties in Europe: Programmatic Profile and Programmatic Coherence of the Party of European Socialists', Paper prepared for presentation at the conference: *Social Justice and the Future of European Social Democracy*, Center for European Studies, Harvard University, Cambridge, MA, March 18–19.

—— and Fuchs, D. (1995). *Beliefs in Government, volume I: Citizens and the State*. Oxford: Oxford University Press.

Knichewski, G. (1996). 'Postwar National Identity in Germany', in B. Jenkins and S. A. Sofos (eds.), *Nation and Identity in Contemporary Europe*. London: Routledge.

References

Knill, C. (2001). *The Europeanization of National Administrations*. Cambridge: Cambridge University Press.

—— and Lehmkuhl, D. (1999). 'How Europe Matters: Different Mechanisms of Europeanization', *European Integration Online Papers*, EIOP 3(7), http://eiop.or.at/eiop/texte/1999

—— and Lenschow, A. (1998). 'Coping with Europe: The Impact of British and German Administrations on the Implementation of EU Environmental Policy', *Journal of European Public Policy*, 5(4): 595–14.

Koehane, R. (2002). 'Ironies of Sovereignty: The European Union and the United States', *Journal of Common Market Studies*, 40(4): 743–65.

Kohler-Koch, B. (1995). 'The Strength of Weakness: The Transformation of Governance in the EU', Working paper, Mannheimer Zentrum für Europäishe Sozialforschung, ABIII/no. 10, Mannheim.

—— (1996). 'Catching up with Change: The Transformation of Governance in the European Union', *Journal of European Public Policy*, 3(3): 359–80.

—— (1997). 'Organized Interests in European Integration: The Evolution of a New Type of Governance?' in A. Young and H. Wallace (eds.), *Participation and Policymaking in the European Union*. Oxford: Oxford University Press.

—— (2002). 'European Networks and Ideas: Changing National Policies?', *European Integration Online Papers*, Nr. 6, S.

—— and Eising, R. (eds.) (1999). *The Transformation of Governance in the European Union*. London: Routledge.

Koopmans, R. (2004). 'The Transformation of Political Mobilisation and Communication in European Public Spheres', 5th Framework Programme of the European Commission, http://europub.wz-berlin.de

Krasner, S. (1999). 'Globalization and Sovereignty', in D. A. Smith, D. J. Solinger, and S. C. Topick (eds.), *States and Sovereignty in the Global Economy*. London: Routledge.

Kreppel, A. and Hix, S. (2003). 'From Grand Coalition to Left-Right Confrontation: Explaining the Shifting Structure of Party Competition in the European Parliament', *Comparative Political Studies*, 36(1/2): 75–96.

Kritzinger, S. (2005). 'European Identity Building from the Perspective of Efficiency', *Comparative European Politics*, 3(1): 50–75.

Labbé, D. (1990). *Le Vocabulaire de François Mitterrand*. Paris: Presses de la Fondation Nationale des Sciences Politiques.

Ladrech, R. (1994). 'Europeanization of Domestic Politics and Institutions: The Case of France', *Journal of Common Market Studies*, 32(1): 69–88.

—— (1999). 'Political Parties and the Problem of Legitimacy in the European Union', in T. Banchoff and M. P. Smith (eds.), *Legitimacy and the European Union: The Contested Polity*. London and New York: Routledge.

Ladrech, R. (ed.) (2002). '*The Europeanization of Party Politics*', Special Issue of *Party Politics*, 8(4): 387–503.

Laïdi, Z. (2005). *La Norme sans la Force: l'énigme de la puissance européenne*. Paris, Presses de Sciences Po.

Lange, P. and Regini, M. (1989). 'Conclusion', in P. Lange and M. Regini (eds.), *State, Market, and Social Regulation: New Perspectives on Italy*. Cambridge: Cambridge University Press.

Lapalombara, J. (1989). *Democracy Italian Style*. New Haven, CT: Yale University Press.

Larsen, H. (1997). *Foreign Policy and Discourse Analysis*. London: Routledge.

Laurent, A. and Sauger, N. (eds.) (2005). *Le Référendum de Ratification du Traité Constitutionnel Européen du 29 Mai 2005: Comprendre le 'Non' Français*, Cahiers du Cevipof no. 42

Laursen, F. (2001). 'The Danish Folketing and Its European Affairs Committee: Strong Players in the National Policy Cycle', in A. Maurer and W. Wessels (eds.), *National Parliaments on their Ways to Europe: Losers or Latecomers?* Baden-Baden, Germany: Nomos Verlagsgellschaft, pp. 99–116.

Lavignote, G. E. (1999). *Expertise et Politiques Européennes de Développement Local*. Paris: L'Harmattan.

Le Galès, P. (2001). *'Est Maître des Lieux celui qui les Organise*: How Rules Change when National and European Policy Domains Collide', in A. Stone Sweet, W. Sandholtz, and N. Fligstein (eds.), *The Institutionalization of Europe*. Oxford: Oxford University Press.

Lees, C. (2002). 'Dark Matter': Institutional Constraints and the Failure of Party-based Euroscepticism in Germany', *Political Studies*, 50: 244–67.

Lehmbruch, G. (1996). 'German Federalism and the Challenge of Unification', in J. J. Hesse and V. Wright (eds.), *Federalizing Europe? The Costs, Benefits, and Preconditions of Federal Political Systems*. Oxford: Oxford University Press.

Lehmbruch, G. (1997). 'From State of Authority to Network State: The German State in Comparative Perspective', in M. Muramatsu and F. Naschold (eds.), *State Administration in Japan and Germany*. Berlin: de Gruyter.

Leitner, C. (ed.) (2003). *eGovernment in Europe: The State of Affairs* presented at the eGovernment conference (Como, Italy July 7–8). Maastricht: European Institute of Public Administration.

Leonardi, R. (1993). 'The Regional Reform in Italy: From Centralized to Regionalized State', in R. Leonardi (ed.), *The Regions and the European Community*. London: Frank Cass.

Lequesne, C. (1993). *Paris—Bruxelles: Comment se fait la politique européenne de la France*. Paris: Presses de la Fondation Politique Nationale des Sciences Politiques.

Leslie, P. (2001). 'The European Regional System: A Case of Unstable Equilibrium', *Journal of European Integration*, 22: 211–35.

Lijphart, Arend (1999). *Patterns of Democracy: Government Forms and Performance in Thirty-Six Countries*. New Haven: Yale University Press.

Lijphart, A. (1984). *Democracies: Patterns of Majoritarian and Consensus Government in Twenty-One Countries*. New Haven, CT: Yale University Press.

Lindberg, L. (1963). *The Political Dynamics of European Economic Integration*. Stanford, CA: Stanford University Press.

Locke, R. M. (1995). *Remaking the Italian Economy*. Ithaca, NY and London: Cornell University Press.

Lodge, J. (Sept. 1994). 'Transparency and Democratic Legitimacy', *Journal of Common Market Studies*, 32(3): 343–60.

Lord, C. (1992). 'Sovereign or Confused? The "Great Debate" About British Entry to the European Community 20 Years on', *Journal of Common Market Studies*, 30(4).

—— (1998). *Democracy in the European Union*. Sheffield, UK: Sheffield Academic Press.

—— and Beetham, D. (2001). 'Legitimizing the EU: Is there a "Postparliamentary Basis" for its Legitimation?' *Journal of Common Market Studies*, 39(3): 443–62.

Lord, C. and Magnette, P. (2002). 'Notes Towards a General Theory of Legitimacy in the European Union', ESRC *One Europe or Several?* Program Working Papers, 39/02.

Loughlin, J. (2001). *Subnational Democracy in the European Union: Challenges and Opportunities.* Oxford: Oxford University Press.

Lynch, P. (1999). *The Politics of Nationhood: Sovereignty, Britishness, and Conservative Politics.* New York: St Martin's Press.

Magnette, P. (2001*a*). 'European Governance and Civic Participation: Can the European Union be Politicised?', Jean Monnet Program Working Paper no. 6/01.

—— (2001*b*). *L'Europe, l'Etat et la Démocratie.* Bruxelles: Complexe.

—— (2003*a*). 'The Convention and the Problem of Democratic Legitimacy in the EU', Paper presented at the conference: *The European Convention, A Midterm Review*, Harvard Center for European Studies, Cambridge, MA, Jan. 31.

—— (2003*b*). 'European Governance and Civic Participation: Beyond Elitist Citizenship?', *Political Studies*, 51: 144–60.

—— (2003*c*). 'Between Parliamentary Control and the Rule of Law: The Political Role of the Ombudsman in the European Union', *Journal of European Public Policy*, 10(5): 677–94.

Mair, P. (1995). 'Political Parties, Popular Legitimacy and Public Privilege', in J. Hayward (ed.), *The Crisis of Representation in Europe.* London: Frank Cass.

—— (2001). 'The Limited Impact of Europe on National Party Systems', in K. Goetz and S. Hix (eds.), *Europeanised Politics? European Integration and National Political Systems.* London: Frank Cass.

—— (2004). 'Popular Party Democracy and the Construction of the European Union Political System', Paper prepared for presentation to the workshop *Sustainability and the European Union*, ECPR joint session, Uppsala, April.

—— (2006). 'Political Parties and Party Systems', in P. Graziano and M. Vink (eds.), *Europeanization: New Research Agendas.* Palgrave Macmillan (forthcoming).

Majone, G. (ed.) (1996). *Regulating Europe.* London and New York: Routledge.

—— (1998). 'Europe's Democratic Deficit', *European Law Journal*, 4(1): 5–28.

Mancini, G. F. (2000). 'The Italians in Europe', *Australian Journal of Politics and History*, 46(1): 21–32.

Manow, P. (2005). 'National Vote Intention and European Voting Behavior, 1979–2004: Second Order Election Effects, Election Timing, Government Approval and the Europeanization of Elections', MPIfG Discussion Paper 05/11, Max Planck Institute for the Study of Societies

Maor, M. (1998). 'The Relationship Between Government and Opposition in the Bundestag and House of Commons in the Run-Up to the Maastricht Treaty', *West European Politics*, 21(3): 187–207.

March, J. G. and Olsen, J. P. *Democratic Governance.* New York: Free Press.

Marin, B. and Mayntz, R. (eds.) (1991). *Policy Networks. Empirical Evidence and Theoretical Considerations.* Frankfurt am Main: Campus Verlag and Westview Press.

Marks, G. (1993). 'Structural Policy and Multilevel Governance in the EC', in A. W. Cafruny and G. G. Rosenthal (eds.), *The State of the European Community: The Maastricht Debates and Beyond*, vol. 2. Boulder, CO: Lynne Rienner, pp. 391–411.

—— (1996). 'Exploring and Explaining Variation in Cohesion Policy', in L. Hooghe (ed.), *Cohesion Policy, the European Community and Subnational Government.* Oxford: Oxford University Press.

—— and Hooghe, L. (2001). *Multi-Level Governance and European Integration*. Lanham, MD: Rowman & Littlefield.

—— and McAdam, D. (1999). 'On the Relations of Political Opportunities to the Form of Collective Action: The Case of the European Union', in D. della Porta and H-P. Kriesi (eds.), *Social Movements in a Globalizing World*. Basingstoke, UK: Palgrave.

—— and Wilson, C. (2000). 'The Past in the Present: A Cleavage Theory of Party Responses to European Integration', *British Journal of Political Science*, 30(4): 433–59.

—— Hooghe, L., and Blank, K. (1996). 'European Integration since the 1980s: State-Centric versus Multi-Level Governance', *Journal of Common Market Studies*, 34(3): 341–78.

Marquand, D. (1979). *Parliament for Europe*. London: Jonathan Cape.

Marsh, D. and Rhodes, R. A. W. (eds.) (1992). *Policy Networks in British Government*. Oxford: Clarendon Press.

—— and Smith, M. (2000). 'Understanding Policy Networks: Towards a Dialectical Approach', *Political Studies*, 48: 4–21.

Martin, A. and Ross, G. (2001). 'Trade Union Organizing at the European Level: The Dilemma of Borrowed Resources', in D. Imig and S. Tarrow (eds.), *Contentious Europeans*. Lanham, MD: Rowman & Littlefield.

Maurer, A. (2001). 'National Parliaments in the European Architecture: From Latecomers Adaptation to Permanent Institutional Change', in A. Maurer and W. Wessels (eds.), *National Parliaments on their Ways to Europe: Losers or Latecomers?* Baden-Baden, Germany: Nomos Verlagsgellschaft, pp. 27–76.

—— (2003). 'Germany: Fragmented Structures in a Complex System', in W. Wessels, A. Maurer, and J. Mittag (eds.), *Fifteen into One? The European Union and Its Member-States*. Manchester, UK: University of Manchester Press.

—— and Wessels, W. (2001). *National Parliaments on their Ways to Europe: Losers or Latecomers?* Baden-Baden, Germany: Nomos Verlagsgellschaft.

Mayer, N. (1999). *Ces Français qui votent FN*. Paris: Flammarion.

Mazey, S. (1988). 'European Community Action on Behalf of Women: The Limits of Legislation', *Journal of Common Market Studies*, 27(1): 63–84.

—— (1995a). 'French Regions and the European Union', in J. Loughlin and S. Mazey (eds.), *The End of the French Unitary State? Ten Years of Regionalization in France, 1982–1992*. London: Frank Cass.

—— (1995b). 'The Development of EU Equality Policies: Bureaucratic Expansion on Behalf of Women?' *Public Administration*, 73(4): 591–610.

—— and Richardson, J. (eds.) (1993a). *Lobbying in the European Community*. Oxford: Oxford University Press.

—— —— (1993b). 'Environmental Groups and the EC: Challenges and Opportunities', in D. Judge (ed.), *A Green Dimension for the European Community: Political Issues and Processes*. London: Frank Cass.

—— —— (1996). 'EU Policymaking: A Garbage Can or an Anticipatory and Consensual Policy Style?', in Y. Mény P. Muller, and J-L. Quermonne (eds.), *Adjusting to Europe: The Impact of the European Union on National Institutions and Policies*. London: Routledge.

—— —— (eds.) (2002). *Lobbying in the European Community*. Oxford: Oxford University Press.

McAdam, D. (1996). 'Conceptual Origins, Current Problems, Future Directions', in D. McAdam, J. McCarthy, and M. Zald, (eds.), *Comparative Perspectives on Social*

Movements: Political Opportunities, Mobilizing Structures, and Cultural Framings. Cambridge: Cambridge University Press.

McCarthy, P. (1995). *The Crisis of the Italian State*. New York: St Martin's Press.

McCormick, J. (2001). *Environmental Policy in the European Union*. New York: Palgrave.

McKay, D. (2000). 'Policy Legitimacy and Institutional Design: Comparative Lessons for the European Union', *Journal of Common Market Studies*, 38(1): 25–44.

McLaughlin, A. and Jordan, G. (1993). 'The Rationality of Lobbying in Europe: Why are Euro-Groups so Numerous and so Weak? Some Evidence from the Car Industry', in Mazey and Richardson (eds.), *Lobbying in the European Community*.

Mehta, J. (2004). 'Ideas and Politics: Toward a Second Generation', Mss. Harvard University.

Menon, A. (2000). 'France', in H. Kassim, A. Menon, G. Peters, and V. Wright (eds.), *The National Co-ordination of EU Policy Making: The Domestic Level*. Oxford: Oxford University Press.

Mény, Y., Muller, P., and Quermonne, J-L. (1996). 'Introduction', in *Adjusting to Europe: The Impact of the European Union on National Institutions and Policies*. London: Routledge.

Meyer, T. (1995). 'European Public Sphere and Societal Politics', in M. Telo (eds.), *Democratie et Construction Européenne*. Brussels: Presses de l'Université Libre.

Milward, A. (1992). *The European Rescue of the Nation-State*. Berkeley, CA: University of California Press.

Minkenberg, M. (2005). 'Germany: From *Kulturnation* to Europeanization?', in A. Ichijo and W. Spohn (eds.), *Entangled Identities: Nations and Europe*. London: Ashgate.

Mitterrand, F. (1986). *Réflexions sur la Politique Extérieure de la France—Introduction à Vingt-Cinq Discours*. Paris: Fayard.

Moran, M. (2004). *The British Regulatory State*. Oxford: Oxford University Press.

Morass, M. (1997). 'Austria: The Case of a Federal Newcomer in European Union Politics', in C. Jeffery (ed.), *The Regional Dimension of the European Union: Towards a Third Level?* London: Frank Cass.

Moravcsik, A. (1991). 'Negotiating the Single European Act: National Interests and Conventional Statecraft in the European Community', *International Organization*, 45: 651–88.

—— (1994). 'Why the European Community Strengthens the State: Domestic Politics and International Cooperation', Center for European Studies Working Paper 52, Cambridge, MA: Harvard University.

—— (1998). *The Choice for Europe: Social Purpose and State Power from Messina to Maastricht*. Ithaca, NY: Cornell University Press.

—— (November, 2002). 'Reassessing Legitimacy in the European Union', *Journal of Common Market Studies*, 40(4): 603–24.

Morin, E. (1987). *Penser L'Europe*. Paris: Seuil.

Morlino, L. (1998). *Democracy Between Consolidation and Crisis*. Oxford: Oxford University Press.

Mosher, J. and Trubek, D. M. (2003). 'EU Social Policy and the European Employment Strategy', *Journal of Common Market Studies*, 41(1): 63–88.

Muller, P. (1995). 'Les Politiques Publiques comme Construction d'un Rapport au Monde', in A. Faure, G. Pollet, and P. Warin (eds.), *La Construction du Sens dans les Politiques Publiques: Débats autour de la notion de Référentiel*. Paris: L'Harmattan.

Nehring, N. J. 'Parliamentary Control of the Executive' in L. Lyck (ed.), *Denmark and EC Membership Evaluated*. London: Pinter

Newman, M. (1996). *Democracy, Sovereignty and the European Union*. New York: St Martin's Press.

Newton, K. and Norris, P. (2000). 'Confidence in Public Institutions: Faith, Culture, or Performance?', in S. Pharr and R. Putnam (eds.), *Disaffected Democracies*. Princeton, NJ: Princeton University Press.

Nicolaïdis, K. (2001). 'Conclusion: The Federal Vision Beyond the Nation-State', in K. Nicolaïdes and R. Howse (eds.), *The Federal Vision: Legitimacy and Levels of Governance in the US and the EU*. London: Oxford University Press.

—— (2003). 'Our European Demoi-cracy', Paper prepared for presentation at the biannual meetings of the European Union Studies Association, Nashville, TN, March 26–30.

—— (2005). 'UE: Un Moment Tocquevillen', *Politique Étrangère* no. 3: 497–510.

Niedermayer, O. and Simott, R. (eds.) (1995). *Public Opinion and International Governance*. Oxford: Oxford University Press.

Nonon, J. and Clamen, M. (1991). *L'Europe et ses Couloirs: Lobbying et Lobbyistes*. Paris: Dunod.

Nora, P. (1984). *Les Lieux de Mémoire: vol. I: La République*. Paris: Gallimard.

Norris, P. (ed.) (1999). *Critical Citizens: Global Support for Democratic Government*. Oxford: Oxford University Press.

Norton, P. (1996a). 'The United Kingdom: Political Conflict, Parliamentary Scrutiny', in P. Norton (ed.), *National Parliaments and the European Union*. London: Frank Cass.

—— (ed.), (1996b). *National Parliaments and the European Union*. London: Frank Cass.

Olsen, J. (2002). 'The Many Faces of Europeanization', ARENA Working Papers WP 02/2, http://www.arena.uio.no/publications/wp02_2.htm

Padoa-Schioppa, T. (2001). 'Italy and Europe: A Fruitful Interaction', *Daedalus*, 130(2): 13–44.

Page, E. C. (1995). 'Administering Europe', in J. Hayward and E. C. Page (eds.), *Governing the New Europe*. Cambridge: Polity Press.

—— (2001). 'The European Union and the Bureaucratic Mode of Production', in *From the Nation State to Europe? Essays in Honor of Jack Hayward*. Oxford: Oxford University Press.

—— (2003). 'Europeanization and the Persistence of Administrative Systems', in J. Hayward and A. Menon (eds.), *Governing Europe*. Oxford: Oxford University Press.

Parsons, C. (2003). *A Certain Idea of Europe*. Ithaca, NY: Cornell.

Pasquier, R. (2003). 'From Identity to Collective Action: Building Political Capacity in French Regions', in J. Bukowski, S. Piattoni, and M. Smyrl (eds.), *Between Europeanization and Local Societies: The Space for Territorial Governance*. Lanham, MD: Rowman & Littlefield.

—— (2004). *La Capacité Politique des Régions: Une Comparaison France/Espagne*. Rennes: PUR.

Pasquino, G. (1989). 'Unregulated Regulators: Parties and Party Government', in P. Lange and M. Regini (eds.), *State, Market, and Social Regulation: New Perspectives on Italy*. Cambridge: Cambridge University Press.

—— (2003). 'Comparing Democracies: A Critique and a Tentative Research Agenda.' Paper prepared for presentation to the Workshop 'Accountability and Representation in European Democracy.' Harvard University, Center for European Studies (May 2–3).

References

—— (1997). 'No Longer a "Party State"? Institutions, Power and the Problems of Italian Reform', *West European Politics*, 20(1): 34–53.

Paterson, W. (1996). 'Beyond Sovereignty: The New Germany in the New Europe', *German Politics* (2).

—— (1998). 'Helmut Kohl, "The Vision Thing" and Escaping the Semi-Sovereignty Trap', *German Politics*, 7(11): 17–36.

Pederson, T. (2000). 'Denmark', in H. Kassim, G. Peters, and V. Wright (eds.), *The National Co-ordination of EU Policy Making: The Domestic Level*. Oxford: Oxford University Press.

Perrineau, P. (ed.) (2005). *Le Vote Européen, 2004–2005*. Paris: Presses de Sciences Po.

Peters, G. B. (1992). 'Bureaucratic Politics and the Institutions of the European Communit', in A. Sbragia (ed.), *Euro-Politics*. Washington, DC: Brookings,

Peterson, J. (1999). 'Sovereignty and Independence', in I. Holliday, et al. (eds.), *Fundamentals in British Politics*. Basingstoke, UK: Macmillan.

Pharr, S. J. and Putnam, R. D. (eds.) (2000). *Disaffected Democracies: What's Troubling the Trilateral Countries?* Princeton, NJ: Princeton University Press.

Piar, C. and Gerstlé, J. (2005). 'Le Cadrage du Référendum sur la Constitution Européenne: La Dynamique d'une Campagne à Rebondissements', in A. Laurent and N. Sauger (eds.), *Le Référendum de Ratification du Traité Constitutionnel Européen du 29 Mai 2005: Comprendre le 'Non' Français*. Cahiers du Cevipof no. 42: 42–73.

Piattoni, S. (2003). 'Regioni a statuto speciale e politica di coesione. Cambiamenti interistituzionali e risposte regionali', in S. Fabbrini (ed.), *L'Europeizzazione dell'Italia: L'impatto dell'Unione Europea sulle istituzioni e le politiche italiane*. Rome: Laterza.

—— and Smyrl, M. (2003). 'Building Effective Institutions: Italian Regions and EU Structural Funds', in J. Bukowski, S. Piattoni, and M. Smyrl (eds.), *Between Europeanization and Local Societies: The Space for Territorial Governance*. Lanham, MD: Rowman & Littlefield.

Pilkington, C. (1995). *Britain in the European Union Today*. Manchester, UK: Manchester University Press.

Pinder, J. (1994). *European Community: The Building of a Union*. Oxford: Oxford University Press.

Pizzorno, A. (1993). *Le Radici della Politica Assoluta*. Milano: Feltrinelli.

Pochet, P. and De la Porte, C. (2002). *Building Social Europe through the Open Method of Coordination*. Brussels: PIE/PeterLang.

Pogge, T. (1997). 'Creating Supra-National Institutions Democratically: Reflections on the European Union's Democratic Deficit', *Journal of Political Philosophy*, 5(2): 163–82.

Pollack, M. (1997a). 'Delegation, Agency, and Agenda Setting in the European Community', *International Organization*, 51(1).

—— (1997b). 'Representing Diffuse Interests in EC Policymaking', *Journal of European Public Policy*, 4(4): 572–90.

—— and Hafner-Burton, E. (2000). 'Mainstreaming Gender in European Union Policymaking', *Journal of European Public Policy*, special issue on *Women, Power and Public Policy* 7(1).

Popper, K. (1957). *The Poverty of Historicism*. London: Routledge & Kegan Paul.

Portelli, H. (1999). 'Arbitre ou Chef de l'Opposition?', *Pouvoirs*, (91): 59–70.

Preston, P. W. (1994). *Europe, Democracy and the Dissolution of Britain: An Essay on the Issue of Europe in UK Public Discourse*. Aldershot, UK: Dartmouth.

Preuss, U. K. (2004). 'Citizenship and the German Nation', in R. Bellamy, D. Castiglione, and E. Santoro (eds.), *Lineages of European Citizenship: Rights, Belonging and Paricipation in Eleven Nation-States*. Basingstoke, UK: Palgrave Macmillan.

Prodi, R. (2001). 'Italy, Europe', *Daedalus*, 130(2): 7–12.

Prudhomme-Deblanc, C. (2002). *Un Ministère Français face à l'Europe: Le Cas du Ministère de l'Equipement, des Transports et du Logement*. Paris: L'Harmattan.

Putnam, R. D. (1988). 'Diplomacy and Domestic Politics', *International Organization*, 42: 427–61.

—— (1993). *Making Democracy Work*. Princeton, NJ: Princeton University Press.

—— Leonardi, R., and Nanetti, R. (1985). *La Pianta e le Radici*. Bologna, Italy: Il Mulino.

Radaelli, C. (1999). *Technocracy in the European Union*. London and New York: Longman.

—— (2000). 'Whither Europeanization? Concept Stretching and Substantive Change', Paper presented at Political Studies Annual Conference, London, April 10–13.

Radaelli, C. M. (1998). 'Networks of expertise and policy change in Italy', *South European Society and Politics*, 3(2): 1–22.

—— (2002). 'The Italian State and the Euro', in K. Dyson (ed.), *The European State and the Euro*. Oxford: Oxford University Press.

—— (2003). 'The Europeanisation of public policy', in K. Featherstone and C. M. Radaelli (eds.), *The Politics of Europeanisation*. Oxford: Oxford University Press, pp. 27–56.

—— and Schmidt, V. A. (2004). 'Mapping the Scope of Discourse, Learning, and Europeanisation in Policy Change', *West European Politics*, 27(4): 364–79.

Raderchi, P. R. (1998). 'Report on Italy', in Slaughter, Sweet, and Weiler (eds.), *The European Court and National Courts: Doctrine and Jurisprudence*. Oxford: Hart Publishing.

Reif, K. and Schmitt, H. (1980). 'Nine Second-Order National Elections: A Conceptual Framework or the Analysis of European Election Results', *European Journal of Political Research*, 8: 3–44.

Reif, K.-H. (1997). 'Reflections: European Elections as Member State Second-Order Elections Revisited', *European Journal of Political Research*, 31(1): 115–24.

Rein, M. and Schön, D. A. (1994). *Frame Reflection: Toward the Resolution of Intractable Policy Controversies*. New York: Basic Books.

Renan, E. (1947). 'Qu'est-ce qu'une Nation?', in *Oeuvres Complètes*, vol. 1. Paris: Calmann-Lévy, pp. 887–906.

Reynié, D. and Cautrès, B. (2001). *L'Opinion Européenne*. Paris: Presses de Sciences Po.

Rhodes, M. and de la Porte, C. (2004). 'EU Employment Policy: Between Experimentalism and Effectiveness', Paper prepared for presentation to the American Political Science Association Meetings, Chicago, IL: Sept. 2–5.

Rhodes, R. A. W. and Marsh, D. (1992). 'New Directions in the Study of Policy Networks', *European Journal of Policy Research*, 21: 181–205.

Richardson, J. J. (1993). 'Interest Group Behavior in Britain: Continuity and Change', in J. J. Richardson (ed.), *Pressure Groups*. Oxford: Oxford University Press.

—— (1994). 'Doing Less by Doing More: British Government 1979–1993', in W. C. Müller and V. Wright (eds.), *The State in Western Europe: Retreat or Redefinition*. London: Frank Cass.

—— (2000). 'Government, Interest Groups and Policy Change', *Political Studies*, 48: 1006–25.

Richardson, J. J. and Jordan, A. G. (1979). *Governing Under Pressure: The Policy Process in a Post-Parliamentary Democracy*. Oxford: Martin Robertson.

Risse, T. (2001). 'A European Identity? Europeanization and the Evolution of National Identities', in M. Cowles, J. Caporaso, and T. Risse, (eds.), *Transforming Europe*. Ithaca, NY: Cornell, pp. 198–218.

Risse, T. (2003). 'An Emerging European Public Sphere? Theoretical Clarifications and Empirical Indicators', Paper prepared for presentation at the Biannual Meetings of the European Union Studies Association, Nashville, TN, Mar. 26–30.

Rittberger, B. (2003). 'The Creation and Empowerment of the European Parliament', *Journal of Common Market Studies*, 41(2): 203–25.

Rizzuto, F. (1996). 'The French Parliament and the EU: Loosening the Constitutional Straitjacket', in P. Norton (ed.), *National Parliaments and the European Union*. London: Frank Cass.

Roederer-Rynning, C. (2002). 'Farm Conflict in France and the Europeanization of Agricultural Policy', *West European Politics*, 25(3): 105–24.

Romano, S. (1993). *L'Italia Scappata di Mano*. Milan: Longanesi.

Rometsch, D. and Wessels, W. (eds.) (1996). *The European Union and Member-States: Toward Institutional Fusion*. Manchester, UK: Manchester University Press.

Rosanvallon, P. (1992). *L'État en France: De 1789s à Nos Jours*. Paris: Seuil.

—— (2004). *Le Modèle politique français : La société civile contre le jacobinisme de 1789 à nos jours*. Paris: Seuil.

Rosati, M. (2000). *Il Patriotismo Italiano: Culture Politiche e Identità Nazionale*. Roma: Laterza.

Rose, C. (1992). *The Dirty Man of Europe: The Great British Pollution Scandal*. London: Simon & Schuster.

Ross, G. (1995). *Jacques Delors and European Integration*. Oxford: Polity Press.

Roussel, E. (1994). *Georges Pompidou, 1911–1974*. Paris: Lattes.

Rucht, D. (2002). 'The EU as a Target of Political Mobilisation: Is There a Europeanisation of Conflict?', in R. Balme, D. Chabanet, and V. Wright (eds.), *L'action collective en Europe*. Paris: Presses de Sciences Po.

Ruggie, J. (1993). 'Territoriality and Beyond: Problematizing Modernity in International Relations', *International Organization*, 47(1): 139–75.

Saalfeld, T. (1996). 'The German Houses of Parliament and European Legislation' in P. Norton (ed.), *National Parliaments and the European Union*. London: Frank Cass.

Sabatier, P. A. (1998). 'The Advocacy Coalition Framework: Revisions and Relevance for Europe', *Journal of European Public Policy*, 5(1): 98–130.

—— and Jenkins-Smith, H. C. (eds.) (1993). *Policy Change and Learning: An Advocacy Coalition Approach*. Boulder, CO: Westview.

Saguy, A. (2003). *What Is Sexual Harassment? From Washington D.C. to the Sorbonne*. Berkeley, CA: University of California Press.

Sandholtz, W. (1996). 'Membership Matters: Limits of the Functional Approach to European Institutions', *Journal of Common Market Studies*, 34: 403–29.

Saurugger, S. (2002). 'Europeaniser les Interets? Les Groupes d'intérêt économiques de l'élargissement de l'Union Européenne', Ph.D. dissertation, Institut d'Études Politiques, pp. 88–9.

Sbragia, A. (1992). 'Italia/CEE Un Partner Sottovalutato', *Relazioni Internazionali* (2): 78–86.

—— 'The European Community: A Balancing Act', *Publius*, 23.

—— (1994). 'From "Nation-State" to "Member-State": The Evolution of the European Community', in P. M. Lutzeler (ed.), *Europe After Maastricht: American and European Perspectives*. Providence, RI: Berghahn.

—— (2001). 'Italy', in M. G. Cowles, J. Caporaso, and T. Risse, (eds.), *Transforming Europe: Europeanization and Domestic Change*. Ithaca, NY: Cornell University Press

Scharpf, F. W. (1988). 'The Joint Decision Trap: Lessons from German Federalism and European Integration', *Public Administration*, 66(3): 239–78.

—— (1994). 'Community and Autonomy: Multi-Level Policymaking in the European Union', *Journal of European Public Policy*, 1(2).

—— (1997). 'Economic Integration, Democracy and the Welfare State', *Journal of European Public Policy*, 4(1): 18–36.

—— (1999). *Governing in Europe*. Oxford: Oxford University Press.

—— (2000b). 'Interdependence and Democratic Legitimation', in S. Pharr and R. Putnam (eds.), *Disaffected Democracies*. Princeton, NJ: Princeton University Press.

—— (2002). 'The European Social Model: Coping with the Challenges of Diversity', *Journal of Common Market Studies*, 40(4): 645–70.

—— (2003a). 'What a European Constitution Could and Could not Achieve', Paper prepared for presentation for the Harvard Conference, *The European Convention: A Midterm Review*, Center for European Studies, Harvard University, Jan. 31.

—— (2003b). Legitimate Diversity: The New Challenge of European Integration' in T. Börzel and R. Cichowski (eds.), *The State of the European Union*. Oxford: Oxford University Press.

—— and Schmidt, V. A. (2000). *Welfare and Work in the Open Economy. vol. 1: From Vulnerability to Competitiveness*. Oxford: Oxford University Press.

Schild, J. (2001). 'National v. European Identites: French and Germans in the European Multi-Level System', *Journal of Common Market Studies*, 39(2): 331–51.

Schmidt, S. K. (1997). 'Behind the Council Agenda: The Commission's Impact on Decisions', MPIfG Discussion Paper 97/4, Max Planck Institute for the Study of Societies, Cologne.

—— (2004). 'Habilitation Treatise'. Hagen: Fern Universität.

Schmidt, V. A. (1990). *Democratizing France: The Political and Administrative History of Decentralization*. Cambridge: Cambridge University Press.

—— (1996a). *From State to Market? The Transformation of Business and Government in France*. Cambridge: Cambridge University Press.

—— (1996b). 'Loosening the Ties that Bind: The Impact of European Integration on French Government and Its Relationship to Business', *Journal of Common Market Studies*, 34(2): 223–54.

—— (1997). 'Discourse and (Dis)Integration in Europe: The Cases of France, Great Britain, and Germany', *Daedalus*, 126(3): 167–98.

—— (1999a). 'European "Federalism" and Its Encroachments on National Institutions', *Publius*, 29(1): 19–44.

Schmidt, V. A. (1999*b*). 'National Patterns of Governance Under Siege: The Impact of European Integration', in B. Kohler-Koch and R. Eising (eds.), *The Transformation of Governance in the European Union*. London: Routledge.

—— (1999*c*). 'The Changing Dynamics of State–Society Relations in the Fifth Republic', *West European Politics* (October): 141–65.

—— (2000). 'Values and Discourse in the Politics of Adjustment', in F. W. Scharpf and V. A. Schmidt (eds.), *Welfare and Work in the Open Economy: vol. 1*. Oxford: Oxford University Press.

—— (2001*a*). 'Federalism and State Governance in the EU and the US: An Institutional Perspective', in K. Nicolaïdis and R. Howse (eds.), *The Federal Vision: Legitimacy and Levels of Governance in the US and the EU*. London: Oxford University Press.

—— (2001*b*). 'The Politics of Adjustment in France and Britain: When Does Discourse Matter?', *Journal of European Public Policy*, 8: 247–64.

—— (2002*a*). *The Futures of European Capitalism*. Oxford: Oxford University Press.

—— (2002*b*). 'The Effects of European Integration on National Governance: Reconsidering Practices and Reconceptualizing Democracy', in J. Gröte and B. Gbikpi (eds.), *Participatory Governance: Theoretical, Political, and Societal Implications*. Opladen, Prussia: Leske and Budrich.

—— (2002*c*). 'Europeanization and the Mechanics of Policy Adjustment', *Journal of European Public Policy*, 9(6): 894–912.

—— (2002*d*). 'Does Discourse Matter in the Politics of Welfare State Adjustment?', *Comparative Political Studies*, 35(2): 168–93.

—— (2003*a*). 'How, Where, and When Does Discourse Matter in Small States' Welfare State Adjustment?', *New Political Economy*, 8(1): 127–46.

—— (2003*b*). 'The Boundaries of "Bounded Generalizations": Discourse as the Missing Factor in Actor-Centered Institutionalism', in R. Mayntz and W. Streeck (eds.), *Die Reformierbarkeit der Demokratie: Innovationen und Blockaden*. Frankfurt a. m.: Campus.

—— (2004). 'The European Union: Democratic Legitimacy in a Regional State?', *Journal of Common Market Studies*, 42(4): 975–99.

—— (2005*a*). 'Democracy in Europe: The Impact of European Integration', *Perspectives on Politics*, 3(4): 761–79.

—— (2005*b*). 'Institutionalism and the State', in C. Hay, D. Marsh, and M. Lister (eds.), *The State: Theories and Issues . . .* Basingstoke, UK: Palgrave.

—— and Radaelli, C. (2004). 'Conceptual and Methodological Issues in Policy Change in Europe', in C. Radaelli and V. Schmidt (eds.), Symposium issue 'Policy Change and Discourse in Europe', *West European Politics*, 27(4): 1–28.

Schmitter, P. (1970). 'A Revised Theory of Regional Integraton', *International Organization*, 24: 836–68.

—— (1996). 'Some Alternative Futures for the European Polity and their Implications for European Public Policy', in Y. Mény, P. Muller, and J-L. Quermonne (eds.), *Adjusting to Europe: The Impact of the European Union on National Institutions and Policies*. London: Routledge.

Schmitter, P. C. (1985). 'Neo-Corporatism and the State', in W. Grant (ed.), *The Political Economy of Corporatism*. New York: St Martin's Press.

—— (2000). *How to Democratize the European Union and Why Bother*. London: Rowman & Littlefield.

Schnapper, D. (1994). *La Communauté des Citoyens*. Paris: Gallimard.

Schwarz, H.-P. (ed.) (1975). *Konrad Adenauer: Reden, 1917–1967: Eine Auswahl*. Stuttgart, Germany: Deutsche Verlags-Anstalt.

Scott, A., Peterson, J., and Millar, D. (March 1994). 'Subsidiarity: A "Europe of the Regions" v. the British Constitution?', *Journal of Common Market Studies*, 32(1): 47–68.

Seldon, A. (1998). *Major—A Political Life*. London: George Weidenfeld & Nicholson.

Shackleton, M. (2005). 'The European Parliament: Is the Destination Still Unknown?', in N. Jabko and C. Parsons (eds.), *With US or Against US? European Trends in American Perspective*. Oxford: Oxford University Press.

Shonfield, A. (1965). *Modern Capitalism: The Changing Balance of Public and Private Power*. Oxford: Oxford University Press.

Shor, C. (2000). *Building Europe*. London: Routledge.

Siedentop, L. (2000). *Democracy in Europe*. London: Penguin.

Skocpol, T. and Sommers, M. (1980). 'The Uses of Comparative History in Macro Social Inquiry', *Comparative Studies in Society and History*, 22: 174–97.

Slaughter, A.-M. (2001). 'In Memoriam: Abram Chayes', *Harvard Law Review*, 114(3): 682–9.

Smismans, S. (2003). 'Representation Through Interest Committees: The Case of the Tripartite Advisory Committee for Safety, Hygiene and Health Protection at Work', in S. Saurugger and B. Irondelle (eds.), *Les modes de représentation dans l'Union européenne*. Paris: L'Harmattan.

Smith, G. (1992). 'Britain in New Europe', *Foreign Affairs*, 71(4).

Smith, J. (2005). 'A Missed Opportnity? New Labour's European Policy, 1997–2005', *International Affairs*, 81(4): 703–21.

Solozábal, J. J. (1996). 'Spain: A Federation in the Making?', in J. J. Hesse and V. Wright (eds.), *Federalizing Europe? The Costs, Benefits, and Preconditions of Federal Political Systems*. Oxford: Oxford University Press, pp. 260–3.

Sommier, I. (2003). *Le Renouveau des Mouvements Contestataires à l'heure de la mondialisation*. Paris: Flammarion.

Sørensen, H. and Waever, O. (1992). 'State, Society and Democracy and the Effect of the EC', in L. Lyck (ed.), *Denmark and EC Membership Evaluated*. London: Pinter.

Stefanizzi, S. and Tarrow, S. (1989). 'Protest and Regulation: The Interaction of State and Society in the Cycle of 1965–74', in P. Lange and M. Regini (eds.), *State, Market, and Social Regulation: New Perspectives on Italy*. Cambridge: Cambridge University Press.

Stein, E. (1981). 'Lawyers, Judges, and the Making of a Transnational Constitution', *American Journal of International Law*, 75: 1–27.

Stone Sweet, A. (1998). 'Constitutional Dialogues in the European Community', in A-M. Slaughter, A. Stone Sweet, and J. H. H. Weiler (eds.), *The European Court and National Courts—Doctrine and Jurisprudence*. Oxford: Hart Publishing.

—— (2000). *Governing with Judges: Constitutional Politics in Europe*. Oxford: Oxford University Press.

—— (2004). *The Judicial Construction of Europe*. Oxford: Oxford University Press.

—— and Brunnell, T. (1998). 'Constructing a Supranational Constitution: Dispute Resolutioin and Governance in the European Community', *American Political Science Review*, 92: 63–81.

Stone Sweet, A. and Sandholtz, W. (1997). 'European Integration and Supranational Governance', *Journal of European Public Policy*, 4: 297–317.

Stone, A. (1992). *The Birth of Judicial Politics: The Constitutional Council in Comparative Perspective*. New York: Oxford University Press.

Streeck, W. and Schmitter, P. (1991). 'From National Corporatism to Transnational Pluralism: Organized Interests in a Single European Market', *Politics and Society*, 19(2): 133–64.

Suleiman, E. N. (1974). *Politics, Power, and Bureaucracy in France: The Administrative Elite*. Princeton, NJ: Princeton University Press.

Szarka, J. (2000). 'Environmental Policy and Neo-Corporatism in France', *Environmental Politics*, 9(3): 89–109.

—— (2001). 'European Policy and France', in *The Shaping of Environmental Policy in France*. New York: Berghahn Books.

Szukala, A. (2003). 'France: The European Transformation of the French Model', in W. Wessels, A. Maurer, and J. Mittag (eds.), *Fifteen into One? The European Union and Its Member-States*. Manchester, UK: University of Manchester Press.

Taggart, P. and Szczerbiak, A. (2001). 'Parties, Positions and Europe: Euroscepticism in the EU Candidate States of Central and Eastern Europe', Paper presented at the annual meeting of the Political Studies Association, Manchester, UK, April 10–12.

Tapio, R. and Hix, S. (2001). 'Backbenchers Learn to Fight Back', in K. Goetz and S. Hix (eds.), *Europeanised Politics? European Integration and National Political Systems*. London: Frank Cass.

Tarrow, S. (1988). *Democracy and Disorder: Protest and Politics in Italy, 1965–1975*. Oxford: Oxford Unversity Press.

Tesoka, S. (1999). 'Judicial Politics in the European Union: Its Impact on National Opportunity Structures for Gender Equality', Max Planck Institute, MPIfG Discussion Paper no. 99/2 (September).

Thatcher, M. (1993). *The Downing Street Years*. London: HarperCollins.

Thatcher, M. (1999). *Politics of Telecommunications*. Oxford: Oxford University Press.

—— (2002). 'Analyzing Regulatory Reform in Europe', *Journal of European Public Policy*, 9(6): 859–72.

—— (2004). 'Winners and Losers in Europeanisation: Reforming the National Regulation of Telecommunications', *West European Politics*, 27(2): 284–309.

—— (2005). 'The Third Force? Independent Regulatory Agencies and Elected Politicians in Europe', *Governance*, 18(3): 347–74.

Thaysen, U. (1994). 'The Bundesrat, the Länder and German Federalism', *German Issues*, (13) Washington, DC: American Institute for Contemporary German Studies.

Thiel, E. and Schröder, I. (1998). 'Germany', in *The European Union and National Macroeconomic Policy*. J. Forder and A. Menon (eds.), London: Routledge.

Thielemann, E. R. (2002). 'The Soft Europeanisation of Migration Policy: European Integration and Domestic Policy Change', Paper presented at the 2002 ECPR joint session of workshops, Turin, March 22–27.

Thoenig, J-C. (1987). *L'Administration en Miettes*. Paris: Fayard.

Tilly, C. (1978). *From Mobilization to Revolution*. Englewood Cliffs, NJ: Prentice-Hall.

Todd, E. (1998). *L'Illusion Économique*. Paris: Gallimard.

Transparency International (2005). 'Corruption Perceptions Index', http://www.transparency.org/policy_and_research/surveys_indices/cpi/2005

Triandafyllidou, A. (2005). 'Italy and Europe: Internal Others and External Challenges to National Identity', in A. Ichijo and W. Spohn (eds.), *Entangled Identities: Nations And Europe* London: Ashgate.

Tsebelis, G. (1995). 'Decision Making in Political Systems: Veto Players in Presidentialism, Parliamentarism, Multicameralism and Multipartism', *British Journal of Political Science*, 25: 289–325.

Unwin, D. (1995). *The Community of Europe*, 2nd edn. London: Longman.

van der Eijk, C. and Franklin, M. (1996). *Choosing Europe?* Ann Arbor, MI: University of Michigan Press.

—— —— (2004). 'Potential for Contestation on European Matters at National Elections in Europe', in G. Marks and M. R. Steenbergen (eds.), *European Integration and Political Conflict*. Cambridge: Cambridge University Press.

—— —— and Marsh, M. (1996). 'What Voters Teach Us About Europe-Wide Elections: What Europe-Wide Elections Teach Us About Voters', *Electoral Studies*, 15: 149–66.

Van Keesbergen, C. (2000). 'Political Allegiance and European Integration', *European Journal of Political Research*, 37(1): 1–17.

Verdun, A. (2000). *European Responses to Globalization and Financial Market Integration: Perceptions of EMU in Britain, France and Germany*. Basingstoke, UK: Macmillan.

Viansson-Ponté, P. (1963). *Les Gaullistes, Rituel et Annuaire*. Paris: Seuil.

Visser, J. (2005). 'The OMC as Selective Amplifier for National Strategies of Reform: What the Netherlands Wants to Learn from Europe', in J. Zeitlin and P. Pochet with L. Magnusson (eds.), *The Open Method of Co-ordination in Action: The European Employment and Social Inclusion Strategies*. Brussels: Peter Lang.

Vogel, D. (1986). *National Styles of Regulation: Environmental Policy in Great Britain and the United States*. Ithaca, NY: Cornell University Press.

Waever, O. (1997). 'Imperial Metaphors: Emerging European Analogies to Pre-Nation State Imperial Systems', in O. Tunander, P. Baev, and V. I. Einagel (eds.), *Geopolitics in Post-Wall Europe*. London: Sage.

Wallace, H. (1996). 'Relations Between the European Union and the British Administration', in Y. Mény, P. Muller, and J-L. Quermonne (eds.), *Adjusting to Europe: The Impact of the European Union on National Institutions and Policies*. London: Routledge.

Wallace, W. (1983). 'Less than a Federation, More than a Regime: The Community as a Political System', in H. Wallace et al. (eds.), *Policy-Making in the European Community*. Chichester, UK: John Wiley.

—— (1986). 'What Price Independence? Sovereignty and Interdependence in British Politics', in *International Affairs*, 62(3).

—— (1994). *Regional Integration: The West European Experience*. Washington, DC: Brookings.

—— (1996). 'Governance Without Statehood. The Unstable Equilibrium', in H. Wallace and W. Wallace (eds.), *Policymaking in the European Union*, 3rd edn., Oxford: Oxford University Press, pp. 439–60.

Warin, P. (1997). *Quelle Modernisation des Services Publics? Les Usagers au Coeur des Réformes*. Paris: La Découverte.

References

Warleigh, A. (2001). 'Europeanizing Civil Society', *Journal of Common Market Studies*, 39(4): 619–39.

Warner, C. (2001). 'Mass Parties and Clientelism in France and Italy', in S. Piattoni (ed.), *Clientelism, Interests, and Democratic Representation*. Cambridge: Cambridge University Press.

Watkins, A. (1992). *A Conservative Coup*. London: Duckworth.

Weber, E. (1976). *Peasants into Frenchmen: The Modernization of Rural France, 1870–1914*. Stanford, CA: Stanford University Press.

Webster, R. (1998). 'Environmental Collective Action: Stable Patterns of Cooperation and Issue Alliances at the European Level', in J. Greenwood and M. Aspinwall (eds.), *Collective Action in the European Union: Interests and the New Politics of Associability*. London: Routledge.

Weil, P. (1991). *La France et ses Etrangers*. Paris: Gallimard.

Weiler, J. H. H. (1991). 'The Transformation of Europe', *Yale Law Review*, 100(8): 2403–83.

—— (1994). 'A Quiet Revolution: The European Court of Justice and Its Interlocutors', *Comparative Political Studies*, 26(4): 510–34.

Weiler, J. H. H. (1995). 'The State 'uber alles': Demos, Telos and the German Maastricht Decision', Jean Monnet Working Paper Series 6/95, Cambridge: Harvard Law School.

—— (1999). *The Constitution of Europe: 'Do the new Clothes have an Emperor?' and other essays on European Integration*. Cambridge: Cambridge University Press.

Weisbein, J. (ed.) (1998). *Le Dialogue National pour l'Europe* Cahiers du CEVIPOF, no. 19. Paris: CEVIPOF.

—— (2002). 'La Question de l'Espace Public Européen', in B. Cautrès and D. Reynié (eds.), *L'Opinion Européenne* Paris: Presses de Sciences Po.

Wendt, A. (1995). 'Constructing International Politics', *International Security*, 20(1): 71–81.

Wessels, W. (1990). 'Administrative Interaction', in W. Wallace (ed.), *The Dynamics of European Integration* London: Pinter.

—— (1997). 'An Ever Closer Fusion? A Dynamic Macropolitical View on Integration Processes', *Journal of Common Market Studies*, 35(2): 267–99.

—— (1999). 'Comitology as a Research Subject: A New Legitimacy Mix?' in C. Joerges and E. Vos (eds.), *EU Committees: Social Regulation, Law and Politics*. Oxford: Hart Publishing, pp. 259–69.

Williams, P. (1966). *Crisis and Compromise: Politics in the Fourth Republic*. New York: Doubleday.

Williams, S. (1991). "Sovereignty and Accountability in the European Community" in R. Keohane and S. Hoffmann (eds.), *The New European Community*. Boulder, CO: Westview.

Wilson, F. L. (1983). 'French Interest Group Politics: Pluralist or Neocorporatist?', *American Political Science Review* (77).

Wincott, D. (1995). 'The Role of Law or the Rule of the Court of Justice? An "Institutional" Account of Judicial Politics in the European Community', *Journal of European Public Policy* 2(4).

—— (1996). 'Federalism and the European Union: The Scope and Limits of the Treaty of Maastricht', *International Political Science Review*, 17(4): 403–15.

Winkler, J. T. (1976). 'Corporatism', *European Journal of Sociology*, 17(1).

Woodhouse, D. (2001). 'The Law and Politics: More Power to the Judges—and to the People?', *Parliamentary Affairs*, 54: 223–37.

Woodward, A. (2003). 'European Gender Mainstreaming: Promises and Pitfalls of Transformative Policy', *Review of Policy Research*, 20(1): 65–88.

Wright, V. (1994). 'Reshaping the State: Implications for Public Administration', *West European Politics*, 17: 102–34.

Young, A. R. (1998). 'European Consumer Groups: Multiple Levels of Governance and Multiple Logics of Collective Action', in J. Greenwood, and M. Aspinwall (eds.), *Collective Action in the European Union: Interests and the New Politics of Associability*. London: Routledge.

Young, H. (1998). *This Blessed Plot: Britain and Europe from Churchill to Blair*. Basingstoke, UK: Macmillan.

Zeitlin, J. and Pochet, P., with Magnusson, L. (eds.) (2005). *The Open Method of Coordination in Action: The European Employment and Social Inclusion Strategies*. Brussels: Peter Lang.

Ziblatt, D. (2003). 'Constructing a Federal State: Political Development, Path Dependence, and the Origins of Federalism in Modern Europe, 1815–1871', Ph.D. Berkeley.

Zielonka, J. (2001). 'How new enlarged borders will reshape the European Union,' *Journal of Common Market Studies*, 39(3): 507–536.

Zimmer, M. (1999). 'From the National State to the Rational State and Back? An Exercise in Understanding Politics and Identity in Germany in the Twentieth Century', *German Politics*, 8(3): 21–42.

Zolner, M. (1999). 'National Images in French Discourses on Europe', Paper presented at the ECSA Sixth Biennial International Conference, Pittsburgh, June 2–5.

Zürn, M. (2000). 'Democratic Governance Beyond the Nation-State', in M. Greven, and L. W. Pauly, (eds.), *Democracy Beyond the State? The European Dilemma and the Emerging Global Order*. Lanham, MD: Rowman & Littlefield.

Zweifel, T. (2002). 'Who Is Without Sin Cast the First Stone: The EU's Democratic Deficit in Comparison', *Journal of European Public Policy*, 9: 812–40.

Index